New England
Middle Atlantic
Midwest
South
Southwest
West
1 VERMONT
2 NEW HAMPSHIRE
3 MASSACHUSETTS
4 CONNECTICUT
5 RHODE ISLAND
6 NEW JERSEY
7 MARYLAND
8 DELAWARE
ANADA
SOTA
WISCONSIN
MICHIGAN
IOWA
Chicago
ILLINOIS
INDIANA
Detroit
OHIO
MISSOURI
ROUTE 66
Niagara Falls
NEW YORK
Boston
PENNSYLVANIA
Philadelphia
New York City
Washington D.C.
WEST VIRGINIA
VIRGINIA
KENTUCKY
NORTH CAROLINA
TENNESSEE
SOUTH CAROLINA
ARKANSAS
Mississippi
MISSISSIPPI
ALABAMA
GEORGIA
ATLANTIC OCEAN
LOUISIANA
New Orleans
uston
Gulfstream
GULF OF MEXICO
FLORIDA
Everglades National Park
Miami
Gulfstream
THE UNITED STATES OF AMERICA

Red **Line**
4

Herausgeber: Dr. Frank Haß

Ernst Klett Verlag
Stuttgart • Leipzig

Red Line 4 für Klasse 8 an Realschulen und gemäß den Bildungsstandards Klasse 8.

Herausgeber: Dr. Frank Haß, Kirchberg; unter besonderer Mitwirkung von Harald Weisshaar, Bisingen

Autoren: Marion Horner M. A., Cambridge; Jennifer Baer-Engel, Göppingen; Rolf W. Roth M. A., Idar-Oberstein (Lost in the USA) sowie Pauline Ashworth M. A., Stuttgart

Unter besonderer Mitwirkung von:
Hamida Aziz, Tübingen; Sheila McBride, Stuttgart

Berater: Friederike Bachmann, Remscheid; Sandra Haberland, Recklinghausen; Elga Hartwig, Oer-Erkenschwick; Elke Lüdeke, Möckmühl; Dieter Vilimek, Helmstadt-Bargen

Zusatzmaterial für Schülerinnen und Schüler zu diesem Band:

Workbook mit Audio-CD	978-3-12-581145-4
Workbook mit Audio-CD und Lernsoftware	978-3-12-581245-1
Lernsoftware CD-ROM (Einzelversion)	978-3-12-990694-1
Fit für Tests und Klassenarbeiten	978-3-12-581141-6
Vokabellernheft	978-3-12-581147-8

1. Auflage **ISBN** 978-3-12-581140-9 (fester Einband) 1 10 9 8 | 2016 2015

1. Auflage **ISBN** 978-3-12-581240-6 (flexibler Einband) 1 10 9 8 | 2016 2015

Alle Drucke dieser Auflage sind unverändert und können im Unterricht nebeneinander verwendet werden. Die letzte Zahl bezeichnet das Jahr dieses Druckes.

www.klett.de

Redaktion: Joanne Popp, William Sears, Iris Seiler
Gestaltung: Meike Haas, Ulrike Wursthorn
Illustrationen: David Norman, Meerbusch; Sylvia Wolf, Wiesbaden; Steffen Wolff, Düsseldorf (Grammar); Christian Dekelver, Weinstadt (Karten)
Umschlaggestaltung: Koma Amok, Stuttgart
Umschlagfoto: Corbis (March), Düsseldorf

Satz: Marion Köster, Stuttgart (Grammar)
Reproduktion: Meyle + Müller, Medien-Management, Pforzheim
Druck: PHOENIX PRINT, GmbH

Printed in Germany
ISBN 978-3-12-581140-9 (fester Einband)
ISBN 978-3-12-581240-6 (flexibler Einband)

9 783125 811409 9 783125 812406

Welcome back to Red Line!

Im vierten Band deines Englischbuchs geht es um die USA. Du erfährst einiges über die Regionen und die jungen Leute dort – und du lernst amerikanisches Englisch kennen.

Es gibt wieder fünf **Units** (Kapitel) mit folgenden Unit-Teilen:

Check-in: Neue Wörter und Landeskunde
Language: Redemittel und Grammatik
Talkwise: Sprechen am Beispiel von Alltagssituationen
Text: Interessante Geschichten und Texte
Wordwise: Alles rund um Wörter, Wortarbeit und Wortspiele
Check-out: Alles klar? Prüfe am Ende der Unit, was du gelernt hast.

Neben den Units findest du folgende Buchteile:

Das Buch beginnt mit **Zoom-in**, dem Reisetagebuch der jungen Britin Kelsey.
Nach jeder Unit kannst du in den **Skills workshops** z. B. gezielt dein Hören, Lesen und Schreiben trainieren.
Auf die Standardprüfungen kannst du dich mit Hilfe der **Test practice**-Seiten vorbereiten.

Im hinteren Teil des Buches kannst du auf den **Passing on information**-Seiten zeigen, dass du zwischen zwei Sprachen dolmetschen kannst.
Unter **Extras** findest du interessante Zusatzinformationen zu den USA, Projekte und eine spannende Geschichte.
Auf die Extras folgt **Grammar** (der Grammatikanhang) mit vielen Regeln, Beispielen und Tipps. Dort kannst du auch überprüfen, ob du alles verstanden hast.
Am Ende des Buches findest du den **Vocabulary**-Teil (die Vokabelliste). Hier stehen alle neuen Wörter einer Unit mit ihren deutschen Übersetzungen.
Das **Dictionary** (Wörterbuch) listet die Vokabeln von Red Line alphabetisch auf. Es ist auch zum Nachschlagen gedacht, wenn du einmal ein Wort vergessen hast.

Das Wichtigste zum Schluss: Bis auf Zoom-in, das ja von der Britin Kelsey geschrieben wurde, wird in Red Line 4 amerikanisches Englisch und die amerikanische Schreibweise verwendet.

Alles klar? Dann los und viel Spaß!

Erläuterungen:

Real talk	Wir sprechen echtes Alltagsenglisch.
Listening	Wir hören zu.
Your turn	Hier kannst du über dich, deine Familie und Freunde sprechen oder schreiben.
Revision	Wiederholung
(CD-Symbol)	Diese Teile sind auf den Begleit-CDs enthalten.
(2 Personen)	Partnerarbeit
(3 Personen)	Gruppenarbeit
(Mappe)	Hier entsteht ein Produkt für deine Sammelmappe.
(Stift)	Wir schreiben.
*	Diese Übungen sind besonders knifflig.
( )	Diese Übungen sind fakultativ.
→ WB 3,1	Workbook-Verweis
→ G1	Grammatik-Verweis

HOLLYWOOD BLVD

Zoom-in Around the US

Hi there! My name's Kelsey and this is the web album of my journey across the US! It's for my stay-at-home friends in the UK and Germany, and it'll have the best photos from my journey. I hope you'll like it!

My US blog

March

San Francisco

Guess where I started my US journey from west to east. Yep, in San Francisco. It's a cool city! You can see the old cable car here. Oh, and California's beaches make it a great place to surf, too.

Look at the photos on this and the next three pages. Which scenes look typically American? Say why.

March

Silicon Valley

This is Silicon Valley, the home of the PC. Some of the first computer companies started here, thirty years ago.

Walk of Fame

When I was in Los Angeles (LA) I saw the Walk of Fame. There's a star here for every … er … star. More than 2,000 of them! Here's my favourite!

Look at the map at the front of your book and find where the journey started. Which state are the cities in? What other big city is in this state?

April

Monument Valley

From California I went east to Arizona, and Monument Valley. If you have ever seen a western, you will recognize this fantastic scenery. These are some of the most famous rocks in the world.

May

A Native American village

It wasn't far from Monument Valley to this Native American village. (But Native Americans don't always wear traditional clothes like the ones in this photo!)

What do you know about Native Americans from what you have read, or seen in films?

June

Cheerleaders

Everything's BIG in Texas – the schools are, too! I looked at a middle school there.
There's a lot of fun at American schools. The schools have all these after-school activities and lots of sports to take part in and watch. The cheerleaders are always full of energy – and they're LOUD! American pupils work hard, too, if they want to go to college later.

What American sports do you know?

The US flag

While I was at middle school I found out why the US flag has fifty stars and thirteen stripes. Do **you** know why?

If you don't, the answer is on page 173.

July

Independence Day

There's a big party every year on 4th July, or Independence Day, when Americans celebrate their freedom from England. Everybody wears the colours of the American flag and goes out in the evening to watch the fireworks.

When did you last see fireworks?

August

The Midwest

I stopped for lunch at this typical small town in the huge Midwest, the area between Kansas and Ohio. "Nice folks here," as the Americans say – but the Midwest is not the most interesting place in the world. All you see here is corn and wheat for hundreds and hundreds of miles. That's why they call this part of the US the 'Corn belt'.

September

New England

The white people started to come to the US from Europe in the early 1600s. They built what are the oldest towns of the US, in New England. I took this photo near Boston.

Why do you think this part of the US is called New England?

October

The White House

I spent a day in Washington D.C., the capital. The President of the United States lives here, in the White House. He didn't have any time for me, so I went on to New York City.

Who is the US President at the moment?

November

West Side Story

I like to be in America!
OK by me in America!
Everything free in America,
For a small fee in America!

I love musicals, and one night I went to see a real classic: West Side Story. It's got SO many good songs, like 'America'. What do you think of it? The story is about immigrants in New York and their problems.

Sondheim, Stephen © Leonard Bernstein Music / Chappell-Co Inc.

You can find out more about the musical on the Internet.

November

Empire State Building

My last stop was New York City! I LOVE the city's energy, its size, its huge SKYSCRAPERS, like the Empire State Building. I hope you'll love it, too.

Number plates

Each of the 50 states has a different number plate (in the US: license plate). Here are some of the plates I saw on my journey.

Find the four states on the map at the front of the book. Which states are in the east, which are in the west?

US facts

Here are some more US facts:

- There are more than 290 million Americans. Everyone who is born in the US gets an American passport.
- The state of Alaska is bigger than Germany, France and Spain together.
- The journey from LA to NYC takes five and a half hours by plane. (It's about 2,400 miles.)
- There are six time zones in the US. Hawaii is five hours behind New York City, which has East Coast time.

Make your own list of US facts. Here are some ideas:
- How many states?
- Important days?
- Capital?

You could also collect information about an American city or movie star for a US file. Why not add to the file as you work through this book?

→ WB 3, 1

1 Central Park, Manhattan, from the top of a skyscraper

Unit 1 I ♥ New York City

1 A big city

a) *Look at the photos and the information on these two pages with a partner. Find as many of the places as you can on the map at the back of the book.*

b) *Explain the numbers.*

Example: 5: There are five boroughs in New York.

1. 12,000
2. 8,000,000
3. 2,800+
4. 2,000+
5. 305
6. 2,880,000

→ WB 4, 1

2 Listening: In the city

a) *Listen to the first text: A tourist guide is talking in New York.*

1. Which sight does she talk about?
2. What information does she give about the sight? Take notes.

b) *Listen to the second text.*

1. Which sight are the people looking at?
2. What do you find out about it? Take notes.

→ WB 4, 2

The Statue of Liberty

3 The Empire State Building

FACTS AND INFORMATION

More than 8 million people live in New York City.

There are five boroughs, or parts of the city: Manhattan, Brooklyn, Queens, Staten Island and the Bronx.

A Brooklyn neighborhood

5 Chinatown

DID YOU KNOW?

- New York is a city of immigrants. Today 36% of New Yorkers were born outside the US.
- NYC has more than 12,000 yellow cabs. Many drivers are immigrants whose first language isn't English.
- Except for the Bronx, all of the boroughs are islands. The city has a lot – more than 2,000 – of bridges and tunnels.
- France gave the US the Statue of Liberty as a present. It is 305 feet tall, and a symbol of freedom for Americans.
- Chinatown has lots of Chinese restaurants and stores. NYC's first Chinese immigrants lived here.
- On September 11, 2001 terrorists destroyed the twin towers of the World Trade Center. Over 2,800 people died.

3 Your turn: More about NYC

a) *Find out about ONE of these things in a group. Use the library or the Internet.*

the Empire State Building | September 11, 2001 | the Statue of Liberty | Central Park

b) *Give a short talk to your class. Use your notes to tell them what you found out.*

VOCBOX

in the foreground ['fɔːgraʊnd] – *im Vordergrund*
in the background ['bækgraʊnd] – *im Hintergrund*
skyscraper ['skaɪˌskreɪpə] – *Wolkenkratzer*
banner ['bænə] – *Fahne*
kickboard ['kɪkbɔːd] – *Kickboard*
story *(AE)* ['stɔːri] – *Stockwerk*
elevator *(AE)* ['elɪveɪtə] – *Aufzug*
torch [tɔːtʃ] – *Fackel*

A meal in Manhattan

New York City is a great place for food. Chinese, Italian, Polish, it's all there! Delis (short for 'delicatessens') have interesting meals and are usually cheaper than restaurants and cafés.

THE MANHATTAN MONSTER

1 Revision: The monster → G1

a) *Write down three or more of the ingredients in a 'Manhattan Monster'. Would you like to try one? Say why or why not.*

b) *Write two or three sentences for each picture of the cartoon. Start like this:*

1. Diego goes away for an hour to deliver … . José looks after … .
2. The man wants … .

c) *What can you eat at snack bars in your town? How are they different from Diego's Deli?*

GRAMMAR

You use the simple present for facts and for things that happen regularly (every day, week, …).
You also use it when you give a summary of a story.

- Diego **goes away** for an hour.
- José **doesn't know** what is in Diego's specials.

→ WB 5,1 → G1

2 Real talk: At the deli

DIEGO'S DELI

Coffee to go	$2.60	Big sandwiches cream cheese or egg, two slices of bacon, pastrami or turkey with lettuce, tomato and French fries	$6.49
Coffee to go & Danish or cupcake	$4.60	Diego's special sandwich	$5.95
Empire State Breakfast pancakes with maple syrup, eggs, sausage, bacon, potatoes, bagel or toast and coffee	$7.49	Milkshakes strawberry, cherry, banana	$2.90

a) *Look at the menu. Match the pictures with the words on the menu.*

b) *Work with a partner. One of you orders something to eat and drink at the deli. The other partner is the waiter/waitress.*

→ WB 6, 2

USEFUL PHRASES

A: Hi! What can I get you?
B: I'll have a …, please.
A: Would you like it with …?
A: Enjoy your meal!
A: That's …, please.
B: Here's … . You can keep the change.

3 Money

How much money is there each time?

1. One dollar bill, a dime and two quarters.
2. Two dollar bills, a quarter and two nickels.
3. Three dimes and three cents.
4. A quarter, a nickel and two cents.
5. Three quarters and three dimes.
6. Five dollar bills, five nickels and a cent.

→ WB 6, 3

a cent

a dime (10 cents)

a dollar ($1 = 100 cents)

a quarter (25 cents)

a nickel (5 cents)

4 Your turn: A special sandwich

Make your own recipe for your favorite sandwich. Write a list of ingredients. Add instructions and a picture of the sandwich.

→ WB 6, 4

US immigration

Between 1892 and 1954 more than twelve million immigrants landed at Ellis Island, close to the Statue of Liberty in New York Harbor. Many of them came to America to escape from poverty, war and oppression in Europe. The lucky ones went from the island to a new life in America.

1626
Dutch immigrants founded New Amsterdam.

1630
The Dutch bought Little Oyster Island from Native Americans.

1664
After the English had taken New Amsterdam from the Dutch, they named it New York.

1785
Samuel Ellis bought Little Oyster Island. He named it Ellis Island.

1820
Large numbers of immigrants began to sail to New York. They landed at Manhattan.

1845
A terrible famine in Ireland started and millions of poor and hungry Irish people left on ships to New York. The journey was awful and many were seasick. Some hadn't eaten for days when they arrived.

1892
They closed the immigration station in Manhattan and opened one on Ellis Island. The first immigrant was a young Irish girl.

1907
Sick people were no longer allowed to enter the US. The officials sent them back to Europe.

1921
The US started quotas for immigrants from Eastern Europe. They set a limit for the number of immigrants from each country. A Polish woman had a baby on a ship. When she landed, the Polish quotas had just run out. The officials said, "You can stay, but not your baby." Suddenly one man had an idea. "The ship was late," he said, "and the baby was early. So the baby is American."

1954
The Ellis Island immigration station closed.

The 1960s
The journey for some immigrants got easier. Planes brought them to airports in the US.

Today
It is still hard to immigrate into the US. Most people who do it come from Mexico, India and China.
On Ellis Island there is now a museum about immigration.

1 The journey to the US

When did these things happen? Complete the sentences.

Say the years like this:
In 1626: in sixteen twenty-six
In 1990: in nineteen ninety
In 2008: in two thousand and eight

Example: In 1892 they closed the immigration station in Manhattan.

1. … the Dutch founded …
2. … the English took the city and named it …
3. … Samuel Ellis gave … a new name: …
4. … Irish immigrants came because …
5. … they opened … on …
6. … the officials started to send …
7. … they started quotas …
8. … immigrants started to fly to …

→ WB 7,1

2 Revision: What happened first? → G3, G4

Look at these sentences. Which happened first, the blue or the green action?

1. The ship arrived after the Polish woman had had her baby. Green
2. After the English had taken the city, they named it New York. Blue
3. Before the famine started, other Irish immigrants had come to New York. Green

GRAMMAR

The simple past is for actions in the past.
▶ Many Irish immigrants **arrived** in 1845.

The past perfect is for actions before other past actions.
▶ Some **hadn't eaten** for days when they arrived.

→ WB 7,2

3 Revision: Ellis Island → G3, G4

Use the simple past or the past perfect to complete these sentences.

1. After the immigrants … (*land*) at Ellis Island, they … (*wait*) in the immigration hall.
2. They … (*be*) often still weak because they … (*be*) seasick on the journey.
3. Many … (*not/eat*) for days when they … (*leave*) the ship.
4. After the doctors … (*check*) the immigrants, the officials … (*ask*) them a lot of questions.
5. Some people … (*have to*) go back because the quota for their country … (*run out*).
6. After the lucky ones … (*show*) their money to the officials, they … (*leave*) Ellis Island and … (*start*) their new life.

→ WB 8,3–4

4 Pros and cons

What do you think it is like to be an immigrant today? Make a list of the pros and cons. Talk about them in a small group.

USEFUL PHRASES

Yes, but …
I think … / I don't think …
I agree / I don't agree because …

5 Your turn: In your class

a) *Make notes about someone who came from another country to live in Germany. (It can be someone you know, or a famous person, like a football star.)*

Name? | Age? | Born in? | Came to Germany because … | …

b) *Tell the class about the person you chose.*

→ WB 9,1–2

Words and feelings

1 What can people's faces tell you?

a) *Find a 'feelings' word for each picture. Which words don't you need?*

worried | surprised | embarrassed | mad | happy | sympathetic

A

B

C

b) *When do you feel surprised / happy / mad … ? Write a sentence for each word.*

I feel … when … . I always feel … when … .

→ WB 10, 1

2 Listening: A trip to New York

a) *The Goodman family, from a small town in Iowa, are going to spend a vacation in New York. Listen to some short scenes. After each scene say how the Goodmans feel.*

b) *Copy the list of useful phrases. Listen again. Add the words and phrases which the Goodmans use to say how they feel.*

USEFUL PHRASES

Surprised:	That's amazing!
	…
Sympathetic:	How terrible!
	…
Happy:	I'm really enjoying it.
	…

→ WB 10, 2

3 How do you feel?

Work in groups of three or four and choose a picture. You are the young people in the picture. Find a 'feelings' word for the picture. Then make a dialogue and say how you feel in this situation. Use the useful phrases from exercise 2. Your face can help to show how you feel, too.

1

2

3

→ WB 10, 3

New York songs

1 Before you start

Before you listen to the songs and read the lyrics, think:
What songs about places (cities, towns, countries) do you know?

An open letter to NYC, by the Beastie Boys

Dear New York, I hope you're doing well.
I know a lot's happened, and you've been through hell.
So, we give thanks for providing a home,
Through your gates at Ellis Island we passed in droves.

((Chorus:)) Brooklyn, Bronx, Queens and Staten,
From the Battery to the top of Manhattan,
Asian, Middle-Eastern and Latin,
Black, White, New York, you make it happen.

...

Shout out the South Bronx, where my mom hails from,
Right next to High Bridge, across from Harlem.
To the Grand Concourse, where my mom and dad met,
Before they moved on down to the Upper West.
I see you're still strong, after all that's gone on,
Life long we dedicate this song.
Just a little something to show some respect,
To the city that blends and mends and tests.
Since 9/11 we're still livin',
And lovin' life we've been given.
Ain't nothing gonna take that away from us,
We're lookin' pretty and gritty, 'cause in the city we trust.

Dear New York, I know a lot has changed,
Two towers down but you're still in the game.
Home to the many, rejecting no one,
Accepting peoples of all places, wherever they're from.

Brooklyn, Bronx, Queens and Staten,
From the Battery to the top of Manhattan,
Asian, Middle-Eastern and Latin,
Black, White, New York, you make it happen.

Brooklyn, Bronx, Queens and Staten ...

The Beastie Boys

Naturally 7

New York, by Naturally 7

Close to the edge,
I'm like a bomb ticking slowly,
Just don't push me if you know what's good for you,
I'm not that holy.
I'm an island, I'm a rock,
On an island made of rock.
Concrete flowers, falling towers,
To tell the time, who needs a watch?

Ain't that just like New York?
Ain't that just like TV?
There's nothin' like New York,
Don't you believe what you see.

It gets so crazy (it gets so crazy)
It gets so crazy sometimes,
(It gets so crazy sometimes.)

((Chorus:)) I got this love for New York, New York
I think it's more than she knows.
I said goodbye to New York, New York
But my heart won't let her go.

I've seen a few things,
I've seen fire, I've seen rain,
What I haven't seen is much sunshine.
Through my window, shades of gray,
Baby's crying, Mommy's trying her very best to make ends meet,
Daddy's spot is on the corner, made at least three G's last week.

Ain't that just like New York?
Ain't that just like TV?
There's nothin' like New York,
Don't you believe what you see.

2 The songs

a) *Which song do you like better? Why? (How does it make you feel?) What kind of music is each song?*

STUDY SKILLS

Understanding songs
A song is more than just the lyrics, and you don't need to understand every word! Look at the chorus first. This usually has the most important ideas of the song. How the singers sing can also tell you about the message of the song.

b) *In which song are the singers positive about New York? In which song aren't they sure what they think about it?*

3 The lyrics

a) *Match these phrases to lines of the songs.*

1. A lot of things are different now.
2. Life has been very hard for you.
3. Be careful with me.
4. New York is a very special place.
5. You're fine after all that has happened.
6. I can't forget the city.

* b) *Which event in New York's history do both songs mention?*

4 The bands

a) *Work with a partner. Use the Internet to find out more about the two bands. Collect information in a grid like this.*

Name of band	Number and names of members	Name and date of first CD	One other (interesting!) piece of information
Naturally 7	…	…	…
Beastie Boys	…	…	…

b) *Compare your information with what the other pairs found. Which piece of information do you find most interesting?*

STUDY SKILLS

Take notes on the pages you find on the Internet, and don't print out more information than you need.
It's a good idea to set a time limit when you look for information on the Internet.

5 Your turn: Where you live

a) *Write a short rap or a poem about the place where you live (or would like to live). Write how you feel about the place, and name some of the things you can see and do there. You can work alone or in groups.*

b) *Perform your rap or your poem. You can also record it as a sound file.*

→ WB 11,1

1 New York City: A mind map

Make a mind map with information about New York City. Here are some ideas for the groups in the mind map.

VOCABULARY SKILLS A B C

Mind maps can help you to organize what you know. You can put words into groups and you can also connect different words, groups and ideas.

There is no right or wrong way to make a mind map. Why not compare your mind map with a partner's when you have both finished?

2 In Central Park

Look at the picture. What are the people doing? Describe four or more (groups of) people. You will need your dictionary to talk about some of the people.

in the foreground | in the background | on the right | on the left | …

3 Sounds: Sentences

a) *Read these sentences to a partner. Put the stress on the words in* blue.

1. Can you look after things for an hour?
2. It gets so crazy sometimes.
3. I hope you're doing well.
4. NYC has more than 12,000 yellow cabs.
5. Would you like it with French fries?
6. I'm really enjoying it.

COMMUNICATION SKILLS

With normal sentences, think: What is the **most important** part of the sentence? With questions, be an actor! The question should **sound** like a question.

b) *Listen to the sentences on the CD and say them again.*

4 American and British English

a) *American English (AE) has some words which are different from British English (BE). Find the British words for these American words from the unit and start a list.*

cab | vacation | French fries | store

AE	BE
cab	…

b) *The AE words in* blue *are new, but the pictures will help you to match them with the BE words on the right. Add the pairs to your list from a).*

bill | rubbish | film | toilet | queue

* c) *Some spellings are different in AE, too. Complete the BE spellings. What are the rules?*

- neighborhood, color, harbor
- center

- neighbourhood, …
- …

5 My grandfather

Find the right word and complete the sentences.

young | popular | manager | plane | immigrant | Chinese | money | cab | during | well | opened | delicious | United States

My grandfather was an [1] from China. He came to the [2] when he was a [3] man because he believed he could do [4] here. He came by [5] in 1948. For many years he worked in a friend's store [6] the day. In the evenings he drove a [7] because he needed more [8]. After twenty years he [9] our [10] restaurant here in Chinatown. The restaurant is very [11] today, and the food is really [12]. I should know. I'm the [13].

‹› 6 What's the word?

Find the word.

1. A person who moves to another country is an … .
2. The first people from Europe travelled to the US by … .
3. If you are …, this means you get sick on a ship because of the waves.
4. Many Irish people decided to go to the US because there was a … in Ireland.
5. Today a lot of people who … into the US come from Mexico.
6. The limit on the number of people who can come to the US from a country is a … .

→ WB 12, 1–2

1 New Yorkers and their jobs (simple present → G 1)

Daisy, 22

Tony, 55

Frank, 27

Bruce, 15

Write three sentences about each New Yorker. Use the notes.

Example: 1. Daisy is 22. She works … .

1. work for a computer company • go jogging every Saturday
2. drive a cab in Brooklyn • not speak very good English
3. clean skyscraper windows • sometimes have lunch 200 feet above the city
4. take dogs for walks in Central Park • not get much money

2 James in NYC (simple past → G 3)

a) *Look at the map and the pictures. What did James, a tourist, do / see / visit, and when? Make a chart.*

time	place
8:00	Hotel Rome in …
…	…

b) *Use the chart and say what he did in New York. Start like this:*

At eight o'clock James had breakfast in his hotel in … . At … .

3 The history of Central Park (simple past, past perfect → G 3, G 4)

Read the text and put in the right form of the verb, simple past or past perfect.

Before they [1] (*come*) to the US, many immigrants [2] (*live*) in small villages. After they [3] (*be*) in New York for a year or two, they [4] (*start*) to miss the trees and fields of home. They also [5] (*want*) a place for their families, a park where their children [6] (*can*) play or do sports. After officials [7] (*argue*) for about three years, they finally [8] (*decide*) where to put it. After they [9] (*draw*) the plans, they [10] (*talk*) to people who [11] (*live*) in the area which they [12] (*choose*). After the people [13] (*leave*) their homes, workers [14] (*destroy*) their houses and [15] (*start*) to work on the park project. They [16] (*change*) a huge area in the middle of Manhattan into a beautiful park. 20,000 people [17] (*work*) on the area which is now Central Park. This [18] (*be*) the first public park in the US. Work on the project [19] (*start*) in 1858 and it [20] (*take*) eight years to finish it.

→ WB 13, 1–3

* 4 9/11 (mixed exercise)

Read the text and put in the right word each time.

Until that awful day, the World Trade Center had [1] one of the tallest buildings [2] the world. 50,000 people [3] in the offices there, and lots of visitors also went [4] in the elevators to enjoy the view of Manhattan [5] the top. Then, [6] September 11, 2001, everything changed. Terrorists flew two planes [7] the twin towers, and the buildings fell to the ground in a terrible cloud [8] smoke and steel. More [9] 2,800 people died that day. Most of them were already in the World Trade Center [10] the planes hit [11]. But some were firefighters [12] arrived later. They lost [13] lives when [14] tried to save people. New Yorkers [15] never forget these heroes.

NOW YOU CAN

✓ Talk about food in New York.	→ Name three things you can buy in a deli.
✓ Talk about US immigration.	→ Name four groups of immigrants to the US.
✓ Use American money.	→ How many dimes are there in a dollar?
✓ Say how you feel in English.	→ A friend tells you something sad. What can you say?
✓ Talk about actions before other actions in the past.	→ Say two things that had already happened when you got up this morning.

Skills workshop 1 Listening

LISTENING SKILLS

In a conversation, you can always ask the other person to say something again, so don't panic if you don't understand the first time! The other person's face can also give you clues. Is he / she smiling? Does he / she look sad / worried / …? Before the conversation starts, think about the situation. What do you think the other person will ask or tell you? What would **you** want to know in that situation?

1 Don't panic!

a) *Find a useful phrase for each situation.*

1. You don't understand a word someone has just said.
2. You didn't hear part of a sentence because there was suddenly a loud bang.
3. It is hard to understand because the other person is talking very fast.
4. When the tour guide talks to you, she always uses the wrong name.
5. You aren't sure you'll remember the address of a deli someone is telling you about.

USEFUL PHRASES

I'm sorry. Could you speak more slowly, please?
Sorry, that's not quite right. It's … .
Could you write that down for me, please?
Sorry, what was the person's name again?
Sorry, could you say that word again?
Excuse me, that noise was so loud that I didn't hear what you just said.

b) *Which phrase didn't you use? Think of a situation where you could use it.*

2 Delis and karaoke

Look at dialogue 1: A's keywords are in ***blue****. What are A's keywords in dialogue 2?*

1. A: Don't eat at this **deli**. The one round the **corner** has much **better food**.
   B: OK, I'll get my breakfast round the corner. Thanks for the tip!
2. A: If you happen to like karaoke, we could go to this great club I know downtown.
   B: Oh yes, I really like karaoke. I'd love to go to the club with you.

LISTENING SKILLS

Keywords

The keywords are the most important words in a sentence. They often answer the questions 'What …?' 'Who …?' 'Where …?' 'When …?' or 'Why …?'

It is always easier to find the keywords if you know what the situation is. You should also listen for the words which the speaker puts the most stress on.

3 Listening: In New York

These people stop you in the street in New York.

a) *What do they say? Listen and write down the keywords.*

b) *Now write down an answer for each person.*

1

2

3

4 Listening: How Americans speak

a) *You can recognize American English because some sounds are different from British English. Read the information, and then listen to a cab driver. Which words sound typically American?*

b) *Now listen to some passengers in the cab. Do they come from the US or the UK?*

American pronunciation

★ Words like **after**, **aunt** or **half** have the sound [æ], like in the word 'cat'.

★ You hear the **r** in words like **sure**, **car** or **work**.

★ In words like **beautiful** or **British**, the **t** often sounds like a **d**.

5 Be a good listener!

LISTENING SKILLS

Be a good listener! The other person will think that you are not polite if you don't listen, or don't show that you are listening.

Remember to look at the other person's face when he / she speaks, and try to react the right way to good or bad news.

Two tourists are on vacation in New York City. One of them went shopping on Fifth Avenue yesterday, and is telling the other one about the trip.

Work with a partner. Act the conversation. Partner A went shopping. Where there is a [B]*, partner B uses one of the useful phrases to show that he / she is listening.*

I went shopping on Fifth Avenue yesterday. [B] It was so busy! I've never seen so many people! [B] The stores are fantastic, but some of the clothes are very expensive! [B] So we didn't buy any. [B] Then we had lunch at a great deli. [B] When we got back to our hotel, my dad didn't have his bag with him. [B] We were worried, because his passport was in it. [B] But it was OK. He'd left it at the deli. [B] One of the waiters had found the bag and put it behind the counter. [B]

USEFUL PHRASES

Really? / Is that right? / Hmm?
That's very interesting.
That's nice! / Oh, good! / Cool! / Wow!

I see. / I understand. / OK.
Oh, I'm sorry. / Oh dear. / That's sad.

A: I went shopping on Fifth Avenue yesterday.
B: Cool!
A: Yes, it was so busy! I've …

→ WB 15, 1–2

Global Kids

"Did you know that many people in the world are poor because they're sick?" Eddie asks. "No? That was news to me, too, when I joined Global Kids two years ago." Eddie is excited about a lot of the things he has learned in the last two years.

He is a student at Canarsie High School in Brooklyn. Most of the kids there are from poor families, and many of them are immigrants. Only a few top students do well and go to college when they have finished; some drop out of school. This is the kind of school where Global Kids tries to get kids interested in the problems that people have in their own neighborhood and in other countries.

"We did this project with Global Kids about poor people all over the world," Eddie explains. "Although kids like us have enough money problems of their own, it wasn't boring; it helped me to understand things better. We even made a radio program about our project. Man, was I scared when I had to speak!"

"The media are very important in our projects," says Cristina, one of the organizers. "A software firm has just helped some of our students to create a computer game about the problems of the world's poor."

CREATING LEADERS THROUGH EXPERIENCE

Global Kids

Global Kids started in 1991. Since then 'GK' has shown thousands of young people that they can make a difference. Eddie's classmate Shelley is working on another Global Kids project in her free time.

"We're telling New Yorkers about the difficult situation many high school students are in," she explains. "Students who are illegal immigrants. They can go to school – that's free for everyone in the US.

But most of them can't go to college. For some kids it's too expensive. And many of them don't want to give colleges any information about their families. They're scared they will have to go back to their own country. We did a theater project about the problem and performed it on the streets of Manhattan last month." Shelley sounds excited. "People stopped to watch and ask us questions. I loved it because I got the feeling that I was really doing something to help these students!"

"That's what Global Kids is all about," says Cristina. "The students learn that things can only get better – in Africa or in Brooklyn – if people are active."

A Reading

1 *Right or wrong? Correct the wrong sentences.*

a Eddie's school is in New York.
b Kids like Eddie don't have any problems with money.
c Christina has a job with a software firm.
d Shelley isn't in the same class as Eddie.
e Most illegal immigrants don't go to college.
f Nobody was interested in the theater project.

2 *Answer the questions.*

a When did Global Kids start?
b What does the organization try to do?

B Language

Find the word or phrase in the text.

a to leave school before you have finished
b to design and make or build something
c someone who has entered a country but isn't allowed to be there
d without (much) money
e the part of town where someone lives
f to change things

C Passing on information

Luis, an American student, wants to do a job in your town. He has found this leaflet. Read the leaflet and answer Luis's questions.

a 'Brot' means bread, doesn't it? Do Hand-in-Hand make bread for poor people?
b What jobs can I do with Hand-in-Hand?
c When do they need people?
d I can't work for more than a few hours on Sundays. Is that OK?
e Do the people have to pay for the food?

Hand-in-Hand

Nicht alle Menschen haben genug zu essen – dennoch werden jeden Tag einwandfreie Lebensmittel weggeworfen! Die Initiative Hand-in-Hand sammelt Brot und andere Lebensmittel an Samstagnachmittagen nach Ladenschluss ein. Die Lebensmittel werden samstagabends und sonntags kostenlos an bedürftige Personen verteilt.
Hand-in-Hand sucht ehrenamtliche Helferinnen und Helfer, die beim Sammeln, Zubereiten und Verteilen des Essens mitwirken können. Ein paar Stunden am Wochenende genügen, Ihren Beitrag zu leisten. Ausführliche Infos im Internet unter www.ha

D Listening

Two high school kids are talking about what they did with Global Kids. Listen and complete the sentences.

a The first speaker joined Global Kids … ago.
b He worked on a project that was about … .
c They found out how clean the water was in the lake in … .
d The second speaker found out about kids who … .
e She found the project interesting, but … .
f She sometimes forgets to … .

E Writing

1 *Which of the 'GK' projects you have read and heard about would you like to work on? Write 4–5 sentences to say why.*

2 *Write a text (80–100 words) about the immigrant Rosa Sanchez. Use the notes.*

1993: born in small town – Mexico
1997–2000: family tried to enter US 3 times
2000: family entered Texas
2003: moved to New York, Rosa – school
2006: started to play the guitar
2007: started at high school in Brooklyn
2008: joined Global Kids – made radio program about immigrants in NY – fun, learned a lot

1

Unit 2 School life

1 School in the US

a) *Talk about the photos with a partner. Which of the scenes could happen during your school day? Which couldn't? Say why.*

b) *Read the 'Did you know?' texts. Which things could be a good idea for your school? Which wouldn't you like? Say why.*

2 Listening: School scenes

a) *Listen. Match each scene with a photo.*

b) *In two of the scenes there is a problem. What are the problems? Take notes.*

* c) *For which scene is there no photo? How could the photo look?*

→ WB 18, 1

VOCBOX

to pass [pɑːs] – *weitergeben*
microscope ['maɪkrəskəʊp] – *Mikroskop*
serious ['sɪəriəs] – *ernst*
pompom ['pɒmpɒm] – *Pompom (bunte Quaste)*
to chant [tʃɑːnt] – *rhythmisch rufen*
to date [deɪt] – *sich verabreden*

Steve Lopez, 8th Grade Schedule: Monday – Friday

1st period	9:00 – 9:40	English
2nd period	9:43 – 10:23	Math
3rd period	10:33 – 11:13	P.E.
4th period	11:16 – 11:56	Science
Lunch	11:56 – 1:00	Lunch
5th period	1:00 – 1:40	History
6th period	1:43 – 2:20	Orchestra

Time for sports and other activities
15:20 End of school day

3

5

DID YOU KNOW?

- School buses in the US are yellow, because the color is easy to see on dark mornings. The buses are free, and pick students up near where they live.
- Students say the Pledge of Allegiance at the start of every day. It shows that they support their country.
- Each year students receive 2–4 report cards with their grades.
- At many schools, students have the same classes every day. They go to a different room for each period.
- Cheerleaders support the school teams at football and baseball games. Cheerleading is also a national sport.
- In many schools there are elections to decide who is the most popular student in each class.

3 The schedule

a) *Look at Steve's schedule.*

1. When does school start and finish?
2. Which subject has different spellings in American and British English?
3. There are three minutes between most of the periods. Why?

b) *Would you like to have the same schedule every day? What are the pros and cons?*

4 Your turn: School FAQs

a) *American schools often have 'frequently asked questions' on their home pages for visitors and new students. Write five FAQs to help American visitors to your school.*

Is there …? | Where can I …? | What happens if …? | When …?

b) *Write the answers to your partner's FAQs.* ✓

→ WB 18, 2

The Growl

Berry Middle School is in Mesquite, Texas. The school is for students in the sixth, seventh and eighth grades. Its magazine is 'The Growl'.

Dear students!
Welcome to this semester's magazine!
We have news, information and advice for all our students.

Student Council corner

Student Council's next big charity event this year is the Fall Dance on November 28 from 7–10 pm. Tickets cost $10. The money will go to poor families in Mesquite. Do you have a date yet?

This month's special charity pencils are for sale during lunch for 50¢. Get yours now and write a personal note to go with it. Give it back to us with the name of the person you want to send it to. We'll deliver it in 5th period, Monday November 3.

Student Council shares students' ideas and problems with teachers and the principal. If you want them to hear your voice, then you ought to vote for your class Council member at the elections on December 4.

From the principal

All students should remember these important school rules:

1. Students will receive detention after school if they arrive late to school or class three times.

2. Students must follow the new school dress code. Important points: boys must not wear earrings; girls' jewelry must not be too large; boys' hair must not be longer than their shirt collar. Pants must not be the same color as sweatshirts and T-shirts. We will send home students who do not follow the dress code.

3. Students must not smoke in school.

1 Berry Middle School

a) *Work with a partner. Talk about these questions.*

1. What happens at Berry if students are late? Is your school stricter?
2. Is your partner following the Berry dress code? Do you think the dress code is fair for boys and girls?
3. What's happening on November 28?
4. Why do students send charity pencils? Is there an event like this at your school?
5. Why should students vote on December 4? Does your school have elections?

b) *Who, or what is it? Explain in your own words.*

Example: A semester is a part of the school year.

1. a middle school
2. the Student Council
3. a charity event
4. a dress code
5. an election
6. the principal
7. a detention
8. the fall

2 Revision: Students at the school → G7

Make sentences about Berry Middle School.

Example: students – wear the wrong clothes / they – have problems at school
If students wear the wrong clothes, they'll have problems at school.

1. students – buy a ticket for the dance / they – help poor people in Mesquite
2. they – want to go to the dance / they – need a date
3. they – not listen in class / they – not get good grades
4. they – vote at the elections / the teachers and the principal – hear their voice
5. they – not follow the dress code / the principal – send them home
6. they – arrive late three times / they – receive detention
7. they – not read the school magazine / they – not find out about school events
8. a student – want to send a pencil / the Student Council – deliver it

→ WB 19, 1

3 Listening: Dress code or uniform?

Listen. A student from Berry Middle School is on vacation in Florida. He talks to a girl from the UK. Which of these things is the boy not allowed to wear at school?

LISTENING SKILLS

Always think about the topic before you listen. What do you already know about the dress code? What do you know about schools in the UK?

4 Real talk: Advice for a friend

What advice can you give a friend in these situations? Act a dialogue.

1. Your friend has to stay at home Friday because he / she got bad grades.
2. Your friend has borrowed someone's camera but has lost it.
3. Your friend is taking French this semester but doesn't like the other students.
4. Your friend wants to buy a computer but has no money.

USEFUL PHRASES

Maybe you could …	You really ought to …
You should / shouldn't …	Why don't you … ?

→ WB 20, 2–3

5 Your turn: Rules at your school

An American student is going to visit your school next week. Write an e-mail to tell him or her about five of your school rules (or your classroom rules).

Dear …,

You'll like our school. But there are some rules, too. …

Dating tips

Dating is a hot topic at middle school. If you want a date, you have to ask someone. But asking someone out on a date isn't always easy. If you do it wrong, you could get a 'no' for an answer. On the evening of the date there are clear rules, too. OK, you like watching movies but you hate going alone? Or you still don't have a date for the next school dance? Well, you need to learn fast!

1 Dating

a) *What should you do before and during an American date? What shouldn't you do?*

* b) *Are there rules like this for you and your friends? How are they different?*

2 Ideas for a date

What do you think of these ideas?

Example: watch football games

I wouldn't like that. I hate watching football games.

1. go to concerts
2. skateboard
3. dance
4. go for long hikes
5. swim
6. play badminton

GRAMMAR

You can use a gerund to say what you think of an action.

▶ *I like **watching movies**.*

▶ ***Dating** is fun.*

→ G9

I love … • I enjoy … •
I like … / I don't like … •
I hate … / I can't stand …

→ WB 21, 1–2

3 Good and bad ideas on a date

a) *Look at what some middle school kids said about their dates. Which were good ideas and which were bad? Make two lists.*

Good ideas 🙂	Bad ideas ☹
Being polite	Falling …
…	…

"He was polite when Dad opened the door."
"She fell asleep during the movie!"
"He danced with three other girls."
"She said thanks at the end of the evening."
"He was late when he picked me up."
"She talked on her cell phone for an hour."
"He bought the cokes."
"She wore nice clothes."

b) *What was the best / worst idea? Talk with a partner.*

A: I think dancing with three other girls was a terrible idea.   B: Yes, but …

→ WB 22, 3–4 → G9

4 Real talk: Dates

Imagine you are in a US movie for teenagers. Your character has to ask someone out on a date. Act the scene as a role play. Here are some ideas.

Friday – movies – seven o'clock

Saturday – ice skating rink – three o'clock

Saturday – school dance – eight o'clock

USEFUL PHRASES

Would you like to …?
Well, let me check. I think that's OK.
Thank you, but I'm dating someone else.
Oh. That's a pity.
What time should we meet?
I can pick you up at …
I have to be back home by …
OK. See you around.

5 Your turn: Pros and cons

What do you think of American-style dating? Write about the pros and cons. ✓

Language in different situations

Europeans usually find that Americans are very casual. But that doesn't mean that you can talk casually to every American. 'Teen talk', for example, is not the right thing for a tourist information office. Just like in your own language, you should talk differently – or use a different 'register' – in different situations.

1 Different registers

Think of situations where you need to use different registers. Write them in two groups. Think of two or three situations for each group.

Polite	Casual
talking to …	…

WB 24, 1

2 Phrases

Look at the phrases below and find the pairs with the same meaning.

1 What did you say?
2 Would you like something to drink?
3 Excuse me, could you help me, please?
4 If you want a drink, get it yourself.
5 Hello, could I speak to Mr. Brian Jones, please?
6 Hey, give me some help!
7 I'm sorry, could you repeat that, please?
8 Hi, is Brian there?

WB 24, 2

3 Listening: What do you say?

a) *Listen to two phone calls. Which register do the speakers use in each call? How does the register change in the second call?*

b) *How could the conversations end? With a partner, choose one of the scenes and collect ideas for the rest of the conversation. Be careful with the register!*

c) *Act out your phone calls for your class.*

Here are some more tips for when you meet Americans:

TIP

Teenagers don't shake hands when they meet, even the first time.
Friends don't kiss when they meet. That's European.
When you meet a friend's parents, always use Mr. / Mrs. / Ms. and their last name.

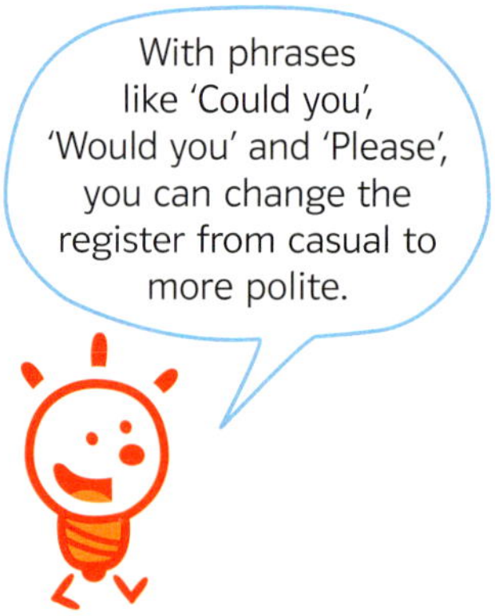

Before the dance

1 The Fall Dance

Before you read, think: what do you already know about the Fall Dance at Berry Middle School?

Steve

Brittany

Tiffany

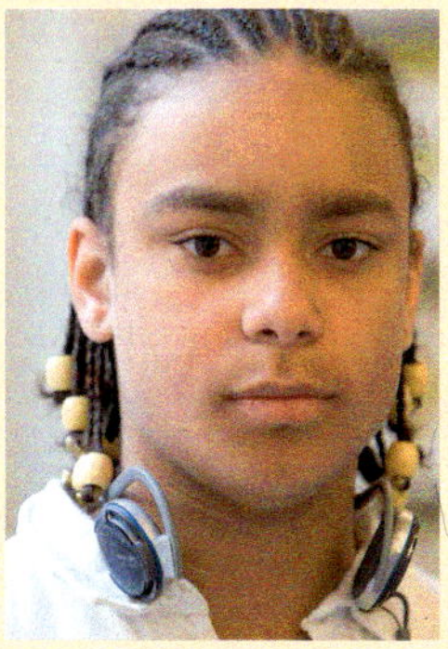
Joshua

Steve had been late to Math class three times this semester, so he didn't see the posters until he came out of detention. It was one of Student Council's most important charity events of the year, the one no one wanted to miss: the Fall Dance in November.

Dating was very important at Berry Middle School. The girls always asked the boys to the Fall Dance. Steve liked dancing, but he didn't think his chances were very good; he hadn't had a date in 7th grade, and the new school dress code didn't help. What girl went crazy about khaki pants?

It was Monday, 5th period. This month, Student Council was selling 'Berry Bear' pencils for poor families in Mesquite. You could send them to your friends, with a note. They were delivering today. But Steve hadn't sent any pencils. Boys only did that if they had a girlfriend, so he was surprised when he heard his name.

"Hey, the orchestra geek got a pencil," Cody, the school bully, shouted.
Steve didn't answer. He put the pencil into his backpack. He didn't have time to look at it.

While Steve was walking to the Music room for his 6th-period class, Brittany Kolden saw him and asked, "Did you get the pencil?"
"Huh?" Steve said. "Oh, yeah. The pencil."
The bell rang and they had to run. The pencil was from Brittany? Cool.

Back at his locker after 6th period, Steve looked into his backpack. The pencil was at the bottom, under the sandwich he hadn't eaten for lunch. The mayonnaise had left stains on the note, so he couldn't read everything, only 'dance', 'with me', 'Love,' and the letters 'ny' at the end. He smiled as he took out his jacket. Suddenly his friend Joshua was there.
"What are you smiling about?" Joshua asked.
"Um ... Brittany asked me to the dance."
"Brittany Smith, the principal's daughter?"
"No, Brittany Kolden, the cheerleader."
"What?! She looked great at the game Saturday," said Joshua. "Hey, can she get me a date with her friend Tiffany?" he added.

In front of the school, Brittany was getting onto the school bus.
"Brittany!" Steve shouted. "I'll go!"
"So cool!" she answered. "Bye!"

"Steeeeeve! Telephone!" called Kerry, Steve's little sister. "It's a giiiiirl!"
Steve went to the phone.
"Hi, Steve. It's Tiffany. I just wanted to tell you what color my dress is."
"Your dress?"
"Yeah, for the dance on Saturday. It's red-orange. What are you wearing?"
"Um, um … Do you need to know?"
"No, silly. It's not like I'm buying you flowers. You're buying me flowers."
What? Did he have two dates?
"… so I'll see you tomorrow. Bye, Steve!"
"Yeah, see you, Tiffany."

Steve went into his bedroom and looked at himself in the mirror. "Hey, you are one lucky guy. Brittany and Tiffany are crazy about you. Cody will never call you a geek again. They may even elect you to Student Council!"

The next day in 1st period before the Pledge of Allegiance, Steve was bragging to the guys.
"So, do you think I can take them both? One on each arm?" he joked, but he could really imagine it. Having two dates was just awesome.

At lunch he could see that people were whispering about him when he walked past. He liked being the subject of gossip – like the popular kids. But after lunch, Steve felt that kids were laughing at him. How could that be? Laughing at the guy with two dates?

After 6th period, Steve saw Brittany.
"Hey, Brittany. You ought to tell me the color of your dress."
She looked at Steve a little strangely before she told him.
"I like yellow, too," said Steve. "It'll look good on you."
Brittany waited for what seemed like forever before she replied, "Um, yeah. I hope Scott likes it, too."

Steve was at his locker when he saw Tiffany.
"Steve," she said in a quiet voice. "Are you already going to the dance with Brittany?
I can't believe she would do this to me.
She knew I was sending you the pencil!
And I can't believe *you* would do this to me!
Well, I've got some news for you, cool guy!
My date for the Fall Dance is your friend, Joshua!"

2 Before the dance

a) *Answer the questions.*

1. Who sent Steve the pencil?
2. Who is Brittany's date for the dance? Who is Tiffany's?
3. How does Steve feel at the end of the story? Why does he feel that way?

b) *What do you think? Was Steve stupid?*

c) *Right or wrong? Correct the wrong sentences.*

1. At Berry Middle School's Fall Dance, the girls ask the boys to the dance.
2. Steve is in 7th grade this year.
3. Steve has Science 6th period.
4. Brittany Kolden is the principal's daughter.
5. The boys have to buy flowers for their dates.
6. Steve felt cool after lunch the second day.
7. He wanted to wear yellow to the dance.
8. Tiffany was mad with Joshua at the end.

→ WB 25,1

3 Who's who?

a) *Make a list of all the characters in the story. Put the names into a mind map and write information under the names to show who's who.*

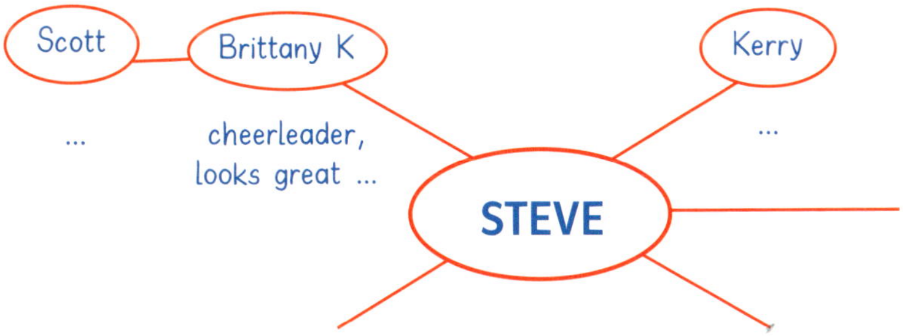

⟨ ⟩ b) *Make a mind map like this for yourself and four or five people you know well.*

4 Your turn: At lunch

WRITING SKILLS

Writing a dialogue

Make a plan for the dialogue before you write it. What do the characters feel about each other? (You can use what you already know about them from the story.)

Remember that the characters should be the same in the dialogue as they are in the story. Brittany is still a cheerleader, and Steve still – probably! – likes bragging.

a) *Steve, Tiffany and Brittany all have lunch at school the next day. Write a dialogue for a scene in which they meet.*

b) *Read someone else's dialogue. Tell the other person what you think and give him/her some advice. Be positive!*

USEFUL PHRASES

This part is great.
I like the end of the dialogue.
Maybe you should change this part.
I don't really understand this sentence.

⟨ ⟩ 5 A song: First date

In the car I just can't wait,
To pick you up on our very first [1].
Is it [2] if I hold your hand?
Is it wrong if I think it's lame to dance?
Do you like my [3] hair?
Would you guess that I didn't know what to [4]?
I'm too [5] of what you think
You make me [6] so I really can't eat.
Let's go, don't [7], this night's almost over.
Honest, let's make this [8] last forever
Forever and ever, let's make this last forever.

Tr. L. Barker / Th. DeLonge / M. Hoppus © Fun with Goats / EMI April Music Inc.

a) *Read the lyrics. What could the missing words be?*

b) *Listen and find the missing words.*

c) *How does the singer feel? Why?*

1 Triangles

a) *Make AE-BE-German word triangles with these words.*

Example: student

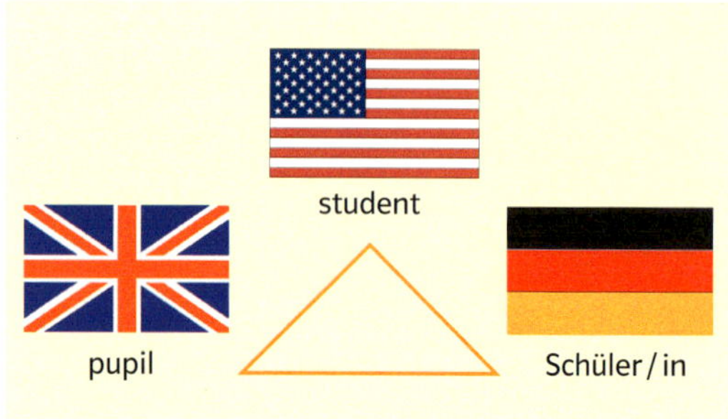

1. principal
2. Math
3. schedule
4. pants
5. fall
6. backpack
7. (8th) grade
8. (good) grade

b) *Why do you need to be careful when you talk about pants? Look the word up in an English – German dictionary and find all the meanings.*

* c) *Make more word triangles with other AE words you know. Use your dictionary.*

2 Monday morning, first period

a) *Look at the picture for two minutes, then close your books. Write down all the things you can remember about the picture.*

b) *Exchange lists with a partner. How many things could your partner remember? Give one point for each thing he / she remembered and another point if the spelling is correct each time.*

3 Sounds: Difficult words

a) *Read the words to yourself and then read four of them to your partner.*

1. mayonnaise
2. semester
3. allegiance
4. register
5. European
6. casual
7. orchestra
8. information

b) *Now listen and check. Did your partner say the words correctly?*

4 One of a group

a) *Find the right group for each noun.*

Example: earring → jewelry

subject | flower | fruit | color | fish | jewelry ✓ | bag | building | furniture

1. cherry
2. station
3. yellow
4. daffodil
5. table
6. backpack
7. Math
8. tuna

* b) *Find three more words for each group.*

5 Verb friends

Put the parts together correctly.

1. to follow
2. to wear
3. to receive
4. to vote
5. to buy
6. to shake
7. to laugh
8. to ask

someone out on a date
at someone
flowers for someone
a detention
the dress code
earrings
in an election
hands with someone

6 At your school

How can you explain these words in English?

Example: 'Projektwoche' is a week when we do projects and we don't have normal classes.

1. Klassensprecher
2. SMV (SV)
3. Klassenlehrer
4. Entschuldigung
5. Aula
6. Nachhilfestunde
7. Schullandheim
8. Wandertag
9. Zeugnis
10. Abschlussprüfung

USEFUL PHRASES

It's something which …
It's someone who …
It's a place where …
It's a kind of …

7 In Art class

Scott is taking Art class this semester. Look at what the teacher says and find the right word each time.

away | up | off ✓ | out | off | down | up | away

Example: Scott, could you take **off** those earrings, please? You know the dress code!

1. Brittany, could you go to the principal's office and pick … some books for me?
2. Hey, don't throw those cards … ! We can use them to make something else.
3. Hey, Tiffany, turn … that MP3 player and put it … now.
4. Let's cut the triangles … now, OK?
5. If you don't know what the word means, why don't you look it … in your dictionary?
6. OK, guys, here's the homework. Can you write it … now, please?

STUDY SKILLS A B C

We call verbs that go with a preposition or an adverb 'phrasal verbs'. Try to learn them together with a noun.

to take off earrings
to pick up some books
…

→ WB 26, 1–3

1 Tiffany and her mom (conditional sentences with 'will' → G 7)

a) *When Tiffany wants something, she often promises to do something for her mom. What does she promise?*

Example:

If you buy me a new dress for the Fall Dance, I'll help you in the garden.

let me / go / disco	→	wash / car
drive me / school	→	cook / supper
wash / my sports clothes	→	do / shopping
lend me / digital camera	→	clean / windows
let me / use / new laptop	→	make / family website

b) *Sometimes Tiffany doesn't do what she promised. What does her mom say?*

Example: If you don't help me in the garden soon, I won't buy you a new dress!

2 A school project (gerund as subject → G 9)

Jody is talking about a school project he did in Science class. Put in the gerund of the verbs.

listen to | work | find out | look for | talk | use | answer | write

1. Our Science project was cool. **Finding out** about water was interesting.
2. … information on the Internet took hours. But we found some good pictures.
3. … the microscope was interesting. Our water isn't as clean as I thought!
4. … cards with notes for the presentation helped us to remember what to say.
5. … other groups' presentations gave us some ideas.
6. … the questions at the end of the presentation wasn't too difficult.
7. … about the presentation after you've done it is important.
8. … in a group was fun. I did the work and Steve made the jokes!

3 Say what you think! (gerund as subject → G 9)

Look at what these students say about different activities. Rewrite the sentences with a gerund.

Example: "Buy a Berry pencil! It will help poor people in Mesquite."
→ **Buying** a Berry pencil will help poor people in Mesquite.

1. "I joined the orchestra last semester. It was a good idea!"
2. "I sometimes go to the movies. It costs a lot of money!"
3. "Some kids laugh when a student gives the wrong answer. That's awful!"
4. "We drew pictures of our teacher in Art class this morning. It was fun!"
5. "We went on a trip to the Space Center in Florida. It taught us a lot about Science."
6. "My dad runs every weekend. It's good for him!"
7. "I always listen to my MP3 player on the bus. It helps me forget about school."
8. "A lot of the older kids smoke. That isn't cool."

4 The kids in 8th grade (gerund as object → G 9)

Write about the kids in Steve's 8th grade class.

Start like this: 1. Brittany **loves cycling.**

1 Brittany – to love

2 Scott – to like

3 Joshua – to enjoy

4 Carol – to hate

5 Tiffany – to like

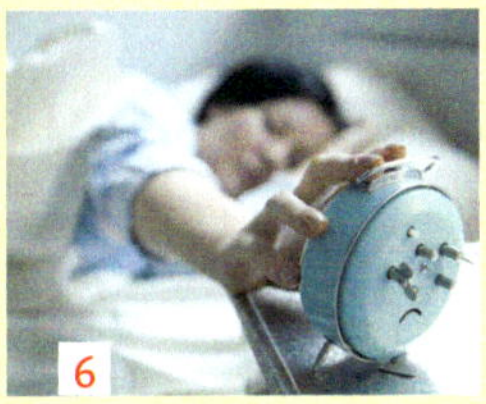
6 Kate – to hate

7 Steve – to not like

to skateboard • to wait for the bus • to go to the movies • to cycle • to swim • to play baseball • to get up early

→ WB 27, 1–3

5 Cheerleaders at the middle school (mixed exercise)

Choose the right tense each time.

Student Council corner

November 2

Hi everyone,

Our cheerleaders [1] a great job at our football games every week. With their chants and cool uniforms, they always [2] the 'Berry Bears' team. The cheerleaders [3] to a special workshop last weekend. You can see what they [4] there at the next football game! [5] to join the team, girls? Try-outs for the spring games [6] on November 13 from 3:30 to 5:30 pm. We [7] the team lists up by 9 am the next day. New 7th grade cheerleaders [8] their uniforms at the first practice on January 8. Good luck at the try-outs, everyone!

See you!

1 do / did
2 help / helped
3 go / went
4 learn / learned
5 Do you want / Did you want
6 were / will be
7 put / will put
8 received / will receive

NOW YOU CAN

- ✓ Talk about life at a US middle school. → Write three sentences about Berry Middle School.
- ✓ Talk about dates and dating. → Name three dating rules.
- ✓ Say what you think of activities. → Name two things you like doing and two things you can't stand doing.
- ✓ Say what will happen if … → Say what you will do if it rains all day Sunday.
- ✓ Give advice. → What can you say to someone who is tired every morning?

Skills workshop 2 Using computers

It's a good idea to use the Internet to find information before you do a presentation. You can also use a computer to show pictures and information on 'slides'. This workshop will help you to find information more quickly. It also has tips for presentations with a computer.

1 Collecting information

STUDY SKILLS

Decide what you are looking for before you start. If you use a **search engine**, choose your search term carefully. (Often typing in a question, or a phrase from the question, will help you to find the answer.)
You can use **online encyclopedias**, too. But be careful! In some encyclopedias, anyone can write the entries, and they sometimes have mistakes in them!

Here are some more tips:
- Skim the text on the website quickly. If it isn't a useful website, go back to the search engine.
- Change the language on the search engine to find pages in English (or German) only.
- Don't print more than one page. Why not copy the text you need into a file on your computer? You can save images, too.

a) *Use the tips in the skills box and find out about the American city, Detroit. Find the answers to these questions.*

1. Which state is Detroit in?
2. How many people live in Detroit?
3. What industry is Detroit famous for?
4. Which of these flags is Detroit's flag?

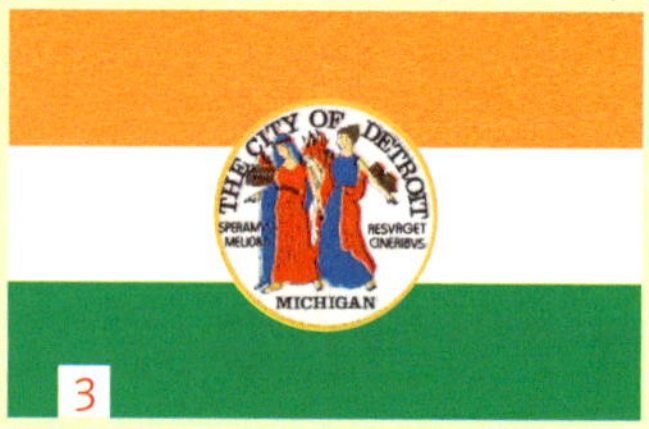

5. Which sport do the Detroit Red Wings play?
6. Find images of Detroit. What can you see in typical photos of the city?

b) *Now find similar information about another American city (not Detroit or New York City!) for a presentation. You can also add other interesting pictures or pieces of information!*

New Orleans | San Francisco | Seattle | Boston | Kansas City | …

2 Preparing the presentation

a) *Make a plan for your presentation on paper first. Think about these questions.*

How long do you want to speak?
Which pictures and information do you need?
What is the best order for the parts of your presentation?

b) *Make five or six computer slides for your presentation. Use the tips in the skills box.*

PRESENTATION SKILLS

Keep the slides simple and don't put too much information on each one. The slides can have pictures, animation, and even sound or video clips.

But remember: the slides are only a part of the presentation. What you say and how you say it is very important, too!

c) *Make a handout for your audience. It should have the important information and pictures from the slides. It could also have a list of the new words in your presentation.*

3 The presentation

PRESENTATION SKILLS

Talking to an audience

1. Don't hide! Stand close (but not too close!) to the audience.
2. Don't stand in front of the screen!
3. Check that everybody has understood before you go to the next slide.
4. Look at the audience and be friendly.
5. Don't talk too fast. It's a presentation, not a race!
6. If there is a problem with the slides, keep cool. The audience will understand!
7. Ask if there are any questions at the end.

a) *Read the tips in the skills box, and look at this speaker. What mistake is he making in each picture?*

b) *Now present what you have found out about your American city to the class. Good luck!*

c) *After the presentation, talk about it with the audience. What did they find most interesting? What went well? How can you make your next presentation better?*

STUDY SKILLS

Listen carefully while other people do their presentations. They can give you ideas.

Watching others can also help you not to make the same mistakes.

→ WB 29,1

1

Unit 3 In the Southwest

1 A sight to remember?

a) *What do you already know about the American Southwest?*

b) *Look at picture 1.*

1. How do you think the people feel?
2. What do you think they are saying to each other?

2 Facts and photos

a) *Find a keyword for each 'Did you know?' text. Match each keyword with a photo.*

b) *Which piece of information do you find most interesting? Say why.*

→ WB 32,1

VOCBOX

dry [draɪ] – *trocken*
platform ['plætfɔːm] – *Plattform*
dizzy ['dɪzi] – *schwindelig*
dusty ['dʌsti] – *staubig*
truck *(AE)* [trʌk] – *Lastwagen*
to gamble ['gæmbl] – *(Glücksspiele) spielen*

The states of the American Southwest:

- Arizona
- New Mexico
- Oklahoma
- Texas
- parts of Nevada

4

DID YOU KNOW?

- Route 66 runs for more than 2,000 miles from Chicago to California, through the hot, dry desert in the Southwest.
- The Southwest is famous for its cowboys. But today they sometimes use motorcycles instead of horses.
- Tourists come to Las Vegas from all over the world. They win or (lose!) money in its casinos.
- The Grand Canyon is a deep river gorge in Arizona. It is in Grand Canyon National Park, one of the huge national parks which protect America's plants and animals. From the 'Skywalk' above the canyon you can look one mile (1.6 km) down to the Colorado River. The Skywalk has a glass floor.

3 Listening: The Grand Canyon

Listen to the answering machine message at the Grand Canyon visitor center. Take notes to answer these questions.

1. When is the center open?
2. When do the tours into the canyon start?
3. How much do the tours cost?
4. What should people be careful about before they go down?

→ WB 32, 2

4 Your turn: The Southwest

a) *Collect information under these headings.*

states | cities | sights | climate | landscape | …

b) *Use the information to make a fact card about the Southwest.* ✓

The most beautiful place in the world

Lindy Turner is a ranger in Grand Canyon National Park. Today Lindy is telling a reporter about her job in the park.

Reporter: Did you always want to be a ranger?

Lindy: Well, I've been crazy about hiking and other outdoor sports since I was a kid. When I was 14, we went to Grand Canyon National Park on vacation and I fell in love with the place. That's when I decided I wanted to be a ranger.

Reporter: What do you do?

Lindy: There are two sides to the job. We organize programs for visitors. That's fun. Rangers need to be good at explaining things and answering questions. And we look after the park and protect nature. I often work alone for that part of the job, but I never worry about that. I know how to look after myself.

Reporter: Do you always enjoy your work?

Lindy: I've been a ranger for ten years, but I never get tired of showing the Grand Canyon to visitors. It's the most beautiful place in the world. I always look forward to seeing it when I've been away.

Reporter: Are there parts of the job you don't like?

Lindy: Well, tourists sometimes leave garbage in the Canyon. We have to pick it up. I'm not crazy about that! And then there are all the reports we have to type. A lot of rangers don't like that, but I'm used to doing it now.

Reporter: Thanks for your time, Lindy!

Lindy: You're welcome!

1 A great job?

a) *Would you like to be a park ranger? Say why or why not.*

b) *Make a list of the pros and cons of the job, as Lindy sees it. Do you agree with her?*

2 Crazy about picking up garbage?

Complete the sentences about Lindy.

1. She's been crazy about … since she was a kid.
2. For her job, she needs to be good at …
3. She never worries about …
4. She never gets tired of …
5. She always looks forward to …
6. She isn't crazy about …
7. She's used to … now.

GRAMMAR

Rangers are **good at talking** about nature.

→ WB 33, 1–2 → G 10

3 What about you?

a) *What about you? Write five sentences about yourself.*

I'm	crazy about, tired of, good at, interested in, not so good at, looking forward to	run, visit, see, meet, do, watch, …

b) *Compare your list with a partner's. Are you the same?*

A: Hey, I'm crazy about running, too! But I'm not interested in running in a marathon!
B: I didn't know you were interested in going to the US one day!

VOCABULARY SKILLS A B C

There are lots of phrases that take a gerund. Why not start a list? You can add to your list as you find more phrases of this kind in the texts you read.

- good at …
- interested in …
- …

c) *Write a short profile of your partner. Say what your partner is / isn't good at, crazy about and looking forward to doing.*

→ WB 34, 3

4 Listening: Native Americans at the Canyon

The Skywalk above the Grand Canyon belongs to the Hualapai Native Americans.

LISTENING SKILLS

In exercises like this, read the sentences carefully before you listen. Think about what information you need to listen for.

When a sentence is wrong, take notes with the right information. Use your notes when you do part b).

a) *Read the sentences and listen. Are the sentences right or wrong?*

1. The Hualapai are the only tribe that lives near the Grand Canyon.
2. The tribe has 1,000 members.
3. They get their name from the trees near the Canyon.
4. It's not very polite to call Native Americans 'Indians'.
5. They have always lived near the Canyon.
6. All the tribe members wanted the Skywalk.
7. It opened in 2004.

b) *Correct the wrong sentences.*

→ WB 34, 4

5 Your turn: A beautiful place

Write about a beautiful place that you know. Say where the place is, describe it and say why it is special. ✓

Summer camp

Lots of American kids go to summer camps. They stay away from home and they get the chance to do lots of activities. But not all kids enjoy summer camp …

+++ Forest Springs Summer Camp, Arizona +++

Fun and adventure from $650 per week!
Our campers are 7–16 years of age.

You'll live in cabins in the woods near the Grand Canyon. We offer 80 different activities. Choose from
+ making a movie
+ white water rafting
+ making campfires and cooking on them
+ enjoying campfire events (games, singing)
+ learning about animal tracks and plants

Dear Lynn,
My parents thought I would have a great time if I went to Forest Springs.
They were wrong! I hate it here! If I were at home, I would go out with you and the others every night. Here in the country, all we do is look at plants during the day and sit around a campfire with boring people and sing stupid songs in the evening. I thought about running away. But if I tried to run away, they would send a police boat down the Colorado River to find me, or a helicopter. It would be great! I'd probably be on TV if they found me! But Mom would be SO worried if she didn't know where I was. That would be awful! So I guess I'll have to stay here.
If you were here, it would be much more fun.
Love,
Abby

1 Forest Springs

a) *Which activities would you do if you spent a week at Forest Springs Summer Camp? Which wouldn't you do? Say why.*

b) *What doesn't Abby like about the camp? Why doesn't she run away?*

2 Abby

What would happen if …? Put the parts of the sentences together.

1. Abby would go out with her friends	she'd be on TV.
2. If she liked singing,	if Lynn was with her.
3. If she ran away,	she'd enjoy the evenings more.
4. If the police found her,	she'd be very worried.
5. If her mom didn't know where she was,	if she was at home.
6. It would be awful	the police would try to find her.
7. The vacation would be more fun,	if her mom was worried about her.

→ WB 35, 1

GRAMMAR

Look at the difference between these sentences.

▶ *If I **go** to summer camp, it **will be** fun.* (The speaker will probably go.)

▶ *If I **won** a million dollars in Las Vegas, I **would buy** a helicopter.* (This probably won't happen.)

→ G 11

3 What would you do?

a) *What would you do in these situations? How would you feel?*

Example: You meet Matt Damon and you can ask him anything you like.
If I met Matt Damon, I'd ask him about his next movie.

1. Someone gives you a plane ticket to anywhere in the world. (And back!)
2. You win a white water rafting vacation in the Grand Canyon. It's for you and one other person.
3. You find fifty euros outside the station in the town where you live.
4. One of your parents gets a fantastic new job. It's in a town in Arizona.
5. A famous rap musician wants you as an extra in his next video.
6. You have to live on an island for a year. You are only allowed to take one piece of music with you.

* b) *Make up three more situations. Write what you would do and how you would feel in each situation.*

→ WB 36, 2–3

4 Real talk: City or country?

a) *What do you think is better, life in the city or in the country? First make notes to support your opinion.*

b) *Talk with a partner. You can use the useful phrases. Do you and your partner agree?*

USEFUL PHRASES

I think living in a city is better, because …
In my opinion, …
I'm quite sure that …
It's a fact that …

That's true, but …
I can see what you mean, but …
Yes, but you're forgetting something.
I wouldn't say that!

c) *Write about 80 words to say what you think is better, the city or the country.*

5 Your turn: Away from home

Where would you go if you got the chance to spend two weeks away from home, without your family? What would you do? What wouldn't you do?

I'd go skiing with my friends …

A happy ending

Something happened in a canyon in Arizona this morning.
A girl, a young man and a park ranger are talking about it on TV.

24 Hours **Top News**

Accident in Arizona

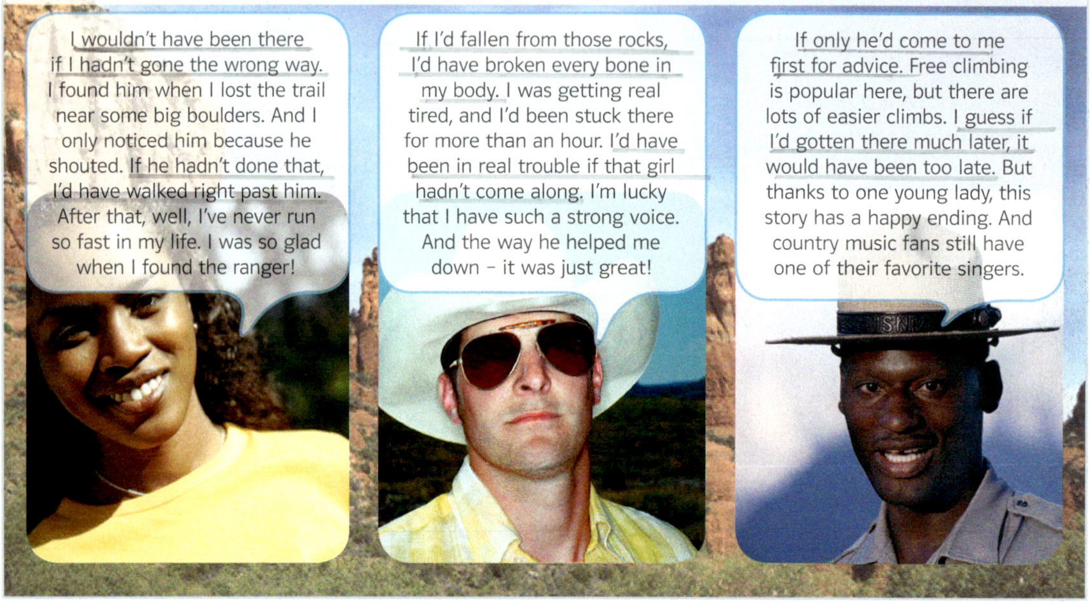

1 What happened?

a) *Work in small groups. Look at what the three people say. Find clues about what happened. Put the facts in the right order.*

WRITING SKILLS

Remember to give your report a headline. You should only put facts in the report, and not your opinions.

b) *Write a report for a newspaper about what (nearly) happened in the canyon. Start like this:* A young man was free climbing in Arizona this morning. …

→ WB 37,1

2 Looking at English

GRAMMAR

We can use conditional sentences to talk about things in the past. They often tell us about things that nearly happened, or nearly didn't happen.

- ***I'd*** *(= I would)* ***have been*** *in real trouble if that girl* ***hadn't come*** *along.*
  (The man didn't get into real trouble.)
- *If only* ***he'd*** *(= he had)* ***come*** *to me first for advice.*
  (The person didn't come for advice.)

Read the grammar box, then find the other sentences in the text with 'I'd' or 'he'd' in them. What is the ***'d*** *short for each time?*

→ G12

3 It would have been different

Complete the sentences about the story.

Example: If the girl hadn't found the ranger, … (the story • end • differently)
If the girl hadn't found the ranger, the story **would have ended** differently.

1. If the girl had gone the right way, … (she • not be • there)
2. She wouldn't have heard the man if … (he • not shout • so loudly)
3. If he hadn't shouted, … (she • walk • past him)
4. The ranger would have arrived too late if … (the girl • not run • so fast)
5. If the man had talked to the ranger first, … (he • tell him • about an easier climb)
6. It would have been too late if … (the ranger • arrive • much later)
7. If the man had chosen an easier climb, … (he • not need • any help)
8. The man would have been in real trouble if … (the girl • not come • along)

* 4 If he had fallen …

Find three different endings for this sentence.

If the young man had fallen, … | … would have … | … wouldn't have … |

5 If …

a) *Put the parts of the sentences together.*

1. If I went free climbing,	we'd have moved to New Mexico.
2. If I had taken a map on the hike,	he wouldn't have lost his money!
3. If Dad had got that job last year,	you'll never forget it.
4. If I go to a summer camp in August,	I'll probably get wet.
5. If I went for a hike in a canyon,	I'd try an easy climb first.
6. If I try white water rafting,	we wouldn't have gotten lost!
7. If he hadn't gone to the casino,	I'd wear a hat and take some water.
8. If you go to the Southwest,	I'll try white water rafting.

* b) *Choose five of the first halves from part a). Write your own second parts.*

→ WB 37, 2; 38, 3 → G 13

6 Your turn: A dangerous situation

Write about a dangerous situation you have been in. Describe the situation, and what nearly happened, or nearly didn't happen. Write 80–100 words.

When and where did it happen? • Who was there? • What was dangerous about the situation? • What would/would not have happened if …

Polite small talk

In the US, people who don't know each other well often ask questions that sound personal. Really they are just being polite, and they don't want a full answer to the question. We call this kind of conversation small talk, but the word 'small' doesn't mean it isn't important! Being friendly and polite to each other in public is very important for Americans.

1 Listening: At the supermarket

a) *Listen to three short conversations at a supermarket. In which conversations is the customer friendly?*

b) *Look at the useful phrases and listen again. Which of the useful phrases do the people use?*

c) *The next time you are waiting in line in a supermarket, listen. Do people in your country use small talk in the same way?*

USEFUL PHRASES

Hi, how are you today?
I'm fine, what about you?
Hey, sounds great!
I see your (T-shirt) there. It's really nice.
The weather's great …
Yeah, isn't it just beautiful today?
You're right about that.
Thanks, have a nice day.

2 Polite small talk

Imagine the cashier is speaking to you. What can you say each time?

1. "Hi – everything OK?"
2. "Isn't it a nice day today?"
3. "So are you having a good day?"
4. "What are you going to do today?"
5. "I haven't seen you here before."
6. "What kind of accent is that?"

→ WB 40, 1–2

3 With people you don't know well

Imagine you're at a party in the US and you don't know most of the people. With a partner, use these prompts to start a short conversation. Don't forget to use the useful phrases, too.

1. Someone says to you, "Isn't it hot this summer? Wow!"
2. Someone is talking about the Grand Canyon. You want to see it, too.
3. Someone tells you, "The food is great."
4. You hear someone with an accent that is different from yours.
5. You see someone your age with a T-shirt with the name and picture of your favorite US city.

TIP

These phrases can help if the other person isn't very friendly:
OK, I was only wondering.
Oh, I see. / Sure, that's OK.

Downriver

This story is about some teenagers at a summer camp. The activities were not exciting enough for them, so they 'borrowed' two rafts and rowed down the Colorado River to the Grand Canyon. Now, a week later, they know it is important to stop and 'scout', or look carefully at the dangerous rapids, Granite Falls, before they go farther. But Al, from the summer camp, and the police, are chasing them. Jessie, one of the girls in the group, tells the story.

READING SKILLS

This is part of a novel for American teenagers, but you can enjoy it, too. Try to get the 'gist' of the story. Who's who in the story, what's happening, and where? Don't worry if there are some words that you don't know.

We began to hear the noise of Granite Falls downriver. As we all started looking around for where to scout, Freddy said, "Helicopters."

On the left side, where we would have to scout, two helicopters were parked, and Al stood above the beach with three other men. We couldn't scout on the right side. It was all cliff over there.

They've got us, I thought. They know we'll have to scout Granite. Game's over.

"They don't have us, you know," Troy said. "Only if we give ourselves up."

"I'm not ready to quit, no way," Rita said.

"Maybe we should go closer," I said. "We could talk to them."

Troy wasn't too happy with me.

"What about? Are we going to believe what they say? And they'll try to scare us about the rapids."

"Live free or die," sang Adam and Pug.

"I love the river," Star said. "I want to stay with the rest of you for as long as I can."

Troy was pleased. "Freddy?"

I remembered when Troy had suggested the trip. Freddy was the only one, I knew now, who had had any idea what it might be like.

"Let's run it," Freddy said.

We moved into the current that would take us into the rapids. The men on the beach were waving their arms, but we couldn't stop now. The adrenaline was making my heart go crazy. Troy was standing up on his seat and scouting.

Behind us Freddy was standing up in the other raft. He wasn't as close yet as we were.

"Good water on the right," Troy shouted. "Rocks center and left. Watch where I enter – stay away from the cliff! Looks nasty!"

Nasty is right. We shot into the rapids, a long line of huge waves that exploded between the rocks in the center and the cliff on the right. It was over fast. At the bottom we rode the tall waves and I saw with joy that Freddy's boat had also made it. Troy was pointing back and laughing at Al.

After a few miles of calm water we came to Hermit Rapids, with the helicopters above us. Hermit wasn't scary at all, and we were sure enjoying having the audience.
Then we began to hear thunder from the black clouds downriver. As soon as the lightning started, the helicopters turned and flew away.
Troy was laughing. "Looks like our friends can't take a little weather." The next moment a dark wall of rain was marching up the canyon.
We couldn't see Crystal Rapids when we got near, but we could sure hear them. We got out of the boats and went down a trail, then through a field of boulders. Between us and the cliff wall opposite, the whole river went into a narrow slot and then fell into a deep hole. The violence of the water was shocking.
"What do you think, Freddy?" Troy said. "We can make it, right?"
He explained his plan, and Freddy listened. Then Freddy said, "No. Water's too strong, that hole's too bad. But there's no reason we can't carry everything around it."
"You mean walk?" Troy said. "Do you guys have any idea how much work that would be? Look, have we had any trouble so far? How many times have I flipped, tell me that. That's right – zero. Let's get started."
"Sorry," Freddy said. "I'm walkin'. If we lose the boats in there, what happens to us?"
Only Freddy, I realized, would be brave enough to stand up to Troy. The rest of us were sheep, and had been, all the way.
"We'll carry the other boat and be ready," Freddy said helpfully, "if anything happens."
"You're so sure we're going to flip," Troy sneered. "You'd love to rescue us, wouldn't you, Freddy? Adam, will you come with me?"

The rain stopped. The rest of us said "Good luck" to Adam and Troy and lifted the other raft onto our shoulders. We had just got to the boulder field when we heard a shout above the noise of the rapids. We looked back to see a brave, silly sight: Troy was rowing, while Adam was holding a rope in the boat with one hand and waving his free hand like a bronc rider. Troy was rowing hard, was trying to pull against the current. He was working … working … but he wasn't making it. A violent wave lifted the boat up and over the hole. The boat fell, and then it flipped.
"Quick!" Freddy shouted, and we started running through the boulders.
They're going to die, I thought. What are we doing here?
Halfway down, we saw the boat close to one of the rocks in the river. No sign of Troy or Adam.
"Holy mother," Rita said. "Holy mother."

From *Downriver*, by Will Hobbs (adapted)

1 The story

a) *Did you enjoy the story? How does the ending make you feel?*

b) *Finish the sentences with 'because'.*

1. The kids couldn't scout Granite Falls …
2. They couldn't stop before the rapids …
3. The helicopters flew away …
4. Freddy wanted to walk …
5. Troy wanted to ride through …
6. The kids ran through the boulder field …

because …

2 Parts of the story

a) *Each heading describes a part of the story. Put the headings into the right order.*

They can't stop now | An argument | Near Granite Falls | Goodbye | Near Crystal Rapids | Disaster? | Hermit Rapids

b) *Write one or two sentences for each heading to make a summary of the story.*

3 Words from the story

VOCABULARY SKILLS A B C

Does the rest of the sentence give you a clue about the meaning of the word? Is the word similar to a word in German or another language you know? Have you met the word somewhere else (computer programs, songs, sport …)?

Think what these words from the story could mean:

to quit (line 14)	adrenaline (line 32)
to make it (68)	to march (57)
the current (29)	shocking (66)
shoulder (90)	a bronc rider (96)

4 Listening: About the novel

Listen to the conversation. Find out …

1. … if the speakers liked the novel.
2. … if Troy and Adam die.
3. … how the trip ends.
4. … what kind of guy Al is.

5 Your turn: A book you have read

Write a report (80–100 words) about a novel or story you have read and enjoyed. Your report should answer these questions:

Who wrote the novel or story? • Who are the most important characters? • What happens (in two or three sentences)? • Why did you enjoy it?

1 Summer camp

a) *What can visitors do at Crazy Horse Summer Camp? Find five or more activities.*

b) *Check your partner's list. Are his / her words correct?*

2 Nature words

a) *Put the words into the right groups.*

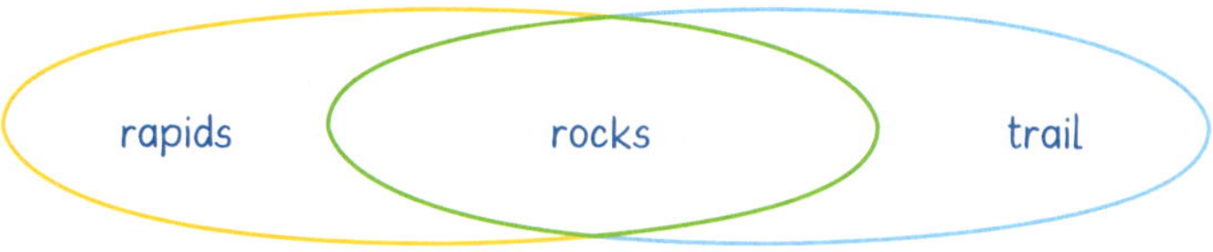

nature (water) | nature (land and water) | nature (land)

rapids ✓ | to row | to go for a hike | wave | boulder | raft | current | cliff | trail ✓ | animal tracks | rocks ✓

b) *Add more words to the groups. You can use your dictionary, too.*

3 Word building

Use the verbs to make nouns for the sentences. Use your dictionary if you are not sure.

1. Today's cowboys are often very good motorcycle …, too. (to ride)
2. In the novel 'Downriver', there is a … between Freddy and Troy. (to fight)
3. The man who was stuck in the canyon was a famous … (to sing)
4. … is hard for lots of Native Americans. (to live)
5. Millions of … come to America's national parks every year. (to visit)
6. What did the … want to say? (to speak)
7. Have you ever tried free …? (to climb)
8. Look at this beautiful … of the Grand Canyon. (to paint)

4 What can you say?

Some people at a party say these things to you. Think of nice answers.

1. Hey, you're not from here, are you? You have a different accent.
2. Are you having fun this evening?
3. You're from Europe? So how do you like America?
4. Have you been to Texas before?
5. Wasn't it just a beautiful day today?
6. German people wear those funny mountain hats, don't they?

5 Sounds: Stress

Listen. Put the words and phrases into two groups.

everything • umbrella • plane ticket • reporter • tomorrow • animal • vacation • summer camp • opinion • Grand Canyon • favorite • wondering

●••	•●•
everything …	umbrella …

→ WB 42, 1–3

6 A song: Route 66

Bobby Troup © Burke & Van Heusen Inc.

If you ever plan to motor [1], travel my way,
Take the highway that's the [2] –
Get your kicks on Route 66.

It winds from Chicago to LA,
More than two thousand [3] all the way.
Get your kicks on Route 66.

Now you go through Saint Louis, Joplin,
Missouri, and Oklahoma City looks mighty [4].

You [5] Amarillo, Gallup, New Mexico,
Flagstaff, Arizona, don't [6] Winona,
Kingman, Barstow, San Bernardino.

Won't you get hip to this timely [7]:
When you make that California [8]
Get your kicks on Route 66.

a) *Listen carefully and write down the missing words.*

b) *How many of the places in the song can you find on the map at the front of your book?*

1 A boy at Forest Springs (gerund after prepositions → G 10)

Tim was at Forest Springs Summer Camp, too. Complete the sentences about his week there.

to | about | at | about ✓ | listen to | eat | row | go back

of | about | in | to | get up | sing | find out | find ✓

1. Before he went, Tim worried **about finding** friends at Forest Springs.
2. He was crazy [2] on the Colorado River.
3. He got used [3] sausages every night.
4. He wasn't very good [4] around the campfire.
5. He wasn't crazy [5] early every morning.
6. He was interested [6] about animal tracks.
7. He got tired [7] kids who weren't enjoying their time at summer camp.
8. Now he is looking forward [8] to Forest Springs next summer.

2 What would they do? (conditional with 'would' → G 11)

What would the speaker do in each situation?

Example: If I had no money, I would try to borrow some from my parents.

1 go to … – wear …

2 spend a week at … – make …

3 see … – run a mile

4 eat too many … – feel sick

5 meet … – ask about his new CD

6 win … – buy a fast car

3 On vacation (conditional with 'would' → G 11)

Finish the sentences. What does the speaker say about these situations?

1. "If I lost my cell phone on vacation, …" (I – go crazy)
2. "I would go to a museum if …" (it – rain)
3. "If someone stole my bags, …" (I – call the police)
4. "If I got lost on a hike, …" (I – try to find my way back to the trail)
5. "I would send a text message to my friend if …" (I – get bored)
6. "I would call my parents if …" (I – miss my flight home)

*

4 Vacation problems (conditional 3 → G 12)

Some people are talking about problems they had on their vacations. Finish their sentences. Choose the right part, a – f.

Example: If we'd had better weather, we … (enjoy) our vacation more.
If we'd had better weather, we would have **enjoyed** our vacation more.

1. "If we'd checked the plane times, …
2. "If I'd been more careful when I was free climbing, …
3. "If I'd taken a map on that hike, …
4. "If we'd taken our MP3 players, …
5. "If I'd looked before I sat down, …
6. "And if I'd listened to the weather report that morning, …

1

a … I … (not – break) my arm."
b … I wouldn't have …" (See picture 1.)
c … the long trip in the car … (not – be) so boring."
d … I … (get back) to the cabin much earlier!"
e … I …" (See picture 2.)
f … we (not – miss) our flight home."

2

→ WB 43, 1 – 3

5 Abby's friend (mixed conditional sentences → G 13)

Abby's English friend, Max, sends her this e-mail. Use the words in the boxes and complete it.

Dear Abby,
First I'd like to answer the [1] which you asked in your last mail. If I [2] in the US, I would live in LA. It's a huge [3] so there must be lots to do there. I'm sure I [4] never be [5] there. And it isn't [6] from the coast. I wouldn't like to be in a place like Utah, hundreds of [7] from the nearest beach. If I [8] rich, I would have an apartment in New York and a [9] in the mountains, too. If you [10] interested, [11] send you some photos of my home. We live in an [12] cottage. It's in the country, near Manchester.

Love,
Max

would | are | far | miles | I'll | cabin | old | bored | were | question | city | lived

NOW YOU CAN

✓ Talk about the American Southwest. → Name two states and two cities of the Southwest.
✓ Talk about summer camp. → Say what you would do if you were at Forest Springs.
✓ Use conditional sentences. → What would you do if you won a million dollars?
✓ Read part of a longer novel for teenagers. → Tell a friend (in German) what happens in 'Downriver'.
✓ Use polite small talk. → Someone in an American café asks if you are from Germany. What can you say?

1

Unit 4 Our smart world

1 In space and on Earth

a) *Look at picture 1. What can you see? What do you think is happening?*

b) *Read the information in the 'Did you know?' box and look at the other pictures. Talk with a partner. What was new for you? What did you know already?*

I didn't know that … I've heard about …

c) *Use the photos and the information to start a 'space technology' mind map. Add to your mind map as you work through the unit.*

→ WB 48, 1

2 Listening: Two people

Listen to the two people and take notes to answer these questions.

1. What are their jobs?
2. How have their jobs changed?

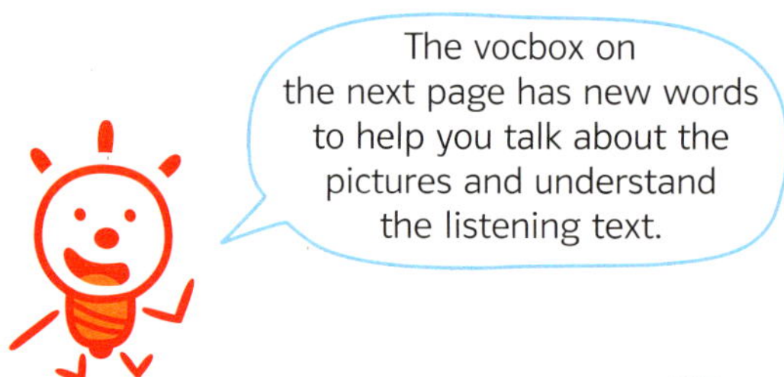

→ WB 48, 2

4 Vacation problems (conditional 3 → G 12)

Some people are talking about problems they had on their vacations. Finish their sentences. Choose the right part, a – f.

Example: If we'd had better weather, we … (enjoy) our vacation more.
If we'd had better weather, we would have **enjoyed** our vacation more.

1. "If we'd checked the plane times, …
2. "If I'd been more careful when I was free climbing, …
3. "If I'd taken a map on that hike, …
4. "If we'd taken our MP3 players, …
5. "If I'd looked before I sat down, …
6. "And if I'd listened to the weather report that morning, …

a … I … (not – break) my arm."
b … I wouldn't have …" (See picture 1.)
c … the long trip in the car … (not – be) so boring."
d … I … (get back) to the cabin much earlier!"
e … I …" (See picture 2.)
f … we (not – miss) our flight home."

→ WB 43, 1 – 3

5 Abby's friend (mixed conditional sentences → G 13)

Abby's English friend, Max, sends her this e-mail. Use the words in the boxes and complete it.

Dear Abby,
First I'd like to answer the [1] which you asked in your last mail. If I [2] in the US, I would live in LA. It's a huge [3] so there must be lots to do there. I'm sure I [4] never be [5] there. And it isn't [6] from the coast. I wouldn't like to be in a place like Utah, hundreds of [7] from the nearest beach. If I [8] rich, I would have an apartment in New York and a [9] in the mountains, too. If you [10] interested, [11] send you some photos of my home. We live in an [12] cottage. It's in the country, near Manchester.

Love,
Max

would | are | far | miles | I'll | cabin | old | bored | were | question | city | lived

NOW YOU CAN

- ✓ Talk about the American Southwest. → Name two states and two cities of the Southwest.
- ✓ Talk about summer camp. → Say what you would do if you were at Forest Springs.
- ✓ Use conditional sentences. → What would you do if you won a million dollars?
- ✓ Read part of a longer novel for teenagers. → Tell a friend (in German) what happens in 'Downriver'.
- ✓ Use polite small talk. → Someone in an American café asks if you are from Germany. What can you say?

Skills workshop 3 Words and spelling

1 New words

a) *First read the text without a dictionary and answer these questions.*

1. What good points of the movie does the writer mention?
2. What's not so good?

ALASKA *104 minutes, USA (1996)*

Rating: ★★½☆☆

This movie is a family adventure with beautiful landscapes, a cute polar bear, two teenagers and a poacher.
Jake Barnes (Dirk Benedict) moves to Alaska from Chicago to find happiness after his wife dies, with his teenage children, Jessie and Sean. He starts an air transport service, but one night his plane crashes far from home in bad weather, so the kids begin a journey full of danger to rescue him. On the way they become friends with a lonely young polar bear, Cubby. The heartless poacher, Perry (Charlton Heston), who has killed the bear's mother, follows the group. Some of the views of Alaska are awesome. But the story is predictable and the screenplay is so weak that the actors are not able to do much with their roles. However, there are some exciting action scenes near the end and it really is a movie that adults and children can watch and enjoy – in parts – together.

b) *Find these words in the text and think: what could they mean? If you're not sure, look them up in your dictionary.*

heartless | happiness | danger | predictable | screenplay | poacher

VOCABULARY SKILLS A B C

You can often find the meaning of a new word if you know a part of the word. The endings '-ful' and '-less' are similar in German (wundervoll, ratlos).

beauty + -ful = beautiful (full of beauty)
heart + -less = heartless (without a heart)
happy + -ness = happiness (the feeling of being happy)

c) *Use the parts to make the right word for each sentence.*

1. People who are … often sleep on the streets.
2. … can kill when you are driving.
3. We can't win. It's a … situation.
4. Umbrellas are very … when it's wet.
5. I'll never forget your …
6. Maybe all cities will have … trains one day.
7. I'm … that my grades will get better!

kind	hope	+	-ness
home	tired		-less
use	driver		-ful
hope			

* 2 Compounds

The word 'screenplay' is a compound. It's a play, with dialogue and action, for the screen, or cinema. Put the parts together to make new words to fit the definitions. Check in your dictionary if you aren't sure.

wind • ball • mini • youth • clock • board✓ • mail • field

hostel • box • walk✓ • bus • work • sock • radio • park

1. You can walk along it at the beach. That's a boardwalk.
2. You find letters or e-mails here.
3. a small bus
4. experiments and research outside for Biology
5. a cheap place to stay for young people
6. a stadium for baseball and other games
7. It shows pilots how windy it is.
8. an alarm clock that wakes you up with music

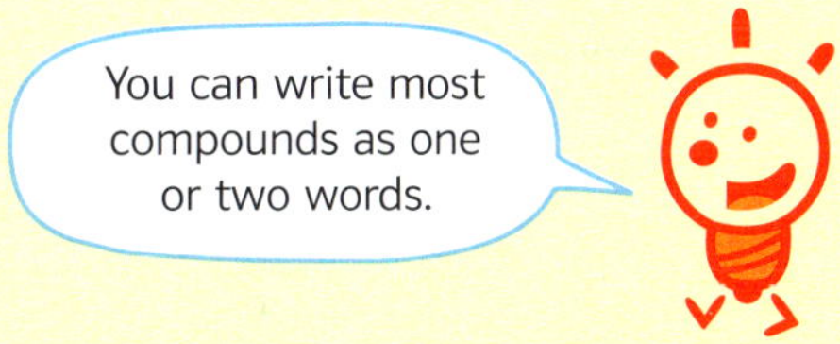

3 Spelling mistakes

STUDY SKILLS A B C

Make a checklist to help your spelling. Here are some ideas.

1. You often don't hear the letters 'gh'. But don't forget they are there when you write!
   → **fight**, **bought**, **weight**
2. Never put a 'k' in front of a 't'!
   → action, October
3. Many words are similar in English and German, but not quite the same.
   → **simple** – simpel, **title** – Titel
   → **phone** – Telefon, **photo** – Foto
4. Remember that there are often double letters in -ing and past forms.
   → stop – **stopped**, **stopping**;
   → plan – **planned**, **planning**
5. The letter 'y' often changes to 'ie'.
   → carry – she **carries**, they **carried**
   → party – two **parties**
   → happy – **happier**
6. Verbs that end with the letter 'e' lose it in the -ing form.
   → write – **writing**, take – **taking**

Ask your partner to spell words 1–6. Your partner can ask you to spell words 7–12.

A: Your first word is 'luckiest'. Can you spell that?
B: I think it's L-U-C-K-I-E-S-T. Is that right?
A: That's right!

1. luckiest	4. daughter
2. example	5. dropped
3. hiking	6. phrase

7. circle	10. joking
8. cries	11. cell phone
9. getting	12. height

STUDY SKILLS

It's always easier to find spelling mistakes in a text that someone else has written. Show your next piece of writing to a partner. How many mistakes can he / she find in three minutes? What other tips can he / she give you?

→ WB 45,1

A letter to a magazine

Dear Newtech,

Your article on the Skywalk last month describes the new platform as 'a great piece of tribal technology'.

I am one of the oldest members of the Hualapai tribe and I am worried. I see the Skywalk as a big problem: Our land is for everyone, for us, for our ancestors, for our children and our children's children. We get all our food from our land, and water from its rivers and lakes. So we must look after it.

The Skywalk will bring too many tourists to our land. These people are not interested in the Hualapai and their culture. They just want to look down into the Grand Canyon. They will take our rocks as souvenirs and damage the land. They will leave all their garbage and they will use our water. We already do not have enough water – they will come and use it all for their toilets and showers!

Some land is very sacred to the Hualapai people. This means we must not build anything on it. Now our tribal council has let others do this on sacred Hualapai land!

The Skywalk is like a huge, hungry monster which shows no respect for our ancestors. The people who built it are only interested in money and do not care about our ancient traditions. It could stop people on their way to better lands after they die.

I am sure that one day the people from our tribe who said 'yes' to this monster will be sorry. But by then it will be too late!

Yours,

Rory Quasala, Peach Springs

A Reading

1 *Read the text and find the right answer.*

a The letter is …		
1 a technology park.	2 a new platform.	3 a monster film.
b Rory Quasala is …		
1 a tourist.	2 a member of a tribe.	3 an ancestor.
c He thinks the Skywalk will …		
1 bring too many children.	2 be good for the land.	3 be bad for his tribe.
d The tourists will use …		
1 too many rocks.	2 the tribe's water.	3 a lot of garbage.
e It's on land which is …		
1 full of souvenirs.	2 better for tribes.	3 important to the Hualapai.

2 *Collect reasons why Rory is against the Skywalk. Write your answers as notes.*

B Language

Find the word in the text.

a a group of Native Americans
b very old
c things that people throw away
d important (in a religion)
e the people of a family who lived a long time ago

C Passing on information

Imagine you are at the Skywalk. Help a German friend whose English isn't very good.

Friend: Können wir echt keine Fotos machen hier? Frage den Mann doch, ob das stimmt.
You: …
Guide: I'm sorry. Visitors are not allowed to take pictures on the Skywalk. It's because the canyon is a sacred place for us.
You: …
Friend: Gibt es wenigstens ein paar Postkarten?
You: …
Guide: Of course. You can buy them in the Visitor Center over there. The center also has posters and books about the canyon.
You: …

D Listening

1 *Right or wrong? Listen to the first part of the radio chat show.*

a Today's guest is Louisa Quasala.
b She works in a café.
c She lives on the reservation.
d Louisa's cousin is Rory Quasala.
e She says that he is very angry, and worried.

2 *Listen to part two. Which of these reasons does Louisa give to support the Skywalk?*

a The Hualapai need money.
b The platform gives jobs to her people.
c It wasn't very expensive.
d Visitors can learn about the Hualapai.
e There are lots of other platforms.
f The platform is very beautiful.

E Writing

1 *Do you agree with this opinion? Write 4-5 sentences.*

"Teenagers should always show respect for older people."

2 *Write a letter to Newtech magazine. Say if you agree with Rory or not, and why. Use your notes from part A. Write 80 – 100 words.*

1

Unit 4 Our smart world

1 In space and on Earth

a) *Look at picture 1. What can you see? What do you think is happening?*

b) *Read the information in the 'Did you know?' box and look at the other pictures. Talk with a partner. What was new for you? What did you know already?*

I didn't know that … I've heard about …

c) *Use the photos and the information to start a 'space technology' mind map. Add to your mind map as you work through the unit.*

→ WB 48, 1

2 Listening: Two people

Listen to the two people and take notes to answer these questions.

1. What are their jobs?
2. How have their jobs changed?

The vocbox on the next page has new words to help you talk about the pictures and understand the listening text.

→ WB 48, 2

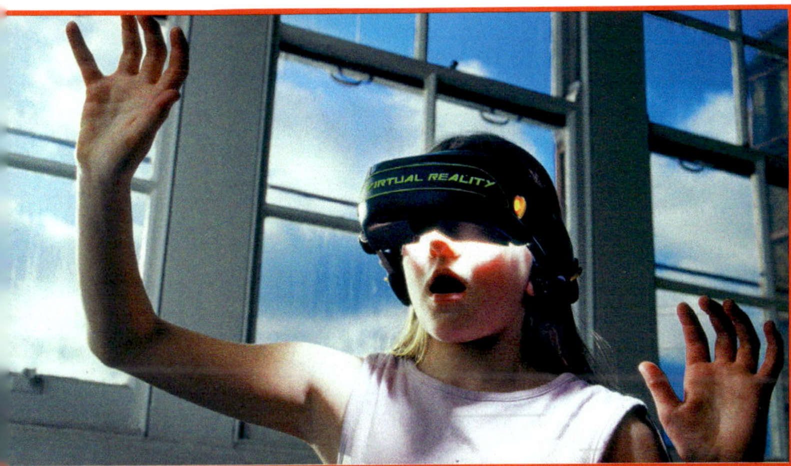

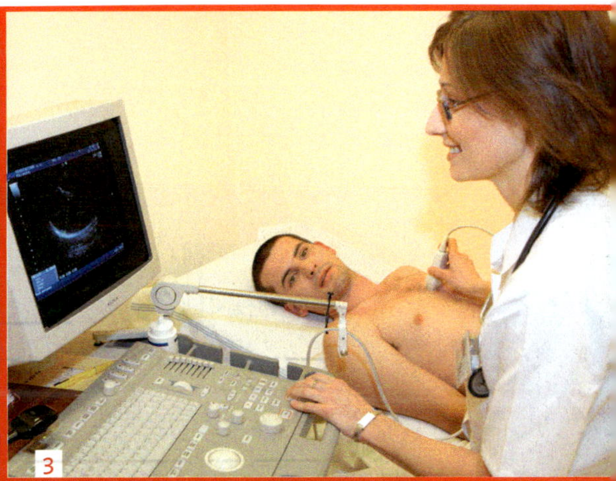

DID YOU KNOW?

- Many of today's inventions started as projects of the US space agency, NASA.
- Robots with remote control do jobs in space for astronauts. Similar robots do dangerous jobs on Earth.
- Virtual reality (VR) equipment helps astronauts to 'practice' being in space. Some computer games use this technology.
- Scientists put devices onto astronauts' bodies to check that the astronauts are OK. Doctors use the same technology in pacemakers for people with heart problems.
- Modern farmers use satellites with GPS (global positioning system) technology to check that the rows in their fields are straight. Scientists also use GPS for weather reports.

3 Your turn: Devices

a) *Think of three devices that make life easier, safer or more fun for us. Make a list.*

b) *Talk to an older person in your family or neighborhood and take notes. Which of the inventions didn't they have when they were your age? What did they use instead of them?*

c) *Write a report about what you found out.*

VOCBOX

astronaut [ˈæstrənɔːt] – *Astronaut/-in*
space station [ˈspeɪs ˌsteɪʃn] – *Raumstation*
to repair [rɪˈpeə] – *reparieren, ausbessern*
gravity [ˈɡrævəti] – *Schwerkraft*
electrical [ɪˈlektrɪkl] – *elektrisch*
scan [skæn] – *Ultraschall(untersuchung)*
to transmit [trænzˈmɪt] – *funken, senden*
mechanic [mɪˈkænɪk] – *Mechaniker/-in*

In space

The US and 15 other countries are working together in space to build the International Space Station (ISS) 217 miles above the Earth. The ISS travels around the Earth 15 times a day, at more than 17,000 miles an hour. But what is life in space really like?

WEIGHTLESSNESS
In space things have no weight. Astronauts – and all the other things on the space station – float. This makes eating, drinking, sleeping and going to the bathroom very difficult. Astronauts must be able to live and work in 'zero gravity'. So scientists give them training and advice before they leave.

LONELINESS
Astronauts have lived on the ISS since 2000. They usually spend four months in space before they can go home, and life there can be very lonely. But they can send messages to their friends and families regularly and tell them their news.

SPACE TOURISTS
There have already been tourists in space. NASA promises them an unforgettable adventure. But the journey into space is dangerous and it isn't cheap (25 million dollars a trip)! Maybe one day NASA will offer tourists less expensive vacations in space.

THE EARTH IN SPACE
When the first rockets went into space, they took pictures of the Earth. Before that, nobody knew what the Earth looked like.

1 Space and the ISS

a) *Do you think you could live and work in space? Would you like to be a space tourist?*

b) *Collect facts about the ISS from the text. Make a list with these headings:*

1. how fast?
2. how high above Earth?
3. astronauts' trips – how long?
4. trips – how much money?
5. how many countries?
6. problems?

c) *Find information about the ISS on the Internet. How many people are there now and what countries are they from?*

2 Looking at English

Read the sentences in the grammar box. Find more sentences like these in the text.

GRAMMAR
Look at these ways of saying the same thing.
- Scientists give **the astronauts training.**
- Scientists give **training to the astronauts.**
- Scientists give **them training.**

→ WB 49,1 → G 14

3 Verbs with two objects

Say it with 'to'.

Example: Astronauts send their families messages.
Astronauts send messages **to their families**.

1. Scientists give astronauts advice before they go into space.
2. NASA offers rich people vacations in space.
3. Journeys into space give tourists a fantastic adventure.
4. Astronauts can't send their families e-mails.
5. The first astronauts sent scientists their pictures from space.
6. One astronaut promised his daughter a piece of moon rock.

→ WB 49, 2

4 The right order

Put the words in the right order to make a second sentence.

1. You can see the ISS in the sky at night. Should … I / it / show / you / to?
2. Your brother would like a book about space? Let's buy one and … it / send / him / to.
3. Trips into space? One day NASA will … to / offer / everybody / them.
4. I'm going to get a virtual reality space game. My parents … me / it / to / promised.
5. Did you hear the joke about the astronaut on the Moon? My sister … it / to / me / told.
6. You want information about stars and planets? The NASA website … you / to / it / gives.

→ WB 49, 3; 50, 4

5 How fast, how much, how often?

a) *Write the information as phrases.*

Example: 3x / day: three times a day

1. 15x / day
2. $25 million / trip
3. 17,000 m / hour
4. 1x / year
5. 186,000 m / second
6. 2x / year

→ G 15

* b) *Make a sentence for each of the pieces of information in a).*

vacations in space cost • light travels at • the Earth goes round the sun • the ISS travels at • the ISS goes round the Earth • the day is as long as the night

STUDY SKILLS

Don't forget to use what you know from other subjects and from outside school! What have you learned in Physics about light, for example, or in Geography about how long the day and night are at different times of the year?

→ WB 50, 5

6 Your turn: Four months in space

If you lived in space for four months, what would you miss the most? Why? How often would you send messages, who would you send them to and what would you say? Write 80–100 words.

How intelligent is your home?

Imagine you and your family are on your way home after your vacation. It's getting dark. Your mom sends a text message to your apartment in the city. The lights are switched on and off a few times so that any burglars are frightened away. Then the refrigerator is checked. There are no eggs for breakfast tomorrow, so you must stop at the supermarket on the way home. Pictures of all the rooms are sent by cameras to your cell phone. Everything looks OK. But there's water under the bathroom sink. Is it leaking? Or did you leave the plug in and forget to turn off the faucet? Just as your parents start to worry, the faucet is turned off and the floor is dried. An apartment like this is called a 'smart' or intelligent home. All the work is done by computers.
But sometimes there are problems. Imagine another day, and another journey home. Your mom sends a message to the apartment, but this time the lights aren't switched on and off, so the burglars aren't frightened away. You can't see the burglars because the cameras aren't working. The water isn't turned off and when you get home everything is wet. Burglars have stolen all your electrical devices, even your microwave and your hairdryer! And the refrigerator is empty.
You see, smart homes are only smart if they have electricity. If this is cut off, even the most intelligent homes have problems. And every winter in the US there are lots of blackouts.

1 Smart?

Make a list of the pros and cons of a home like this.

2 When it works …

Put the parts of the sentences together to make sentences.

1. The lights	is	frightened away.
2. Burglars	are	called 'smart'.
3. The faucet in the bathroom		done by remote control.
4. The floor		turned off.
5. Homes with technology like this		switched on and off.
6. The work		cut off.
7. The refrigerator		dried.
8. There's a problem if the electricity		checked to see if it has any food.

GRAMMAR

We often use the passive voice to talk about actions where the person or thing that does the action isn't important.

▶ A message is sent. ▶ The lights are switched off.

WB 51, 1–2 → G16

3 Jobs at a motel

Lots of Americans stay at motels on their way home from vacation.
What jobs are done at a motel? Make sentences.

Example: Someone cleans the rooms every morning.
The rooms **are cleaned** every morning.

1. They switch on the TV at reception at 6 am.
2. Someone else switches it off at 11.30 pm.
3. Someone checks the e-mails every day.
4. They take the trash out three times a week.
5. They change the beds when guests leave.
6. Someone does the shopping downtown.
7. They sell maps and postcards.
8. Someone carries luggage to the rooms.

4 Listening: Problems

a) *Before you listen, look at the picture. Find these things in the motel room in the picture.*

1. microwave
2. hairdryer
3. light bulb
4. remote control
5. refrigerator
6. faucet

b) *Listen to three phone calls. What's the problem each time? Take notes.*

WB 52, 3

5 Real talk: In a motel

You have just arrived at a motel. But there's a problem with your room.
You call the reception desk and your partner answers. Act the phone conversation.

SPEAKING SKILLS

Decide with your partner what the problem is before you start the dialogue.

Why not sit back to back with your partner to make it more like a phone conversation?

USEFUL PHRASES

How can we help you?
Oh, I'm sorry about that.
We'll send someone right away.
Are you sure about that?
Yes, of course. We'll be with you soon.

There's something wrong with …
We don't have a … in our room.
Can you send someone to repair it, please?
Can we have a new one, please?
The … is very dirty. Can someone clean it?

WB 52, 4

6 Your turn: At home

a) *How many electrical devices are there in your home? Make a list of the ones that do work for you and your family. (You will need your dictionary.)*

b) *What work is done by the devices? Write about five devices.*

Meet halfway

1 Before you listen

Some conversations become fights while others stay friendly.

a) *Look at these tips. Make a list of the tips which would help a conversation to stay friendly.*

Get mad. • Ask what the other person thinks. • Shout. • Show that you understand what the other person feels. • Always agree with the other person. • Cry – then the other person will be nice to you. • Explain your feelings or ideas. • Stay cool. • Show you are listening. • Tell the other person, "I knew you would say that!" • Be polite. • Look at your watch if you think the other person is saying something boring. • Always let the other person finish what he / she is saying. • Be careful when you say something negative.

b) *Compare your list with a partner. Are your lists the same?*

→ WB 54, 1

2 Listening: Conversations

a) *You are going to hear conversations between two girls and their parents. Listen and take notes about:*

1. what the girls want
2. which conversation goes well, and why
3. which conversation goes badly, and why

b) *How many of the useful phrases did you hear in the conversation that went well?*

→ WB 54, 2

USEFUL PHRASES

Can we talk about … ?
What do you think … ?
How do you feel about … ?
I see …
That's true, but …
I know, but …
I've got an idea. Maybe …
Maybe we can meet halfway.
OK, it's a deal!

3 Role play: Meet halfway

a) *Look at the situation. Act a role play with your partner. Can you meet halfway?*

Situation: Your class has some money after a school event. Now you want to spend it. Partner A wants to give the money to a very poor family in your town; Partner B wants to spend it on a class party or a class trip to the movies.

* b) *Make up your own situation and act another role play where you meet halfway. These phrases can help if the conversation doesn't go well:*

USEFUL PHRASES

I didn't mean it like that.
Are you sure about that?
Maybe we ought to talk again later.
Don't get mad! (to someone you know well)

→ WB 54, 3

Alien invader

1 Before you read

An American teenager wrote this story. Before you read it, think about these questions:

1. What science fiction stories do you already know from TV, movies and books?
2. What would you do if you thought one of your friends was an alien?

I've always wondered about Roy Dwight, ever since I saw him jump. One day, I was walking around the corner of Main Street in Greensburg, my hometown, when a car zoomed past me, turned sharply and went straight for Roy.
"Watch it, Roy!" I shouted.
He turned round, seeing the car, which was about three yards away from him, and leaped. And I mean leaped! He went soaring above the car and landed about seven yards behind it. The driver, a short, fat man, climbed out of the car and started cursing at Roy. Roy turned and ran, naturally. The driver added a few more angry words to his little speech, then jumped back into his car, slammed the door and drove off.

Here's the problem: I think Roy's an alien. If he could jump seven yards, he must be used to stronger gravity.

Roy has a long thin face, light brown hair and pointed ears. Maybe it was his ears that made me first think he was an alien. They always reminded me of Spock in that dumb *Star Trek* show on TV. When he first came to Greensburg, one and a half years ago, everyone called him 'Spooky Spocky', but we all got sick of it, so we quit. His eyes always look like they are squinting. If he's not from Earth, he's probably squinting because his sun is less bright than ours, or he lives further away from the sun than we do. He's got a long, drooping nose. But his main feature is his I.Q. It is 183. Show me a kid with an I.Q. of 183 and I'll show you an alien.

I still had doubts about whether he was an alien or not, but yesterday in the park I finally decided. We were playing football in the park stadium, and Roy was sitting in the stands with a radio beside him. Of the whole park, our favorite place is the stadium. The guard always lets us play, which is nice of him.

Well, Roy was sitting in the stands, but he was doing something pretty weird. He wasn't only listening to the radio, he was also talking into it! I guessed it was his transmitter, and he was using it to talk to his people. Then Bill had to go home and clean up his room, so we were one player short. We shouted to Roy and asked if he wanted to play. He agreed, and slid off the bench. As he slid, his leg hit his 'radio' and it fell to the ground and split apart. Its contents were totally different from those of a normal radio. There was this greenish fluid coming out, and the electronics were very, very compact. The antenna had an enormous booster that probably helped in transmitting over long distances.

Right then I knew for sure: Roy is not from Earth. I told the other guys I had to go shopping for my mom, and before they could say anything, I ran home.

When I finally got there, I ran into my room and hurried to my long, wooden desk. I felt under it until I found a button and pushed it. With the hum of electronic motors, my desk transformed into a communications terminal. My fingers went flying over the keyboard, typing area codes and frequencies. Every time I pushed a button, a beep sounded. Then I took my microphone and said into it, "Zargon to Pluto Station, Zargon to Pluto Station, I have found an alien. He is not from Earth, nor is he one of us. Delay the invasion until I have investigated further."

by Peter Yared (adapted), from the Merlyn's Pen New Library of Young Adult Writing at www.merlynspen.org

2 A story by a teenager

What do you think of the story? Are there any parts of the story that you would change?

3 Story facts

Find the story facts.

narrator's name? | other characters? | setting?

STUDY SKILLS

Talking about texts
Collect words and phrases for talking about texts. Make a list and keep it in your file for the next time you read and talk about a story in English.

narrator – the person who tells the story
characters – the people in the story
setting – where the story happens
beginning – the first part of the story
end or ending – …

4 Roy

a) *Find out everything you can about Roy from the story. Where does he live? (What does he look like? What is strange about him? …) Take notes.*

b) *Use your notes to write a short profile of Roy.*

5 Words in the story

Find the word in the story that means the same thing.

1. moved quickly
2. jumped
3. of course
4. stupid
5. next to
6. strange
7. huge, very big
8. changed

6 Your turn: Roy's story

How would Roy tell a scene from the story? Write what happens in one of the scenes, but with Roy as the narrator. Think about these questions:

What does Roy do in each scene? • What could he think to himself? • What was he saying into his radio? • What does he think about the narrator of the story? • Does he know that the other boy is an alien? • …

WRITING SKILLS

In a text like this, you can decide what to write! Find the scenes with Roy in them and think about the questions carefully.

Don't forget that a partner can read your story and give you advice about how to make it better.

→ WB 55, 1

7 A song: No doubt about it

If someone tells you there's no other form of life,
And you believe in that, too.
I'm gonna tell you 'bout the other night,
I swear that it's true!
A cloud of white, and green, and flying ships,
I've never seen came into my view.

Was I frightened? Was I scared?
Was I thrown into confusion?
As they glided down so silently,
It wasn't an illusion,
No no, no doubt about it,
Oh no, no doubt about it.

What kind of magnetism kept me in this place?
Was it out of my control?
What was the ship from outer space?
What was this creature that appeared before
my eyes? Was it good? Was it evil,
On the ship from other skies?

I was frightened, I was scared,
I was thrown into confusion,
As they stood right there in front of me
It wasn't an illusion,
No no, no doubt about it,
Oh no, no doubt about it.

Think about these questions while you listen to the song.

1. What did the singer see?
2. How did he feel about what he saw?

1 Word fields

a) *Put these words from the unit into two lists, 'space' and 'home'.*

refrigerator • zero gravity • faucet • hairdryer • plug
remote control • planet • astronaut • sink • alien • satellite

space	home
…	…

* b) *Add more words to your lists.*

2 A crazy motel room

a) *Mr. Fox gets this motel room. Look at the picture for three minutes, then close your book.*

b) *How many of the things that are broken, damaged – or just crazy – can you and your partner remember? Make notes and then check.*

3 Sounds: Hard to say?

a) *Read words 1–4 to yourself and then read them to your partner. Your partner reads words 5–8.*

1. electricity	3. faucet	5. weird	7. scientist
2. doubt	4. conversation	6. rows	8. refrigerator

b) *Now listen to all the words and check. Did you and your partner say the words correctly?*

4 That's wrong!

Correct the sentences.

Example: A ghost is someone who stays at a motel.
That's wrong! A **guest** is someone who stays at a motel.

1. A scientist is someone who steals things from people's homes.
2. An alien is someone who goes into space.
3. A tourist is someone who tells a story.
4. A farmer is someone who does experiments.
5. A narrator is someone from another planet.
6. A burglar is someone who travels to other places on vacation.
7. An astronaut is someone who has fields and drives a tractor.
8. A guest is someone who comes out at night and wears white.

5 Word friends

a) *Make pairs.*

Example: weather report

weather | electrical | remote | bulb | rock | fiction | gravity

science | virtual | moon | light | reality | control | report

bathroom | device | zero | sink

* b) *Write a sentence with each pair to show what it means.*

6 Word building

Read the sentences. Put in a word from the same 'word family'.

1. The alien sent a message to her planet with a large … (to transmit)
2. A trip to the moon would be … (to forget)
3. On a space station, … means that everything floats. (weight)
4. There is lots of … for astronauts before they go into space. (to train)
5. They talk to scientists … (regular)
6. … can be a problem on the ISS. (lonely)

→ WB 56, 1–3

1 A motel and its guests (verbs with two objects → G 14)

Mr. and Mrs. Rose are the owners of the Rose Motel. Find the right order for the words of the sentence.

Example: The Roses [messages] [give] [guests] [to] when someone calls them.
The Roses give messages to guests when someone calls them.

1. The Roses [the President's Room] [to] [offer] [always] important guests.
2. They [to] [give] [a free map of the area] [their guests] when they arrive.
3. Mr. Rose [his guests] [tells] [to] [often] [stories] about people who have stayed at the motel.
4. They [to] [guests] [Christmas cards] [send] who have stayed more than once.
5. They [guests] [the town] [to] [don't show].
6. Mrs. Rose [the rooms on the quiet side of the building] [gives] [older guests] [to].

2 Signs

Write the information on the signs in sentences.

1

2

3

4

5

… an hour. … a day. … a glass. … an hour. … a pound.

1. The apples cost …
2. You can drive at …
3. You can use the Internet here for …
4. The motel is open …
5. The lemonade costs …

3 What is it called? (the passive voice → G 16)

Put the parts of the sentences together.

1. The satellite system for farmers	is called	the moon.
2. The technology some computer games use	are called	*Star Trek.*
3. The strange things some people see at night		VR.
4. The famous TV show about space travel		Roy and Zargon.
5. The two boys in 'Alien Invader'		GPS.
6. The people who travel into space		the sun.
7. The space station 217 miles above the Earth		astronauts.
8. The Earth's satellite		UFOs.
9. The nearest star to the Earth		the ISS.

4 On the ISS (the passive voice → G16)

Put these sentences about astronauts' lives on the ISS into the passive voice.

Example: They do lots of experiments on the ISS.
Lots of experiments **are done** on the ISS.

1. Sometimes they repair satellites.
2. They check the equipment every day.
3. They take photos of the Earth and the stars.
4. They write a report at the end of every day.
5. They speak English on the ISS.
6. They build new parts of the space station.
7. They don't play card games. (The cards would fly away!)
8. They drink tea from special cups.

5 Robots (mixed exercise)

Read the text. Put in the right verbs.

think | don't wash | repairs | isn't done ✓ | is cooked | are done | don't get | is | is cleaned | does | wash | is used | don't need | are put away | is done | are done

A lot of work in intelligent homes **isn't done** by people. It [1] by machines. People [2] their hands wet when they [3] clothes. And their food [4] for them, in a microwave. They [5] the plates after the meal – another machine [6] to wash them. In a real smart home the jobs [7] by a robot. Imagine! Your room [8] while you are at school. Your shoes [9] and the robot even [10] your bike for you. It [11] all the other jobs like shopping or washing up, too. Some of you probably [12] that these things [13] for you already. You [14] a robot. Your mom or dad [15] your robot. Lucky you!

→ WB 57, 1–2

NOW YOU CAN

- ✓ Talk about technology at home. → Name two devices and say what you do with them.
- ✓ Talk about life on a space station. → Name three facts about the ISS.
- ✓ Use the passive voice. → Say what is usually done for people who are ill.
- ✓ Say how fast something travels. → Say how fast most people ride their bikes.
- ✓ Help a conversation to go the right way. → You want to ask someone for something. How can you start the conversation?

Skills workshop 4 Writing a factual text

WRITING SKILLS

Factual texts

Factual texts give information and statistics. You should not give your opinion when you write a factual text, or say what your feelings are about the subject. Reports, encyclopedia entries and summaries of stories are all examples of factual texts.

It's a good idea to write a factual text in three parts:

1. a short introduction (to catch the reader's interest)
2. the 'main part' (a few paragraphs with your main points / information)
3. an ending with one or two sentences that give a summary of what you have written.

- Remember to connect your sentences. Use words like 'but', 'and', 'although', 'so that', 'because' ... (conjunctions).
- Don't repeat a word in the same or the next sentence. For example, for 'students', you can use 'they', or 'the class'.

1 Beginnings

a) *Look at these beginnings of different texts. Which of them are from factual and which are from personal texts? Decide with a partner.*

Baseball is a game that is played between two teams of nine players each. ... 1

May 24: I got up and had breakfast with Dad. It was a warm, sunny morning ... 2

This is a story about a boy and his friend, Roy. In the first part of the story ... 3

Two people died yesterday when a car crashed outside St Louis on Route ... 4

It was a dark, cold day in March. 'Will it ever be spring?' John asked himself. 5

Hey, Scott saw U with Janice yesterday. Did U ask her out on a date???? 6

b) *What is the text each time?*

2 Connecting sentences

Use the conjunction to make a longer sentence out of two short ones.

Example: Ellis Island is famous. It's where lots of immigrants landed. (because)
Ellis Island is famous **because** it's where lots of immigrants landed.

1. Free climbing is a popular sport. It can be dangerous. (but)
2. Lots of old people need a pacemaker. They have problems with their hearts. (because)
3. Middle schools have lots of rules. Many have a dress code. (and)
4. Parents often get mad. Kids play their music too loud. (when)
5. Some people listen to MP3 players on flights. They don't have to talk to the person next to them. (so that)
6. The weather wasn't too bad today. It was awful yesterday. (although)

3 Statistics and a factual text

Topic of survey: Free time and vacations				
Survey group: 7th and 8th grades, Boulder Middle School, California			**Number:** 200	
What's your favorite kind of vacation?	beach 72%	summer camp 14,5%	city trip 9%	other 4.5%
What's your favorite place (in US)?	California 45%	Hawaii 26%	Las Vegas 2%	other 27%
What's your favorite place (outside US)?	Mexico 55%	Canada 19%	Europe 7%	other 19%

- These statistics are from a survey of 200 7th and 8th grade students at a Californian middle school.
- The topic was 'Free time and vacations'. The questions were about vacations and favorite places.
- First of all, if you look at the results, you'll see that less than a sixth of the young people chose summer camp as their favorite type of vacation and only nine per cent wanted to visit a city. But almost three quarters of the class said a beach vacation was best. Less than five per cent wanted a different type of vacation.
- Secondly, California was more popular than Hawaii or Las Vegas in the US. But outside the US, Mexico was the most popular country. In fact, over half the class chose it. Canada was the second most popular foreign country. And very few students, less than one tenth, chose a vacation in Europe.
- So the results show that a beach holiday was the most popular type of vacation in this survey group and that Mexico was the most popular place.

a) *Look at the statistics and the report. Find the three parts of the report.*

b) *Answer these questions about the statistics and the report.*

1. What is the students' favorite kind of vacation?
2. What are the most popular and second most popular places in the US?
3. Which country do they like better – Canada or Mexico?

4 Your turn: A survey and a report

a) *Do a similar survey in your class and collect statistics.*

favorite kind of vacation	skiing …%	beach …%	…
favorite place (in Germany)	… …%	… …%	…
favorite country (in Europe)	… …%	… …%	…

b) *Write a short report about the survey. The useful phrases can help you.*

USEFUL PHRASES

First of all / Secondly … .
The results show that … .
the most / second most popular
… are more popular than …
very few / less than a third of / a quarter of
… per cent of … / over half of
In fact, …
So the results show that …

WRITING SKILLS

Don't forget to look at your text when you have finished. A checklist can help you to find mistakes and make the text better.

Here are some ideas for your checklist:
spelling? tenses?
paragraphs? …

→ WB 59, 1–4

1 Jamie Foxx and Morgan Freeman

Unit 5 At the movies

1 Hollywood

a) *What do you think of when you hear the words 'Hollywood' and 'the Oscars'?*

b) *Look at the people in photos 1 and 5. How do you think they feel, and why?*

c) *Read the 'Did you know?' texts. What did you find most interesting?*

2 Kinds of movies

a) *Photos 2–4 are all from movies*. Match each scene with the kind of movie it is from.*

gangster movie • fantasy movie • comedy • love story • western

b) *What other kinds of movies are there? Start a list for your folder.* WB 62, 1

VOCBOX

statue ['stætʃuː] – *Statue, Standbild*
proud [praʊd] – *stolz*
overwhelmed [ˌəʊvə'welmd] – *überwältigt*
romantic [rə'mæntɪk] – *romantisch*
to get divorced [dɪ'vɔːsd] – *sich scheiden lassen*
handsome ['hænsəm] – *gut aussehend*

*You can find out which movies photos 2–4 are from on page 95.

2

3

4

5 Drew Barrymore

DID YOU KNOW?

- Hollywood is a part of LA. The first movie makers chose California because of its good weather. They could shoot there almost every day of the year.
- The first movies were silent. When sound came, in the late 1920s, stars suddenly had to learn how to talk in movies. For some, this was the end of their career.
- The Oscars ceremony takes place in LA every spring. The dresses the women wear are often talked about more than the awards they win.
- More than 2,000 actors, directors and singers have a star on Hollywood's Walk of Fame. There are also stars for the most famous TV and movie characters.

3 Listening: Stars in the news

Listen to the news about the stars. Correct the wrong sentences.

1. Tiffany and Shane want to marry.
2. Tiffany is working on a new CD.
3. Kyle Newman is 41.
4. He went to a party on Friday.
5. Cristina Rodrigo's new movie is a western called 'A lady and an officer'.
6. Cristina has made lots of movies with Eddie Jones.

› WB 62, 2–3

4 Your turn: Stars

a) *Make notes about a famous movie or music star.*

born? | best movie or song? | also famous for …? | …

b) *Work in small groups. Each person tells the others about his/her star, but doesn't name the star.*
Can the others guess who the star is?

Movie firsts

A trip to the moon, 1902

Tron, 1982

The first movies were made in Paris, France, by the Lumière brothers. They directed very short movies. One of them was made in 1895 and showed a train as it arrived at a station. The train seemed to come towards the audience. It was as if a real train was coming. The movie was so real that people screamed the first time it was shown.

The first science fiction movie, **A trip to the moon** (1902), was made in France, too. It was directed by Georges Méliès. Trick photography was used to show a rocket that was moving through 'space'.

The Oscars started in 1929. The best movies of the year were given a prize. Later awards were also introduced for movies with the best screenplay, music, and even costume and make-up.

Gone with the wind, a great Hollywood love story, was made in 1939. It was one of the first long movies that was shot all in color. The first movies had been made in black and white.

Since **Tron** (1982), computer graphics have been used a lot in Hollywood. They make it easier and cheaper to show battle scenes in space, for example. In some movies, the computer graphics and special effects are as important as the characters and the story.

By 2000, more movies were being made in India than in Hollywood. 'Bollywood' movies (the name is a compound of Bombay, the Indian city Mumbai's old name, and Hollywood) are romances with singing and dancing. The boy and the girl usually live happily ever after.

1 What happened?

Complete with 'was' or 'were' and the third form of the verb.

1. The first movies … (to make) in France.
2. People screamed in one of them when it … (to show) for the first time.
3. Lots of computer graphics … (to use) in *Tron*.
4. A famous long color movie … (to make) in 1939.
5. In the years after 1929, more Oscars … (to introduce).
6. Trick photography … (to use) in *A trip to the moon*.
7. Mumbai, the home of Bollywood, … (to call) 'Bombay' before its name changed.

GRAMMAR

To use the passive voice in the past, you need 'was' or 'were' and the third form of the verb.
- The movie **was made** in 1939.
- People screamed when the movies **were shown**.

→ WB 63, 1 → G17

2 Another science fiction movie

E.T. is one of the most famous Hollywood science fiction movies. Use the passive voice and a phrase with 'by' each time.

Example: Millions of people [watched] [E.T.]
[E.T.] [**was watched by**] millions of people.

1. Drew Barrymore [played] [the girl in the movie].
2. Lots of journalists [interviewed] [Drew].
3. Steven Spielberg [directed] [the movie].
4. A team of twelve people [did] [the special effects].
5. A few years ago a magazine [did] [a movie survey].
6. Many readers [chose] [E.T.] as their favorite movie.

→ WB 63, 2–3

3 Oscars for music

Complete the sentences. Use the passive voice. You need 'by' in some of the sentences.

The first Oscar for music in a movie … (to win/a musical). It … (to call) *One night of love*. In the 1930s musicals were popular and they … (to make/a lot of studios). Later the awards for best song and best music … (to win/other kinds of movie). In 1970, for example, the Beatles … (to give) a special award for *Let it be*. In other years the music award … (to receive/movies) that were not about music. In 2003 the best song and best music awards … (to give) to *Lord of the Rings*.

→ WB 64, 4–5

4 Listening: My kind of movie!

Listen to Alison, Paul and Kerry. They are all talking about movies. Take notes about what each person likes and doesn't like.

LISTENING SKILLS

Always read the instructions carefully and think before you listen. How many people will you hear? What will they be talking about? What kind of words do you need to listen for?

5 Real talk: I like it!

Ask a partner about the movies he/she likes and doesn't like. Ask about three kinds of movies. Start like this.

A: What kind of movies do you like?
B: Well, I love watching …
A: Do you like … ? … What about …?

USEFUL PHRASES

I love watching … (kind of movie).
I think it's great when …
That's the kind of thing I like.
I don't like watching … (kind of movie).
They're too (scary / brutal / silly / …)
I can't stand it when …

6 Your turn: A movie report

Write a report about a movie you have seen. Put this and other information in your report.

When and where was it made? • What kind of movie is it? • Who are the stars? • Who was it directed by? …

And the winner is ...

The Oscars ceremony is the biggest night in the year for everyone in Hollywood. Millions watch it on TV. And the winners of the awards always make a speech ...

In 2002 Halle Berry became the first black woman to win the award for best actress, with the movie *Monster's ball*. In her speech she said that she wanted to thank her mom. Her mom had always believed in her and had made her strong. She added that her manager had been the only father she had ever known. Then she told the audience that the moment was much bigger than her, and that the award had opened a door for other black women. She said she was sure that these nameless, faceless women would now have a better chance in life.

Jamie Foxx won an Oscar as best actor in 2004 for his role as the blind singer Ray Charles in *Ray*. When he got close to the end of his speech, he said that this would be the most difficult part for him. He thanked his grandmother, Marie. He explained that she had been his first acting teacher. She had whipped him when he had been wild, because she had wanted him to be a gentleman. He said that she still talked to him now, but only in his dreams. And he added that he couldn't wait to go to sleep that night, because he wanted to talk to her again.

1 Speeches

a) *What do the speeches tell you about the stars' families when they were growing up?*

b) *Whose speech could each sentence be from?*

1. "She wanted me to be a gentleman."
2. "It has opened a door for other black women."
3. "This moment is much bigger than me!"
4. "I want to talk to her again."
5. "They will now have a better chance."
6. "She was my first acting teacher."
7. "I want to thank my mom."
8. "He has been the only father I've ever known."
9. "I can't wait to go to sleep tonight."
10. "This will be the hardest part for me."

GRAMMAR

Look at the difference between what the people said and how it is reported. Can you make a rule?

"I enjoyed making the movie."

▶ She said (that) she had enjoyed making the movie.

→ G18

2 A new movie

A director talked about his new movie last week. Report what he said.

1. "My new movie is a comedy." → He said that his … new movie was a comedy.
2. "I wrote the screenplay with my wife." → He added that he had …
3. "The movie has lots of funny characters." → He told us that …
4. "Jamie Foxx plays an old baseball player." → He …
5. "There are some action scenes, too." → …
6. "We worked very hard on the jokes." → …
7. "The movie was fun to make!" → …
8. "People of all ages will enjoy it." → …

TIP
my → his
we → they

→ WB 65, 1

3 The questions

She asked **where we had shot** the action scenes. And she wanted to know **whether we had used** lots of special effects.

Where did you shoot the action scenes?
Did you use lots of special effects?

→ G 19

The director is telling a friend about the interview. Look at the questions and complete what the director tells the friend.

Example: Who are the stars? → She asked me … were / who / the stars
She asked me **who the stars were**.

1. What kind of movie is it? → She asked me … it / what kind of movie / was
2. Where did you make the movie? → … had made / it / where / we
3. Who wrote the screenplay? → … the screenplay / had written / who
4. When will it be in the movie theaters? → … in the movie theaters / would be / when / it
5. Did you enjoy working with Jamie? → … had enjoyed / whether / I / working with Jamie
6. Did you have any problems? → … had had / whether / I / any / problems
7. Are you working on another movie? → … I / on another movie / was working / whether

→ WB 66, 2

4 Your turn: Awards and prizes

a) *Which actors or musicians won movie or music awards this or last year? Use the Internet to find out. You can find out about the Oscars or about other awards.*

Best actor / actress | Best song | Best album | …

b) *Find out what one of the winners said. Write three of their sentences as reported speech.*

Books, movies and games

1 Photos

a) *What can you say about the three photos? What are the people doing in each photo?*

b) *Which of the three activities do you and your friends do most often?*

2 Listening: Phrases that give advice

a) *Listen to two teenagers who are giving advice. What are they talking about: a book, a game or a movie?*

b) *Copy the list of useful phrases and listen again. Add more useful phrases for giving advice, and your own ideas.*

→ WB 68, 1

USEFUL PHRASES

You should …
If I were you, …
I'd recommend …
…

3 What can you ask?

When people tell you about books, films or games, you often want to know more. Collect ideas for questions. Some questions can go in more than one group.

Books	Movies	Computer games
What's it about? Is it easy to read? …	What kind of movie is it? Who's in it? …	What do you have to do? Is it exciting? …

4 Your turn: What would you recommend?

Talk in small groups about the books, movies or computer games you know.

- Say which ones you would or wouldn't recommend, and explain why.
- Try to find out more about the things your friends mention.

Use your useful phrases and questions from exercises 2 and 3.

→ WB 68, 2

The Drew Barrymore story

Drew Barrymore, who comes from one of America's old show-business families, suddenly became famous at the age of seven. She played the little girl in one of the biggest Hollywood movies of all time, *E.T. – The Extra-Terrestrial.* But being a child star isn't always easy.

READING SKILLS

This text is taken from a biography. A biography tells the story of a person's life. The writer is not allowed to invent anything in this kind of text.

As you read, remember that the things that are described really happened. What would you do and how would you feel in a similar situation?

1 Before you read

Before you read, think: what problems do you think a child star in Hollywood could have?

Drew's fame didn't come slowly – with a TV show here, a magazine article there, and then a bigger part later. It came like a fast train. Drew was an overnight sensation. On the night of the *E.T.* premiere, Drew was spending a quiet evening in a hotel room with her two child co-stars. It was her last night as a private person.

E.T. opened and Drew suddenly became very popular. Autograph seekers and photographers were all screaming her name, they were trying to ask questions, and always wanted something. "From the time I became famous in *E.T.*, my life got really weird," Drew explained. "In the evening I was a little girl, and the next day I was being mobbed by people who wanted my autograph or who wanted to photograph me, or just to be near me. It was frightening. I was this seven-year-old who was expected to be twenty-nine."

Before she started her next movie project, she had to spend six months at a new school, her third in the three years since *E.T.* "I went to a regular school, but one that let me go away to shoot films," she explained in an interview. "I loved learning, but I was never very good with authority because I grew up alone."

Drew was simply a lot more 'adult' than the other third-graders. By working with adults for so long, she was forgetting how to relate to people her age. Most of the time, she didn't even see a reason to try. The adults whom she knew well were some of the most attractive and exciting people in the world, the people who seemed to have perfect Hollywood lives. Drew was a regular guest at cool parties and on talk shows. She knew all the entertainment industry's old stars and the hot, new stars.

"By the time I was eight and a half, I felt like I was some weird, crazy girl," she admitted. "I could walk up to the door of any nightclub and they'd say, 'Hi, you're that little girl! Come in!' Around this time I quit hanging out with people my own age. I didn't think that they could understand the kind of life I had."

Six years later Drew Barrymore is 13. She is back in L.A. after four months in New York City, where she made another movie. Drew is now using drugs and alcohol.

Drew snorted her first line of cocaine at a school dance. She had returned to Los Angeles and fallen back in with her high school crowd. Life in Manhattan had been exciting, especially when she had had her first real boyfriend while she was there. But it felt good to be back in familiar surroundings and with her regular crowd. It felt even better after Drew finally gave in to cocaine. She was addicted right from the start. For fifteen wonderful minutes, the drug took all of Drew's troubles away. She didn't worry about her weight problems or why she hated herself. While she was high, life felt beautiful for her. As soon as her good feelings started to wear off, all she had to do was snort another line and, like magic, she was happy again. From the moment she tried it, Drew could think of nothing else but cocaine, cocaine, cocaine – and drinking.

When the next summer vacation arrived, Drew had all the time in the world for her addictions. She had spent so many summers in studios that she had almost forgotten what it felt like to have a summer break. This summer, she could do just as *she* wanted, and didn't have to worry about getting up early the next morning. But she soon found out that she had been hired to work on yet another movie, and the cameras were starting in July. That gave Drew only one month of freedom for her addictions. The moment of truth came two weeks into her vacation. She went to a movie with some friends and got drunk on beer. The group stayed out until very late, past Drew Barrymore's curfew. But breaking that rule was the least of her crimes: terribly drunk, she called her mom and told her to find somewhere else to sleep for the night.

"When I got home," Drew told *People* magazine, "I screamed, 'What the hell are you doing here?!' I wanted her out of the house – I said it was *my* turn to be Mom. She just stood there and looked at me. I started to throw things … I went to get another beer and was swearing at my mother when the front door opened. 'Oh shit, the cops!' I thought. But a friend came through the door, someone who had checked into a rehabilitation program to get sober. By that time, I couldn't walk or function. She and my mother pulled me into the car."
"Where are you taking me?!" Drew wanted to know.
"The hospital."
'Good answer,' thought Drew as she silently thanked her lucky stars for her breakdown. Of course, she was not just going to the city hospital. Finally, and before it had become too late, Drew Barrymore was on the painful road to rehabilitation.

adapted from: *Happily Ever After – The Drew Barrymore Story*, by Leah and Elina Furman

2 What do you think?

a) *Do you feel sorry for Drew Barrymore? Do your feelings change during the story?*

b) *Talk about these questions in small groups.*

1. Why did Drew take drugs?
2. Do you know anyone with similar problems?
3. What other reasons are there for taking drugs? Do they really solve problems?
4. Should kids like Drew be protected?

→ WB 69, 1–2

3 Friends and family

a) *Skim the story for all the friends that are mentioned. Which do you think are good friends, which are not so good? Take notes from the story to support your answer.*

* b) *What do you think Drew's mother felt about Drew's life after she became famous, and what she did as a teenager?*

READING SKILLS

Sometimes information about the people or events in a text is 'hidden'. What a person says or does, for example, often shows you how he or she is feeling. Reading a text for this kind of information is called 'reading between the lines' of the text. What a person **doesn't** say or do can also give you clues.

4 Your turn: A friend

Write the last part of the story as if you are the friend who helps Drew. Start like this:

I saw Drew outside her house. It was late, and she was very drunk …

5 A song: Miss California

She's Miss California, hottest thing in West L.A.,
House down by the water, sails her yacht across the bay.
Drives a Maranello, Hollywood's her favorite scene,
Loves to be surrounded with superstars that know her name.

She's a rich girl from the top of the food chain,
Love and material things.
Kinda lonely, till I met her at the Grammys,
Ten mill on a diamond ring.
She invites me to spend a day on the jet skis,
At first it didn't mean a thing.
Then she told me I'm the one that she searched for,
It was hard to believe.

Vada J Nobles / Rasheem Sharrief Pugh © Kilosheem Pub / VNM Publ.

a) *What kind of person is Miss California?*

b) *What do you think 'Mr. California' could look like?*

1 Hollywood and the movies

Make a mind map with words about Hollywood and the movie industry.

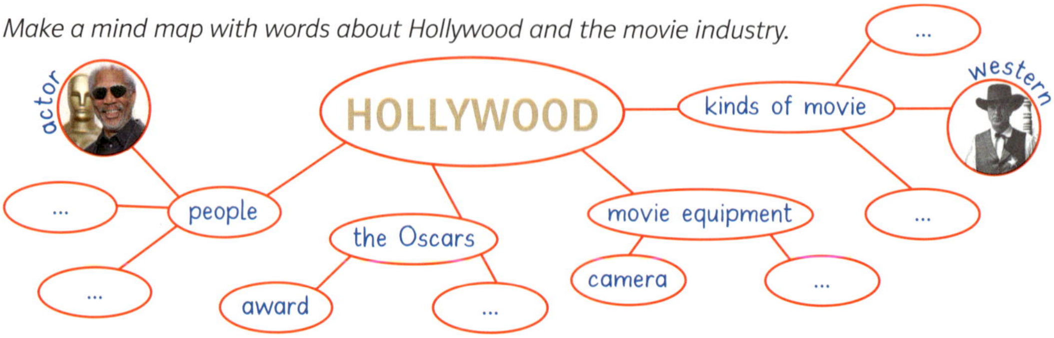

2 Old science fiction movies

A director used some things from his home when he made a science fiction movie. What did he use?

Start like this:
1. The robot is really an old …
2. The director used …

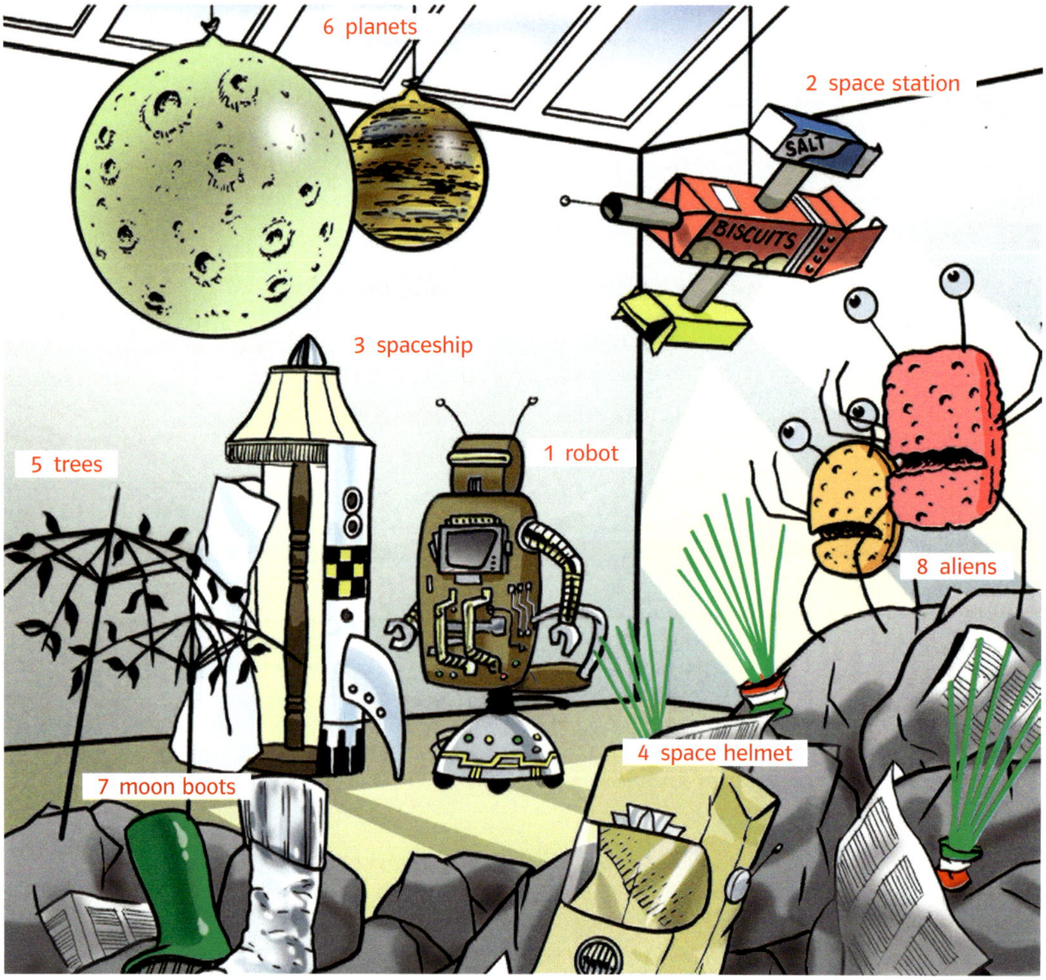

balloons • sponges • lamp • fast food bag • wellies • chair • boxes • umbrella

3 Sounds: Odd one out

a) *Say the words to a partner carefully. Which is the odd one out each time?*

1. park • award • farther • harbor
2. scream • freedom • wear • seem
3. grade • break • fame • leak
4. novel • motel • moment • joking
5. silent • license • hiking • liberty
6. boulder • council • crowd • doubt

b) *Listen and check your answers. Were you right?*

4 American and British words

Make a grid for words which are different in American English and British English. Add as many words as you can.

	AE	BE
1. Spelling	center …	centre …
2. Vocabulary	movie theater …	cinema …

5 A puzzle: Another word

a) *Find another word for … (the words were all in this unit!)*

1. strange: w****
2. a funny movie: a c*****
3. a prize: an a****
4. without noise: s*****
5. the book of a life: a b********
6. good-looking: h*******
7. good-looking: a*********
8. the first time a movie is shown: a p*******
9. very good: w********
10. very violent: b*****

b) *Make a word puzzle like this for your partner. Can he/she find the words? (And did you get the number of stars right?)*

6 Word families

Complete the sentences with a word from the same word family.

1. Bollywood movies are often very … (romance)
2. … sometimes wait outside stars' homes. (to photograph)
3. Do you want to know more about the stars? Have a … at this website. (to look)
4. Tell me what happened. I want to know the … (true)
5. Steven Spielberg is a movie … (to direct)
6. Some of the special effects in *Tron* were …, when the movie was made. (to believe)

WB 70, 1–3

7 Which movies? (From page 84)

Photo number 2 is from the movie *King Kong* (1933). Number 3 is from *Gone with the wind* (1939). Number 4 is from *High Noon* (1952).

Do you know the German titles of the movies?

1 An actor's things (the passive voice → G17)

Where were the actor's things made?

Example: His hat was made in the UK.

2 The first … (the passive voice → G17)

Make sentences with the passive voice and 'by'.

Example: the first stories / to tell / people around campfires / thousands of years ago
The first stories **were told by** people around campfires thousands of years ago.

1. the first books / to print / people in Europe / more than 500 years ago
2. the first photograph / to take / a man in France / in the 1820s
3. the first cars / to build / a German / in 1886
4. the first plane / to fly / two American brothers / in 1903
5. the first westerns / to make / directors in the US / in the 1900s
6. the first people / to send / to the moon / the US / in 1969
7. the first hip hop music / to perform / DJs / in the 1970s

You need the third forms of the verbs. You can find them in the list on page 224.

3 Oscar winners (reported speech → G18)

Look at what some Oscar winners said. Put the sentences into reported speech.

1 I'm so proud! It's the best night of my life!

2 I've made lots of movies but it's my first Oscar. Wow!

3 I want to thank my mom and dad for all they did for me!

4 I really enjoyed making the movie. I'll never forget it.

5 I'm very happy! It's as if all my dreams have come true!

6 We're glad to be in LA! And it's a wonderful surprise!

1. He said that he … . It …
2. She explained that she … but that this …
3. She said she … for all they …
4. She told the audience she … and that …
5. He said that he … . It …
6. They said that they … and that it …

4 A date (reported speech → G 18, G 19)

Sarah and Jamie went out on a date together last night. Now Sarah is telling a friend about the evening. Change the sentences and questions into reported speech.

Example: Jamie: I like *The Lord of the Rings*.
He said that he liked *The Lord of the Rings*.

1. Jamie: I'm crazy about science fiction. → He said …
2. Jamie: Have you ever seen *Tron*? → He asked me whether …
3. Sarah: I haven't seen it. → I said …
4. Jamie: What computer games do you like? → He …
5. Sarah: I don't really like games. → I said …
6. Sarah: It has been a nice evening. → I added that …
7. Jamie: I'll see you around. → He …

5 A dangerous job (mixed exercise)

Read the magazine article and find the right word each time.

When I **was** a kid at school, I [1] want to be a fire fighter or policewoman, like my [2]. Jobs like that were too [3] for me. I decided to make movies. I was [4] my first camera when I was ten and I [5] pictures of everything: my school, my family, my dog, [6] moon and the stars. But they weren't movies, they [7] just photos.
When I was twelve, Dad lent me [8] movie camera. It was summer. We were all on [9] in California. I made short movies about everyone in my [10], even about my older sister. She [11] mad about that. One sunny day we were all on the [12]. I had my dad's new movie camera. My sister was [13] beach volleyball with some friends and I was [14] a movie of them. I was [15] near the water. Suddenly the ball came straight at me. I turned too quickly and was [16] by a big wave. I fell on my back into the [17]. I got wet but I saved the movie camera. I held it above my head until I was pulled out of the water [18] my dad. After that I decided it was [19] dangerous to be a director so I [20] a policewoman.

friends | family | vacation | water | beach | given | became | took | standing | hit | making | playing | were | was ✓ | was | didn't | his | the | dangerous | by | too

→ WB 72, 1–2

NOW YOU CAN

✓ Talk about stars. → Find three adjectives to describe a Hollywood star.
✓ Talk about different kinds of movies. → Name three kinds of movies. Describe your favorite kind.
✓ Use the passive voice in the simple past. → Say where one of your sweatshirts or T-shirts was made.
✓ Report what someone else said. → Report an announcement that your teacher made during your last English class.
✓ Give advice about a book, movie or game. → Recommend a book, movie or game to your partner.

Skills workshop 5 Working with texts

1 Notes

READING SKILLS

When you read texts for a project or a presentation you can take notes. This will help you to remember the most important parts of what you have read.

With a short text, write down the 3–4 most important points. You needn't write full sentences, but you must write so that you will be able to understand the notes later!

a) *Read Text A on page 99.*

b) *Look at these notes a student made about Spanish in California. Are any of the points in the notes not important? What important information isn't in the notes?*

- first language: many people and businesses
- useful for jobs
- Spanish classes: more and more popular
- Shirlyn Jackson: can't wait to start course

2 Clusters

STUDY SKILLS

Clusters are another way of taking notes. You can make a cluster about an idea, a person or a thing in the text.

Clusters are like small mind maps. The subject of the cluster goes in the middle.

a) *Look at this cluster about Oscar Negrete. What other information could you add?*

b) *Compare your cluster with a partner's. Do you have the same information?*

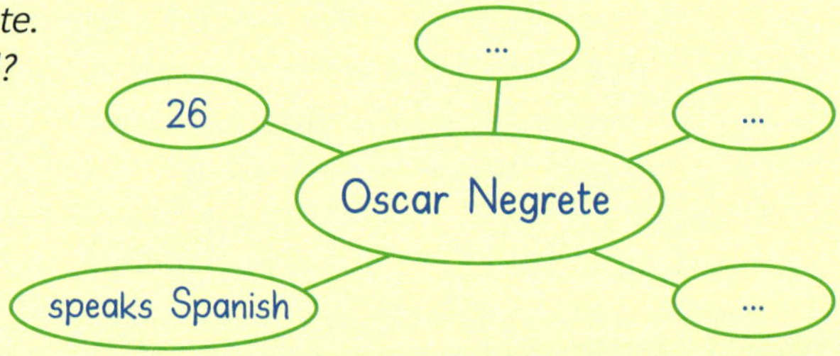

3 Your turn: A one minute talk

a) *Read Text B on page 99. Take notes about Hollywood at the different times (16th century, the years after 1769, …) that are mentioned in the text.*

b) *Make a cluster about one of the people in the text.*

c) *Use your notes or your cluster to give a one minute talk to your partner about one of the times or one of the people.*

STUDY SKILLS

Your talk
Remember to talk clearly and not too fast. Three or four points are enough for one minute!

Your partner's talk
Remember to listen carefully to the talk and to give your partner tips at the end of the talk. Do you have any questions?

A Hispanics want the good life

Life is good for 26-year-old Oscar Negrete of San Diego. Selling cars brings him $ 6,000 per month, a lot of money for someone his age. Now Oscar feels that he's living his 'American Dream'. He has been with the same company for a few years, but his old job there only paid $ 1,800 per month. Oscar got his new job because he speaks Spanish. It is the first language of many people in the region, and like many local businesses, Oscar's company saw that speaking Spanish would help to sell more cars.
Over the next 20 years the number of Hispanics – people whose first language is Spanish or who grew up in families where Spanish was spoken – in California is expected to rise to 50 per cent of the population. Carlos Gomez, a Spanish teacher at a college in San Diego, reports that Spanish classes are becoming more and more popular each year. Shirlyn Jackson is one of the new students. Shirlyn is sure her Spanish lessons will help her job chances, and she can't wait to start her course next week. The Spanish language and the Hispanic population of California are sure to play important roles in the state's future.

B The real Hollywood

Many people think that the history of Hollywood began at the beginning of the 20th century when the first movie studios were opened. But Hollywood was 'born' many years before that. The area which is now known as Hollywood was first discovered by Spanish explorers in the 16th century. At that time several tribes of Native Americans were living in the area. In the years after 1769 the land was divided into two huge ranches and the farmers grew grain, pineapples and bananas.
These ranches were later divided into smaller ranches. In 1886 Harvey Henderson Wilcox from Kansas bought one of the smaller ranches. Mr. Wilcox was not a farmer, he sold real estate. He made a new community out of the ranch. He paved the street which is now Hollywood Boulevard and sold land to rich Americans who wanted to spend their winters in California. His wife, Daedia Wilcox was busy, too. She collected money to build churches, schools and a library. By 1900 they had a population of 500 and everything that a town needed – except for water. So they turned to their larger neighbor, Los Angeles, for help. In 1910 they became a part of this city, which then gave them all the water they needed. After the first studio was opened in 1911 by the Nestor Company, Hollywood started to grow. And since then the name has stood for one of the largest movie industries in the world.

A working journey

More and more families in the UK and the US are deciding to leave home and look for adventure in other places. This magazine article is about a trip that Marlene Smith, 17, and her family took through America.

Just another family camping trip, you'd have thought, as my mother and I put things into the Volkswagen. But what a trip! My father, mother, brother and I were leaving our farm in Missouri for a year's journey through all fifty states of the US. My mother had suggested the trip as a way to get to know our country better. It would mean a year out of school for fifteen-year-old Joe and the start of college a year later for me, but we wanted to do it.

July found us working in Washington State's Wenatchee Valley, full of fruit farms and skeptical farmers. They knew we had no experience as fruit pickers, but they gave us a chance. We learned quickly, with only a few accidents. The money we earned in the next six weeks paid for the 2,000 mile trip through the Canadian wilderness to Alaska.

Back from Alaska, we were again picking fruit, this time in California, where we learned about the life of migrant workers. The early morning frost killed the feeling in our fingers, while the midday sun gave us headaches. One day, when the police checked our group for Mexicans working illegally in the US, some of our new friends were sent back.

Sometimes we found jobs just in time. In Louisiana, it took two days of searching for a way to pay our motel bill before my father and Joe were hired by a cable-TV company. In Virginia, my mother worked in a flower shop, and I worked in a snack shop. Traveling 40,000 miles across America taught us about different lifestyles – the slow easy-going south and the hustle-bustle of the north. Sometimes we just got tired of all the driving and missed having a permanent home, but there were also some nice surprises. And there was a fantastic feeling of success when we saw the 'Welcome to Iowa' sign and proudly entered state number fifty.

A Reading

1 *Read the text and decide if these sentences are right or wrong.*

a Marlene's family went through every state of the US during their working journey.
b The farmers in Washington State didn't give the family work.
c Some friends of the family had trouble with the police in California.
d The Smiths had no problems with their bills.
e The Smiths found that life was slower in the north than in the south.
f The last state of the journey was Iowa.

2 *Finish the sentences.*

a The Smiths went on the trip because …
b After they had worked in Wenatchee Valley, they …
c A cable company … when the family was in Louisiana.
d Although they got tired of driving, they …

B Language

Explain these words and phrases in one or two sentences.

a a migrant worker
b to work illegally
c a lifestyle
d easy-going
e hustle-bustle
f a permanent home

C Passing on information

A German teenager has found this information about a summer job in the US on the Internet. Her parents aren't sure it's a good idea. Answer the parents' questions in German.

Junior counselors
Live and work with boys and girls (8–13) in a beautiful outdoor setting in California.
Counselors will teach 3–4 of these activities: tennis, golf, climbing, circus, painting and drawing, drama, mountain biking, rock music, water sports, cooking, tennis, golf, horseback riding and more.
All meals are served in the camp dining hall by our camp cooks. Each counselor is given 2 hours off during the day. All counselors have cabins that they share with 2–4 other staff. They have access to Internet, phone, washer/dryer during their time off.

a Man muss doch sehr sportlich sein, um im „summer camp" zu arbeiten, oder?
b Müssen „counselors" dort für sich selbst kochen?
c Müssen sie wirklich nur zwei Stunden pro Tag arbeiten?
d Wie ist es mit Übernachtung? Gibt es Zelte für die „counselors"?

D Listening

Michelle, a student from France, wants to work in a summer camp in the US. Listen to her interview. What makes Michelle right – or not right – for the job? Take notes.

E Writing

1 *Michelle got the job. Write her e-mail to her American friend in New York. Use the notes.*

- arrived at summer camp last Friday
- kids: nice (some of the smaller ones loud)
- food: OK (great sausages last night!)
- another student from France, Julie
- go climbing with kids tomorrow 🙂

2 *Write your opinion in 80–100 words.*

"Every young person should try to see all the different parts of his or her country."

Passing on information

Unit 1 In a New York cab

COMMUNICATION SKILLS

Beim **sinngemäßen Übertragen** von einer Sprache in die andere kommt es darauf an,

- das Wichtige vom Unwichtigen zu unterscheiden
- sich auf das Wichtigste zu beschränken
- nicht Satz für Satz zu übersetzen
- wichtige Wörter, die du nicht auf Englisch kennst, zu umschreiben.

Es geht also darum, den Sinn einer Aussage wiederzugeben.

Du bist mit deinen Eltern in New York, und ihr wollt Ellis Island besuchen. Ihr nehmt ein Taxi. Da deine Eltern nicht so gut Englisch können, musst du ihnen bei der Unterhaltung mit dem Fahrer helfen.

Driver: Hi there, where would you folks like to go today?
Mom: We like … uh …
You: Lass mich das machen, Mama. We'd like to go to Ellis Island.
Driver: Aaah, Ellis Island, ha ha. But I can't drive you there, you know. I can only take you as far as Battery Park. That's where you have to buy your tickets for the ferry.
Mom: Warum schüttelt er seinen Kopf und lacht? Kann er uns nicht hinfahren, oder was?
You: …
Dad: Frag ihn doch, wo wir die Tickets kaufen können.
You: …
Driver: Tickets? That's easy. I'll show you exactly where to buy the tickets.
You: …
Mom: Wie nett von ihm. Frag ihn, wo er herkommt.
You: …
Driver: Me? I'm from Ecuador.
Dad: Oh, Ecuador! Ist er schon lange hier?
You: …
Driver: I've been in New York City for 13 years and I've had my own cab for ten. I work hard. Last year I bought a second cab. My cousin drives that now – but I'm the owner!
You: …
Dad: Wie ist er nach Amerika gekommen? Musste er auch nach Ellis Island?
You: …
Driver: I came in 1994. I'd worked in a shoe factory in Ecuador for 10 years, but I'd always wanted to live in New York. My uncle had already been here for five years so I decided to come, too. This is home for me and my family now. We love it here!
You: …
Dad: Und hat er gesagt, ob er in Ellis Island ankam, oder nicht?
You: …
Driver: Ellis Island? No, man. Ellis Island closed in 1954. I flew to Miami and took a bus to New York!
You: …
Driver: Ah, here we are at beautiful Battery Park. Look over there, see that long line of people? That's where you have to buy your tickets. Good luck, and I hope you enjoy New York!
You: Goodbye and thank you!
Mom: Was war noch? Was hat er gemeint? Wo müssen wir hin?
You: Kein Problem, Mama, alles klar …

Unit 2 School rules

COMMUNICATION SKILLS

Auch hier geht es nicht darum, Satz für Satz zu übersetzen. Konzentriere dich auf das, was die andere Person wissen will und gib nur das Notwendigste weiter.

Ein amerikanischer Austauschschüler sieht dieses Plakat mit der Schulordnung einer Realschule in Deutschland.

1. Das Schulgelände darf während der Unterrichtszeit nur mit ausdrücklicher Genehmigung eines Lehrers verlassen werden.
2. Im Schulgebäude und auf dem Schulgelände gilt ein allgemeines Nikotin- und Alkoholverbot, auch für Schüler, die über 16 Jahre alt sind.
3. Auf dem Schulgelände müssen Handys, MP3-Player and andere elektronische Geräte zu jeder Zeit ausgeschaltet sein und dürfen nicht sichtbar getragen werden.
4. Schüler dürfen während des Unterrichts nur mit Erlaubnis der unterrichtenden Lehrkraft essen und trinken. Kaugummi ist auf dem gesamten Schulgelände verboten.

Beantworte die Fragen des Austauschschülers auf Englisch.

1. Are you guys allowed to go across the road and buy some food during PE? I saw a cool shop there this morning.
2. Someone was checking his messages on a cell phone during History. Are cell phones really allowed at school?
3. Is it really true that kids aren't even allowed to drink water during classes? That's stricter than my school!
4. Hey, what's that about 'Nikotin' and kids over 16?

Unit 3 At the airport

COMMUNICATION SKILLS

Am Flughafen hört man häufig Ansagen, die nicht immer leicht zu verstehen sind. Konzentriere dich deshalb auf Schlüsselwörter wie Namen, Zeit- und Ortsangaben sowie Zahlen. Die Hauptinformation wird meistens wiederholt.

Du bist mit deiner Familie in den USA und ihr wollt gerade den Rückflug nach Frankfurt antreten. Aus irgendwelchen Gründen verzögert sich das Einchecken noch. Ihr hört vier verschiedene Durchsagen. Deine Mutter befürchtet, dass ihr etwas Wichtiges überhört haben könntet. Wie beruhigst du sie jeweils?

1. Sie denkt bei Ansage 1: Ihr müsst jetzt am Gate 26 einchecken.
2. Sie denkt bei Ansage 2: Ihr sollt euch in der Abfertigungshalle melden.
3. Sie denkt bei Ansage 3: Ihr sollt jetzt zum Gate 42 gehen.
4. Sie denkt bei Ansage 4: Etwas mit eurem Gepäck ist nicht in Ordnung.

Unit 3 The Everglades National Park

COMMUNICATION SKILLS

In Broschüren stehen bestimmte Informationen, wie z.B. Preise und Öffnungszeiten, im Vordergrund. Die Bedeutung unbekannter Wörter (wie bei „fishing license") kannst du oftmals aus dem Kontext erschließen. Du brauchst nicht Wort für Wort zu übersetzen, sondern kannst den Sachverhalt mit deinen eigenen Worten ausdrücken.

Du bist zu Besuch im Everglades National Park in Florida mit einem deutschen Freund und seiner Familie. Ihr wollt den morgigen Tag zusammen planen. Dein Freund spricht nur wenig Englisch. Fasse die drei Aktivitäten für deinen Freund auf Deutsch zusammen.

Free two-hour hikes with a ranger are available Mon – Fri at 8 am, 11 am, 2 pm and 5 pm. Hiking is allowed on our boardwalk trails from dawn to dusk. Remember to bring along plenty of water!

Boat rentals at the ranger station:
$10 / hour, half day $30, full day $65. Fishing license needed. We recommend fishing from a boat rather than from the shore.
Good fishing guaranteed!

Ninety-minute boat tours daily (except holidays):
Apr. – Sept. 6 am – 9 pm
Oct. – Mar. 8 am – 5 pm.
$15 per person. The boat captains will make sure that your trip is unforgettable!

Unit 4 A fast car

Du besuchst mit deiner Familie Freunde in den USA. Zur Familie dort gehört auch ein zwölfjähriger Junge, für den du als Geschenk ein ferngesteuertes Spielzeugauto mitgebracht hast. Leider ist die Gebrauchsanweisung auf Deutsch, und daher musst du dem Jungen die wichtigsten Informationen auf Englisch erklären. Lies dir die Gebrauchsanweisung auf der nächsten Seite durch und stelle dem Jungen das Auto auf Englisch vor. Konzentriere dich dabei auf folgende Punkte:

1. Welche Ausrüstung gehört dazu?
2. Wie oft muss der Akku aufgeladen werden?
3. Welche Funktionen hat das Auto?
4. Braucht man noch weiteres Zubehör?
5. Funktioniert das Ladegerät auch bei anderen Voltangaben? (In den USA sind sie anders.)

Dieses schnelle Auto fegt durch die Straßen und garantiert viel Spaß. Fahrakku, Fernsteuerung und Batteriebox gehören mit zur Ausrüstung.

Technische Daten: Länge: 540 mm; Breite: 280 mm; Höhe: 220 mm; Gewicht: 1,6 kg; Fahrakku 9,6 V (hält ca. 20 Stunden)

Funktionen: fährt vorwärts, rückwärts, links, rechts; Türen und Dach öffnen automatisch; Scheinwerfer

Für den Fahrakku benötigen Sie ein Extra-Ladegerät. Bei anderen Voltangaben muss ein Adapter benutzt werden.

Unit 5 Oscar information

COMMUNICATION SKILLS

Lies dir zunächst die Fragen in der Aufgabe durch, um dann gezielt nach diesen Informationen im Text suchen zu können. So kannst du die Fragen beantworten, ohne dich um schwierige Wörter, wie z. B. „box office" oder „Academy of Motion Picture Arts and Sciences" kümmern zu müssen.

Deine kleine Schwester hat diese Informationen über die „Oscars" im Internet gefunden. Leider ist ihr Englisch nicht so toll und sie bittet dich um Hilfe … Beantworte die Fragen deiner Schwester.

1. Was ist diese Academy? Sind das nur berühmte Schauspieler?
2. Wer war Onkel Oscar? Hat er die Statue angefertigt?
3. Müssen Filme schon erfolgreich sein, bevor sie Oscars bekommen können?
4. Den Namen Marilyn Monroe kenne ich doch … Hat sie einen Oscar gewonnen?

Who awards the Oscars?

The Oscars, or Academy Awards, are chosen by some of the 6,000 members of the Academy of Motion Picture Arts and Sciences (called 'the Academy' for short). They are important people in the US movie industry.

Why the funny name?

Where the name Oscar comes from is a mystery. One idea is that at the first awards, in 1929, a member of the Academy said that the statue looked just like her Uncle Oscar. And the name stuck. But nobody really knows.

Why are they so important?

Actors often get more work and can be in bigger movies after they've been in a movie that has won an Oscar. And movies that haven't done very well at the box office can suddenly turn into big hits after Oscar night. But not all great movies win Oscars, and some of Hollywood's greatest stars, like Richard Burton and Marilyn Monroe, never won an Academy Award.

A project English and Science

Step 1: What do we need energy for?

What do we need energy for? Talk in groups and make clusters.

Step 2: Find out about energy changes

a) *Read this page from an English Science book:*

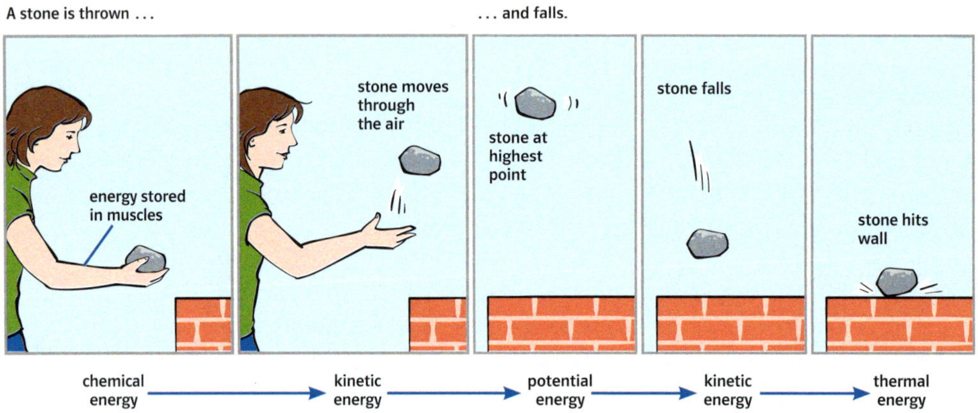

To do work, you have to spend energy. But, like money, energy doesn't disappear when you spend it. It goes somewhere else! People talk about 'using energy', but energy is never used up. It just changes into different forms.

The pictures above show a sequence of energy changes. The last one is from kinetic to thermal energy. When the stone hits the wall, it makes the atoms and molecules in the stone and the wall move faster, so the materials get hotter. During each change, the amount of energy stays the same.

adapted from: *Complete Physics* – by Stephen Pople

b) *Which energy is it? Use the information in the pictures and the text.*

1. ... energy is another word for 'heat'.
2. ... energy is the energy stored in food, fuels and batteries (and muscles!)
3. ... energy is the energy in objects that move.
4. ... energy is the energy stored in objects that have been raised.

kinetic | thermal | potential | chemical

stored [stɔ:d] – *gespeichert,* muscle ['mʌsl] – *Muskel,* chemical ['kemɪkl], kinetic [kɪ'netɪk], potential [pəʊ'tenʃl], thermal ['θɜ:ml], to spend [spend] – *einsetzen,* to disappear [dɪsə'pɪər] *verschwinden,* to use up [ju:z‿'ʌp] – *aufbrauchen,* sequence ['si:kwents] – *Abfolge,* atom ['ætəm], molecule ['mɒlɪkjʊ:l], material [mə'tɪəriəl] – *Stoff,* amount [ə'maʊnt] – *Menge,* heat [hi:t] – *Hitze,* fuel ['fju:el] – *Treibstoff,* to raise [reɪz] – *hochheben*

Step 3: Energy changes

Energy changes happen all around us, every day.

Example: When a car is driven …

chemical energy (in the fuel) → kinetic energy (the car moves)
chemical energy (in the fuel) → thermal energy (the engine gets hot!)

Use the example as a model. Show the energy changes that happen …

1. … in a light bulb, when the light is switched on.
2. … in a campfire.

chemical energy | electrical energy | thermal energy | light

Step 4: An experiment with thermal energy

Thermal energy is 'lost' every day, for example when warm water cools down. (But remember: energy that is 'lost' like this does not disappear. It just spreads out so thinly that it becomes very difficult to do anything with the energy.)

a) *How can you keep a liter of warm water warmer longer? Try out the three methods in the picture. Measure the temperature of the water at the beginning and the end of the experiment. Which method was best?*

bottle | bottle in a bag | thermos flask

b) *Write a report about the experiment. Use the tips below.*

WRITING SKILLS

1. **Hypothesis.** What did you think would happen before you did the experiment? (We wanted to show that … We expected … because …)
2. Give a list of the **equipment** you used.
3. Describe your **method.** (First we … Then we …)
4. Give your **results.** You can show the results in a table / in a list …
5. Write your **conclusion.** What do the results tell you? (We were right. The results show that … We were not right. We expected that … but …)

* c) *Think about how you could use the results of this experiment to save energy at home and at school.*

engine ['endʒɪn] – *Motor,* to cool down [kuːl 'daʊn] – *abkühlen,* to spread out [spred‿'aʊt] – *sich verteilen,* liter ['liːtə] – *Liter,* method ['meθəd] – *Methode,* to measure ['meʒə] – *messen,* temperature ['temprətʃə] – *Temperatur,* thermos flask ['θɜːmɒs ˌflɑːsk] – *Thermoskanne,* hypothesis [haɪ'pɒθəsɪs] – *Hypothese, Annahme,* conclusion [kən'kluːʒən] – *Schlussfolgerung*

A project English and Mathematics

Step 1: Thinking about surveys and data

Surveys are a way of collecting information. The information is often about how people spend their lives, or what they think about a topic. The information that is collected is called data.

Have you ever done, read about or taken part in a survey? What did it try to find out?

Step 2: Looking at pie charts

When data has been collected in a survey, it can be shown as a pie chart.

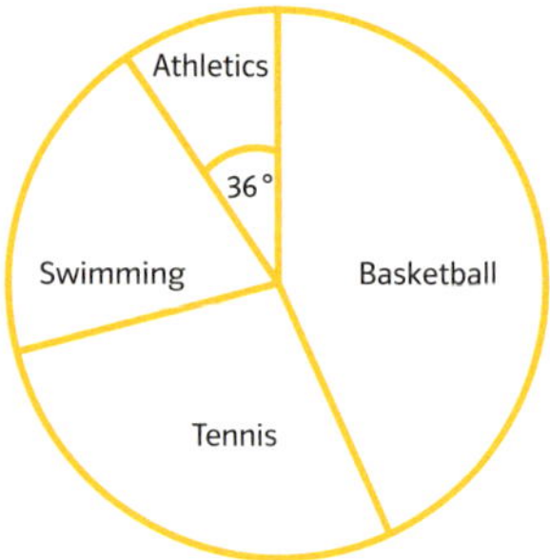

a) *One summer the 30 students of an eighth grade class were allowed to choose what they did in their PE lessons. Look at this pie chart which shows what they chose. What was the most popular sport?*

b) *How many students did athletics? How did you find out? If you aren't sure, look at Step 3.*

Step 3: Drawing a pie chart

To show results as a pie chart, we need to put in each piece of data as a proportion of 360, because that is how many degrees there are in a circle. In a survey about food, if 20 out of 90 people say their favorite meal is pizza, this will be (20 ÷ 90) x 360 = 80 degrees of the pie chart.

TIP

+ = plus
− = minus
÷ = divided by
x = times

a) *Calculate the proportions of the pie chart for each of these results.*

Survey of the favorite meals of 90 middle school students

spaghetti / other pasta meals: 38

pizza: 20

hamburger with French fries: 17

other: 15

b) *Now draw the pie chart to show the results. You will need to measure the angles with a protractor. Before you draw, remember to check that the parts add up to 360°!*

data ['deɪtə] – *Daten,* pie chart ['paɪ ˌtʃɑːt] – *Tortendiagramm,* proportion [prə'pɔːʃən] – *Anteil,* degree [dɪ'griː] *Grad,* to calculate ['kælkjəleɪt] – *berechnen,* plus [plʌs] – *plus,* minus ['maɪnəs] – *minus,* divided by [dɪ'vaɪdɪd baɪ] – *geteilt durch,* times [taɪmz] – *mal,* to measure ['meʒə] – *messen,* angle ['æŋgl] – *Winkel,* protractor [prə'træktə] – *Winkelmesser, Geometrie-Dreieck*

Step 4: Bar charts

Data that has been collected can also be shown as a bar chart.

a) *Look at this bar chart with the results of another survey.*
How many people took part in the survey?

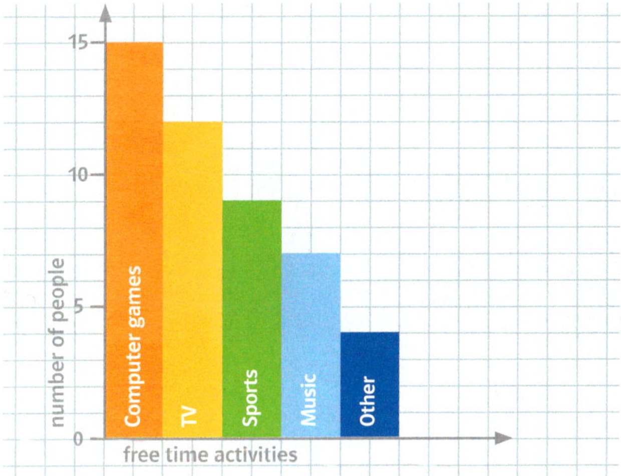

TIP

You should always label the axes of your bar chart. This means that you should say what is shown by the x-axis (in this example, the activities) and the y-axis (here, the number of people).

If you aren't sure of the answer, think what the chart is telling you.
Fifteen people did the first activity, twelve did the second activity, nine …

15 + 12 + 9 + . . . + . . . + . . . = . . .

b) *Now put these results from another survey into a bar chart. Remember to label the axes.*

Ages of guests who stayed at the Rose Motel on a Saturday night in May.

Age	Under 21	21-30	31-40	41-60	Over 60
Number of guests	8	15	18	12	7

Step 5: Your turn: A survey

a) *Think of a topic for your own survey. Here are some ideas:*

the styles of music people listen to • the TV channels people watch • the countries people would like to visit • …

b) *Do your survey and collect the data. You should ask twenty people or more.*

c) *Show your data as a pie chart or a bar chart.*

bar chart ['bɑː ˌtʃɑːt] – *Balkendiagramm,* to label ['leɪbl] – *beschriften, kennzeichnen,*
axis, pl. axes ['æksɪs, 'æksiːz] – *Achse*

A calendar Special days in the US

1

2

3

4

A July 4th, or **Independence Day**, is a holiday, so nobody goes to work. The American flag is everywhere, and people put on red, white and blue clothes (the colors of the flag) and paint their faces in these colors, too. There are lots of parades, parties and fireworks.

B Most American families put a pumpkin in their window for **Halloween** (October 31st). In Ireland and other Celtic countries, this was the night when people tried to frighten bad spirits away. Now young kids put on scary costumes, ring on their neighbors' doorbells and say 'trick or treat'. For older kids it's also a chance to put on a costume and to have a good time at a party!

C "I have a dream ..." is a phrase from one of the most famous speeches in American history. Martin Luther King said it when he was fighting to get the same rights for black and white Americans in the 1960s. King was murdered in 1968, but every year on **Martin Luther King Day** (the third Monday in January), there is a holiday so that Americans remember this great leader.

D **Labor Day** is a holiday at the end of the summer in the US. It is always on the first Monday in September. This is the day when America remembers its workers. It's a great day for a hike in the country, or for a barbecue in the backyard with grilled fish or sausages!

1 Different or the same?

a) *Read the texts and find the right picture for each one.*

b) *Which of the special days are celebrated in Germany, too? Which other special days do you know, for example in other countries?*

holiday ['hɒlɪdeɪ] – *Feiertag*, pumpkin ['pʌmpkɪn] – *Kürbis*, Halloween [hæləʊ'i:n] – *Halloween*, Celtic ['keltɪk] – *keltisch*, to frighten away [ˌfraɪtn‿ə'weɪ] – *verscheuchen*, bad [bæd] – *übel*, spirit ['spɪrɪt] – *Geist*, 'trick or treat' [trɪk‿ə 'tri:t] – *„Süßes oder Saures"*, right [raɪt] – *Recht*, leader ['li:də] – *Führer/-in*, Labor Day ['leɪbə ˌdeɪ] – *Tag der Arbeit*, barbecue ['bɑ:bɪkju:] – *Grillfest*, backyard [ˌbæk'jɑ:d] – *Garten (hinter dem Haus)*, grilled [grɪld] – *gegrillt*

6

7

8

E

On **St. Patrick's Day** (March 17th) everything in the US is green! St. Patrick is the patron saint of Ireland, but the day isn't only for Americans whose families came from that country. Lots of people dye their hair green, wear green clothes, and in Chicago they even dye the river green for the day!

F

The early English settlers in America were glad when Native Americans helped them to grow food in 1621, their first year in New England. So they had their first **Thanksgiving** meal to say 'thank you'. Today Americans still get together on this holiday. It is always the last Thursday in November, and many people travel from one end of the country to the other to be with their family. They eat turkey with stuffing and cranberry sauce, and the dessert is a delicious pumpkin pie.

G

Memorial Day is the last Monday in May. It's the holiday when Americans remember the soldiers who died for their country in war.

H

President's Day is a holiday on the third Monday in February in most states. On this day Americans remember all their presidents. One of the most famous presidents was John F. Kennedy, who will always be special for the people of Berlin. In 1963 he visited the city and said, "Ich bin ein Berliner!", to show that he understood their problems.

2 Dates

a) *Which holiday is it?*

1. It's at the end of May.
2. It's at the end of November.
3. It's in the first week of September.
4. It's in the second half of January.
5. It's in the middle of February.

b) *On which date is or was each of these holidays this year?*

St. Patrick's Day [sənt 'pætrɪks deɪ] – *Namenstag von Sankt Patrick,* patron saint [ˌpeɪtrən 'seɪnt] – *heiliger Schutzpatron,* to dye [daɪ] – *färben,* settler ['setlə] – *Siedler/-in,* Thanksgiving [ˌθæŋks 'gɪvɪŋ] – *Erntedankfest,* stuffing ['stʌfɪŋ] – *Füllung,* cranberry ['krænberi] – *Preiselbeere,* Memorial Day [mɪ'mɔːriəl ˌdeɪ] – *Heldengedenktag,* soldier ['səʊldʒə] – *Soldat/-in*

A project Scenes from American history

Christopher Columbus

The first people probably came to the American continent from what is now Russia in about **40,000 B.C.** They were the first Americans.

In **1492** Christopher Columbus sailed across the Atlantic from Spain and landed on an island near America. He called the people he found there 'Indians', because he thought that he was in India.

40,000 BC 1400 1500 1600 1700

In **1620** the ship the *Mayflower* brought 102 people from England to America. These 'pilgrims' started a colony where they could practice their religion in freedom. Today Americans celebrate the pilgrims' first harvest as 'Thanksgiving' every November.

The *Mayflower*

The signing of the Declaratic

By the **1770s** the people in the colonies were unhappy about how Britain treated them, and about the taxes that they had to pay to the 'mother country' across the Atlantic. So they signed the Declaration of Independence on July 4 1776 and became a new country, the United States of America. After that George Washington's American army fought the War of Independence against the British and won. Washington later became the first president of the US.

An information stand

Plan a stand about American history for your next school project week and tell the visitors about different topics (first settlers, Declaration of Independence ...). Follow steps 1–3.

Step 1: Before you start

Make groups of four or five and decide in class which group should do which topic(s).

continent ['kɒntɪnənt] – *Kontinent*, B.C. (= before Christ) [biː 'siː] – *vor Christi Geburt*, Atlantic [ət'læntɪk] – *Atlantik*, pilgrims ['pɪlgrɪmz] – *Pilgerväter*, to start [stɑːt] – *begründen*, colony ['kɔːləni] – *Kolonie*, harvest ['hɑːvɪst] – *Ernte*, Thanksgiving [ˌθæŋks 'gɪvɪŋ] – *Erntedankfest*, to treat [triːt] – *behandeln*, tax [tæks] – *Steuer*, Declaration of Independence [dekləˌreɪʃən‿əv‿ɪndɪ'pendəns] – *Unabhängigkeitserklärung*, stand [stænd] – *(Info-) Stand*

Slaves in one of the states of the South

During the nineteenth century the North and the South of the US drifted apart. Farmers in the South used slaves that had been brought from Africa. In the North there was more heavy industry, and people thought that slavery was wrong. From **1861–1865** there was a terrible war between the two groups of states. When the states of the North won the war they freed the slaves.

00 1850 1900 1950 2000 today

dence

Rosa Parks

After the end of slavery there was still discrimination against black Americans. Martin Luther King and others fought – without violence – so that black people could have the same rights that white people had. It all started in **1955**, when a bus driver told a black woman, Rosa Parks, to give her seat to a white man and she said no. In the 1960s there were new laws to end discrimination.

The World Trade Center on September 11 2001

On September 11 **2001** terrorists attacked the World Trade Center and more than 2,800 people died. Many Americans realized that they were less safe than they had thought, even in the US. But the 'war against terrorism' that the US has fought since 2001 has been difficult to win.

Step 2: Organize your work

Make a list of the jobs for your topic (Internet research, making posters, writing texts …). Make a plan so that you all know what you have to do, and when.

Step 3: Plan your stand

When you have everything you need (texts, pictures …), plan the stand with your teacher.

to drift apart [drɪft ə'pɑːt] – *hier: sich auseinanderentwickeln,* slave [sleɪv] – *Sklave/Sklavin,* slavery ['sleivəri] – *Sklaverei,* to free [friː] – *befreien,* discrimination [dɪskrɪmɪ'neiʃn] – *Diskriminierung,* right [raɪt] – *Recht,* law [lɔː] – *Gesetz,* to attack [ə'tæk] – *angreifen,* terrorism ['terərɪzəm] – *Terrorismus,* research [rɪ'sɜːtʃ] – *Recherche*

History pages The wild, wild West

1 History in pictures

a) *What do you think of when you hear the phrase 'wild West'? Start a mind map.*
b) *Look at the pictures and read the texts to find out more. Add words and phrases to your mind map.*

1. Before the Europeans arrived, in 1492, all of what is now the US belonged to the Native Americans. There were lots of different tribes in the country.

2. In the middle of the 19th century European settlers took land from the Native Americans, who they called 'Indians'. The Native Americans fought back and there were wars.

3. But the Native Americans couldn't stop the settlers and they had to move farther West. Many of them died on the way.

4. Many white settlers were farmers with huge farms. The men who helped them were called 'cowboys'.

5. When work on a railroad from East to West started, more land was taken from the Native Americans. They called the train the 'Iron Horse'. The railroad was finished in 1869.

6. Thousands of people went West when gold was found there in 1848. Some of them were outlaws. They robbed banks and trains.

* c) *Why do you think this part of the US was called 'the wild West'?*

settler ['setlə] – *Siedler/-in,* railroad ['reɪlrəʊd] – *Eisenbahn,* iron ['aɪən] – *eisern,* outlaw ['aʊtlɔː] *Gesetzloser/Gesetzlose, Bandit/Banditin*

2 1869 – today

Between 1869 and 1890, when the last battle between Native Americans and whites took place at Wounded Knee, many thousands of Native Americans died and the West was 'won' by the whites. After 1890 the whites gave some of the West back to the Native Americans, as 'reservations'. Most of the land was in the desert, and it was difficult to grow things there. Today reservations make up 2.3% of the land of the US.

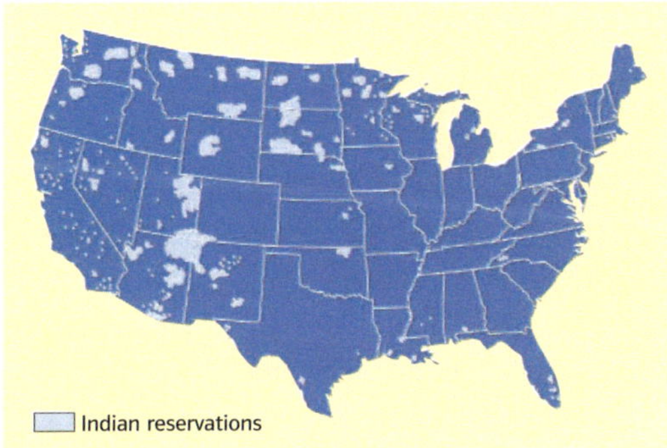

a) *Look at the map and find the largest reservation. Which states is it in?*

* b) *Where are most of the reservations? Why do you think they are in this part of the country?*

3 A rap: Does Hawk know why?

a) *Listen to the rap about the Diné, or Navajo tribe of Native Americans.*

Dear Rocks – millions of years old
New steel – new, hard and cold
Hear! Wounded Mountain lets out a cry
And Hawk up high wonders why,
Flies round and round – over the ground
Do the Diné not hear his loud, warning sound?
No, they're too busy betraying Mother Earth
Nowhere do we care – for what she is worth!

Dear Father – so good, wise and old
Yes, it is steel – and maybe it's gold
But hear! Wounded Diné – hear how we cry
Now, I wonder, does Hawk know why?
From o'er the reservation he looks down on the ground,
Where some drunk, jobless Diné are just hanging around.
That's history – no mystery – of us Diné on Earth
So it's time, too, to care – for what WE are worth!

Kai Desheny (Willow Tree)

The name 'Navajo' is a Spanish word. The tribe's own name for itself is Diné, which just means 'the people' in the Navajo language. This language is taught in Navajo schools, and the tribe even has its own police.

b) *Do you like the rap? Say why or why not.*

c) *Talk about these questions in small groups.*

1. Who is speaking in each verse? What do you think?
2. Which problems that the Navajo have are mentioned in the rap?

wounded ['wu:ndɪd] – *verwundet*, reservation [resə'veɪʃn] – *Reservat*, Hawk [hɔ:k] – *Falke*, Diné [di:neɪ], Navajo ['nævəhəʊ] – *Namen eines Indianerstammes*, cry [kraɪ] – *Schrei*, warning ['wɔ:nɪŋ] – *Warnung*, to betray [bɪ'treɪ] – *verraten*, nowhere ['nəʊweə] – *nirgendwo*, worth [wɜ:θ] – *wert*, wise [waɪs] – *weise, klug*, o'er [əər] – *über*, to hang around [hæŋ‿ə'raʊnd] – *warten, herumhängen*, verse [vɜ:s] – *Strophe*

A project Reading

READING SKILLS

A reader's diary

1. A reader's diary is more than just a report. You will need a new exercise book, a folder or a real diary for it. You can write about any texts which you have read, for example about a science fiction story, a magazine article or even about a whole book. A reader's diary can help you to remember the important parts of a text.
   You can put this information about what you have read into your diary:
   - the title,
   - the names of the characters in the text,
   - adjectives which describe the characters in the text,
   - a summary of each chapter,
   - a time line,
   - … .
2. You can also write about what you liked or didn't like in the text.
3. You can use lists, mind maps, clusters, pictures or cartoons and maps in the diary. You can write articles, different endings for the text, dialogues, reports and poems.

Step 1: Before you start

You are going to look at some pages from a diary about a book called *Lost in the USA*.

a) *Think about the title. What could the text be about?*

b) *What other texts do you know about lost things or lost people?*

Step 2: More information

Now look at parts from the first page of a reader's diary for the story Lost in the USA. *What can you find out about the story? Share your ideas with a partner and write 4–6 sentences.*

chapter ['tʃæptə] – *Kapitel*, to improve [ɪm'pru:v] – *verbessern*, cattle ['kætl] – *Vieh*

Step 3: The second page

Read the summary of the first five chapters and put the pictures below in the right order.

A summary - chapters 1-5

Frank, a German boy, flies to the US to spend his Easter holidays with his aunt. He wants to improve his English. At the airport in New York he gets into a van. He thinks it is a shuttle bus to the place where his aunt lives. But the van goes to Manhattan. The three men in the front are not bus drivers - they are gangsters called Smitty, Pancho and Fats. They kidnap Frank, take his passport and lock him in a hotel room. Fats, who brings Frank food and drinks, feels a bit sorry for him. Later the three men take Frank by private plane to a lonely place. Frank grabs a pouch before he leaves the plane. He knows his passport is in it but he doesn't know that there are diamonds in the pouch, too. The gangsters fly off. Frank finds a road and ends up in a gas station. The gangsters can't find the diamonds and realize that Frank must have them. They go back to look for him and almost find him at the gas station. He escapes in a cattle truck and meets Linda who has run away from home. When the truck slows down, they jump off and hide.

Step 4: A mind map

Draw a mind map with the characters in the story. Who belongs to whom?

Step 5: Your own diary

Use the diary and add to it when you read the chapters from Lost in the USA *on pages 118–121.*

shuttle bus ['ʃʌtl ˌbʌs] – *Zubringerbus,* in the front [ˌɪn ðə 'frʌnt] – *auf dem Vordersitz,* to kidnap ['kɪdnæp] – *entführen,* to grab [græb] – *schnappen,* pouch [paʊtʃ] – *Brustbeutel,* diamond ['daɪəmənd] – *Diamant,* to end up [end‿'ʌp] – *landen,* gas station ['gæs ˌsteɪʃn] – *Tankstelle,* to slow down [sləʊ 'daʊn] – *langsamer werden*

A story Lost in the USA by Rolf W. Roth

a) *Read what happens in chapters 6 and 7.*

The train was very long. It just went on and on, and the children waited until they saw an open boxcar. Then they ran, faster and faster, and finally jumped and were on the train. In the boxcar Frank and Linda sat on the floor and watched the prairie fly by through the open door.

"In Winslow you have to go to the police right away," Linda said. "They can help you."

"Come with me, Linda."

"No! They will take me back home."

They were quiet then.

"Why are those men after you? You must have something they want."

"But I don't. The only thing I have is this pouch here," Frank said and took it from around his neck. "And I don't want that. I don't want anything from them." He took his passport and the ticket out, put them in his jeans pocket and threw the pouch out through the open door.

b) *Why does he do this?*

They were quiet again after that – until Frank said, "I want to go home. You should go home, too. Come to the police with me."

Linda shook her head and looked out of the door. "Was there anything in that pouch? I mean besides your passport and ticket?" she asked.

Now Frank shook his head. "No, just some paper at the bottom. That's all."

"What kind of paper?"

"I don't know. Just paper. Bags often have paper in them to keep their – er –"

"Their shape," Linda helped him with the word. "Yes, I know, but maybe there was something important on the paper."

Frank looked at her. "Maybe, but I don't think so. And it's gone now."

"Yes," Linda said and got up. She walked to the door and looked out – then pulled her head in again fast. "Hey, Frank, come here!"

Frank went to the door and looked out with her. The pouch was hanging on a piece of metal and flapping in the wind.

"Quick, let's get it back," Linda said and leaned out. "Hold onto me."

"No, Linda, it's too dangerous," Frank told her, but she was already hanging out of the door, and Frank held onto her quickly. The wind was strong as Linda stretched and tried to get the pouch – and just as it was about to fly off, she grabbed it, and Frank pulled her back in.

"Boy, that was close," she said.

"You'll see, it's only paper," Frank said to her – and then they sat down again and opened the pouch.

c) *What's wrong in the picture?*
Draw the correct picture in your diary.

on and on [ɒnˌənd'ɒn] – *weiter und weiter,* boxcar *(AE)* ['bɒkskɑː] – *Güterwaggon,* prairie ['præri] – *Prärie,* to fly by [flaɪ 'baɪ] – *vorbeifliegen,* to be after sb. [bɪ 'ɑːftə] – *jmd. verfolgen,* besides [bɪ'saɪdz] – *außer,* to hang ['hæŋ] – *hängen,* metal ['hæŋˌɒn] – *Metall,* to flap [flæp] – *flattern,* to lean out [liːnˌaʊt] – *(sich) hinauslehnen,* to stretch [stretʃ] – *sich strecken,* to be about to [bɪ ə'baʊt tə] – *gerade im Begriff sein etw. zu tun,* close [kləʊs] – *knapp*

Pancho, Fats and Smitty were waiting for the train in Winslow.
"I'm sure he's on that train," Pancho said.
"He has to be!" Smitty said, "Or you two will be in real trouble."
"He has to be," Fats said. "We found tracks."
"What if he doesn't get off here?" Pancho asked.
"Then we'll get on the train and find him," Smitty said.

d) *What do the three men want from Frank? Who is the boss? Which line tells you this?*

e) *What do you think the men look like? Find pictures in a magazine that match the characters and put them in your diary.*

For a long moment the friends just sat there and looked at the stones on the floor.
"Well," Linda finally said, "everything's clear now. I'm sure they're diamonds, and they want them back."
"How much are they, Linda?"
"You mean, how much are they worth?"
"Yes, worth."
"I don't know, but you have to take them to the police now. Those men will not stop hunting you as long as you have them. And you will be OK here. They don't know you're on the train."
"Yes, I will go, in Winslow," Frank said and looked at her.
"No," Linda said. "I won't come with you."
When the train stopped in Winslow, Frank looked out and when he didn't see anyone, he got off quickly. Linda came to the door, waved to him and then went back into the boxcar.
Frank looked around. There wasn't even a station here – just a place for the train to stop and a little town on the other side of the tracks. Frank crossed them and walked towards the houses.

f) *What is Frank thinking? Write down his thoughts in your diary.*

Behind a wooden building near him, Pancho, Fats and Smitty were waiting.
"Let's get him now," Pancho said and started to run out.
"No, you idiot," Smitty said and held him back. "Somebody might see us."
"Yeah, but we have to get him before he can go to the police."
"Just wait."

Frank was on Main Street now. It looked just like the ones he had seen in films: it was very wide, cars were parked on both sides and there were shops in low buildings on both sides, too. There were only a few people on the sidewalks. The town was peaceful.
A young woman with a little girl came by then, and Frank spoke to her. "Can you tell me the way to the police station, please?" he asked her.
The woman smiled. "Sure, honey. It's –"
"Mum, I know that boy," her little girl said then. "I saw his picture on TV."
"Sure you did, Peggy," her mother laughed.
"She watches too much TV," she said to Frank. "Now, young man, you go down this street and then –"
"But, Mum, I really did –"
"Now you hush, Peggy, when I'm talking

boss [bɒs] – *Chef/-in*, worth [wɜːθ] – *wert*, wide [waɪd] – *breit*, low [ləʊ] – *niedrig*, sidewalk *(AE)* ['saɪdwɔːk] – *Gehweg*, peaceful ['piːsfl] – *friedlich*, to come by [kʌm 'baɪ] – *vorbeikommen*, honey ['hʌni] – *Liebling*, Sure you did! [ʃɔː jʊ dɪd] – *Ja, natürlich (ironisch)*, to hush [hʌʃ] – *ruhig sein*

to somebody! OK, young man, down this street and then you turn north at the second traffic light. It'll be the low red building on the west side. Did you understand?"
Frank said 'yes' and thanked her and left fast before Peggy could start again.

g) *How could the girl know him from TV?*

"We have to move now," Pancho said. "I'm sure he asked her about the police station. That's where he's going. It's down that way. I saw it when we drove in."
"OK, OK, just wait until he's off the main street. Let's get to the car."
"It'll be too late. The police station's just around the corner."
"Let's hurry then," Smitty said.
Frank walked down the street fast. Now what had she said? The second traffic light – and turn north. Which way was that? Frank tried to remember what he had learned about the sun. It was almost noon. Frank looked up at the big blue sky. The sun should be right in the south now. Yes, there it was to his left. So north was to the right. He walked on, got to the second traffic light and went around the corner.
It all happened very fast after that: Frank came around the corner, a car door opened suddenly, someone pulled him in and put a hand over his mouth, the door closed and the car raced away.
"Hey, that was close," Frank heard Fats say next to him, and on his other side Smitty said, "OK, where are the diamonds?"
"Thought we were gone, didn't you?" Pancho laughed.
"Shut up and drive!" Smitty shouted.
"Look what I've got here, Frank," Fats said and gave him his baseball hat. "We found it."
Frank took it and put it on. "Thanks," he said to Fats.
"Hey, what is this?" Smitty was angry. "A reunion? Where are the diamonds?"

"I don't know what you mean," Frank said.
"Where's the pouch?" Smitty shouted and grabbed Frank.
"The what?" Frank tried to look puzzled.
"The little bag you took, you idiot!"
"Oh that. I threw it away."
"Threw it away?" Smitty said in a funny way.
"Well, you had it when you were on the road. We know that. And your passport was in it. You didn't throw that away?"
"No, I've got that right here." Frank started to take it out of his pocket, but Smitty grabbed his hand and took it out for him. "But I threw the pouch out of the train," Frank added.
"Sure you did, but you took your passport out first," the thin man held it up, "and that means you've got the rest, too. Stop the car somewhere, Pancho. We will search him," Smitty ordered.

h) *The three men are different. Find words or sentences in the text that tell you about their characters. Write down in your diary what you have found out.*

When Pancho had found a good place to stop, the men searched Frank. He fought

to hurry ['hʌri] – *sich beeilen,* noon [nu:n] – *Mittag,* to race [reɪs] – *rasen,* Shut up! [ʃʌt‿'ʌp] – *Halt den Mund!,* reunion [ri:'ju:nɪən] – *Wiedersehenstreffen,* puzzled ['pʌzld] – *verwirrt,* to search sb. [sɜ:tʃ] – *jmd. durchsuchen,* to order ['ɔ:də] – *befehlen*

them, but they held him down and Fats found the diamonds in his back pocket.
"All right, then," Smitty smiled for the first time. "We've got them. We're back in business. Let's get to the plane, Pancho. Fast."
"Right, boss. We'll leave this car in the bushes and then we'll be off to Mexico."
"Shut up, you idiot! Don't tell him where we're going," Fats said.
"Doesn't matter," Smitty answered. "This time we'll do the job right. He won't be able to talk to anybody."
Pancho raced down the road another mile, then turned off onto a dirt road with small trees on both sides. He drove on until they came to an open place. The plane was there.
"Just leave the car over there and let's go. Everything will be OK," Smitty was happy.
"Yeah," Pancho laughed and showed all his big teeth. "For us, but not for him," he said as they pulled Frank over to the plane.

i) *What does Frank feel in this situation? What do you think?*

Inside the plane, Smitty went to the cockpit right away while his partners took Frank to the back. Smitty tried to start the plane, but the engine wouldn't turn over. He tried again. "Damn!" he said. "There's a problem!"
"There's a problem back here, too," a strange voice said behind him. Smitty turned round fast – and saw a policeman with a gun.
Outside the plane, the police handcuffed Smitty and his men, and took them over to some police cars, which were now there.
"Great," an older police officer said to Frank. "We found you, and you're OK! And we got these guys with all their diamonds. You know there's a big reward for this."
"Reward?" Frank asked.
"Money for catching them," somebody said behind him. Frank turned round.
"Linda!" Frank shouted, and hugged her.
"She saved you," the officer said.
"It's good to see you, Frank," she laughed.
"But you were on that train."
"Yes, but as it was leaving, I saw those three guys. So I jumped out and went to the police as fast as I could."

j) *What did Linda tell the police? Write the dialogue in your diary.*

"But now, Linda, the police will take you –" Frank started but didn't go on.

k) *Here's the summary of a possible ending. Do you like it? Say why / why not.*

At his aunt's house in Oklahoma Frank meets his parents, who flew to the US when they heard that Frank had disappeared. Linda also gets back home. Her parents are very angry with her and she has to go to a boarding school. Frank is worried about Linda. But he can't help her. Linda's parents think she ran away because of Frank. So they don't want her to keep in touch with him. They have to send e-mails secretly. Later Linda has a boyfriend and forgets Frank. They never meet again.

l) *Write a different ending in your diary.*

m) *Did you like the story? Write in your diary what you liked / didn't like about it.*

n) *Interested? Read the whole book by Rolf W. Roth (Klett English readers) and find out what really happened.*

to hold down [həʊld 'daʊn] – *festhalten,* Doesn't matter [ˌdʌznt 'mætə] – *Macht nichts!,* dirt road ['dɜ:t rəʊd] – *Schotterweg,* cockpit ['kɒkpɪt] – *Cockpit,* to turn over [tɜ:n‿'əʊvə] – *anspringen,* Damn! [dæm] – *Verdammt!,* to handcuff ['hænkʌf] – *Handschellen anlegen,* reward [rɪ'wɔ:d] – *Belohnung,* to hug [hʌg] – *umarmen,* boarding school ['bɔ:diŋ ˌsku:l] – *Internat,* because of [bɪ'kɔ:s‿əv] – *wegen,* to keep in touch [ˌki:p‿ɪn 'tʌtʃ] – *in Kontakt bleiben*

Grammar

Hallo! Hier sind wieder die Grammatikseiten deines Schülerbuchs. Erinnerst du dich? Wir sind Jack und Jane und helfen dir auch in diesem Jahr durch das Dickicht des Grammtikdschungels. Unser Freund Chippy ist auch wieder dabei und hilft dir, besonders schwierige Nüsse zu knacken. So bringen wir dich sicher ans Ziel und versprechen dir, dass wir auch eine Menge Spaß zusammen haben werden.

GRAMMAR SKILLS

- Jeden Grammatikpunkt kannst du am besten verstehen, indem du ihn mit deinen eigenen Worten erklärst.

  1. Lege dir dazu in deinem *folder* ein Kapitel *My grammar* an oder arbeite mit *grammar cards*. Notiere darauf die Überschrift des Grammatikpunkts und einige Beispiele. Formuliere nun die Regel.
  2. Überprüfe alle Teile der Regel an Beispielen. Arbeite dabei mit verschiedenen Farben, Unterstreichungen usw.
  3. Du kannst oft eine kurze Bildungsformel entwickeln, z. B. ***to be + ing*** für das *present progressive*.
  4. Zusammenhänge und Regeln lassen sich auch grafisch darstellen. Hierfür kannst du deine eigenen Symbole entwickeln oder diese verwenden:

- - - - -➤	Dauer einer Handlung	X	Zeitpunkt
└───▲	Wort/Satzglied wird an eine andere Stelle gesetzt	- - - - -➤|	Ende einer Handlung

     Du hast sicher selbst noch viele Einfälle.

- Reime und Eselsbrücken helfen beim Einprägen. Du kannst natürlich auch selbst reimen!
- Zum Schluss kannst du an einer kleinen Aufgabe in *Test yourself* überprüfen, ob du alles verstanden hast. Die Lösungen findest du ab Seite 230.

G1 Revision Die einfache Form der Gegenwart
The simple present

→ p. 16.1

Mit dem ***simple present*** kannst du ausdrücken, dass etwas …

Tourists <u>often</u> **visit** the Empire State Building.
She <u>usually</u> **goes jogging** in Central Park.

What sights **do** tourists **visit**?
Does he **work**?
– Yes, but he **doesn't start** until 7 pm.

… **regelmäßig**, aus Gewohnheit, oft, manchmal oder nie geschieht.
Signalwörter:
usually, every (day / week / month), often, always, sometimes, never

New York **is** a very big city.
More than 8 million people **live** there.

… eine **Tatsache** ist.

Pass gut auf bei der **Verneinung**:
weiß nicht → don't know / doesn't know (nicht: „not know")
Sorry, but I **don't know** the way.

Du benutzt das ***simple present*** auch, um eine Inhaltsangabe (***summary***) zu machen und eine Geschichte, einen Witz usw. zu erzählen.

Harry Potter **is** about a boy whose life suddenly **changes** on his 11th birthday. This **is** when he **finds** out that he **is** really a wizard. …

My grammar
Schreibe je zwei Beispielsätze für Aussage, Verneinung und Frage, in denen es um New York geht.

Test yourself
Complete the sentences of this story.

A man from England decides to go and live in New York. "You'll love it in New York," people … (*say*). "The streets … (*be*) full of gold!" So he … (*take*) the next ship to America. The journey … (*be*) awful and he … (*not sleep*) very well. When he … (*leave*) the ship, he … (*be*) very tired and hungry. He … (*start*) to look for a hotel. Then he … (*look*) down and … (*see*) a ten dollar bill in the road. He … (*stop*) to pick it up, but … (*think*) again. "No," he … (*say*) to himself and … (*smile*). "Why should I hurry? I … (*be*) too tired now. I'll start tomorrow!"

Weitere Verwendung

Das ***simple present*** wird auch verwendet, wenn es um **feste Termine**, wie in **Fahrplänen (z. B. Züge)** oder **Programmen (z. B. Kino)**, geht. Im Deutschen benutzt man hier auch die Gegenwart.

My train **leaves** at 10.15. It **arrives** at 14.35.
The game **starts** at 15.30.

What time **does** the movie **begin**?

G2 Revision Die Verlaufsform der Gegenwart
The present progressive

Das ***present progressive*** benutzt du für …	
The phone **is** ring**ing**. Can you answer it? – Sorry, I can't. **I'm** wash**ing** my hair. Can you talk now? – Yes, I can. **I'm not** work**ing** at the moment.	… Handlungen, die **gerade im Verlauf** sind und nicht gewohnheitsmäßig passieren. **Signalwörter**: *look, just, now, at the moment, today*
I'm meet**ing** Malek and Louise tonight. What **are** you do**ing** tomorrow? – **I'm** go**ing** to a concert.	… feste Vereinbarungen (***arrangements***) in der näheren Zukunft. **Zeitangaben**, wie z. B. *tomorrow, tonight*, sind hier wichtig, damit man nicht an die Gegenwart denkt.

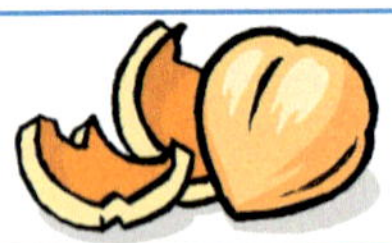

Kurzer Mitlaut wird verdoppelt:
to hit → hi**tt**ing, to put → pu**tt**ing, to run → ru**nn**ing
Stummes „-e" wird abgekoppelt: to argu**e** → arguing, to hat**e** → hating

The simple present and present progressive

The simple present	**The present progressive**
Das ***simple present*** beschreibt Dinge, die aus **Gewohnheit** passieren.	Das ***present progressive*** verwendest du für Handlungen, die zum Zeitpunkt des Sprechens noch **andauern**.
What **do** you **have** for breakfast?	I often have a sandwich. But right now **I'm** eat**ing** some cornflakes.
How **does** Tobias usually **spend** his vacations?	He spends them with his parents in Texas. But now he **is** spend**ing** the summer in New York. He**'s** stay**ing** with his uncle.

My grammar

1. Betrachte die Beispiele zu *simple present* und *present progressive*: Was drückt die jeweilige Zeitform aus? Wann verwendest du die eine, wann die andere Form?
2. Finde eine knappe Formel (z. B. „wenn …, dann …") für den unterschiedlichen Gebrauch.

Test yourself

Complete the sentences with the right form, simple present or present progressive.

1. Man (outside a deli): I … (*get*) hungry now. Let's buy something to eat!
2. Woman (in the street): Excuse me, … (*you – speak*) English?
3. Old man (on a train): Excuse me, … (*anybody – sit*) here?
4. Girl (at a party): Hey, … (*you – play*) baseball?
5. Boy (at a party): Not really, but my sister … (*play*) every weekend.

G3 Revision Die einfache Form der Vergangenheit
The simple past

→ p. 19.2

Das ***simple past*** verwendest du, …

They **opened** the new immigration station on Ellis Island in 1892. Between 1892 and 1954 more than twelve million immigrants **landed** at Ellis Island. She **wasn't allowed to** enter the US. Where **did** most immigrants **come** from?	… für Handlungen, die in der **Vergangenheit** stattgefunden haben (auch: **historische** Ereignisse). **Signalwörter**: *yesterday, (a week/month/year) ago, last (week/month/year), in (1892)*
In 1845 there **was** a famine in Ireland. So millions of poor and hungry Irish people **left** their country for New York. The journey by ship **wasn't** easy in those days and many people **were** seasick.	… in einer Geschichte, in einem Bericht, wenn du **mehrere Ereignisse der Reihe nach erwähnen** möchtest.

My grammar

1. Was musst du beim *simple past* beachten? (Bildungsformel, Signalwörter, (un)regelmäßige Formen)
2. Wiederhole regelmäßig die Formen der unregelmäßigen Verben (*List of irregular verbs*, S. 224–225). Versuche, dir das Lernen zu erleichtern, indem du Gruppen bildest: z. B. *to put, put, put/to cut, cut, cut* usw. oder *to drink, drank, drunk/to sing, sang, sung* usw.

Test yourself

Complete the questions and answers with the simple past.

Friend: What … (*you – do*) last summer?
Jack: We … (*go*) on a trip downriver.
Friend: … (*Chippy – travel*) with you?
Jane: Yes, … . (*short answer*)
Friend: What … (*you – see*)?
Jack: We … (*see*) lots of wild animals.

G4 Revision Die vollendete Form der Vergangenheit
The past perfect

→ p. 19.2

Wenn du ausdrücken möchtest, dass ein Ereignis **weiter in der Vergangenheit zurückliegt** als ein anderes, benutzt du das ***past perfect***. Die **nachfolgende Handlung** steht dann im ***simple past***. Das ***past perfect*** folgt häufig in Nebensätzen, die mit *after* oder *when* beginnen und nach Nebensätzen, die mit *before* und *when* beginnen.

After Dutch immigrants **had founded** New Amsterdam, the English **named** it New York.

When they **arrived** at the immigration station, they sometimes **hadn't eaten** for days.

My grammar
Suche aus der Zeittabelle auf Seite 18 noch weitere Beispielsätze heraus. Stelle die Handlungen grafisch dar. Markiere die frühere Handlung grün und die nachfolgende rot.

Test yourself
Complete the sentences.

1. Chippy … (*get up*) early yesterday.
2. After he … (*have*) breakfast, he … (*go*) to play in the jungle.
3. When he … (*finish*) his game, he … (*climb*) into a tree.
4. He … (*eat*) a banana. When he … (*eat*) it, he … (*sleep*) for an hour.
5. Then it … (*be*) time to go home.

The simple past and the past perfect

The simple past	The past perfect
Mit dem ***simple past*** drückst du aus, dass etwas in der Vergangenheit geschah und bereits **abgeschlossen** und **vorbei** ist.	Mit dem ***past perfect*** betonst du, dass ein Ereignis noch **vor** einem anderen **in der Vergangenheit** stattgefunden hat.
Did Fiona **come** to the concert yesterday? – Yes, she **did**.	Did Paul come to the concert, too? – No, he **had** already **seen** the band the day before. Die Verwendung des *past perfect* macht deutlich, dass Paul bereits vor den anderen im Konzert war.

My grammar
1. Betrachte das Beispiel zu *simple past* und *past perfect* und stelle es auf einer Zeitleiste grafisch dar. (Vergiss nicht, den Zeitpunkt das Sprechens mit einzuzeichnen.)
2. Schreibe eine kurze Bildungsformel für die jeweilige Zeitform.

G5 Revision Das Perfekt
The present perfect

Das ***present perfect*** benutzt du für eine Handlung, die …	
I'**ve lost** my wallet. (= I don't have it now.) Paul **has had** an accident. He's in hospital now. She **hasn't answered** my e-mail yet. Let's have lunch together. Or **have** you already **eaten**?	… in der Vergangenheit stattfand und deren **Ergebnis bis in die Gegenwart** hineinwirkt. **Signalwörter**: *already, ever, never, (not …) yet*
They'**ve** just **arrived**.	… **gerade erst** abgeschlossen wurde. **Signalwort**: *just*

Sollen *already, never* und *just* richtig passen, musst du sie zwischen den Verbteilen lassen.

They'**ve** already **arrived**.
I'**ve** never **done** this before.
Ausnahme: I **haven't seen** this movie yet.

Test yourself
Jack and Jane are organizing a jungle party. What have they done? What haven't they done yet?

Das *present perfect* mit *since* + *for*

Mit dem ***present perfect*** und ***since*** + ***for*** kannst du ausdrücken, dass ein Zustand, der in der Vergangenheit anfing, schon eine bestimmte Zeit **andauert**.	
since (= seit) (betont Zeitpunkt)	**for** (= … lang) (betont Zeitraum)
She has lived in Paris **since 2003**. He has been here **since two o'clock**.	She has lived in Paris **for over five years**. He has been here **for 30 minutes**.

Beachte! Im Deutschen verwendest du hier die Gegenwart.
Sie **wohnt** (schon) seit 2003 in Paris. = She **has lived** in Paris since 2003.
Sie **wohnt** (schon) fünf Jahre lang in Paris. = She **has lived** in Paris for five years.

Weitere Form des *present perfect*

Mit dem ***present perfect progressive*** kannst du ausdrücken, dass eine Handlung bis jetzt **angedauert** hat (und noch weiter andauern kann).
He **has been waiting** here for 30 minutes. (= he is still waiting) How long **have** you **been learning** English? (= you are still learning English) Vergleiche: I didn't hear the phone. I'**ve been cooking** lunch in the kitchen. (= die Person war die ganze Zeit über in der Küche und hat dadurch das Telefon nicht gehört) I'**ve cooked** some fish. We can eat now. (= das Kochen ist beendet; Ergebnis: es kann gegessen werden)

The present perfect and the simple past

The present perfect	**The simple past**
Das ***present perfect*** betont, dass eine Handlung, die in der Vergangenheit begonnen hat, noch in einer **Beziehung zur Gegenwart** steht, z. B. weil man das Ergebnis sehen kann.	Das ***simple past*** betont, dass etwas in der Vergangenheit geschah und bereits **abgeschlossen** und **vorbei** ist.
Have you ever **been** to New York? – Yes, I'**ve been** there twice.	When **did** you first **go** there? – When I **was** twenty.
They'**ve** just **had** dinner. (They aren't hungry now.)	They **had** dinner half an hour ago.
I'**ve lost** my bag. (I don't have it now.)	I **lost** it on the bus. (I'm no longer on the bus.)
Have you **seen** Rachel this morning? (It is still morning.)	**Did** you **see** Rachel this morning? (It is now afternoon or evening.)

My grammar

1. Betrachte die Beispiele zu *present perfect* und *simple past*: Was drückt die jeweilige Zeitform aus? Wann verwendest du die eine, wann die andere Form?
2. Finde eine knappe Formel (z. B. „wenn …, dann …") für den unterschiedlichen Gebrauch.
3. Schreibe eine kurze Bildungsformel für die jeweilige Zeitform.

Test yourself

What's the right form each time?

1. Who has invented / invented the phone?
2. Ow! I've cut / I cut my finger.
3. What have you done / did you do yesterday?
4. In 1845 there has been / was a famine in Ireland.
5. Look! There has been / was an accident.
6. When have they come / did they come home?

G6 Revision Das *will*-Futur
The will-future

Das ***will*-Futur** verwendest du, …	
It **will be** cold and windy tomorrow. My grandma **will be** 62 next August. When **will** you **get** your test back? Next year we **will move** to Amsterdam.	… um über etwas zu sprechen, das du **nicht beeinflussen** kannst (z. B. das Wetter, das Alter). Es geschieht ganz unabhängig von deinen Plänen.
Maybe we **will meet** again. I'm sure we **will meet** again. Do you think she **will phone** him?	… wenn du **vermutest**, dass etwas geschehen wird. **Signalwörter**: *probably, I think, maybe, I'm sure, I promise, I hope, I know*
Don't worry, I'**ll do** the washing up. I forgot to phone Fiona. I'**ll phone** her now.	… wenn du dich **spontan** für etwas entscheidest (z. B. bietest du jemandem deine Hilfe an).

Wenn du etwas bereits **fest vereinbart** hast (***arrangements***):
present progressive für die Zukunft: I'm meeting Sally tonight.

Wenn du etwas bereits **geplant** hast oder **beabsichtigst**:
going to-Futur: I'm going to watch that film on TV tonight.

My grammar
Schreibe deine eigenen Beispiele und Regeln für Pläne, Vereinbarungen *(arrangements)*, spontane Entscheidungen, Vermutungen und Dinge, wie z. B. das Wetter.

Test yourself
What's the right form each time?

1. My dad will be / is 49 next week.
2. I think Paul plays / is playing tennis with Linda this afternoon.
3. That's a heavy bag! I am going to carry / I'll carry it for you.
4. I'm sure you are getting / will get a good grade in the test tomorrow.
5. We're going to spend / We spend our vacation in Florida this year.
6. The weather will change / is changing tomorrow.

Weitere Form des Futurs

Eine weitere Form neben dem *will-future* ist das ***future progressive*** (*will be* + Endung *-ing* am Verb). Es drückt aus, dass jemand (zu einem bestimmten Zeitpunkt in der Zukunft) dabei sein wird, etwas zu tun.

This time tomorrow he will be sitting on the plane for New York.
At 10 o'clock tomorrow she will be working.

G7 Revision Bedingungssätze mit *will* (Typ 1)

Conditional sentences with 'will' (Type 1)

→ p. 35.2

Bedingungssätze bestehen aus zwei Teilen: einem *if*-Satz und einem Hauptsatz. Im *if*-Satz drückst du eine Bedingung aus: *If I go to bed late, …* Im Hauptsatz sagst du, was passiert, wenn die Bedingung erfüllt wird: *… I'll be tired in the morning.* Die Bedingung (Typ 1) erscheint wahrscheinlich und damit **erfüllbar**.
If kann am Anfang oder in der Mitte des Satzes stehen. Steht der *if*-Satz am Anfang, dann brauchst du ein Komma vor dem Hauptsatz.
Im ***if*-Satz** verwendest du das ***simple present***. Im **Hauptsatz** wird meist das ***will-future*** verwendet.

Bedingung im *if*-Satz:	**Folge im Hauptsatz:**
If students **arrive** late to school three times,	they **will receive** detention after school.
If you **forget** your sister's birthday,	she**'ll be** unhappy.
Folge im Hauptsatz:	**Bedingung im *if*-Satz:**
Students **won't have** problems	if they **follow** the dress code.
What **will happen**	if students **arrive** late to school?

Merke: Kein „will" im *if*-Satz!

My grammar
Schreibe einen der *if*-Sätze in dein Heft. Markiere die erfüllbare Bedingung grün und das, was dann passiert, rot. Erkläre deinem / r Partner / in, warum die Bedingung erfüllbar ist.

Test yourself
Complete the sentences.

1. If you … (*not take*) an umbrella with you, you … (*get*) wet.
2. If you … (*ask*) Mrs. Smith, she … (*help*) you.
3. She … (*catch*) the plane if she … (*hurry*).
4. What … you … (*do*) if you … (*not find*) your money?
5. Mum … (*not be*) happy if we … (*not go*) shopping for her.
6. If you … (*not work*) harder, you … (*not get*) a good grade.
7. We … (*have*) dinner together if Paul … (*come*) home early.

G8 Revision Modale Hilfsverben im Überblick
Modal auxiliaries – a summary

Mit den **modalen Hilfsverben** *can / can't, may, must, mustn't, needn't, could, should, shall* kannst du sehr verschiedene Dinge mit unterschiedlichem Grad ausdrücken. Du verwendest sie, wenn du von einer **Fähigkeit**, einer **Bitte**, einer **Erlaubnis**, einem **Verbot**, einer **Notwendigkeit/ Verpflichtung** oder einem **Vorschlag** sprechen willst.
Sie sind für alle Personen gleich und können nur im *simple present* verwendet werden (Ausnahme: *can / can't – could / couldn't*).

I **can** play the piano, but I **can't** sing very well.	Mit *can / can't* kannst du ausdrücken, dass jemand **fähig** oder unfähig ist, etwas zu tun.
Can / Could you turn on the lights, please?	*Can / Could ...?* kannst du auch gebrauchen, um eine **Bitte** auszudrücken.
May I use your toilet, please?	Mit *May I ...?* kannst du **sehr höflich** um etwas **bitten**. (Du kannst hier auch *Can / Could I ...?* verwenden; *May I ...?* klingt jedoch noch höflicher.)
Will you switch on the TV, please? **Would you** help me with my bags, please?	Mit *Will you ...? / Would you ...?* kannst du auch eine **Bitte**, einen Wunsch ausdrücken. Dabei klingt *would* noch höflicher als *will*.
Students **must** follow the school dress code. I don't feel well. I **must** see a doctor.	Mit *must* kannst du ausdrücken, dass etwas **notwendig** ist.
You **shouldn't** sleep in class. She **should** write the e-mail today.	Mit *should* kannst du einen **Rat geben** und ausdrücken, dass etwas gemacht werden müsste, **sollte**.
You **needn't** tell your parents.	Mit *needn't* drückst du aus, dass etwas **nicht notwendig** ist.
They **mustn't** be late for school. You **mustn't** smoke.	Mit *mustn't* drückst du aus, dass etwas **verboten** oder **nicht erlaubt** ist.
You **may** close the door. You **may** leave the room now.	Mit *may* kannst du auch ausdrücken, dass jemand etwas **darf**. (Du kannst hier auch *can* verwenden, da *may* recht förmlich klingt.)
I **won't** clean my room. I **wouldn't** walk home alone last night.	Mit *won't / wouldn't* kannst du ausdrücken, dass du dich **weigerst**, etwas zu tun.
Shall I answer the phone? **Shall we** go to the concert?	Mit *Shall I ...? / Shall we ...?* kannst du jemandem etwas anbieten, etwas **vorschlagen**.

Mit *ought to* kannst du etwas vorschlagen, einen **Rat geben**:
She **ought to** tell her parents about her bad grades.
Mit *may* und *might* kannst du eine **Möglichkeit** ausdrücken:
Lisa **may / might** know Rachel's number. (= Perhaps Lisa knows Rachel's number.)

My grammar
Welche modalen Hilfsverben kannst du verwenden, um eine Bitte, eine Erlaubnis, ein Verbot, eine Notwendigkeit, einen Vorschlag oder einen Ratschlag auszudrücken? Lege dir *grammar cards* an und schreibe deine eigenen Beispiele.

Test yourself

a) *Read the notices on the tree. Now write the jungle rules.*

b) *Your friend has got some problems. What advice can you give?*

1. Your friend hurts his / her foot.
2. Your friend has borrowed someone's CD but can't find it anymore.
3. Your friend has found a lot of money.
4. Your friend has bought a T-shirt but doesn't like it.

Ersatzformen der Modalverben

Für die modalen Hilfsverben *can, may, must, needn't, mustn't* gibt es die **Ersatzformen** *to be able to, to be allowed to* und *to have to*. Diese können parallel zu den Formen im *simple present* verwendet werden. Du benötigst die Ersatzformen in jedem Fall für alle **anderen Zeiten**.

can → **be able to**	I'm able to meet you. (= I can meet you.) We were / weren't able to get tickets for the concert.
may → **be allowed to**	Are we allowed to come in? (= May we come in?) I was allowed to go to the party.
must → **have to**	She has to go to hospital. (= She must go to hospital.) You will have to clean your room.
needn't → **not have to**	You don't have to write him. (= You needn't write him.) They didn't have to pay.
mustn't / may not → **not be allowed to**	You're not allowed to smoke. (= You mustn't smoke.) She wasn't allowed to go to the party.

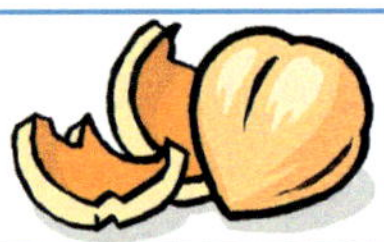

Die Verneinung von „must" (= müssen) ist nicht „mustn't" (= nicht dürfen), sondern „not have to":
I **must** go now. (= I have to go now.) → I **don't have to** go now.

Unit 2

G9 Das *gerund* als Subjekt und Objekt des Satzes

→ p. 37.2; 3

The gerund as subject and object of the sentence

Ein ***gerund*** wird aus einem **Verb und** der **Endung *-ing*** gebildet. (Daher wird diese Form auch *-ing*-Form genannt.) Ist das *gerund* **Subjekt** des Satzes, steht es am Satzanfang. Dann wird es wie ein Nomen gebraucht. Das gibt es auch im Deutschen, aus „schwimmen" wird „das Schwimmen" in Sätzen, wie z. B. Ihre Hobbys sind Schwimmen und Kochen.

Gerund as subject

Dating is a hot topic at middle school.
Cooking is fun.
Being polite is always a good idea.
Swimming is a great hobby.

Das ***gerund*** steht häufig **nach Verben**, die **Vorliebe** (z. B. *to love, to like, to enjoy*) oder **Abneigung** (z. B. *not like, to hate, can't stand*) ausdrücken. Dann wird es zum **Objekt** des Satzes. Im Deutschen werden *gerunds* gerne umschrieben, z. B. sie lieben es, Chinesisch essen zu gehen; ich kann es nicht ausstehen, wenn ich in der Schlange anstehen muss; usw.

Gerund as object

She **likes watching** movies,
but she **hates going** alone.
They **love eating** Chinese food.
We **enjoy sitting** in our garden.
I **can't stand waiting** in a line.

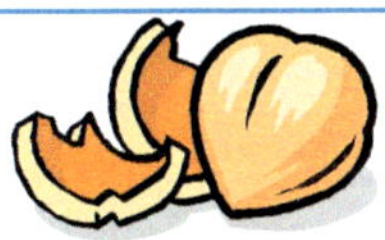

Beachte folgenden Unterschied:
I **like going** to the movies. (= ich gehe gerne ins Kino)
I **am going** to the movies. (= ich gehe gerade ins Kino)

My grammar

Schreibe dir je einen Satz mit *gerund* als Subjekt und einen Satz mit *gerund* als Objekt aus dem Text auf Seite 36 heraus. Markiere die *gerunds*, um ihre unterschiedliche Stellung in den Sätzen hervorzuheben.

Test yourself

Choose the right verb and form the gerund to complete the sentences.

get up eat live play swim

1. Jane and Jack like … the drums.
2. Chippy loves … nuts.
3. … in the river is sometimes dangerous.
4. Jack hates … early in the morning.
5. … in the jungle is fun.

Unit 3

G10 Das *gerund* nach Präpositionen
Gerunds after prepositions

→ p. 50.2

Das ***gerund*** steht auch häufig **nach Verben und Adjektiven**, auf die eine **Präposition** folgt.

verb + preposition

to look forward to:	I'm **looking forward to meeting** my exchange partner.
to worry about:	Are you **worried about traveling** on your own?

adjective + preposition

interested in:	Would you be **interested in visiting** the Grand Canyon?
crazy about:	Yes, I'm **crazy about going** there.
tired of:	Lindy Turner never gets **tired of working** in the national park.
good at:	If you are **good at working** in a team, we will give you the job.
used to:	Rangers are **used to working** hard.

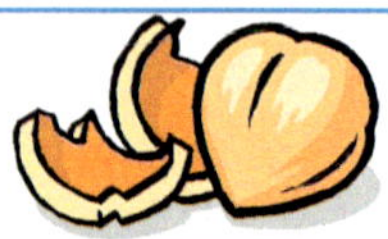

Anstelle des *gerund* kann auch ein Nomen auf diese Konstruktionen folgen:

She is looking forward to **seeing the movie**.	They are used to **working hard**.
She is looking forward to **the movie**.	They are used to **hard work**.

My grammar
Schreibe deine eigenen Beispielsätze. Markiere die Präposition mit einer Farbe und das *gerund* mit einer anderen Farbe.

Test yourself
Complete the sentences of the e-mail with the right preposition.

Dear Mr. Roberts,
I am writing because I am interested … working at Forest Springs Summer Camp this summer. I am used … working with younger children and I never get tired … playing games and singing with them. I am also quite good … sports and playing the guitar.
I am looking forward … hearing from you. Thank you.
Best wishes,
Caroline Baker

Weitere *gerunds*

Das ***gerund*** kann auch **nach einem Nomen und einer Präposition** stehen:

noun + preposition

in danger of:	The car was **in danger of crashing**.
the idea of:	**The idea of swimming** from Europe to the US is crazy.

G11 Bedingungssätze mit *would* (Typ 2)
Conditional sentences with 'would' (Type 2)

→ p. 52.2

Du kennst bereits den Bedingungssatz mit *will* (Typ 1) (→ G7). Beim Typ 1 geht es immer um eine wahrscheinliche Situation: *If I go to bed late, I'll be tired in the morning.* Die Bedingung, die im *if*-Satz formuliert wird, gilt als erfüllbar.

Beim **Bedingungssatz mit *would* (Typ 2)** geht es um eine theoretisch mögliche, aber relativ unwahrscheinliche Situation: Rachel würde Lisa gerne eine E-Mail schicken, aber leider kennt sie ihre Adresse nicht.
Sie denkt: *If I knew her address, I would send her an e-mail.*
Sie stellt sich also vor, wie es wäre, wenn sie Lisas Adresse kennen würde – dann würde sie ihr nämlich eine E-Mail schicken. Die Bedingung gilt als nur **theoretisch erfüllbar**, denn Rachel hat die Adresse nicht.
Im ***if*-Satz** verwendest du das ***simple past***, das jedoch nicht auf etwas Vergangenes verweist, sondern eine gedachte Möglichkeit ausdrückt.
Im **Hauptsatz** wird meist ***would* + Grundform** (Infinitiv) verwendet.

Bedingung im *if*-Satz:	**Folge im Hauptsatz:**
If you **were** here,	it **wouldn't be** so boring.
If I **was / were** American,	**I'd live** in California.
If she **had** more money,	she **would go** on holiday more often.

Folge im Hauptsatz:	**Bedingung im *if*-Satz:**
Abby **would enjoy** the summer camp more	if her friend **was** with her.
What **would** it **be** like	if they **won** a million dollars?

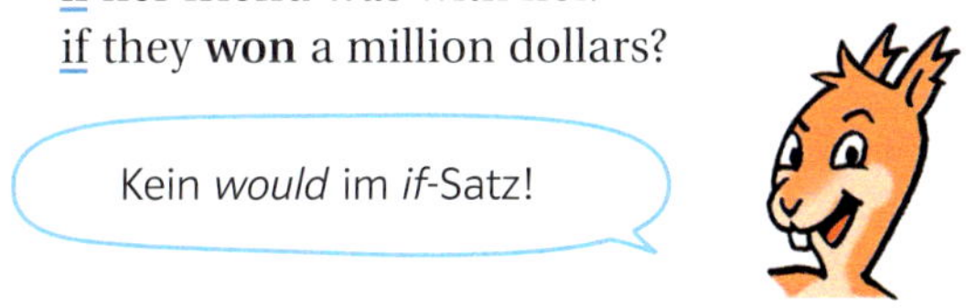

Beachte den Unterschied zum Deutschen:
Wenn ich im Lotto gewinnen würde, … = If I **won** the lottery, …

Beachte den Unterschied zwischen „when" und „if":
When I went to New York last year, I visited Chinatown. = Als ich …
If I went there again, I would go to Ellis Island. = Wenn/Falls ich …

My grammar
Erkläre den Unterschied zwischen dem Bedingungssatz Typ 1 und dem Bedingungssatz Typ 2.

Test yourself
Complete the sentences. Where do you need 'would'?

1. If I … (*have*) more money, I would give you some of it.
2. I … (*live*) in Spain if I spoke Spanish.
3. My parents … (*help*) us if they were here.
4. If my computer … (*be*) faster, I would be able to play more games on it.
5. If I … (*need*) a bike, my friend would lend me his.
6. I … (*watch*) TV more often if I wasn't so busy.

G12 Bedingungssätze (Typ 3)
Conditional sentences (Type 3)

→ p. 55.3

Beim **Bedingungssatz Typ 3** geht es um eine Situation, die bereits in der Vergangenheit liegt und damit nicht mehr eintreten kann: Peter traf neulich seinen Freund Josh wieder, der ihm erzählte, dass er vor ein paar Tagen große Probleme gehabt hatte.
Peter denkt sich: *If I had known about his situation, I would have helped him.*
Peter stellt sich also vor, wie es gewesen wäre, wenn er von Joshs Problemen gewusst hätte – dann hätte er sich nämlich bei seinem Freund gemeldet, um ihm zu helfen.
Die Bedingung gilt als **nicht mehr erfüllbar**, da die Situation bereits in der **Vergangenheit** liegt und vorbei ist.
Im ***if*-Satz** verwendest du das ***past perfect***, das hier auf die Vergangenheit verweist.
Im **Hauptsatz** wird meist ***would*** + ***have*** + ***past participle*** (= 3. Verbform) verwendet.

Bedingung im *if*-Satz:	**Folge im Hauptsatz:**
If they **hadn't watched** TV until late,	they **wouldn't have been** so tired.
If only she **had asked** me before,	she **wouldn't have had** any problems.

Folge im Hauptsatz:	**Bedingung im *if*-Satz:**
The man **would have been** in real trouble	if that girl **hadn't found** him.
What **would have happened**	if he **had fallen** from those rocks?

Die Kurzform „'d" kann „would" oder „had" sein:
If I**'d** known him before, I**'d** have invited him to my party.
= If I **had** known him before, I **would** have invited him to my party.
Merk dir einfach: Kein „would" im *if*-Satz!

If only …

Sätze mit „If only …" können auch ganz alleine stehen.
Sie drücken häufig einen Wunsch aus:
Jack: If only we had taken an umbrella.
(= I wish we had taken an umbrella.)

My grammar
Erkläre den Unterschied zwischen dem Bedingungssatz Typ 2 und dem Bedingungssatz Typ 3 anhand dieses Beispiels:
If I had some money, I would buy a new DVD.
If the weather had been better yesterday, we would have gone cycling.

Test yourself
Sally's grandma often thinks about the past. Complete the missing parts of the sentences.

1. If I had had more time when the kids were young, I … (*look*) for a job.
2. I wouldn't have met your grandpa if I … (*stay*) at home that night in 1952.
3. We wouldn't have married if our parents … (*say*) no.
4. I … (*take*) French classes if our school had had a French teacher.
5. If we … (*have*) more money, we would have moved to California in 1963.

G13 Bedingungssätze im Überblick (Typ 1, 2, 3)
Conditional sentences (Type 1, 2, 3)

→ p. 55.5

Typ 1

erfüllbare Bedingung im *if*-Satz: ***simple present***	**Folge** im Hauptsatz: ***will-future***
If students **read** this advice,	they **won't have** problems at school.
Das *simple present* im *if*-Satz beschreibt eine wahrscheinliche Situation.	

→ G7

Typ 2

nur theoretisch erfüllbare Bedingung im *if*-Satz: ***simple past***	**Folge** im Hauptsatz: ***would + infinitive***
If Abby's friend **was** there,	summer camp **would be** real fun.
(Abby's friend isn't there, but if she was, …)	
Das *simple past* im *if*-Satz drückt aus, dass die Situation zwar theoretisch möglich, aber relativ unwahrscheinlich ist.	

→ G11

Typ 3

nicht mehr erfüllbare Bedingung im *if*-Satz: ***past perfect***	**Folge** im Hauptsatz: ***would + have + past participle***
If the man **had fallen** from those rocks,	he **would have broken** his leg.
(The man was lucky. He didn't fall, because the girl saved his life. But if he had fallen, …)	
Das *past perfect* im *if*-Satz verweist hier auf eine Situation, die in der Vergangenheit liegt.	

→ G12

Unit 4

G14 Verben mit zwei Objekten
Verbs with two objects

→ p. 70.2

Verben wie *to give, to offer, to show, to write* usw. werden – ähnlich wie ihre deutschen Entsprechungen – mit zwei Objekten verwendet:
She gave ***him the book***. = Sie gab **ihm das Buch**.
Es gibt ein direktes Objekt (*the book*), das eine Sache beschreibt, und ein indirektes Objekt (*him*), das sich auf eine Person bezieht.
Im Englischen hast du die Möglichkeit, den Satz noch auf eine andere Art und Weise auszudrücken: *She gave* ***the book*** *to* ***him***.
Allerdings musst du hier ein „to" vor dem „Personenobjekt" ergänzen. Der Inhalt dieser beiden Sätze ist derselbe.

	„Personenobjekt"	„Sachobjekt"
Astronauts send	their families	messages.
They show	them	their pictures from space.
Scientists give	the astronauts	advice.
NASA offers	tourists	a journey into space.

	„Sachobjekt"		„Personenobjekt"
Astronauts send	messages	to	their families.
They show	their pictures from space	to	them.
Scientists give	advice	to	the astronauts.
NASA offers	a journey into space	to	tourists.

G15 Der unbestimmte und der bestimmte Artikel
The indefinite and the definite article

→ p. 71.5

The indefinite article

Der unbestimmte Artikel ***a / an*** wird meistens genauso verwendet wie im Deutschen.
Nach Zeit- und Maßangaben sowie bei Berufsbezeichnungen steht im Englischen immer der unbestimmte Artikel.

Zeit- und Maßangaben

She works eight hours **a day**
and five days **a week**.
He gets sixty thousand euros **a year**.
They go on vacation twice **a year**.
Dad always drives at fifty-five miles **an hour**.
Apples cost one dollar **a pound**.
A journey into space costs 25 million dollars **a trip**.

Berufsbezeichnungen

She works as **a shop assistant**.
Isn't your brother **a doctor**?
I'd like to become **a football player**.

The definite article

Wir benutzen den bestimmten Artikel ***the***, wenn wir eine bestimmte Person, eine bestimmte Sache meinen: z. B. *Can you turn off the television, please?* (= the television in the room)
Der bestimmte Artikel steht nicht, wenn von Personen oder Dingen ganz allgemein gesprochen wird: z. B. *I watch television a lot.*
Dies trifft insbesondere auf **abstrakte Begriffe** (*life, love, time, music usw.*), **Verkehrsmittel** (*car, train, bike usw.*) und **Mahlzeiten** (*breakfast, lunch, dinner*) zu.

ohne Artikel	mit Artikel
Life is too short to be unhappy.	I'm interested in **the life of Mozart**.
I couldn't live without **music**.	She liked **the music in the film**.
Money is important.	Did you get **the money from your parents**?
School starts at eight.	Do you like **the school you go to**?
Dad goes to work by **car**.	I've washed **the car**. (= our car)

Familiennamen stehen immer mit dem bestimmten Artikel:
*We know the owners of the motel, **the Roses**, well.* (= Mr. and Mrs. Rose)

My grammar
Der Gebrauch des Artikels im Englischen unterscheidet sich vom Gebrauch des Artikels im Deutschen. Im Englischen wird z. B. bei Berufsbezeichnungen ein Artikel benötigt, während im Deutschen keiner notwendig ist. Vergleiche: My brother is a doctor. = Mein Bruder ist Arzt.
Übersetze jeweils einen Satz aus jeder Kategorie. Was ist im Deutschen anders?

Test yourself
How often do you do these things?

once / twice / three / … times
an hour / a day / a week / a month

Example:
I tidy my room twice a week.

1. tidy your room
2. go to the movies
3. use a computer
4. eat fruit

G16 Das Passiv im *simple present*

The passive voice (simple present)

→ p. 72.2

Die meisten Sätze sind im Aktiv. Der **Aktivsatz** betont, wer etwas tut oder Verursacher der Handlung ist (hier: *we*): z. B. *We keep the butter in the refrigerator.*
Der **Passivsatz** hingegen betont, **was mit einer Person oder Sache geschieht** (hier: *the butter*): *The butter is kept in the refrigerator.*
Hier ist es nicht so wichtig, wer oder was die Handlung verursacht. Wenn der Verursacher der Handlung jedoch im Passivsatz erwähnt werden soll, so wird er mit ***by*** angehängt.
Passivsätze findet man häufig in Zeitungsberichten, historischen Texten oder technischen Beschreibungen.
Aktiv- und Passivsätze spiegeln verschiedene Sichtweisen einer Situation wider.
Passivsätze im ***simple present*** werden mit ***am / are / is*** und dem ***past participle*** (= 3. Verbform) gebildet.

Aussage

All the work **is done** by computers.
The lights **are switched** on and off.
Robots **are used** to do dangerous jobs.

Verneinung

The rooms **aren't cleaned** every day.
The water **isn't turned** off.

Frage

What jobs **are done** by electrical devices?

My grammar

1. Finde drei (weitere) Beispielsätze zum Passiv im Text auf Seite 72.
2. Markiere die Verbformen und erkläre deinem / r Nachbar / in das Passiv.

Test yourself

Most of the jobs at Jane and Jack's house are done by the animals.
Today the animals are on vacation. What happens? Complete the sentences.

1. The shopping … (*not do*).
2. The clothes … (*not wash*).
3. The sandwiches … (*not make*).
4. The floor … (*not clean*).

Unit 5

G17 Das Passiv im *simple past*
The passive voice (simple past)

→ p. 86.1

Du hast bereits das Passiv im *simple present* kennen gelernt. Wiederhole noch einmal die Bedeutung und die Bildung (→ G16). Jetzt kommt das Passiv im *simple past* neu hinzu.
Die Passivform im ***simple past*** wird mit ***was / were*** und dem ***past participle*** (= 3. Verbform) gebildet.

The movie **was directed** by Steven Spielberg.

After *Gone with the wind,* lots of movies **were shot** in color.

Computer graphics **weren't used** until the 1980s.

My grammar
1. Finde zwei weitere Beispielsätze (Aussagen) zum Passiv im Text auf Seite 86. Forme diese Sätze jeweils in einen verneinten Satz und in eine Frage um.
2. Markiere die Verbformen und erkläre deinem / r Nachbar / in, was du bei der Bildung des Passivs beachten musst.

Test yourself
Write full sentences to say what happened yesterday in Jonesboro, a small US town.

Example: twenty DVD players – to steal – from a music shop
Twenty DVD players were stolen from a music shop.

1. three houses – to damage – in stormy weather
2. a UFO – to photograph – in California
3. Jamie Foxx – to see – in downtown Jonesboro
4. four teenagers – to hurt – in a car accident

Die Passivformen in verschiedenen Zeiten

Im Passiv werden die Zeitformen wie im Aktiv gebildet und auch so verwendet.
Du benötigst die jeweilige Zeitform von ***to be*** + ***past participle*** (= 3. Verbform).

simple present:	Today's science fiction movies **are made** with special effects.
present progressive:	Next year's movies **are being made** now.
simple past:	*Tron* **was made** in 1982.
present perfect:	Hundreds of Bollywood movies **have been made** since 2000.
past perfect:	Not many long color movies **had been made** before 1939.
past progressive:	Drew Barrymore missed school while *E.T.* **was being made**.
will-future:	Lots of movies **will be made** in Hollywood in the future.
infinitive:	*The jazz singer* (1927) was the first movie **to be made** with sound.

G18 Direkte und indirekte Rede
Direct and reported speech

→ p. 88.1

Wenn du wiedergeben möchtest, was jemand gesagt hat (= direkte Rede), benutzt du die **indirekte Rede** (*reported speech*).
Sie wird meistens mit Sätzen, wie z. B. *She said / told us (that)* … eingeleitet.
Darauf folgt dann der eigentliche Satz, der wiedergegeben werden soll:
(An actress: "I always look forward to the Oscars ceremony.")
She said (that) she always looked forward to the Oscars ceremony.
Dabei kommt es zwischen der direkten und indirekten Rede zu einer **Verschiebung der Zeiten**.
Steht das einleitende Verb in der Vergangenheit (*said*, *told*), so verschieben sich die Zeiten jeweils in die nächst fernere Vergangenheit.

Direct speech	**Reported speech** (Einleitungssatz im *simple past*)
"I'**m** so happy to be at the Oscars ceremony."	The actress said (that) she **was** so happy to be at the Oscars ceremony.
simple present →	simple past
"I'**ve** already **acted** in over fifty movies."	She told us (that) she **had** already **acted** in over fifty movies.
present perfect →	past perfect
"I **enjoyed** making *E.T.*"	She said (that) she **had enjoyed** making *E.T.*
simple past →	past perfect
"I **will** always **act** in movies."	She added that she **would** always **act** in movies.
will →	would

Vergiss nie,
nach *said* und *told (me/us/…)*
die Zeiten zu verschieben.

My grammar
Schau dir noch einmal die Beispielsätze zur direkten und indirekten Rede an.
Was musst du bei der Umformung eines Satzes in die indirekte Rede beachten?

Test yourself
Yesterday Ben talked to his friend Paul.
a) *Read what he said to him.*

1. "I've acted in a short movie."
2. "I only had a very small role."
3. "I didn't have to say anything."
4. "I wore a funny costume."

b) *Today Ben tells another friend what Paul said. Use reported speech.*

1. Paul said he had acted in a short movie.
2. He added that he only …
3. …

G19 Fragen in der indirekten Rede
Questions in reported speech

→ p. 89.3

Bei **direkten Fragen ohne Fragewort** wird die Frage in der indirekten Rede mit Sätzen, wie z. B. *They asked (me) / wanted to know* + ***whether / if*** (= ob) eingeleitet.

Direct speech (Fragen ohne Fragewort)	**Reported speech** (Einleitungssatz im *simple past*)
"**Do** you **like** the screenplay?"	They asked me whether I **liked** the screenplay.
simple present →	simple past
"**Did** you **like** shooting the action scenes?"	They wanted to know whether I **had liked** shooting the action scenes.
simple past →	past perfect
"**Are** you **working** on another movie?"	They also asked whether I **was working** on another movie.
present progressive →	past progressive

Bei **direkten Fragen mit Fragewort** wird das Fragewort in der indirekten Rede beibehalten: z. B. *They asked (me) / wanted to know* + ***what / when / who***.

Direct speech (Fragen mit Fragewort)	**Reported speech** (Einleitungssatz im *simple past*)
"What kind of movie **is** it?"	They asked me what kind of movie it **was**.
simple present →	simple past
"Who **wrote** the screenplay?"	They wanted to know who **had written** the screenplay.
simple past/present perfect →	past perfect
"When **will** it **be** in the movie theaters?"	They asked when it **would be** in the movie theaters.
will →	would

Die Wortstellung in indirekten Fragesätzen ist dieselbe wie in Aussagesätzen:

"Did you like the movie?" → They asked me whether **I** (Subjekt) **had liked** (Verb) **the movie** (Objekt).

Test yourself

Chippy, Jack and Jane watched a movie on TV yesterday. When Chippy saw his animal friends, they had lots of questions. Write their questions as reported speech.

1. Was it a good movie?
   → They wanted to know whether …
2. Did it have a happy ending?
   → They asked whether …
3. What was the name of the movie?
   → They…
4. Who were the stars? → They …

Grammar words

Deutsch	Englisch	Englisches Beispiel	in:
Artikel: unbestimmter Artikel bestimmter Artikel	articles indefinite article definite article	They go on vacation twice a year. School starts at eight. Do you like the school you go to?	G15 G15
Bedingungssätze: Typ 1 Typ 2 Typ 3	conditional sentences	Students won't have problems if they follow the dress code. If you were here, it wouldn't be so boring. If the man had fallen from those rocks, he would have broken his leg.	Revision G7 G11 G12 G13
Futur: „will" Verlaufsform der Gegenwart	'will'-future present progressive with future meaning	It will be cold tomorrow. Maybe we will meet again. What are you doing tomorrow? – I'm going to a concert.	Revision G6 Revision G2
Gegenwart: einfache Form Verlaufsform	simple present present progressive	She goes to baseball practice on Tuesdays. This Tuesday she is going out for a meal.	Revision G1 Revision G2
Gerund als Subjekt als Objekt nach Präpositionen	gerund as subject as object after prepositions	Cooking is fun. She loves cooking Chinese dishes. Dad isn't used to cooking for himself.	G9 G9 G10
modale **Hilfsverben** und ihre Ersatzformen	modal auxiliaries	May I / Shall I close the door? Lisa ought to call Rachel. We were able to get tickets for the concert.	Revision G8
indirekte Rede	reported speech	She said she had enjoyed the movie. They asked me whether I liked the screenplay.	G18 G19
Passiv im „simple present" im „simple past"	passive voice simple present simple past	All the work is done by computers. Computer graphics weren't used until the 1980s.	G16 G17
Verben mit zwei Objekten	verbs with two objects	Scientists give the astronauts advice. Scientists give advice to the astronauts.	G14
Vergangenheit: einfache Form Perfekt vollendete Vergangenheit	simple past present perfect past perfect	They opened the new immigration station on Ellis Island in 1892. Paul has had an accident. He's in hospital now. The immigrants hadn't eaten for days when they arrived.	Revision G3 Revision G5 Revision G4

Vocabulary

Auf den folgenden Seiten findest du alle englischen Wörter und Ausdrücke aus Band 4. Sie stehen in der Reihenfolge, wie sie im Buch vorkommen.
Die Wortliste ist in drei Spalten aufgeteilt:

- Links stehen die englischen Wörter und Sätze.
- In der Mitte werden sie übersetzt.
- Rechts findest du Beispiele, Erklärungen und Tipps, die dir beim Lernen helfen.

Die fett gedruckten Wörter musst du lernen, die normal gedruckten Wörter nicht.
Gleich nach jedem neuen englischen Wort steht die Lautschrift in eckigen Klammern. Sie zeigt dir, wie das neue Wort ausgesprochen wird. Wie du diese Lautzeichen liest, siehst du unten.

Englische Laute

Mitlaute

[b]	**b**ed	[p]	**p**icture
[d]	**d**ay	[r]	**r**ed
[ð]	**th**e	[s]	**s**ix
[f]	**f**amily	[ʃ]	**sh**e
[g]	**g**o	[t]	**t**en
[ŋ]	morni**ng**	[tʃ]	lun**ch**
[h]	**h**ouse	[v]	**v**ideo
[j]	**y**ou	[w]	**w**e, **o**ne
[k]	**c**an, mil**k**	[z]	ea**s**y
[l]	**l**etter	[ʒ]	revi**s**ion
[m]	**m**an	[dʒ]	pa**ge**
[n]	**n**o	[θ]	**th**ank you

Selbstlaute

[ɑː]	c**ar**
[æ]	**a**pple
[e]	p**e**n
[ə]	**a**gain
[ɜː]	g**ir**l
[ʌ]	b**u**t
[ɪ]	**i**t
[i]	happ**y**
[iː]	t**ea**cher
[ɒ]	d**o**g
[ɔː]	b**a**ll
[ʊ]	b**oo**k
[u]	Jan**u**ary
[uː]	t**oo**, tw**o**

Doppellaute

[aɪ]	**I**, m**y**
[aʊ]	n**ow**, m**ou**se
[eɪ]	n**a**me, th**ey**
[eə]	th**ere**, p**air**
[ɪə]	h**ere**, id**ea**
[əʊ]	hell**o**
[ɔɪ]	b**oy**
[ʊə]	s**ure**

[:] der vorangehende Laut ist lang, z. B. *you* [juː]

['] die folgende Silbe wird betont, z. B. *hello* [he'ləʊ]

Tipps zum Vokabellernen findest du in den Kästen zu Beginn jeder ***Unit***.
Am Ende der ***Units*** kannst du nützliche Ausdrücke für deinen *folder* sammeln, mit denen du dich auf Englisch verständigen kannst.
Außerdem gibt es zu jeder ***Unit*** einen Kasten, in dem du Interessantes zum Leben in Amerika erfährst.

Auf den ***Vocabulary***-Teil folgt das ***Dictionary***, eine alphabetische Wortliste mit allen englischen Wörtern aus den Bänden 1, 2, 3 und 4. Wenn du ein Wort nicht weißt, kannst du es hier nachschlagen.

Abkürzungen und Zeichen

pl	Plural, Mehrzahl	↔	ist das Gegenteil von
p. 10	Auf dieser Seite kommen die Wörter vor.	→	ist verwandt mit
		=	entspricht
AE	American English	*BE*	British English

Zoom-in Around the US

p. 10	to **zoom-in** [ˌzu:m‿ˈɪn]	heranzoomen, nahe herangehen	
	web [web]	*hier:* Web-, Internet-	
	journey [ˈdʒɜ:ni]	Reise, Tour →	When you travel you go on a *journey*.
	yep [jep]	ja *(Umgangssprache)*	
	cable car [ˈkeɪbl ˌkɑ:]	*hier:* Straßenbahn	
	state [steɪt]	Staat, Land; ein Bundesstaat in den USA	
p. 11	**western** [ˈwestən]	Western *(Filmart)* →	west → *western*
	scenery [ˈsi:nəri]	*hier:* Landschaft →	The *scenery* in the mountains is very beautiful.
	rock [rɒk]	Fels; Stein; Gestein	
	Native American [ˌneɪtɪv əˈmerɪkən]	*Ureinwohner/-in von Amerika*, Indianer/-in →	The Sioux are *Native Americans*.
	traditional [trəˈdɪʃənl]	traditionell →	Achte auf die Schreibung und die Aussprache!
	cheerleader [ˈtʃɪəˌli:də]	Cheerleader/-in	
	middle school [ˈmɪdl ˌsku:l]	*Schulform zwischen Grundschule und weiterführender Schule*	
	energy [ˈenədʒi]	Energie →	Cheerleaders have lots of *energy*.
	stripe [straɪp]	Streifen	
p. 12	to **celebrate** [ˈseləbreɪt]	feiern	
	freedom [ˈfri:dəm]	Freiheit →	free → *freedom*
	fireworks [ˈfaɪəwɜ:ks]	Feuerwerk →	There are *fireworks* in Germany at New Year.
	corn [kɔ:n]	*hier:* Mais →	Cornflakes are made from *corn*.
	wheat [wi:t]	Weizen →	Achte auf die Schreibung!
	in the early 1600s [ɪn ði ˌɜ:li ˈsɪksti:n hʌndrədz]	am Anfang/zu Beginn des 17. Jahrhunderts	
	capital [ˈkæpɪtl]	Hauptstadt →	The *capital* of Germany is Berlin.
	president [ˈprezɪdnt]	Präsident/-in →	Achte auf die Schreibung und die Aussprache!
p. 13	**fee** [fi:]	Gebühr	
	musical [ˈmju:zɪkəl]	Musical →	'Mamma Mia', 'Starlight Express' and 'The Phantom of the Opera' are all *musicals*.
	classic [ˈklæsɪk]	Klassiker	
	immigrant [ˈɪmɪgrənt]	Einwanderer/Einwanderin →	An *immigrant* is someone who has left his/her own country to live in another one.
	skyscraper [ˈskaɪˌskreɪpə]	Wolkenkratzer →	A *skyscraper* is a very high building. 
	number plate *(BE)* [ˈnʌmbə ˌpleɪt]	Nummernschild	
	license plate *(AE)* [ˈlaɪsəns ˌpleɪt]	Nummernschild →	*license plate* (AE) = number plate (BE)
	zone [zəʊn]	Zone →	Achte auf die Aussprache!
	movie *(AE)* [ˈmu:vi]	Film →	*movie* (AE) = film (BE)
	file [faɪl]	Ordner	

Unit 1 I love New York City

VOCABULARY SKILLS

Lerntipp: Erinnerst du dich an die Tipps vom letzten Schuljahr?

In den ersten drei Bänden hast du schon viele nützliche Tipps kennengelernt, die dir das Vokabellernen erleichtern. Hier noch einmal eine kleine Zusammenfassung:

- Lerne möglichst immer am gleichen Arbeitsplatz.
- Führe deine Vokabeldatei fort.
- Nimm dir mehrmals am Tag kleine Lernportionen vor, die du dann jeweils für eine kurze Zeit (10 Minuten) bearbeitest.
- Stelle für jedes neue Wort so viele Zusammenhänge wie möglich her.
- Gestalte das Lernen spannender, indem du mit anderen lernst oder Vokabellernspiele spielst.

Check-in

p. 15	**statue** ['stætʃu:]	Statue, Standbild →	The *Statue* of Liberty →
	borough ['bʌrə]	Bezirk, Stadtgemeinde →	Achte auf die Schreibung!
	neighborhood *(AE)* ['neɪbəhʊd]	Gegend, Viertel; Nachbarschaft →	*neighborhood* (AE) = neighbourhood (BE)
	cab *(AE)* [kæb]	Taxi →	*cab* (AE) = taxi (BE)
	tall [tɔ:l]	hoch; groß →	a *tall* building/a big city
	store *(AE)* [stɔ:]	Laden; Geschäft →	*store* (AE) = shop (BE)

New York

In Manhattan verlaufen die Straßen wie mit dem Lineal gezeichnet in einem Raster. Die Straßen haben Nummern statt Namen und verlaufen entweder von Norden nach Süden (*Avenues* genannt) oder von Westen nach Osten (*Streets*). Viele Straßen in New York sind Einbahnstraßen. Hier gilt die Regel: Der Verkehr verläuft in Straßen mit geraden Nummern nach Osten, in Straßen mit ungeraden Nummern nach Westen.

In New York leben etwa 5 000 obdachlose Menschen in stillgelegten U-Bahntunnels. Diese Menschen werden „Mole People" („Maulwurfmenschen") genannt. Sie leben meist in größeren Gruppen zusammen und haben ihre eigene Kultur.

Etwa 35 000 Läufer nehmen jedes Jahr am New-York-City-Marathon teil. Sie laufen am ersten Sonntag im November durch die verschiedenen Stadtteile und werden dabei von 12 000 Helfern betreut.

New Yorks größtes Kaufhaus „Macy's" hat eine Verkaufsfläche von 198 500 m² und bietet über 500 000 verschiedene Produkte an. Touristen erhalten bei der Anmeldung einen Gutschein für einen Rabatt auf alle Produkte. So erhalten z. B. Deutsche in allen Geschäften der Kette 19 % Rabatt.

Würdest du gern in einer Großstadt wie New York leben? Was sind deiner Meinung nach die Vor- und Nachteile einer solchen Stadt im Vergleich zu deiner Heimatstadt?

Unit 1

p. 15	**terrorist** ['terərɪst]	Terrorist/-in	
	to **destroy** [dɪ'strɔɪ]	zerstören; kaputt machen; vernichten	
	twin [twɪn]	Zwilling	
	center *(AE)* ['sentə]	Zentrum →	*center* (AE) = centre (BE)
	foreground ['fɔ:graʊnd]	Vordergrund	
	background ['bækgraʊnd]	Hintergrund →	foreground ↔ *background*
	banner ['bænə]	Fahne	
	kickboard ['kɪkbɔ:d]	Kickboard, Tretroller	
	story *(AE)* ['stɔ:ri]	Stockwerk →	*story* (AE) = floor (BE)
	elevator *(AE)* ['elɪveɪtə]	Aufzug →	*elevator* (AE) = lift (BE)
	torch [tɔ:tʃ]	*hier:* Fackel	
	talk [tɔ:k]	Vortrag →	We gave a *talk* about our trip to New York.

Language 1

p. 16	**Polish** ['pəʊlɪʃ]	polnisch, Polnisch; Pole/Polin	
	deli (= delicatessen) ['deli (= ˌdelɪkə'tesn)]	Imbiss; Feinkostgeschäft →	We bought our breakfast at the *deli*.
	short for [ˌʃɔ:t 'fə]	Kurzform von	
	monster ['mɒnstə]	Monster	
	vacation *(AE)* [və'keɪʃn]	Urlaub, Ferien →	*vacation* (AE) = holiday (BE)
	to **deliver** [dɪ'lɪvə]	(aus)liefern	
	special ['speʃl]	*hier:* Spezialität →	special → a *special*
	dollar ['dɒlə]	Dollar *(US-Währung)* →	How much did you pay for the food? – Six *dollars*.
	to **keep** [ki:p]	*hier:* behalten	
	change [tʃeɪndʒ]	Wechselgeld; Kleingeld; Veränderung, Änderung →	I told the waiter to keep the *change*.
	to **give away** ['gɪv‿əweɪ]	verschenken	
	tip [tɪp]	*hier:* Trinkgeld →	Before you leave a café or restaurant, it's normal to leave a *tip*.
	to **write down** [ˌraɪt 'daʊn]	aufschreiben →	I *wrote down* the message so I didn't forget it.
	ingredient [ɪn'gri:diənt]	Zutat	
p. 17	**coffee** ['kɒfi]	Kaffee →	A lot of people drink tea or *coffee* in the morning.
	to go [tə 'gəʊ]	zum Mitnehmen	
	Danish ['deɪnɪʃ]	*hier:* Plundergebäck →	I'd like a *Danish* and a coffee to go, please.
	cupcake *(AE)* ['kʌpkeɪk]	kleiner Kuchen →	A *cupcake* is a small cake.
	maple ['meɪpl]	Ahorn	
	syrup ['sɪrəp]	Sirup →	Achte auf die Schreibung und die Aussprache!

p. 17	**bagel** *(AE)* ['beɪgl]	Bagel (*weiches, ringförmiges Brötchen*) →	*bagels* → 
	toast [təʊst]	Toast, Toastbrot →	A lot of people eat *toast* for breakfast.
	cream cheese [ˌkriːm 'tʃiːz]	Frischkäse	
	pastrami *(AE)* [pæs'trɑːmi]	geräuchertes Rindfleisch	
	turkey ['tɜːki]	Pute, Truthahn	
	lettuce ['letɪs]	Blattsalat →	Achte auf die Schreibung!
	French fries *(AE)* [ˌfrentʃ 'fraɪz]	Pommes frites →	*French fries* (AE) = chips (BE)
	milkshake ['mɪlkˌʃeɪk]	Milkshake →	milk + shake = *milkshake*
	strawberry ['strɔːbri]	Erdbeere	
	cherry ['tʃeri]	Kirsche →	Strawberries and *cherries* are kinds of fruit.
	waiter ['weɪtə]	Kellner	
	bill *(AE)* [bɪl]	*hier:* Geldschein →	*bill* (AE) = note (BE)
	dime [daɪm]	*amerik. Geldeinheit* →	10 cents are a *dime*.
	quarter ['kwɔːtə]	*amerik. Geldeinheit* →	25 cents are a *quarter*.
	nickel ['nɪkl]	*amerik. Geldeinheit* →	5 cents are a *nickel*.
	cent [sent]	*amerik. Geldeinheit* →	100 *cents* are a dollar.
	favorite *(AE)* ['feɪvrɪt]	Lieblings- →	*favorite* (AE) = favourite (BE)
	instructions [ɪn'strʌkʃnz]	Anweisungen	

Useful phrases: At the deli A B C

Die folgenden *phrases* helfen dir im Restaurant oder im *deli*.

Hi! I'd like … and …, please.	Guten Tag! Ich hätte gerne … und … .
Would you like it with or without … ?	Hätten Sie es gerne mit … oder ohne … ?
Can I also have some … ?	Kann ich auch … bekommen?
Would you like to have anything to drink?	Möchten Sie etwas zu trinken?
OK. That's … dollars and … cents, please.	OK. Das macht … Dollar und … Cent.
Here's … . Give me … and you can keep the change.	Hier sind … . Bitte geben Sie mir … zurück und behalten Sie den Rest.
I hope you enjoy it!	Guten Appetit!

Language 2

p. 18	**immigration** [ˌɪmɪ'greɪʃn]	Einwanderung, Immigration →	immigrant → *immigration*
	close to ['kləʊs‿tʊ]	in der Nähe von	
	harbor *(AE)* ['hɑːbə]	Hafen →	*harbor* (AE) = harbour (BE)
	to **escape** [ɪ'skeɪp]	flüchten, entfliehen, entkommen	
	poverty ['pɒvəti]	Armut →	poor → *poverty*

Unit 1

p. 18	**war** [wɔː]	Krieg →	*War* is when two or more groups or countries fight against each other.
	oppression [əˈpreʃn]	Unterdrückung	
	Dutch [dʌtʃ]	holländisch, niederländisch; Holländisch, Niederländisch; Holländer/-in, Niederländer/-in	
	to **found** [faʊnd]	errichten, gründen	
	to **name** [neɪm]	nennen →	If you *name* something, you give it a name.
	famine [ˈfæmɪn]	Hungersnot	
	seasick [ˈsiːsɪk]	seekrank →	You are *seasick* if you feel bad on a boat or ship.
	station [ˈsteɪʃn]	*hier:* Station, Posten →	Achte auf die Aussprache!
	sick [sɪk]	krank →	*sick* = not feeling very well
	official [əˈfɪʃl]	Beamter/Beamtin	
	quota [ˈkwəʊtə]	Anteil; *hier:* zugelassene Einwanderungsquote →	There were *quotas* for immigrants.
	limit [ˈlɪmɪt]	Grenze, Begrenzung	
	to **immigrate** [ˈɪmɪgreɪt]	einwandern →	*to immigrate* → immigrant, immigration
p. 19	**action** [ˈækʃn]	Handlung	
	pros and cons pl. [ˌprəʊz‿n ˈkɒnz]	Pro und Kontra, Für und Wider	

Talkwise

p. 20	**feeling** [ˈfiːlɪŋ]	Gefühl →	Sometimes it is hard to show your *feelings*.
	embarrassed [ɪmˈbærəst]	verlegen →	Achte auf die Schreibung!
	sympathetic [ˌsɪmpəˈθetɪk]	mitfühlend, verständnisvoll →	Achtung! *sympathetic* = mitfühlend sympathisch = nice
	amazing [əˈmeɪzɪŋ]	erstaunlich; unglaublich; toll →	That's *amazing*! I've never seen anything like it.

Text

p. 21	**by** [baɪ]	von →	A song *by* the Beastie Boys.
	s.o. is doing well [ɪz ˈduːɪŋ ˌwel]	jdm. geht es gut *(Umgangssprache)*	
	hell [hel]	Hölle	
	to **give thanks to s.o.** [ˌgɪv ˈθæŋks]	sich bei jdm. bedanken →	*to give thanks to s.o.* = to thank s.o.
	to **provide** [prəʊˈvaɪd]	zur Verfügung stellen	
	gate [geɪt]	Tor	
	to **pass** [pɑːs]	durchgehen →	We *passed* through the gates of the White House to go on the tour.
	Asian [ˈeɪʒn]	asiatisch, Asiat/-in	
	Middle-Eastern [ˌmɪdl ˈiːstən]	aus dem Nahen Osten	

p. 21	**Latin** ['lætɪn]	lateinamerikanisch; Lateinamerikaner/-in	
	mom *(AE)* [mɒm]	Mama →	*mom* (AE) = mum (BE)
	to **dedicate** ['dedɪkeɪt]	widmen →	My boyfriend *dedicated* a poem to me at the poetry slam.
	to **blend** [blend]	vermischen	
	to **mend** [mend]	reparieren, ausbessern	
	pretty ['prɪti]	hübsch, nett; ziemlich →	That girl is really *pretty*.
	to **reject** [ri:'dʒekt]	ablehnen, zurückweisen, abweisen	
	to **accept** [ək'sept]	akzeptieren, annehmen →	The man *accepted* that he had made a mistake.
	wherever [weə'revə]	egal wo, wo (auch) immer	
p. 22	**edge** [edʒ]	Rand, Kante; Grenze →	I looked over the *edge* of the skyscraper. It was a long way down.
	bomb [bɒm]	Bombe	
	to **tick** [tɪk]	*hier:* ticken	
	concrete ['kɒŋkri:t]	Beton →	Modern cities have lots of *concrete* buildings.

American English – British English I   A B C

Obwohl in den USA ebenfalls Englisch gesprochen wird, gibt es einige Unterschiede zu dem Englisch, das man in Großbritannien spricht. Wir unterscheiden daher zwischen *British English* (BE) und *American English* (AE). Unterschiede gibt es bei der Schreibung und Aussprache, manchmal wird auch im amerikanischen Englisch ein komplett anderes Wort verwendet.

American English (AE)	***British English (BE)***	***German***
cab	*taxi*	Taxi
*cent**er***	*cent**re***	Zentrum
check	*bill*	Rechnung
*col**or***	*col**our***	Farbe
elevator	*lift*	Aufzug
*fav**o**rite*	*fav**ou**rite*	Lieblings-
French fries	*chips*	Pommes frites
*gr**a**y*	*gr**e**y*	grau
*harb**or***	*harb**our***	Hafen
line	*queue*	Schlange
movie	*film*	Film
*neighb**o**rhood*	*neighb**ou**rhood*	Nachbarschaft
license plate	*number plate*	Nummernschild
restroom	*toilet*	Toilette
store	*shop*	Laden
story	*floor*	Stockwerk
trash, garbage	*rubbish*	Müll, Abfall
vacation	*holiday*	Ferien

Unit 1

p. 22	**flower** ['flaʊə]	Blume →	We have lots of *flowers* in our garden.
	watch [wɒtʃ]	Armbanduhr →	You wear a *watch* on your arm.
	sunshine ['sʌnʃaɪn]	Sonnenschein	
	gray *(AE)* [greɪ]	grau →	*gray* (AE) = grey (BE)
p. 23	**positive** ['pɒzətɪv]	positiv →	Achte auf die Schreibung und die Aussprache!
	to mention ['menʃn]	erwähnen	
	to **record** [rɪ'kɔ:d]	aufnehmen →	*to record* → record
	sound file ['saʊnd ˌfaɪl]	Audiodatei	

Wordwise

p. 24	**way** [weɪ]	Art und Weise, Weise	
p. 25	**line** *(AE)* [laɪn]	Warteschlange →	*line* (AE) = queue (BE)
	trash *(AE)* [træʃ]	Müll, Abfall →	*trash* (AE) = rubbish (BE)
	check *(AE)* [tʃek]	Rechnung →	*check* (AE) = bill (BE)
	restroom *(AE)* ['restru:m]	Toilette →	*restroom* (AE) = toilet (BE)
	color *(AE)* ['kʌlə]	Farbe →	*color* (AE) = colour (BE)

Check out

p. 26	**company** ['kʌmpəni]	Firma, Unternehmen	
p. 27	**public** ['pʌblɪk]	öffentlich; Öffentlichkeit	
	ground [graʊnd]	Boden, Erde	
	firefighter *(AE)* ['faɪəˌfaɪtə]	Feuerwehrmann/-frau →	*firefighter* (AE) = fireman/-woman (BE)
	hero ['hɪərəʊ]	Held/-in	

For my folder

New York

In dieser Unit hast du einiges über New York erfahren. Was würdest du unternehmen, wenn du einen Tag in New York verbringen könntest? Suche Fotos und fertige ein Poster mit den verschiedenen Dingen an, die du tun würdest. Schreibe zu jedem Aspekt einen Satz auf Englisch.

Skills workshop 1

p. 28	**conversation** [ˌkɒnvə'seɪʃn]	Gespräch, Konversation →	When people talk to each other they have a *conversation*. Achte auf die Aussprache!
	karaoke [ˌkæri'əʊki]	Karaoke →	
	keyword ['ki:wɜ:d]	Schlüsselwort	
	downtown *(AE)* [ˌdaʊn'taʊn]	im Stadtzentrum, in der Innenstadt →	*downtown* (AE) = in the city/town centre (BE)
p. 29	**passenger** ['pæsndʒə]	Passagier/-in →	There were 100 *passengers* on the plane. They were all going on vacation.
	to **react** [ri'ækt]	reagieren	

Unit 2 School life

VOCABULARY SKILLS

Lerntipp: Sprich verschiedene Sinne an

Das Gehirn merkt sich neue Informationen am besten, wenn so viele Sinnesorgane wie möglich mit der neuen Information beschäftigt werden. Dazu kannst du z. B. so vorgehen:

- Lies dir die neuen Vokabeln erst leise durch.
- Lies die neuen Vokabeln nun laut vor.
- Schreibe die neuen Vokabeln ab. Am besten immer nur fünf auf einmal.
- Lasse dir die Vokabeln von jemand anderem vorlesen.
- Wiederhole das Schema so lange, bis du dir alle Vokabeln merken kannst.

Dieses Prinzip kannst du mit kleinen Änderungen auch für andere Fächer anwenden. Statt wie hier die Vokabeln abzuschreiben, kannst du die zu lernenden Informationen z. B. zu einem Text zusammenfassen, mit dem du genauso vorgehst.

Check-in

p. 32	to **pass** [pɑ:s]	*hier:* weitergeben →	He *passed* me the menu so I could choose my food.
	microscope ['maɪkrəskəʊp]	Mikroskop	
	serious ['sɪəriəs]	ernst	
	pompom ['pɒmpɒm]	Pompom *(bunte Quaste)* →	Cheerleaders dance with *pompoms* in their hands.
	to **chant** [tʃɑ:nt]	rhythmisch rufen	
	to **date** [deɪt]	sich verabreden →	I can't believe I'm *dating* Dave. We're going to the movies together tomorrow.
p. 33	to **pledge** [pledʒ]	geloben	
	allegiance [ə'li:dʒənts]	Treue	
	start [stɑ:t]	Anfang, Beginn	
	grade *(AE)* [greɪd]	Klasse; Note →	*grade* (AE) = year; mark (BE)
	schedule *(AE)* ['skedʒu:l]	Stundenplan →	*schedule* (AE) = timetable (BE)
	Math *(AE)* [mæθ]	Mathe →	*Math* (AE) = Maths (BE)
	student *(AE)* ['stu:dnt]	Schüler/-in	
	to **support** [sə'pɔ:t]	unterstützen	
	to **receive** [rɪ'si:v]	bekommen, empfangen →	*to receive* = to get
	report card *(AE)* [rɪ'pɔ:t ˌkɑ:d]	Zeugnis →	*report card* (AE) = school report (BE)
	class [klɑ:s]	Unterrichtsstunde	
	baseball ['beɪsbɔ:l]	Baseball →	*Baseball* is a popular American sport.
	cheerleading ['tʃɪəli:dɪŋ]	Cheerleading (*Aktivitäten der Cheerleader*)	
	election [ɪ'lekʃn]	Wahl	
	FAQs (= frequently asked questions) [ˌef eɪ 'kju:z]	häufig gestellte Fragen →	These are questions that people often ask.
	home page ['həʊm ˌpeɪdʒ]	Homepage	

Unit 2

Cheerleading

Das Wort „Cheerleading" besteht aus den Begriffen *to cheer* (Beifall klatschen, jubeln) und *to lead* (führen). Cheerleading bedeutet also sinngemäß „das Publikum zum Beifall führen". Mittlerweile trainieren die meisten Cheerleader-Mannschaften jedoch, um möglichst gut bei den Cheerleader-Meisterschaften abzuschneiden.
Die ersten Cheerleader-Teams gab es 1898 an der University of Minnesota. Dort war Cheerleading am Anfang – im Gegensatz zum heutigen Klischee – ein reiner Männersport. Erst im Laufe der Zeit wurden auch Frauen zugelassen.
Typische Sportarten, bei denen Cheerleader auftreten, sind American Football und Basketball, aber auch im Eishockey, Fußball und Handball wächst die Zahl der Cheerleader-Gruppen, die man auch *squads* nennt.

Gibt es bei dir in der Nähe auch einen Cheerleader-Verein? Würde dir *Cheerleading* als Sportart Spaß machen? Stimmt aus deiner Sicht das Klischee, dass *Cheerleading* nur etwas für Frauen ist?

Language 1

p. 34	**semester** *(AE)* [sɪˈmestə]	Semester →	This is the time you are at school between vacations, e.g. from Christmas to Easter.
	advice (no pl.) [ədˈvaɪs]	Rat, Ratschlag →	I didn't know what to do and I asked my teacher for some *advice*.
	student council [ˌstjuːdnt ˈkaʊnsl]	Schülervertretung	
	fall *(AE)* [fɔːl]	Herbst →	*fall* (AE) = autumn (BE)
	dance [dɑːns]	Tanz(veranstaltung), Ball; Tanz	
	date [deɪt]	Verabredung, Date	
	for sale [ˌfɔː ˈseɪl]	zu verkaufen	
	principal *(AE)* [ˈprɪntsəpl]	Schulleiter/-in →	*principal* (AE) = headteacher (BE)
	ought to [ɔːt]	sollen	
	to **vote** [vəʊt]	wählen, abstimmen →	You *vote* for the person you want to win in an election.
	detention [dɪˈtentʃn]	Nachsitzen	
	dress code [ˌdres ˈkəʊd]	Kleiderordnung; Bekleidungsvorschriften →	What you are supposed to wear to school, a dance, a party, …
	earring [ˈɪərɪŋ]	Ohrring	
	jewelry *(AE)* [ˈdʒuːəlri]	Schmuck →	*jewelry* (AE) = jewellery (BE)
	collar [ˈkɒlə]	Kragen	
	pants *(AE)* [pænts]	Hose →	*pants* (AE) = trousers (BE)

Language 2

p. 36	**the movies** *(AE)* [ˈmuːviz]	das Kino	
	awesome [ˈɔːsəm]	toll, super	
	to **overdo sth.** [ˌəʊvəˈduː]	etw. übertreiben →	When you do too much of something you *overdo it*.

p. 36	**jerk** [dʒɜːk]	Idiot/-in, Blödmann *(Umgangssprache)*	
	kiss [kɪs]	Kuss →	She gave me a *kiss* on the mouth and smiled.
	See you around! [ˌsiː jə əˈraʊnd]	Man sieht sich! *(Umgangssprache)*	

Useful phrases: Dating

A B C

Wenn du mit einem Mädchen oder einem Jungen ausgehen möchtest, kannst du die folgenden *phrases* verwenden.

Hi, there! Would you like to go to the movies with me?	Hallo! Hast du Lust, mit mir ins Kino zu gehen?
Do you want to go to the dance with me?	Möchtest du mit mir zur Party gehen?
Oh yes, that would be great!	Oh ja, das wäre toll!
Yes, I'd love to go with you!	Ja, ich würde gern mit dir hingehen!
Thank you, but I've already got other plans for the weekend.	Danke, aber ich habe schon andere Pläne fürs Wochenende.
Oh, I'm so sorry! I'm already going out with	Es tut mir leid, aber ich gehe schon mit ... aus.
Should we meet at ... ?	Sollen wir uns um ... treffen?
I'll pick you up at eight o'clock.	Ich hole dich um acht Uhr ab.
You're looking cute.	Du siehst hübsch aus.
Well, I'll see you around.	Man sieht sich.

p. 37	**gerund** [ˈdʒerənd]	Gerundium	
	I can't stand ... [aɪ ˌkɑːnt ˈstænd]	Ich kann ... nicht ausstehen.	
	cell phone *(AE)* [ˈsel ˌfəʊn]	Handy →	*cell phone* (AE) = mobile phone (BE)
	coke [kəʊk]	Cola	
	ice skating rink *(AE)* [ˈaɪs skeɪtɪŋ ˌrɪŋk]	Eislaufbahn →	*ice skating rink* (AE) = ice rink (BE)
	ice skating [ˈaɪs ˌskeɪtɪŋ]	Schlittschuhlaufen →	I go *ice skating* at the ice skating rink.
	(that's a) pity [ˌðæts ə ˈpɪti]	(Das ist) schade →	Sorry, I can't come to your party. – Oh, *that's a pity.*

Talkwise

p. 38	**casual** [ˈkæʃuəl]	lässig →	You can wear *casual* clothes to the party.
	teen [tiːn]	Teenager; Jugendliche/-r	
	office [ˈɒfɪs]	Büro	
	register [ˈredʒɪstə]	Register, Sprachebene	
	What's up? [wɒtsˈʌp]	Wie geht's? *(Umgangssprache)* →	*What's up?* = How are you?
	to **kiss** [kɪs]	küssen →	I couldn't believe it when he *kissed* me.

Text

p. 39	to **go crazy about sth.** [ˌgəʊ ˈkreɪzi]	nach etw. verrückt sein →	She *goes crazy about swimming.*

Unit 2

p. 39	**geek** [gi:k]	Außenseiter/-in *(Umgangssprache)*	
	bully ['bʊlɪ]	jemand, der andere tyrannisiert	
	backpack *(AE)* ['bækpæk]	Rucksack →	*backpack* (AE) = rucksack (BE) 
	at the bottom [æt ðə 'bɒtəm]	ganz unten	
	mayonnaise [ˌmeɪə'neɪz]	Majonäse →	I love French fries with ketchup and *mayonnaise*.
	stain [steɪn]	Fleck; Verfärbung	
p. 40	**dress** [dres]	Kleid; Kleidung	
	silly ['sɪli]	Dummkopf	
	to **be crazy about** [bi: 'kreɪzi əˌbaʊt]	verrückt sein nach	
	may [meɪ]	könnte(n) vielleicht	
	to **elect** [ɪ'lekt]	wählen →	*to elect* → election
	to **brag (to s.o. about s.th.)** [bræg]	(mit etw.) angeben, prahlen	
	to **joke** [dʒəʊk]	einen Witz machen →	*to joke* → joke
	subject ['sʌbdʒekt]	Thema →	The *subject* of my presentation is American schools.
	gossip ['gɒsɪp]	Klatsch, Tratsch	
	forever [fə'revə]	für immer; ewig →	I will love him *forever*.
	to **reply** [rɪ'plaɪ]	antworten	

Wordwise

p. 42	**triangle** ['traɪæŋgl]	Dreieck	
p. 43	**phrasal verb** [ˌfreɪzl 'vɜ:b]	Phrasal Verb (*Verb mit Präposition oder Adverb*)	

Wordbuilding I A B C

Im Englischen kannst du durch das Anfügen der Endung *-ing* aus vielen Verben ein Nomen machen.

to build	→	*a building*	ein Gebäude
to end	→	*ending*	der Schluss
to feel	→	*a feeling*	ein Gefühl
to mean	→	*the meaning*	die Bedeutung
to meet	→	*a meeting*	ein Treffen
to paint	→	*a painting*	ein Gemälde

Check-out

p. 44	**conditional** [kən'dɪʃnl]	Konditional-, Bedingungs-	
p. 45	**chant** [tʃɑ:nt]	Sprechgesang, Sprechchor	
	try-out *(AE)* ['traɪaʊt]	*hier:* Aufnahmetest für die Mannschaft →	A *try-out* is like an audition but it is for a team.

For my folder
Schools

In dieser Unit hast du einiges über amerikanische Schulen erfahren. Vergleiche die *Berry Middle School* mit deiner Schule. Sammle Gemeinsamkeiten und Unterschiede und mache eine Tabelle.

my school	BMS
smv	Student Council
...	dress code
...	...

Skills workshop 2

p. 46	**slide** [slaɪd]	Folie, Dia	
	search engine ['sɜːtʃ ˌendʒɪn]	Suchmaschine →	You can find things in the Internet with a *search engine*.
	search term ['sɜːtʃ ˌtɜːm]	Suchbegriff	
	online [ˌɒn'laɪn]	online	
	similar ['sɪmɪlə]	ähnlich →	American English is *similar* to British English.
p. 47	**animation** [ˌænɪ'meɪʃn]	Animation	
	clip [klɪp]	Ausschnitt, Clip	
	handout ['hændaʊt]	Handout, Arbeitsblatt →	I gave everybody a *handout* at my presentation.

Unit 3 In the Southwest

VOCABULARY SKILLS

Lerntipp: Lerne die schwierigen Vokabeln wie die Gedächtnisweltmeister

Kaum zu glauben, aber es gibt wirklich Weltmeisterschaften im Begriffemerken. Weltmeister wird derjenige, der sich in einer bestimmten Zeit die meisten vorgegebenen Begriffe in der richtigen Reihenfolge merken kann.

Besonders gut kann man sich schwere Vokabeln merken, wenn man sie mit etwas Bekanntem verbindet. Wenn deine neue Vokabel zum Beispiel *to glow* (leuchten) ist, überlegst du dir zum Beispiel einen deutschen Begriff dazu, mit dem du das Wort „leuchten" verbindest. Das funktioniert auch mit einem Beispielsatz, am besten mit einem ungewöhnlichen:

- *glow* → leuchten → **Gl**ühwürmchen leuchten.
- *expressive* → ausdrucks**stark** → Espresso (klingt ähnlich wie *expressive*) ist ein **starker** Kaffee.

Probiere die Weltmeistermethode aus und du wirst sehen, dass du dir schwierige Vokabeln viel leichter merken kannst.

Check-in

p. 48	**dry** [draɪ]	trocken →	*dry* ↔ wet
	dizzy ['dɪzi]	schwindelig	

Unit 3

p. 48	**dusty** ['dʌsti]	staubig →	It was really *dusty* and I couldn't see anything.
	truck *(AE)* [trʌk]	Lastwagen →	*truck* (AE) = lorry (BE)
	to **gamble** ['gæmbl]	(*Glücksspiele*) spielen	
p. 49	**desert** ['dezət]	Wüste →	*Deserts* can be very hot during the day and very cold at night. 
	cowboy ['kaʊbɔɪ]	Cowboy	
	motorcycle ['məʊtəˌsaɪkl]	Motorrad →	motor + cycle = *motorcycle*
	instead of [ɪn'sted‿əv]	statt, anstelle von	
	casino [kə'si:nəʊ]	Kasino →	You can win or lose a lot of money in a *casino*.
	canyon ['kænjən]	Felsenschlucht, Canyon	
	deep [di:p]	tief →	Don't get into *deep* water if you can't swim.
	gorge [gɔ:dʒ]	Schlucht	
	national park [ˌnæʃnl 'pɑ:k]	Nationalpark, Naturpark →	Yellowstone was America's first *national park*.
	plant [plɑ:nt]	Pflanze	
	climate ['klaɪmət]	Klima	

Las Vegas

Las Vegas, die wohl berühmteste Spielerstadt der Welt, verkörpert das Klischee der USA als Land, in dem man sehr schnell reich werden kann. Sie wurde 1905 gegründet und liegt mitten in der Wüste von Nevada. Neben den unzähligen Spielautomaten, an denen man sieben Tage die Woche rund um die Uhr spielen kann, ist die Stadt vor allem für ihre riesigen Hotels bekannt. Diese bieten neben großen Hallen mit Spielautomaten und Spielcasinos weitere Touristenattraktionen, so dass viele Menschen extra nach Las Vegas kommen, um diese Hotels zu besichtigen.

Vor dem Hotel *Mirage* steht z. B. ein großer Vulkan zwischen Palmen und Wasserfällen. Tagsüber ist er nicht aktiv, nach Einbruch der Dämmerung aber kündigt er seinen Ausbruch mit einem dumpfen Grollen an und speit dann Feuer und Lava bis zu 40 Meter hoch in die Luft.

Auf dem *Stratosphere Tower* (350 m) des Hotels *Stratosphere Las Vegas* befindet sich der höchstgelegene Vergnügungspark der Welt. Dort kann man sich noch einmal 48 Meter nach oben schießen lassen und für einige Sekunden die Schwerelosigkeit genießen. Das futuristische Kettenkarussell *Insanity* dreht sich außerhalb der Aussichtsplattform und ist nichts für schwache Nerven.

Im Hotel *Mandalay Bay* kann man im *Shark-Reef-Aquarium* gefährliche und ungewöhnliche Wassertiere aus aller Welt bewundern, wie z. B. 13 unterschiedliche Haifischarten, Krokodile, Meer- und Süßwasserfische sowie Seeschildkröten.

Im Hotel *Bellagio* spielen die reichsten Pokerspieler um die höchsten Einsätze. Um Zutritt zu erhalten, muss man bereit sein, um mindestens 80 000 Dollar zu spielen.

Würdest du gern nach Las Vegas fahren, wenn du volljährig bist? Warum/warum nicht? Gibt es auch Nachteile einer solchen „Spielerstadt"?

p. 57 to **quit**, **quit**, **quit** [kwɪt, kwɪt, kwɪt]	aufhören; aufgeben →	I don't feel like working on the Biology project for another second. But if I *quit* now, I know I'll never finish it.
no way [ˌnəʊ ˈweɪ]	auf keinen Fall	
might [maɪt]	könnte(n)	
current [ˈkʌrnt]	Strömung →	The *current* in rapids is very, very strong. Achte auf die Aussprache!
adrenaline [əˈdrenəlɪn]	Adrenalin →	
heart [hɑːt]	Herz	
nasty [ˈnɑːsti]	schlimm; böse, gemein; *hier:* gefährlich →	a *nasty* situation = a dangerous/bad situation
p. 58 to **explode** [ɪkˈspləʊd]	explodieren →	There was a really loud bang. Something must have *exploded*.
joy [dʒɔɪ]	Freude →	They felt a lot of *joy*. = They were very happy.
to **make it** [ˈmeɪk ˌɪt]	es schaffen	
thunder (no pl.) [ˈθʌndə]	Donner →	thunder → thunderstorm
lightning (no pl.) [ˈlaɪtnɪŋ]	Blitz →	lightning → 
moment [ˈməʊmənt]	Augenblick	
to **march** [mɑːtʃ]	marschieren →	When an army walks together as a group, it *marches*.
whole [həʊl]	ganz →	Two halves of an apple make a *whole* one.
narrow [ˈnærəʊ]	eng, schmal	
slot [slɒt]	Schlitz →	In public telephones you put your card or your money into the *slot*.
hole [həʊl]	Loch	
violence (no pl.) [ˈvaɪəlns]	Gewalt, Gewalttätigkeit	
shocking [ˈʃɒkɪŋ]	schockierend →	The violence after the football match was *shocking*.
so far [ˌsəʊ ˈfɑː]	bis jetzt	
to **flip** [flɪp]	*(Boot)* zum Kentern bringen; ausflippen	
to **realize** [ˈrɪəlaɪz]	begreifen, erkennen →	I *realized* my mistake when the teacher explained the answer.
to **stand up to s.o.** [stænd‿ˈʌp tə]	sich jdm. gegenüber behaupten	
helpful [ˈhelpfʊl]	hilfreich	
to **sneer** [snɪə]	spotten; spöttisch grinsen →	*to sneer* = to speak in a way that shows you think the other person is stupid, or that you don't like him or her
to **rescue** [ˈreskjuː]	retten →	We got lost and the police *rescued* us.
shoulder [ˈʃəʊldə]	Schulter	
rope [rəʊp]	Seil →	You need *ropes* when you go climbing.
bronc rider [ˈbrɒŋk ˌraɪdə]	Rodeo-Reiter	
to **pull** [pʊl]	ziehen →	to push ↔ *to pull*
violent [ˈvaɪəlnt]	gewaltsam, *hier:* gewaltig	
halfway down [hɑːfˌweɪ ˈdaʊn]	auf halbem Wege nach unten →	*Halfway down* the tree I got my foot stuck in a hole.

Unit 3

p. 58 **Holy mother** [ˌhəʊli ˈmʌðə] — Heilige Mutter →
adapted [əˈdæptɪd] — bearbeitet

You can use phrases like *'Holy mother'* or 'Holy cow' when you are surprised or afraid.

American English – British English II A B C

Zwischen *British English* und *American English* gibt es einige Unterschiede in der Aussprache.

	American English (AE)	British English (BE)
after	[ˈæftə]	[ˈɑːftə]
ask	[æsk]	[ɑːsk]
car	[kɑːr]	[kɑː]
work	[wɜːrk]	[wɜːk]
better	[ˈbedə]	[ˈbetə]
water	[ˈwɔːdə]	[ˈwɔːtə]

Check-out

p. 63 **rich** [rɪtʃ] — reich
apartment *(AE)* [əˈpɑːtmənt] — Wohnung →

apartment (AE) = flat (BE)

For my folder

The USA

In dieser Unit hast du etwas über die verschiedenen Bundesstaaten und Regionen der USA gelernt. Zeichne oder kopiere dir den Umriss der USA. Trage die Bundesstaaten ein und schreibe zu jedem Bundesstaat auf, was du bis jetzt über ihn gelernt hast.

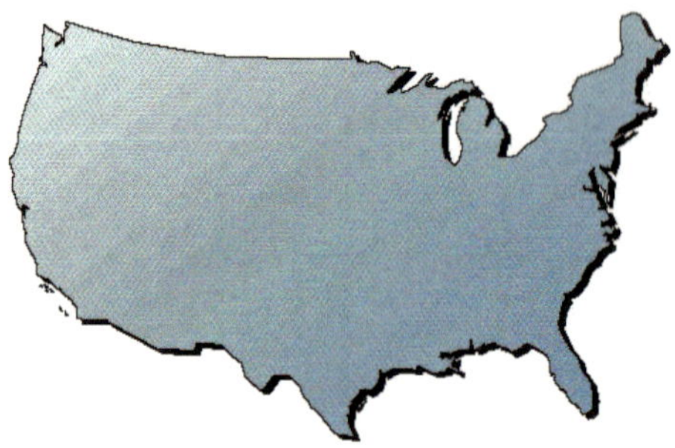

Skills workshop 3

p. 64 to **mention** [ˈmenʃn] — erwähnen →
p. 65 boardwalk [ˈbɔːdwɔːk] — hölzerne Uferpromenade *(am Strand)*
research [rɪˈsɜːtʃ] — Forschung
checklist [ˈtʃeklɪst] — Checkliste, Kontrollliste →
double [ˈdʌbl] — Doppel-, zweimal

Achte auf die Schreibung!

I wrote a *checklist* so I didn't forget anything.

Unit 4 Our smart world

VOCABULARY SKILLS

Lerntipp: Vokabeln nebenbei wiederholen

Lerne deine Vokabeln. Wenn du damit fertig bist, schreibst du die Vokabeln, die dir Schwierigkeiten bereitet haben (beim Lernen oder bei der Aussprache), auf kleine farbige Kärtchen. Verwende pro Vokabel ein Kärtchen. Diese hängst du nun an verschiedenen, gut sichtbaren Stellen bei dir zu Hause auf. Wähle Orte, an denen du öfters vorbeikommst (z. B. Kühlschranktür, Haustür, Telefon, Toilettenspiegel …). Jedes Mal, wenn du ein Kärtchen siehst, sprichst du die Vokabel dreimal laut aus.

Du wirst sehen: Bald kannst du dir die schwierigeren Vokabeln mindestens genauso gut merken wie die einfacheren.

Check-in

p. 68	**smart** [smɑːt]	schlau, klug →	He knew all the answers. He's really *smart.*
	space [speɪs]	Weltraum; Raum	
	Earth [ɜːθ]	Erde →	Our world.
	technology [tek'nɒlədʒi]	Technologie	
p. 69	**invention** [ɪn'venʃn]	Erfindung →	to invent → *invention*
	agency ['eɪdʒntsi]	Agentur, Behörde →	NASA is the US space *agency.*
	robot ['rəʊbɒt]	Roboter	
	remote control [rɪˌməʊt kən'trəʊl]	Fernbedienung →	You need a *remote control* for your TV.
	astronaut ['æstrənɔːt]	Astronaut/-in →	An *astronaut* works in space.
	reality [ri'æləti]	Realität, Wirklichkeit →	real → *reality*
	to **practice** *(AE)* ['præktɪs]	üben →	*to practice* (AE) = to practise (BE)
	device [dɪ'vaɪs]	Gerät, Vorrichtung	
	pacemaker ['peɪsˌmeɪkə]	Herzschrittmacher	
	satellite ['sætəlaɪt]	Satellit →	Achte auf die Aussprache!
	GPS (global positioning system) [ˌdʒiː piː 'es]	GPS *(ein satellitengestütztes Navigationssystem)*	
	row [rəʊ]	Reihe →	The farmer has *rows* of corn in his field.
	space station ['speɪs ˌsteɪʃn]	Raumstation	
	to **repair** [rɪ'peə]	reparieren, ausbessern →	I had a flat tyre, so I had to *repair* it.
	gravity ['grævəti]	Schwerkraft →	If there was no *gravity* on earth we would fly away.
	electrical [ɪ'lektrɪkl]	elektrisch	
	scan [skæn]	Ultraschall(untersuchung)	
	to **transmit** [trænz'mɪt]	funken, senden	
	mechanic [mɪ'kænɪk]	Mechaniker/-in →	A *mechanic* repairs cars, motorbikes, etc.

Unit 4

Die NASA

Die *National Aeronautics and Space Administration* (NASA) wurde 1958 gegründet. Sie ist die zivile US-Bundesbehörde für Luft- und Raumfahrt. Zur Zeit ist die NASA mit anderen Ländern gemeinsam am Bau der Internationalen Raumstation (ISS) beteiligt. Ein weiteres aktuelles Projekt ist das *Constellation*-Programm. Danach sollen 2019 Menschen zum Mond und später auch zum Mars fliegen. Für solche bemannten Missionen wird das *Space Shuttle* eingesetzt. Es ist außen mit hitzebeständigen Kacheln verkleidet, so dass es beim Wiedereintritt in die Erdatmosphäre nicht zu stark beschädigt wird und für weitere Missionen verwendet werden kann.
Viele Projekte der NASA werden jedoch unbemannt durchgeführt, indem Sonden und Roboter zur Erforschung losgeschickt werden. Hierfür verwendet man Raumkapseln, die nur einmal eingesetzt werden können, da sie beim Wiedereintritt in die Erdatmosphäre stark beschädigt werden. Auf unbemannten Missionen erforscht die NASA z. B. den Mond, unser Sonnensystem und vorbeifliegende Kometen.

Gibt es in Deutschland eine ähnliche Einrichtung wie die NASA? Wie viele deutsche Astronauten waren schon im All? Würdest du gern einmal zum Mond oder Mars fliegen?

Language 1

p. 70	to **float** [fləʊt]	schweben; treiben →	Astronauts *float* in space.
	rocket [ˈrɒkɪt]	Rakete →	NASA uses *rockets* to fly to the moon.
p. 71	**planet** [ˈplænɪt]	Planet →	Achte auf die Aussprache!

Language 2

p. 72	**intelligent** [ɪnˈtelɪdʒnt]	intelligent, klug →	An *intelligent* person learns quickly.
	to **switch off** [ˌswɪtʃ ˈɒf]	ausschalten →	to switch on ↔ *to switch off*
	so that [səʊ ˈðæt]	sodass	
	burglar [ˈbɜːglə]	Einbrecher/-in →	a *burglar*
	refrigerator [rɪˈfrɪdʒəreɪtə]	Kühlschrank →	A *refrigerator* keeps food cold and fresh.
	sink [sɪŋk]	Waschbecken, Spülbecken →	You wash your hands and clean your teeth in the *sink*.
	to **leak** [liːk]	auslaufen, lecken →	The bathroom sink is *leaking*.
	plug [plʌg]	Stöpsel; Stecker →	I left the *plug* in the sink and the tap on. There was water everywhere.
	faucet *(AE)* [ˈfɔːsɪt]	Wasserhahn →	*faucet* (AE) = tap (BE)
	microwave [ˈmaɪkrəweɪv]	Mikrowelle →	You can cook food quickly in a *microwave*.
	hairdryer [ˈheəˌdraɪə]	Fön →	hair + dryer = *hairdryer*
	electricity [ˌelɪkˈtrɪsəti]	Elektrizität, Strom →	You need *electricity* for a microwave, a hairdryer, a refrigerator, …

p. 72	to **cut off** [ˌkʌt ˈɒf]	abschneiden, abtrennen; *hier:* abstellen →	We didn't pay the electricity bill, so they *cut* us *off*.
	blackout [ˈblækaʊt]	Stromausfall →	If there is no electricity, there is a *blackout*.
	passive voice [ˌpæsɪv ˈvɔɪs]	Passiv (*Grammatik*)	
p. 73	**motel** [məʊˈtel]	Motel	
	reception [rɪˈsepʃn]	Rezeption, Empfang →	The person at the motel *reception* was very helpful.
	guest [gest]	Gast →	There were only 10 *guests* staying at the motel.
	light bulb [ˈlaɪt ˌbʌlb]	Glühbirne →	A light doesn't work if it hasn't got a *light bulb* in it.

Useful phrases: Something's wrong A B C

Die folgenden *phrases* helfen dir, wenn etwas kaputt ist oder nicht richtig funktioniert.

The light bulb is broken.	Die Glühbirne ist kaputt.
The bathroom sink is leaking.	Das Waschbecken im Bad ist undicht.
The faucet/tap is dripping.	Der Wasserhahn tropft.
The TV isn't working.	Der Fernseher funktioniert nicht.
The battery is dead.	Die Batterie ist leer.
The plug is missing.	Der Stecker fehlt.
The cord is damaged.	Das Kabel ist beschädigt.

Talkwise

p. 74	to **meet halfway** [miːt hɑːfˈweɪ]	sich (auf halbem Weg) entgegenkommen →	I don't agree! But I don't want to fight so let's *meet halfway*.
	negative [ˈnegətɪv]	negativ →	*negative* ↔ positive
	OK, it's a deal! [əʊˈkaɪ ɪts‿ə ˌdiːl]	Abgemacht!	

Text

p. 75	**alien** [ˈeɪliən]	Außerirdische/-r →	*Aliens* come from other planets.
	invader [ɪnˈveɪdə]	Eindringling	
	science fiction [ˌsaɪəns ˈfɪkʃn]	Science-Fiction →	Star Wars is a *science fiction* film and a book.
	ever since [ˌevə ˈsɪnts]	seitdem →	I've been a fan of Tokio Hotel *ever since* I heard their first song.
	to **zoom** [zuːm]	*hier:* rasen	
	sharply [ˈʃɑːpli]	scharf →	I turned the corner *sharply* and didn't see the old man.
	Watch it! [ˈwɒtʃ ˌɪt]	Pass auf!	
	to **turn round** [ˌtɜːn‿ˈraʊnd]	sich umdrehen →	Somebody was behind me. I *turned round* to see who it was.
	yard [jɑːd]	amerik./brit. Längenmaß, ca. 91,5 cm	

Unit 4

p. 75	to **leap**, **leapt**, **leapt** [li:p, lept, lept]	springen	
	to **soar** [sɔ:]	in die Höhe schnellen →	The bird *soared* high in the sky.
	to **curse** [kɜ:s]	fluchen	
	naturally ['nætʃrəli]	natürlich, selbstverständlich	
	speech [spi:tʃ]	Rede, Vortrag; Sprache →	His *speech* about space was really interesting.
	to **slam the door** [ˌslæm ðə 'dɔ:]	die Tür zuknallen →	She *slammed the door* in my face.
	pointed ['pɔɪntɪd]	spitz zulaufend →	Wizards wear *pointed* hats.
	to **remind s.o. of s.th.** [rɪ'maɪnd]	jdn. an etw. erinnern →	I wrote a shopping list to *remind me of what I needed*.
	dumb [dʌm]	blöde, dumm →	Achte auf die Schreibung und die Aussprache!
	to **squint** [skwɪnt]	blinzeln; schielen	
	bright [braɪt]	hell →	The sun was so *bright* I couldn't see the game.
	drooping ['dru:pɪŋ]	nach unten zeigend, herunterhängend	
	feature ['fi:tʃə]	Eigenschaft, Merkmal →	His best *feature* was his fair hair.
	I.Q. [ˌaɪ 'kju:]	IQ (Intelligenzquotient)	
	doubt [daʊt]	Zweifel →	Achte auf die Schreibung und die Aussprache!
	whether ['weðə]	ob	
	stand [stænd]	Tribüne →	In a stadium you sit in the *stands* to watch the match.
	beside [bɪ'saɪd]	neben →	I stood *beside* the statue to have my photo taken.
p. 76	**weird** [wɪəd]	seltsam, komisch →	Achte auf die Schreibung!
	transmitter [ˌtrænz'mɪtə]	Sendegerät, Funkgerät	
	short [ʃɔ:t]	zu wenig →	We didn't have enough players, we were one player *short*.
	to **slide**, **slid**, **slid** [ˌslaɪd, slɪd, slɪd]	rutschen →	He *slid off* the bench.
	bench [bentʃ]	Bank →	There are usually *benches* in parks for people to sit on.
	to **split apart** [ˌsplɪt‿ə'pɑ:t]	auseinanderbrechen	
	fluid ['flu:ɪd]	Flüssigkeit →	Water is a *fluid*.
	electronics [ˌelek'trɒnɪks]	Elektronik	
	compact ['kɒmpækt]	kompakt	
	antenna [æn'tenə]	Antenne →	Achte auf die Schreibung und die Aussprache!
	enormous [ɪ'nɔ:məs]	riesig, enorm, gewaltig →	The Grand Canyon is *enormous*.
	booster ['bu:stə]	Verstärker	
	wooden ['wʊdn]	hölzern, Holz- →	We have got a *wooden* bench in our garden.
	button ['bʌtn]	Knopf →	You can push the *button* to make something work and there are also *buttons* on shirts.
	hum [hʌm]	Brummen, Summen	
	motor ['məʊtə]	Motor →	Achte auf die Aussprache!

p. 76	to **transform** [ˌtræns'fɔ:m]	sich verwandeln	
	communications terminal [ˌkəmju:nɪkeɪʃnz 'tɜ:mɪnl]	Übertragungsterminal	

Die unregelmäßigen Verbformen A B C

Auch wenn Verben unregelmäßige Formen haben, gibt es einige Hilfen, mit denen du sie dir besser merken kannst.

Bei einigen Verben ist die 2. und die 3. Stammform gleich:

to bring	***brought***	***brought***	bringen
to find	***found***	***found***	finden
to have	***had***	***had***	haben
to hear	***heard***	***heard***	hören
to leave	***left***	***left***	verlassen
to meet	***met***	***met***	treffen
to read	***read***	***read***	lesen
to teach	***taught***	***taught***	lehren
to win	***won***	***won***	gewinnen

Bei anderen Verben ist die 1. und 3. Stammform sehr ähnlich, wie z. B.

*to **be***	*was*	***be**en*	sein
*to **do***	*did*	***do**ne*	machen, tun
*to **give***	*gave*	***give**n*	geben
*to **hid**e*	*hid*	***hid**den*	verstecken
*to **rid**e*	*rode*	***rid**den*	fahren, reiten
*to **see***	*saw*	***see**n*	sehen
*to **writ**e*	*wrote*	***writ**ten*	schreiben

area code ['eəriə ˌkəʊd]	(Orts-)Vorwahl →	You have to use the *area code* if you phone someone in another town.
frequency ['fri:kwəntsi]	Frequenz	
not … nor [nɔ:]	weder … noch	
to **delay** [dɪ'leɪ]	aufschieben, hinauszögern →	My brother was sick so we *delayed* going on vacation.
invasion [ɪn'veɪʒn]	Invasion, Einmarsch	
to **investigate** [ɪn'vestɪgeɪt]	ermitteln, untersuchen	
narrator [nə'reɪtə]	Erzähler/-in →	The person who tells a story.
setting ['setɪŋ]	Rahmen, Schauplatz	
beginning [bɪ'gɪnɪŋ]	Anfang →	to begin → *beginning*

Wordwise

p. 78	**broken** ['brəʊkn]	kaputt

Check-out

p. 80	**UFO** ['juː ef 'əʊ]	UFO →	*UFO* = **U**nidentified **F**lying **O**bject

For my folder

Technology

Nun kennst du schon viele Begriffe zum Thema „Technik". Schreibe sie in deinen *folder* und lege für die Begriffe Wortfelder an.

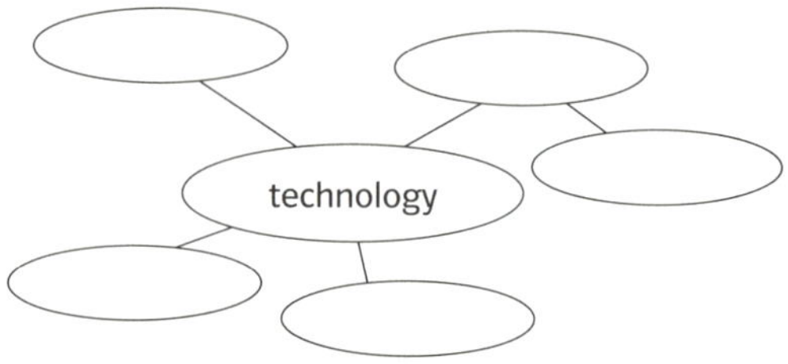

Skills workshop 4

p. 82	**statistics** pl. [stə'tɪstɪks]	Statistik →	*Statistics* are facts and information given in numbers.
	interest ['ɪntrəst]	Interesse	
p. 83	**first of all** [ˌfɜːst‿ɒf‿'ɔːl]	zuerst	
	result [rɪ'zʌlt]	Ergebnis, Resultat →	What was the *result* of the survey?
	type [taɪp]	Typ, Art →	a *type* of holiday = a kind of holiday
	per cent [pə'sent]	Prozent →	100 % = one hundred *per cent*
	secondly ['sekndli]	zweitens	
	in fact [ɪn 'fækt]	tatsächlich	
	foreign ['fɒrɪn]	fremd, ausländisch →	Achte auf die Schreibung!

Unit 5 At the movies

VOCABULARY SKILLS

Lerntipp: Zeitmanagement beim Vokabellernen

Du hast schon gelernt, dass man sich Vokabeln umso besser merken kann, je öfter man sie wiederholt.

Lerne Vokabeln zunächst in deiner aufnahmefähigsten Zeit. Beschäftige dich dann mit etwas anderem. Triff dich z. B. mit Freunden, gehe ins Kino oder treibe Sport. Bevor du schlafen gehst, solltest du dir aber noch einmal fünf Minuten Zeit nehmen und die neuen Vokabeln intensiv und konzentriert durchlesen. Das Gleiche solltest du morgens gleich nach dem Aufwachen tun. Das Gehirn wird so zu verschiedenen Zeiten immer wieder daran erinnert, dass es sich um wichtige Infos handelt, die es speichern muss.

Check-in

p. 84	**proud** [praʊd]	stolz	
	overwhelmed [ˌəʊvə'welmd]	überwältigt →	She was *overwhelmed* when she won the Oscar for the best actress.

p. 84	**romantic** [rə'mæntɪk]	romantisch	
	to **get divorced** [ˌget dɪ'vɔːsd]	sich scheiden lassen →	to get married ↔ *to get divorced*
	handsome ['hænsəm]	attraktiv, gut aussehend →	a *handsome* man = a good-looking man
	gangster movie ['gæŋkstə ˌmuːvi]	Gangsterfilm	
	comedy ['kɒmədi]	Komödie (*Filmart*) →	A *comedy* is a funny film.

Hollywood

Hollywood ist für Viele der Inbegriff der Filmindustrie. Eigentlich ist Hollywood ein Stadtteil von Los Angeles und heißt übersetzt „Stechpalmenwald". 1911 wurde dort das erste Filmstudio gegründet und im selben Jahr siedelten sich noch zehn weitere Filmstudios an. Das sonnige Kalifornien war zum Filmen ideal, da es damals noch kein geeignetes Kunstlicht gab.
Heute sind die wichtigsten Hollywood-Studios *Universal Studios (Miami Vice, The Fast and the Furious, Bridget Jones)* und *Warner Brothers (Herr der Ringe, Matrix, Harry Potter)*. Wer nach Hollywood kommt, erwartet natürlich, überall Stars zu sehen. Aber auch wenn die Wahrscheinlichkeit relativ hoch ist, einen Prominenten zu sehen, wohnen die meisten von ihnen nicht direkt in Hollywood, sondern im nahe gelegenen Beverly Hills, in Malibu oder in anderen Teilen von Los Angeles.

Welche deutschen Filme kennst du? Stimmt das Klischee von Hollywood als reiner Glamourwelt? Gibt es auch Schattenseiten?

p. 85	to **shoot, shot, shot** [ʃuːt, ʃɒt, ʃɒt]	*(einen Film)* drehen →	Many movies are *shot* in Hollywood.
	silent ['saɪlənt]	stumm	
	the late 1920s [ðə 'leɪt ˌnaɪn'tiːnˌtwentiːz]	die späten Zwanzigerjahre des 20. Jahrhunderts	
	ceremony ['serɪməni]	Zeremonie →	The actors get their Oscars at a *ceremony*.
	award [ə'wɔːd]	Auszeichnung →	The Oscar is an important movie *award*.
	director [dɪ'rektə]	Regisseur/-in →	Steven Spielberg is a famous Hollywood film *director*.

Language 1

p. 86	to **direct** [dɪ'rekt]	Regie führen →	*to direct* → director
	as if [æz‿'ɪf]	als ob	
	to **scream** [skriːm]	schreien →	The movie was scary and I *screamed*.
	photography [fə'tɒgrəfi]	Fotografie	
	to **introduce** [ˌɪntrə'djuːs]	einführen; vorstellen →	Movies with people talking were *introduced* after silent ones.

Unit 5

p. 86	**graphics** pl. [ˈɡræfɪks]	Grafiken →	All movies today have computer *graphics* in them.
	special effects [ˌspeʃl ɪˈfekts]	Spezialeffekte *(von Computern erzeugter Bild- und Toneffekt)*	
	romance [rəʊˈmænts]	Liebesfilm; Romanze	
	to **live happily ever after** [lɪv ˈhæpɪli evə‿ɑːftə]	glücklich und zufrieden bis ans Lebensende leben →	A movie has a good ending when everybody *lives happily ever after.*
p. 87	**journalist** [ˈdʒɜːnəlɪst]	Journalist/-in →	*Journalists* write articles for magazines and newspapers.
	to **interview** [ˈɪntəvjuː]	interviewen, befragen →	*to interview* → interview
	studio [ˈstjuːdiəʊ]	Studio →	Not all movies are shot outside, sometimes *studios* are used.
	brutal [ˈbruːtl]	brutal →	Achte auf die Aussprache!

Language 2

p. 88	to **whip** [wɪp]	schlagen; peitschen	
	wild [waɪld]	wild →	quiet, calm ↔ *wild*
	gentleman [ˈdʒentlmən]	Herr, Gentleman	
	to **grow up** [ɡrəʊ‿ˈʌp]	aufwachsen, erwachsen werden	
p. 89	**reported speech** [rɪˌpɔːtɪd ˈspiːtʃ]	indirekte Rede	

Talkwise

p. 90	to **recommend** [ˌrekəˈmend]	empfehlen →	I really liked that movie. I *recommended* it to all my friends.

Words with no plural A B C

Einige Nomen haben im Englischen keine Pluralform. Deshalb braucht man zur Mengenangabe eine Umschreibung wie z. B. *a piece of, some* usw.

advice → *He gave me a piece of advice.* (einen Ratschlag)
furniture → *She has some beautiful furniture.* (Möbelstücke)
information → *There are two pieces of information in the text.* (zwei Informationen)
news → *She told me three pieces of news.* (drei Nachrichten)
thunder → *I heard two claps of thunder last night.* (zwei Donnerschläge)
lightning → *There was a flash of lightning during the storm.* (einen Blitz)

In den meisten Wörterbüchern sind solche Wörter mit einem Hinweis, wie z. B. „kein Plural" oder „nicht zählbar", gekennzeichnet.

Text

			You will find **all** the new words from this text in the Dictionary (from page 174); here are the most important ones.
p. 91	**show-business** ['ʃəʊ ˌbɪznɪs]	Showgeschäft	
	biography [baɪ'ɒgrəfi]	Biografie, Lebensgeschichte →	Achte auf die Schreibung!
	fame [feɪm]	Ruhm →	*fame* → famous
	overnight [ˌəʊvə'naɪt]	über Nacht →	He became famous *overnight*. = He became famous very quickly.
	sensation [sen'seɪʃn]	Sensation →	Achte auf die Aussprache!
	premiere ['premieə]	Premiere, Uraufführung →	Achte auf die Aussprache!
	private ['praɪvɪt]	privat	
	autograph ['ɔ:təgrɑ:f]	Autogramm →	If stars sign their names and give it to their fans, they give them an *autograph*.
	seeker ['si:kə]	Suchende/-r; *hier:* Jäger/-in →	A *seeker* is a person that looks for something.
	photographer [fə'tɒgrəfə]	Fotograf/-in →	*photographer* → photography
	to **photograph** ['fəʊtəgrɑ:f]	fotografieren →	*to photograph* → photographer, photography
	to **expect** [ɪk'spekt]	erwarten →	I *expected* to get a better grade in my German test.
	authority [ɔ:'θɒrəti]	Autorität	
	third-grader [ˌθɜ:d 'greɪdə]	Drittklässler →	first-grader, second-grader, *third-grader*, fourth-grader, …
	attractive [ə'træktɪv]	attraktiv	
	talk show ['tɔ:k ˌʃəʊ]	Talkshow	
	entertainment [ˌentə'teɪnmənt]	Unterhaltung →	Movies, songs and plays are all kinds of *entertainment*.
	to **admit** [əd'mɪt]	zugeben →	I didn't want to go to the movie, but I *admit* it was really good.
	nightclub ['naɪtklʌb]	Disko, Nachtklub	
p. 92	**alcohol** (no pl.) ['ælkəhɒl]	Alkohol →	Achte auf die Schreibung und die Aussprache!
	crowd [kraʊd]	Menschenmenge; *hier:* Clique →	There were a lot of people at the football match. = There was a big *crowd*.
	especially [ɪ'speʃəli]	besonders, vor allem →	I like sport, *especially* baseball and basketball.
	familiar [fə'mɪliə]	vertraut →	Things that you know well are *familiar* to you.
	surroundings pl. [sə'raʊndɪŋz]	Umgebung →	Your *surroundings* are the area where you live.
	to **be addicted to …** [bi ə'dɪktɪd tʊ]	süchtig nach … sein	
	wonderful ['wʌndəfl]	wunderbar →	great – fantastic – *wonderful*
	to **wear off** [weər 'ɒf]	nachlassen →	Her happiness didn't last long. It soon began to *wear off*.
	addiction [ə'dɪkʃn]	Sucht; Abhängigkeit →	to be addicted to → *addiction*
	to **hire** [haɪə]	einstellen; mieten →	*to hire* someone = to give someone a job

Unit 5

p. 92	**yet another** [jet ə'nʌðə]	noch ein/-e	
	truth [tru:θ]	Wahrheit →	true → *truth*
	to **get drunk** [get 'drʌŋk]	sich betrinken	
	beer [bɪə]	Bier →	Achte auf die Schreibung!
	curfew ['kɜ:fju:]	Ausgangssperre; Sperrstunde	
	to **break a rule** [ˌbreɪk‿ə 'ru:l]	eine Regel brechen →	*to break a rule* = not do as a rule says
	least [li:st]	geringste/-r/-s →	*least* ↔ most
	crime [kraɪm]	Verbrechen	
	to **swear, swore, sworn** [sweə, swɔ: swɔ:n]	fluchen; schwören →	It's not very polite *to swear* at people.
	sober ['səʊbə]	nüchtern →	*sober* ↔ drunk
	to **function** ['fʌnkʃn]	funktionieren →	*to function* = to work
	breakdown ['breɪkdaʊn]	(Nerven)zusammenbruch	
	painful ['peɪnfʊl]	schmerzhaft →	*painful* ↔ painless

Wordwise

p. 94	**balloon** [bə'lu:n]	Luftballon →	Achte auf die Schreibung und die Aussprache!
	sponge [spʌndʒ]	Schwamm	

Wordbuilding II A B C

Es gibt verschiedene Möglichkeiten, um aus einem Verb ein Nomen abzuleiten.

1. Du kannst die Endung *-ing* anhängen:

   to build → a building
   to meet → a meeting

2. Manche Nomen werden mit der Endung *-er* oder *-or* gebildet. Solche Nomen bezeichnen meistens eine Person:

   to ride → a rider
   to visit → a visitor

3. Es gibt auch die Endung *-tion*:

   to define → a definition
   to invent → an invention

4. Sehr oft haben Verb und Nomen auch dieselbe Form:

   to call → a call
   to dream → a dream
   to fight → a fight

For my folder
The Oscars

Finde die Namen der Gewinner der letzten Oscarverleihung heraus.
Wer hat den Oscar in diesen Kategorien gewonnen?

- bester Film
- bester Dokumentarfilm
- beste Regie
- beste Hauptdarstellerin
- bester Hauptdarsteller
- bester fremdsprachiger Film

Skills workshop 5

p. 98	**cluster** ['klʌstə]	Cluster *(einfaches Wörternetz)*	
p. 99	**Hispanic** [hɪ'spænɪk]	hispanisch, lateinamerikanisch; Lateinamerikaner/-in	
	Spanish ['spænɪʃ]	spanisch, Spanisch; Spanier/-in →	*Spanish* is spoken in Spain, Latin America and parts of the US.
	local ['ləʊkl]	örtlich, ortsansässig, lokal	
	business ['bɪznɪs]	Geschäft; Branche →	Achte auf die Schreibung!
	population [ˌpɒpjə'leɪʃn]	Bevölkerung →	The *population* is the number of people who live somewhere.
	to **discover** [dɪ'skʌvə]	entdecken →	*to discover* = to find
	several ['sevrəl]	einige, mehrere, verschiedene	
	divided [dɪ'vaɪdɪd]	aufgeteilt	
	ranch *(AE)* [ræntʃ]	Ranch →	*ranch* (AE) = farm (BE)
	grain [greɪn]	Getreide	
	pineapple ['paɪnˌæpl]	Ananas	
	real estate *(AE)* ['rɪəl ɪˌsteɪt]	Immobilien →	*real estate* (AE) = buildings for sale (BE)
	community [kəm'ju:nəti]	Gemeinde →	A group of people who live in an area.
	to **pave** [peɪv]	pflastern	
	boulevard ['bu:ləvɑ:d]	Boulevard	

The US flag (page 11)

There is one star for each of the fifty states of the US. When the US got its freedom from England in 1776, there were only thirteen states in the US. The flag has one stripe for each of those states.

English – German

Dictionary

In dieser alphabetischen Liste ist das Vokabular von *Red Line 1* bis *4* enthalten. Namen werden in einer gesonderten Liste am Ende des Vokabulars aufgelistet (ab Seite 197).
Die mit * gekennzeichneten Verben sind unregelmäßig.
Wendungen, die aus mehreren Wörtern bestehen, werden meist unter mehreren Stichwörtern aufgeführt. So ist z. B. *a little* sowohl unter *a* als auch unter *little* zu finden.
Die Fundstellen verweisen auf das erstmalige Vorkommen der Wörter, z. B.
about [ə'baʊt] über **I** kommt zum ersten Mal in Band I vor.
accident ['æksɪdnt] Unfall **II** kommt zum ersten Mal in Band II vor.
age [eɪdʒ] Alter **III** kommt zum ersten Mal in Band III vor.
action ['ækʃn] Handlung **IV U1,** 19 kommt zum ersten Mal in Band IV, Unit 1, Seite 19, vor.
cable car ['keɪbl ˌkɑː] Straßenbahn **IV ZI,** 10 kommt zum ersten Mal in Band IV, Zoom-in, Seite 10, vor.
Ist die Fundstelle mit Spitzklammern versehen, weist das darauf hin, dass das Wort zum fakultativen Wortschatz zählt.

A

a [ə], **an** [ən] ein/-e **I**
a few [ə 'fjuː] ein paar, einige **I**
a little [ə 'lɪtl] ein bisschen **I**
a long time ago [ə lɒŋ 'taɪm ˌəgəʊ] vor langer Zeit **II**
a lot [ə 'lɒt] sehr; viel **I**
a lot of [ə 'lɒt‿əv] viel/-e, eine Menge **I**
about [ə'baʊt] über; wegen **I**; ungefähr, etwa **II**; umher **III**
above [ə'bʌv] über, oberhalb; oben **I**
abracadabra [ˌæbrəkə'dæbrə] Abrakadabra **II**
accent ['æksnt] Akzent **IV U3,** 56
to **accept** [ək'sept] akzeptieren, annehmen **IV U1,** 21
accident ['æksɪdnt] Unfall **II**
across [ə'krɒs] auf der anderen Seite von; über **I**
to **act** [ækt] spielen **I**; sich verhalten, sich benehmen **II**
action ['ækʃn] Handlung **IV U1,** 19
action movie ['ækʃn ˌmuːvi] Actionfilm **IV U5,** 87
active ['æktɪv] aktiv, tätig ⟨**IV U1,** 30⟩
activity [æk'tɪvəti] Aktivität **III**
activity centre [ˌæktɪvəti 'sentə] Jugendzentrum **III**
actor ['æktə] Schauspieler **I**
actress ['æktrəs] Schauspielerin **I**
actually [ˌæktʃʊəli] eigentlich; übrigens **IV U1,** 14
adapted [ə'dæptɪd] bearbeitet **IV U3,** 58
to **add** [æd] hinzufügen; addieren **III**
addiction [ə'dɪkʃn] Sucht; Abhängigkeit **IV U5,** 92
address [ə'dres] Adresse, Anschrift **II**
adjective ['ædʒɪktɪv] Adjektiv, Eigenschaftswort **I**
admission [əd'mɪʃn] Eintritt; Zutritt, Einlass **III**
to **admit** [əd'mɪt] zugeben **IV U5,** 91
adrenaline [ə'drenəlɪn] Adrenalin **IV U3,** 57
adult ['ædʌlt] Erwachsene/-r **I**
advantage [əd'vɑːntɪdʒ] Vorteil **III**
adventure [əd'ventʃə] Abenteuer **IV U3,** 52
adverb ['ædvɜːb] Adverb, Umstandswort **II**
advice (no pl.) [əd'vaɪs] Rat, Ratschlag **IV U2,** 34
after ['ɑːftə] nach **I**
after that ['ɑːftə ˌðæt] danach **I**
afternoon [ˌɑːftə'nuːn] Nachmittag **I**
aftershave ['ɑːftəʃeɪv] Aftershave, Rasierwasser **III**
again [ə'gen] noch einmal, wieder **I**
against [ə'genst] gegen **II**
age [eɪdʒ] Alter **III**
agency ['eɪdʒəntsi] Agentur, Behörde **IV U4,** 69
. . . ago [ə'gəʊ] vor … **II**
a long time ago [ə lɒŋ 'taɪm ˌəgəʊ] vor langer Zeit **II**
to **agree** [ə'griː] zustimmen **II**
ain't (= is not) [eɪnt] ist nicht *(Umgangssprache)* ⟨**IV U1,** 21⟩
air [eə] Luft **II**
air mail ['eə meɪl] Luftpost **II**
airport ['eəpɔːt] Flughafen **III**
alarm clock [ə'lɑːm ˌklɒk] Wecker **I**
album ['ælbəm] Album **III**
alcohol (no pl.) ['ælkəhɒl] Alkohol **IV U5,** 92
A-Level (= Advanced Level) ['eɪlevl = ˌədvɑːnst 'levl] *brit. Abitur* **III**
alien ['eɪliən] Außerirdische/-r **IV U4,** 75
alive [ə'laɪv] lebendig **III**
all [ɔːl] alle **I**; ganz **II**
allegiance [ə'liːdʒənts] Treue **IV U2,** 33
almost ['ɔːlməʊst] fast, beinahe **II**
alone [ə'ləʊn] allein **I**
alphabet ['ælfəbet] Alphabet **I**
already [ɔːl'redi] bereits, schon **II**
also ['ɔːlsəʊ] auch **I**
although [ɔːl'ðəʊ] obwohl **II**
always ['ɔːlweɪz] immer **I**
am [ˌeɪ'em] vormittags **I**
amazing [ə'meɪzɪŋ] erstaunlich; unglaublich; toll **IV U1,** 20
American [ə'merɪkən] amerikanisch, Amerikaner/-in **III**
ancestor ['ænsestə] Vorfahr ⟨**IV U3,** 66⟩
ancient ['eɪnʃnt] alt, antik **III**
and [ænd; ən] und **I**
angry ['æŋgri] verärgert, wütend **I**
animal ['ænɪml] Tier **I**
animation [ˌænɪ'meɪʃn] Animation **IV U2,** 47
announcement [ə'naʊnsmənt] Ankündigung, Bekanntgabe **II**
another [ə'nʌðə] noch ein/eine(-r/-s), ein(e) weitere(-r/-s) **I**; ein anderer, eine andere, ein anderes **II**
answer ['ɑːnsə] Antwort **I**
to **answer** ['ɑːnsə] beantworten; antworten **I**
answering machine ['ɑːnsrɪŋ məˌʃiːn] Anrufbeantworter **III**
antenna [æn'tenə] Antenne **IV U4,** 76
any ['eni] (irgend)welche **II**; jede/-r/-s **II**

anybody ['enibɒdi] irgendjemand **III**
anyone ['eniwʌn] (irgend)jemand **IV U1,** 20
anything ['eniθɪŋ] (irgend)etwas **II**
anyway ['eniweɪ] sowieso **II**
anywhere ['eniweə] irgendwo **III**
apartment *(AE)* [ə'pɑ:tmənt] Wohnung **IV U3,** 63
to **apologize** [ə'pɒlədʒaɪz] sich entschuldigen **III**
to **appear** [ə'pɪə] erscheinen, auftauchen ⟨**IV U4,** 77⟩
appetite ['æpɪtaɪt] Appetit **II**
apple ['æpl] Apfel **I**
apple pie ['æpl ˌpaɪ] gedeckter Apfelkuchen **II**
application form [ˌæplɪ'keɪʃn ˌfɔ:m] Bewerbungsformular **III**
apprentice [ə'prentɪs] Auszubildende/-r, Lehrling **II**
apprentice wizard [əˌprentɪs 'wɪzəd] Zauberlehrling **II**
April ['eɪprəl] April **I**
architect ['ɑ:kɪtekt] Architekt/-in **III**
area ['eəriə] Gegend; Gebiet **II**
area code ['eəriə ˌkəʊd] (Orts-)Vorwahl **IV U4,** 76
to **argue** ['ɑ:gju:] diskutieren, sich auseinandersetzen; sich streiten **III**
argument ['ɑ:gjəmənt] Streit, Auseinandersetzung; Argument **III**
to have an argument [ˌhæv‿ən‿'ɑ:gjəmənt] (sich) streiten **III**
arm [ɑ:m] Arm **II**
army ['ɑ:mi] Armee **II**
around ... [ə'raʊnd] um ... herum **I**
to **arrange** [ə'reɪndʒ] organisieren, verabreden **III**
arrangement [ə'reɪndʒmənt] Vereinbarung, Abmachung **III**
to **arrest** [ə'rest] festnehmen, verhaften **III**
to **arrive** [ə'raɪv] ankommen, eintreffen **II**
Art [ɑ:t] Kunst **II**
article ['ɑ:tɪkl] Artikel; Gegenstand **III**
as [æz] wie **III**
as ... as [əz ... əz] (genau)so ... wie **II**
as if [əz‿'ɪf] als ob **IV U5,** 86
as long as [əz 'lɒŋ‿əz] solange **III**
as soon as [əz 'su:n‿əz] sobald **III**
Asian ['eɪʒn] asiatisch, Asiat/-in **IV U1,** 21
to **ask** [ɑ:sk] fragen; (eine Frage) stellen **I**
assembly [ə'sembli] Schulversammlung **II**
assistant [ə'sɪstnt] Verkäufer/-in **I**; Assistent/-in **III**
astronaut ['æstrənɔ:t] Astronaut/-in **IV U4,** 69
at [æt; ət] an; auf; in; bei; um **I**
at all [æt 'ɔ:l] überhaupt **II**
at least [ˌət 'li:st] mindestens, wenigstens **IV U1,** 20
at the bottom [æt ðə 'bɒtəm] ganz unten **IV U2,** 39
at the moment [ˌæt ðə 'məʊmənt] im Augenblick, momentan **I**
athletics [æθ'letɪks] (Leicht-)Athletik **III**
attic ['ætɪk] Dachboden, Speicher **II**
attraction [ə'trækʃn] Sehenswürdigkeit **IV U1,** 29
attractive [ə'træktɪv] attraktiv **IV U5,** 91
audience ['ɔ:diəns] Publikum **I**
audition [ɔ:'dɪʃn] Vorspielen, Vorsprechen, Vorsingen, Vortanzen **II**
August ['ɔ:gəst] August **I**
aunt [ɑ:nt] Tante **I**
authority [ɔ:'θɒrəti] Autorität **IV U5,** 91
autograph ['ɔ:təgrɑ:f] Autogramm **IV U5,** 91
autumn ['ɔ:təm] Herbst **I**
awake [ə'weɪk] wach **II**
award [ə'wɔ:d] Auszeichnung **IV U5,** 85
away [ə'weɪ] weg, fort **II**
awesome ['ɔ:səm] Ehrfurcht gebietend **III**; toll, super **IV U2,** 36
awful ['ɔ:fl] schrecklich **I**

B

baby ['beɪbi] pl. **babies** ['beɪbiz] Baby **I**
back [bæk] Rücken **II**; zurück **I**
at the back of the book [æt ðə 'bæk‿əv ðə ˌbʊk] hinten im Buch **II**
back door [ˌbæk 'dɔ:] Hecktür; Hintertür **II**
back pocket [ˌbæk 'pɒkɪt] hintere Hosentasche **II**
background ['bækgraʊnd] Hintergrund **IV U1,** 15
backpack *(AE)* ['bækpæk] Rucksack **IV U2,** 39
bacon ['beɪkn] Speck **II**
bad [bæd] schlecht **I**
badminton ['bædmɪntən] Badminton, Federball **I**
bag [bæg] Tasche; Tüte **I**
bagel *(AE)* ['beɪgl] Bagel (*weiches, ringförmiges Brötchen*) **IV U1,** 17
ball [bɔ:l] Ball **I**
balloon [be'lu:n] Luftballon **IV U5,** 94
ballpark *(AE)* ['bɔ:lpɑ:k] *Stadion für Ballsportarten* **IV U3,** 65
banana [bə'nɑ:nə] Banane **II**
band [bænd] Band **I**
bang [bæŋ] Knall **I**
banner ['bænə] Fahne **IV U1,** 15
bar [bɑ:] Tafel **I**
bark [bɑ:k] Bellen **III**
to **bark** [bɑ:k] bellen **I**
barn [bɑ:n] Stall; Scheune **I**
baseball ['beɪsbɔ:l] Baseball **IV U2,** 33
basement ['beɪsmənt] Kellergeschoss; Untergeschoss **III**
basket ['bɑ:skɪt] Korb **II**
basketball ['bɑ:skɪtbɔ:l] Basketball **I**
bass [beɪs] Bass **III**
bathroom ['bɑ:θrʊm] Badezimmer **I**
battery ['bætri] Akku, Batterie **II**
battle ['bætl] Schlacht, Kampf **II**
bay [beɪ] Bucht ⟨**IV U5,** 93⟩
*to **be** [bi:] sein **I**
Be careful! [ˌbi: 'keəfl] Sei vorsichtig! **I**
to be a pain [ˌbi: ə 'peɪn] jdm. auf den Geist gehen (*Umgangssprache*) **I**
to be able to [bi: 'eɪbl tʊ] können; fähig sein **III**
to be addicted to ... [bi ə'dɪktɪd‿tʊ] süchtig nach ... sein **IV U5,** 92
to be afraid of [ˌbi: ə'freɪd əv] Angst haben **III**
to be allowed to [bi: ə'laʊd tʊ] dürfen **III**
to be bored [bi: 'bɔ:d] sich langweilen **III**
to be crazy about [bi: 'kreɪzi əˌbaʊt] verrückt sein nach **IV U3,** 40
to be disappointed [ˌbi: dɪsə'pɔɪntɪd] enttäuscht sein **III**
to be fed up [bi: fed‿'ʌp] die Nase voll haben **III**
to be frightened [bi: 'fraɪtnd] Angst haben **III**
to be glad [ˌbi: 'glæd] froh sein **IV U3,** 54
to be good at ... [ˌbi: 'gʊd‿ət] ... gut können; gut sein in ... **I**
to be lucky [ˌbi: 'lʌki] Glück haben **II**
to be mad [bɪ 'mæd] wütend sein, sauer sein **II**
to be mad about ... [bi: 'mæd‿əbaʊt] verrückt sein nach **III**
to be mobbed [bi 'mɒbd] umringt sein/werden ⟨**IV U5,** 91⟩
to be scared [ˌbi: 'skeəd] Angst haben **I**

English – German

to be sick of s.th. ['sɪk‿əv] von etw. genug haben **IV U4,** 75
to be stuck [ˌbi: 'stʌk] hängen bleiben **IV U3,** 54
to be worried [ˌbi: 'wʌrɪd] besorgt sein, beunruhigt sein **II**
beach [bi:tʃ] Strand **II**
beard [bɪəd] Bart **III**
*to **beat** [bi:t] schlagen **IV U2,** 32
beautiful ['bju:tɪfʊl] schön, wunderschön, wundervoll **I**
because [bɪ'kɒz] weil, da **I**
*to **become** [bɪ'kʌm] werden **III**
bed [bed] Bett **I**
to go to bed [ˌgəʊ tə 'bed] ins Bett gehen **I**
bedroom ['bedrʊm] Schlafzimmer **I**
beep [bi:p] piep **II**
beer [bɪə] Bier **IV U5,** 92
before [bɪ'fɔ:] bevor; vor; vorher **I**
*to **begin** [bɪ'gɪn] anfangen, beginnen **III**
beginning [bɪ'gɪnɪŋ] Anfang **IV U4,** 76
behaviour [bɪ'heɪvjə] Benehmen, Verhalten **III**
behind [bɪ'haɪnd] hinter **I**
to **believe** [bɪ'li:v] glauben **I**
bell [bel] Glocke; Klingel **II**
to **belong** [bɪ'lɒŋ] angehören; gehören **IV U2,** 35
below [bɪ'ləʊ] unten; unter **II**
bench [bentʃ] Bank **IV U4,** 76
beside [bɪ'saɪd] neben **IV U4,** 75
best [best] beste/-r/-s **I**
Best wishes, [ˌbest 'wɪʃɪz] Viele Grüße (*am Briefende*) **III**
best-selling [ˌbest 'selɪŋ] meistverkauft **III**
*to **bet** [bet] wetten **III**
better ['betə] besser **I**
between [bɪ'twi:n] zwischen **I**
big [bɪg] groß **I**
bike [baɪk] Fahrrad **I**
bike ride [baɪk 'raɪd] Fahrradtour **II**
bike shed [ˌbaɪk 'ʃed] Fahrradschuppen **II**
bill [bɪl] Rechnung **III**
bill *(AE)* [bɪl] Geldschein **IV U1,** 17
billion ['bɪliən] Milliarde **II**
biography [baɪ'ɒgrəfi] Biografie, Lebensgeschichte **IV U5,** 91
Biology [baɪ'ɒlədʒi] Biologie **II**
bird [bɜ:d] Vogel **II**
birth [bɜ:θ] Geburt **III**
birthday ['bɜ:θdeɪ] Geburtstag **I**
biscuit ['bɪskɪt] Keks **III**
black [blæk] schwarz **I**
blackout ['blækaʊt] Stromausfall **IV U4,** 72
to **blend** [blend] vermischen **IV U1,** 21
blind [blaɪnd] blind **III**
blog [blɒg] Blog, Internettagebuch **III**
bloke [bləʊk] Typ, Kerl **III**
blue [blu:] blau **I**
board [bɔ:d] Tafel; Brett **I**
boardwalk ['bɔ:dwɔ:k] hölzerne Uferpromenade *(am Strand)* ⟨**IV U3,** 65⟩
boat [bəʊt] Boot **III**
body ['bɒdi] Körper **III**
bomb [bɒm] Bombe **IV U1,** 22
bone [bəʊn] Knochen **IV U3,** 54
book [bʊk] Buch **I**
bookshop ['bʊkʃɒp] Buchhandlung, Buchladen **II**
booster ['bu:stə] Verstärker **IV U4,** 76
boot [bu:t] Stiefel **III**
boring ['bɔ:rɪŋ] langweilig **I**
born [bɔ:n] geboren **I**
borough ['bʌrə] Bezirk, Stadtgemeinde **IV U1,** 15
to **borrow** ['bɒrəʊ] ausleihen **II**
both [bəʊθ] beide **I**
both ... and [bəʊθ] sowohl ... als auch **I**
to **bother** ['bɒðə] stören, belästigen **III**
bottle ['bɒtl] Flasche **I**
at the **bottom** [æt ðə 'bɒtəm] ganz unten **IV U2,** 39
to the **bottom** [tə ðe 'bɒtəm] bis ganz unten **IV U3,** 49
boulder ['bəʊldə] Felsblock, Felsbrocken **IV U3,** 54
boulevard ['bu:ləvɑ:d] Boulevard **IV U5,** 99
bowl [bəʊl] Napf, Schüssel, Schale **II**
box [bɒks] Schachtel; Karton; Kiste **I**
boy [bɔɪ] Junge **I**
boyfriend ['bɔɪfrend] Freund (*in einer Paarbeziehung*) **III**
to **brag (to s.o. about s.th.)** [bræg] (mit etw.) angeben, prahlen **IV U2,** 40
brave [breɪv] mutig; tapfer **II**
bread [bred] Brot **II**
break [breɪk] Pause **II**
*to **break** [breɪk] kaputt machen, (zer)brechen **III**
to break a rule [ˌbreɪk‿ə 'ru:l] eine Regel brechen **IV U5,** 92
to break down ['breɪk daʊn] zusammenbrechen, abstürzen **II**
breakable ['breɪkəbl] zerbrechlich **III**
breakdown ['breɪkdaʊn] (Nerven)-zusammenbruch **IV U5,** 92
breakfast ['brekfəst] Frühstück **I**
bridge [brɪdʒ] Brücke **I**
bright [braɪt] hell **IV U4,** 75
brilliant ['brɪliənt] fantastisch, hervorragend **II**
*to **bring** [brɪŋ] mitbringen; bringen **I**
to the **brink** [tə ðə 'brɪŋk] an den Rand **III**
British ['brɪtɪʃ] britisch, Brite/Britin **I**
brochure ['brəʊʃə] Broschüre **I**
broken ['brəʊkn] kaputt **IV U4,** 78
bronc rider ['brɒŋk ˌraɪdə] Rodeo-Reiter **IV U3,** 58
brother ['brʌðə] Bruder **I**
brown [braʊn] braun **I**
brownie ['braʊni] Brownie **II**
brutal ['bru:tl] brutal **IV U5,** 87
*to **build** [bɪld] bauen, aufbauen **I**
building ['bɪldɪŋ] Gebäude **III**
bully ['bʊlɪ] jemand, der andere tyrannisiert **IV U2,** 39
burger ['bɜ:gə] Burger **I**
burglar ['bɜ:glə] Einbrecher/-in **IV U4,** 72
bus [bʌs] pl. **buses** ['bʌsɪz] Bus **I**
bus stop ['bʌs ˌstɒp] Bushaltestelle **I**
double-decker bus [ˌdʌbldekə 'bʌs] Doppeldeckerbus **II**
bush [bʊʃ] Busch **III**
business ['bɪznɪs] Geschäft; Branche **IV U5,** 99
busy ['bɪzi] beschäftigt **I**; verkehrsreich, belebt **II**
but [bʌt] aber **I**
button ['bʌtn] Knopf **IV U4,** 76
*to **buy** [baɪ] kaufen **I**
by [baɪ] mit **I**; bis **II**; von **IV U1,** 21
by the way [ˌbaɪ ðə 'weɪ] übrigens **II**
Bye! [baɪ] Tschüss! **I**

C

cab *(AE)* [kæb] Taxi **IV U1,** 15
cabin ['kæbɪn] Hütte; Kabine **IV U3,** 52
cable-TV [ˌkeɪbl 'ti:vi:] Kabelfernsehen ⟨**IV U5,** 100⟩
cable car ['keɪbl ˌkɑ:] Straßenbahn **IV ZI,** 10
café ['kæfeɪ] Café **I**
cafeteria [ˌkæfə'tɪəriə] Cafeteria **I**
cake [keɪk] Kuchen **I**
calendar ['kæləndə] Kalender **I**
call [kɔ:l] Anruf **I**
to **call** [kɔ:l] anrufen; rufen; nennen **I**
to call s.o. back [ˌkɔ:l 'bæk] jdn. zurückrufen **III**
calm [kɑ:m] ruhig **III**

camera ['kæmrə] Kamera, Fotoapparat **II**
camper ['kæmpə] Camper/-in **IV U3,** 52
campfire ['kæmpfaɪə] Lagerfeuer **IV U3,** 52
camping ['kæmpɪŋ] Zelten, Camping ⟨**IV U5,** 100⟩
to go **camping** [ɡəʊ 'kæmpɪŋ] zelten gehen, campen **II**
campsite ['kæmpsaɪt] Campingplatz, Zeltplatz **II**
can [kæn] können **I**
Canadian [kə'neɪdiən] kanadisch; Kanadier/-in ⟨**IV U5,** 100⟩
candle ['kændl] Kerze **I**
cannot ['kænɒt] können nicht, kann/-st nicht **II**
canyon ['kænjən] Felsenschlucht, Canyon **IV U3,** 49
cap [kæp] Kappe, Schirmmütze **I**
capital ['kæpɪtl] Hauptstadt **IV ZI,** 12
capital letter [ˌkæpɪtl 'letə] Großbuchstabe **III**
capsule ['kæpsju:l] Kapsel, Gondel **II**
captain ['kæptɪn] Kapitän **I**
car [kɑ:] Auto **I**
card [kɑ:d] Karte; Spielkarte **I**
to **care** [keə] sich kümmern, sich interessieren, wichtig nehmen **III**
career [kə'rɪə] Karriere **III**
careful ['keəfl] vorsichtig **II**
caretaker ['keəˌteɪkə] Hausmeister/-in **I**
carnival ['kɑ:nɪvl] Karneval **III**
to **carry** ['kæri] tragen **I**
cartoon [kɑ:'tu:n] Cartoon **II**
cashier [kæ'ʃɪə] Kassierer/-in **IV U3,** 56
casino [kə'si:nəʊ] Kasino **IV U3,** 49
castle ['kɑ:sl] Burg, Schloss **II**
casual ['kæʒuəl] lässig **IV U2,** 38
cat [kæt] Katze **I**
*to **catch** [kætʃ] fangen; erreichen; festhalten, festnehmen **III**
cathedral [kə'θi:drl] Dom **III**
'cause (= because) [kɒz] weil, da ⟨**IV U1,** 21⟩
cave [keɪv] Höhle **II**
CD [ˌsi:'di:] CD **I**
CD-Rom [ˌsi:di:'rɒm] CD-ROM **II**
to **celebrate** ['seləbreɪt] feiern **IV ZI,** 12
cell phone *(AE)* ['sel ˌfəʊn] Handy **IV U2,** 37
cent [sent] *amerik. Geldeinheit* **IV U1,** 17
center *(AE)* ['sentə] Zentrum **IV U1,** 15
centre ['sentə] Zentrum; Mitte **I**
tourist information centre [ˌtʊərɪst ɪnfə'meɪʃn sentə] Touristik-Information **I**
century ['sentʃəri] Jahrhundert **III**
cereal ['sɪəriəl] Frühstückscerealien, Getreideflakes **II**
ceremony ['serɪməni] Zeremonie **IV U5,** 85
chain [tʃeɪn] Kette **II**
chair [tʃeə] Stuhl **I**
chance [tʃɑ:ns] Zufall, Möglichkeit **III**
change [tʃeɪndʒ] Wechselgeld; Kleingeld; Veränderung, Änderung **IV U1,** 16
to **change** [tʃeɪndʒ] tauschen, auswechseln; sich umziehen **II**; ändern, (sich) verändern **III**; umsteigen **III**
to change your mind [ˌtʃeɪndʒ jə 'maɪnd] deine Meinung ändern **III**
channel ['tʃænl] Kanal; Programm **III**
chant [tʃɑ:nt] Sprechgesang, Sprechchor **IV U2,** 45
to **chant** [tʃɑ:nt] rhythmisch rufen **IV U2,** 32
character ['kærəktə] Charakter; Person **III**
charge [tʃɑ:dʒ] Preis **III**
charity ['tʃærɪti] Wohltätigkeitsverein **I**
chart [tʃɑ:t] Tabelle **II**
to **chase** [tʃeɪs] verfolgen; jagen; hinterherrennen **I**
chat [tʃæt] Chat; Geplauder **III**
to **chat** [tʃæt] plaudern, sich unterhalten **III**
cheap [tʃi:p] billig, preiswert **II**
check *(AE)* [tʃek] Rechnung **IV U1,** 25
to **check** [tʃek] überprüfen, kontrollieren **II**
to check-in ['tʃekɪn] einchecken **I**
to check-out ['tʃekaʊt] auschecken **I**
to check into [ˌtʃek 'ɪntə] sich anmelden ⟨**IV U5,** 92⟩
checklist ['tʃeklɪst] Checkliste, Kontrollliste **IV U3,** 65
to **cheer** [tʃɪə] jubeln **II**
cheerleader ['tʃɪəˌli:də] Cheerleader **IV ZI,** 11
cheerleading ['tʃɪəli:dɪŋ] Cheerleading *(Aktivitäten der Cheerleader)* **IV U2,** 33
cheese [tʃi:z] Käse **I**
cream cheese [ˌkri:m 'tʃi:z] Frischkäse **IV U1,** 17
chef [ʃef] Koch/Köchin **III**
Chemistry ['kemɪstri] Chemie **II**
cherry ['tʃeri] Kirsche **IV U1,** 17
chess [tʃes] Schach **III**
chicken ['tʃɪkɪn] Huhn, Hähnchen **I**
child [tʃaɪld] pl. **children** ['tʃɪldrn] Kind **I**
Chinese [tʃaɪ'ni:z] chinesisch; Chinese/Chinesin **II**
chips [tʃɪps] Pommes frites **II**
chocolate ['tʃɒklət] Schokolade **I**
chocolate crispie [ˌtʃɒklət 'krɪspi] Schokocrossie **I**
hot chocolate [ˌhɒt 'tʃɒklət] heiße Schokolade, Kakao **III**
choice [tʃɔɪs] Auswahl, Wahlmöglichkeit **II**
choir [kwaɪə] Chor **III**
to **choke** [tʃəʊk] zu ersticken drohen, keine Luft bekommen **III**
*to **choose** [tʃu:z] aussuchen, (aus)wählen **II**
Christmas Day [ˌkrɪsməs 'deɪ] 1. Weihnachtstag **III**
church [tʃɜ:tʃ] Kirche **I**
cinema ['sɪnəmə] Kino **I**
circle ['sɜ:kl] Kreis **III**
city ['sɪti] (Groß-)Stadt **II**
to **clap** [klæp] klatschen **I**
class [klɑ:s] Klasse **I**; Unterrichtsstunde **IV U2,** 33
classic ['klæsɪk] Klassiker **IV ZI,** 13
classical music [ˌklæsɪkl 'mju:zɪk] Klassik *(Musikrichtung)* **III**
classmate ['klɑ:smeɪt] Mitschüler/-in, Klassenkamerad/-in ⟨**IV U1,** 30⟩
classroom ['klɑ:sru:m] Klassenzimmer **I**
clean [kli:n] sauber **I**
to **clean** [kli:n] aufräumen; putzen, sauber machen **I**
clear [klɪə] durchsichtig; deutlich, klar **III**
clever ['klevə] schlau, klug **II**
to **click** [klɪk] klicken **III**
cliff [klɪf] Fels, Klippe **III**
climate ['klaɪmət] Klima **IV U3,** 49
climb [klaɪm] Aufstieg **IV U3,** 54
to **climb** [klaɪm] klettern; steigen, besteigen **III**
free **climbing** ['fri: ˌklaɪmɪŋ] Freiklettern **IV U3,** 54
clip [klɪp] Ausschnitt, Clip **IV U2,** 47
clock [klɒk] Uhr **I**
alarm clock [ə'lɑ:m ˌklɒk] Wecker **I**
clock radio ['klɒk ˌreɪdiəʊ] Radiowecker ⟨**IV U3,** 65⟩
clock tower ['klɒk ˌtaʊə] Uhrturm **II**
to **close** [kləʊz] schließen, zumachen **I**
close to ['kləʊs‿tʊ] in der Nähe von **IV U1,** 18
clothes pl. [kləʊðz] Kleidung, Kleider **I**
cloud [klaʊd] Wolke **II**
club [klʌb] Klub; Verein **I**
clubhouse ['klʌbhaʊs] Klubhaus **I**

English – German

clue [klu:] Hinweis **II**
cluster ['klʌstə] Cluster *(einfaches Wörternetz)* **IV U5,** 98
coach [kəʊtʃ] Coach, Trainer/-in; Reisebus **III**
coal [kəʊl] Kohle **III**
coal mine ['kəʊl maɪn] Kohlenbergwerk, Zeche **III**
coast [kəʊst] Küste **III**
coastline ['kəʊstlaɪn] Küstenlinie **III**
coat [kəʊt] Mantel **III**
cocaine (no pl.) [kə'keɪn] Kokain ⟨**IV U5,** 92⟩
coffee ['kɒfi] Kaffee **IV U1,** 17
coke [kəʊk] Cola **IV U2,** 37
cold [kəʊld] kalt **I**
collar ['kɒlə] Kragen **IV U2,** 34
to **collect** [kə'lekt] sammeln; einsammeln; abholen **I**
collector [kə'lektə] Sammler/-in **I**
college ['kɒlɪdʒ] College; Institut **III**
color *(AE)* ['kʌlə] Farbe **IV U1,** 25
colour ['kʌlə] Farbe **I**
to **colour** ['kʌlə] anmalen, ausmalen; malen **I**
colourful ['kʌləfl] bunt **III**
*to **come** [kʌm] kommen **I**
to come along [ˌkʌm‿ə'lɒŋ] vorbeikommen **IV U3,** 54
to come off [kʌm‿'ɒf] rausspringen **II**
to come over [ˌkʌm‿'əʊvə] herüberkommen **I**
to come true [kʌm 'tru:] wahr werden **III**
comedy ['kɒmədi] Komödie (*Filmart*) **IV U5,** 84
comic ['kɒmɪk] Comic(heft) **I**
communication [kəˌmju:nɪ'keɪʃn] Verständigung, Kommunikation, Vermittlung **I**
communications terminal [ˌkəmju:nɪkeɪʃnz 'tɜ:mɪnl] Übertragungsterminal **IV U4,** 76
community [kəm'ju:nəti] Gemeinde **IV U5,** 99
compact ['kɒmpækt] kompakt **IV U4,** 76
company ['kʌmpəni] Firma, Unternehmen **IV U1,** 26
comparative [kəm'pærətɪv] Komparativ **III**
to **compare** [kəm'peə] vergleichen **I**
competition [ˌkɒmpə'tɪʃn] Wettbewerb; Wettkampf **II**
to **complain** [kəm'pleɪn] sich beschweren **III**
complete [kəm'pli:t] ganze/-r/-s **II**
to **complete** [kəm'pli:t] ergänzen; fertig stellen **III**
compound ['kɒmpaʊnd] zusammengesetztes Wort **III**
comprehension [ˌkɒmprɪ'hentʃn] Verständnis **II**
comprehensive school [kɒmprɪ'hensɪv ˌsku:l] Gesamtschule **III**
computer [kəm'pju:tə] Computer **I**
concert ['kɒnsət] Konzert **II**
concrete ['kɒŋkri:t] Beton **IV U1,** 22
conditional [kən'dɪʃnl] Konditional-, Bedingungs- **IV U2,** 44
confusion [kən'fju:ʒn] Verwirrung, Durcheinander ⟨**IV U4,** 77⟩
conjunction [kən'dʒʌŋkʃn] Konjunktion, Bindewort **I**
to **connect** [kə'nekt] verbinden **I**
to **contact (s.o.)** ['kɒntækt] (sich mit jdm.) in Verbindung setzen **III**
content ['kɒntent] Inhalt **III**
control [kən'trəʊl] Kontrolle ⟨**IV U4,** 77⟩
conversation [ˌkɒnvə'seɪʃn] Gespräch, Konversation **IV U1,** 28
to **cook** [kʊk] kochen **II**
cool [ku:l] cool; klasse **I**
cop *(AE)* [kɒp] Polizist/-in ⟨**IV U5,** 92⟩
copy ['kɒpi] Kopie, Exemplar **III**
copy shop ['kɒpi ˌʃɒp] Copyshop **III**
to **copy** ['kɒpi] abmalen; abschreiben; kopieren **I**
corn [kɔ:n] Mais **IV ZI,** 12
corner ['kɔ:nə] Ecke **I**
correct [kə'rekt] richtig **I**
to **correct** [kə'rekt] korrigieren **I**
co-star ['kəʊstɑ:] ein anderer Hauptdarsteller ⟨**IV U5,** 91⟩
*to **cost** [kɒst] kosten **II**
costume ['kɒstju:m] Kostüm **III**
cottage ['kɒtɪdʒ] kleines Landhaus **III**
could [kʊd] könnte/-n, könntest **II**
council ['kaʊnsl] Gemeinderat, Stadtrat **IV U3,** 51
to **count** [kaʊnt] zählen **I**
counter ['kaʊntə] Theke **II**
country ['kʌntri] pl. **countries** ['kʌntriz] Land **I**
country music [ˌkʌntri 'mju:zɪk] Country-Musik **IV U3,** 54
courier ['kʊriə] Kurier **III**
course [kɔ:s] Kurs, Lehrgang **III**
crash course ['kræʃ ˌkɔ:s] Intensivkurs **III**
cousin ['kʌzn] Cousin/-e **I**
cover ['kʌvə] (Schutz-)Hülle, Umschlag, Einband **II**
cow [kaʊ] Kuh **I**
cowboy ['kaʊbɔɪ] Cowboy **IV U3,** 49
Crash! [kræʃ] Bumm!, Krach! **III**
to **crash** [kræʃ] abstürzen **IV U3,** 64
to **crash ...** [kræʃ] mit ... stürzen; einen Unfall mit ... haben **II**
crash course ['kræʃ ˌkɔ:s] Intensivkurs **III**
crazy ['kreɪzi] verrückt **II**
to drive s.o. crazy [ˌdraɪv ... 'kreɪzi] jdn. verrückt machen **II**
cream [kri:m] Creme; Sahne **II**
cream cheese [ˌkri:m 'tʃi:z] Frischkäse **IV U1,** 17
to **create** [kri:'eɪt] schaffen, kreieren; erfinden ⟨**IV U1,** 30⟩
creature ['kri:tʃə] Geschöpf, Kreatur ⟨**IV U4,** 77⟩
cricket ['krɪkɪt] Kricket **I**
crime [kraɪm] Verbrechen **IV U5,** 92
crisp [krɪsp] Kartoffelchip **I**
cross [krɒs] Kreuz **III**
to **cross** [krɒs] überqueren; kreuzen **I**
crowd [kraʊd] Menschenmenge; Clique **IV U5,** 92
crown [kraʊn] Krone **II**
crown jewels [ˌkraʊn 'dʒu:əlz] Kronjuwelen **II**
to **cry** [kraɪ] rufen, schreien; weinen **II**
culture ['kʌltʃə] Kultur ⟨**IV U3,** 66⟩
cup [kʌp] Tasse **II**
cupboard ['kʌbəd] Schrank **I**
cupcake *(AE)* ['kʌpkeɪk] kleiner Kuchen **IV U1,** 17
curfew ['kɜ:fju:] Ausgangssperre; Sperrstunde **IV U5,** 92
current ['kʌrnt] Strömung **IV U3,** 57
curry ['kʌri] Curry(gericht) **II**
to **curse** [kɜ:s] fluchen **IV U4,** 75
curtain ['kɜ:tn] Vorhang **I**
curve [kɜ:v] Kurve **III**
customer ['kʌstəmə] Kunde/Kundin **I**
Customs pl. ['kʌstəmz] Zoll **III**
*to **cut** [kʌt] schneiden **I**
to cut off [ˌkʌt 'ɒf] abschneiden, abtrennen; abstellen **IV U4,** 72
to cut out [ˌkʌt 'aʊt] ausschneiden **II**
cute [kju:t] süß, niedlich **I**
to **cycle** ['saɪkl] Fahrrad fahren, radeln **II**

D

dad [dæd] Vati, Papa **I**
daffodil ['dæfədɪl] Narzisse, Osterglocke **III**
to **damage** ['dæmɪdʒ] beschädigen **III**

dance [dɑ:ns] Tanz(veranstaltung), Ball; Tanz **IV U2,** 34
to **dance** [dɑ:ns] tanzen **I**
dancer ['dɑ:nsə] Tänzer/-in **II**
danger ['deɪndʒə] Gefahr **IV U3,** 64
dangerous ['deɪndʒrəs] gefährlich **II**
Danish ['deɪnɪʃ] Plundergebäck **IV U1,** 17
dark [dɑ:k] dunkel **II**; Dunkelheit **III**
date [deɪt] Datum **I**; Verabredung, Date **IV U2,** 34
to **date** [deɪt] sich verabreden **IV U2,** 32
daughter ['dɔ:tə] Tochter **I**
day [deɪ] Tag **I**
dead [ded] tot **I**; leer **II**
deaf [def] taub **II**
deal [di:l] Geschäft, Handel **IV U1,** 29
OK, it's a deal! [əʊ'kaɪ ɪts‿ə ˌdi:l] Abgemacht! **IV U4,** 74
Dear ... [dɪə] Liebe/-r ... **I**
death [deθ] Tod **III**
December [dɪ'sembə] Dezember **I**
to **decide** [dɪ'saɪd] entscheiden, beschließen **II**
to **dedicate** ['dedɪkeɪt] widmen **IV U1,** 21
deep [di:p] tief **IV U3,** 49
to **define** [dɪ'faɪn] definieren, näher bestimmen **III**
to **delay** [dɪ'leɪ] aufschieben, hinauszögern **IV U4,** 76
to **delete** [dɪ'li:t] löschen; streichen **II**
deli (= delicatessen) ['deli (= ˌdelɪkə'tesn)] Imbiss; Feinkostgeschäft **IV U1,** 16
delicious [dɪ'lɪʃəs] köstlich, lecker **IV U1,** 20
to **deliver** [dɪ'lɪvə] (aus)liefern **IV U1,** 16
department store [dɪ'pɑ:tmənt ˌstɔ:] Kaufhaus, Warenhaus **I**
to **describe** [dɪ'skraɪb] beschreiben **III**
desert ['dezət] Wüste **IV U3,** 49
to **design** [dɪ'zaɪn] entwerfen **III**
desk [desk] Lehrerpult; Schreibtisch *(zu Hause)* **I**
dessert [dɪ'zɜ:t] Nachtisch **I**
to **destroy** [dɪ'strɔɪ] zerstören; kaputt machen; vernichten **IV U1,** 15
detective [dɪ'tektɪv] Detektiv/-in **III**
detention [dɪ'tentʃn] Nachsitzen **IV U2,** 34
device [dɪ'vaɪs] Gerät, Vorrichtung **IV U4,** 69
dialogue ['daɪəlɒg] Dialog; Gespräch **I**
diamond ring ['daɪəmənd ˌrɪŋ] Diamantring ⟨**IV U5,** 93⟩
diary ['daɪəri] Tagebuch; Terminkalender **I**
dictionary ['dɪkʃənri] Wörterbuch **I**
Did you know? ['dɪd ju: ˌnəʊ] Hast du das gewusst?/Habt ihr das gewusst? **II**
to **die** [daɪ] sterben **II**
diet [daɪət] Diät **II**
to go on a diet [ˌgəʊ ɒn ə 'daɪət] eine Diät machen **II**
difference ['dɪfrənts] Unterschied **IV U3,** 53
different ['dɪfrnt] anders; andere/-r/-s **I**; verschieden, unterschiedlich **II**
difficult ['dɪfɪklt] schwierig; schwer **II**
digital ['dɪdʒɪtl] digital **II**
dime [daɪm] *amerik. Geldeinheit* **IV U1,** 17
dining room ['daɪnɪŋ rʊm] Esszimmer **I**
dinner ['dɪnə] Mittagessen; Abendessen **I**
dinner lady ['dɪnə ˌleɪdi] *Serviererin beim Mittagessen in der Schule* **II**
dinosaur ['daɪnəsɔ:] Dinosaurier **III**
direct [dɪ'rekt] direkt **III**
to **direct** [dɪ'rekt] Regie führen **IV U5,** 86
directions [dɪ'rekʃnz] Angaben, Anweisungen **IV U1,** 29
director [dɪ'rektə] Regisseur/-in **IV U5,** 85
dirty ['dɜ:ti] schmutzig, dreckig **I**
to **disagree** [ˌdɪsə'gri:] nicht zustimmen; nicht einverstanden sein **II**
disaster [dɪ'zɑ:stə] Katastrophe **III**
discman ['dɪskmən] *tragbarer CD-Player* **I**
disco ['dɪskəʊ] Disko **I**
to **discover** [dɪ'skʌvə] entdecken **IV U5,** 99
divided [dɪ'vaɪdɪd] aufgeteilt **IV U5,** 99
divorced [dɪ'vɔ:st] geschieden **I**
dizzy ['dɪzi] schwindelig **IV U3,** 48
DJ [ˌdi:'dʒeɪ] DJ **III**
*to **do** [du:] machen, tun **I**
s.o. is **doing well** [ɪz 'du:ɪŋ ˌwel] jdm. geht es gut *(Umgangssprache)* **IV U1,** 21
doctor ['dɒktə] Arzt/Ärztin **II**
dog [dɒg] Hund **I**
to take the dog for a walk [teɪk ðə 'dɒg fɔ:r‿ə ˌwɔ:k] den Hund ausführen **I**
dollar ['dɒlə] Dollar *(US-Währung)* **IV U1,** 16
Don't worry! [ˌdəʊnt 'wʌri] Mach dir keine Sorgen! **II**
door [dɔ:] Tür **I**
back door [ˌbæk 'dɔ:] Hecktür; Hintertür **II**
doorbell ['dɔ:bel] Türklingel **II**
doorstep ['dɔ:step] Eingangsstufe **III**
double ['dʌbl] Doppel-, zweimal **IV U3,** 65
double-decker bus [ˌdʌbldekə 'bʌs] Doppeldeckerbus **II**
doubt [daʊt] Zweifel **IV U4,** 75
down [daʊn] entlang; herunter, hinunter, nach unten **I**
to **download** [ˌdaʊn'ləʊd] herunterladen, downloaden **II**
downriver [daʊn'rɪvə] flussabwärts, stromabwärts **IV U3,** 57
downstairs [ˌdaʊn'steəz] unten *(im Gebäude)* **I**
downtown *(AE)* [ˌdaʊn'taʊn] im Stadtzentrum, in der Innenstadt **IV U1,** 28
Dr ['dɒktə] *Kurzform für 'Doctor'* **II**
dragon ['drægn] Drache **III**
drama ['drɑ:mə] Schauspiel **I**
Drama Club ['drɑ:mə ˌklʌb] Theaterklub **I**
*to **draw** [drɔ:] zeichnen; malen **I**
dream [dri:m] Traum **I**
*to **dream** [dri:m] träumen **II**
dress [dres] Kleid; Kleidung **IV U2,** 40
dress code [ˌdres 'kəʊd] Kleiderordnung; Bekleidungsvorschriften **IV U2,** 34
to **drill** [drɪl] bohren **II**
drink [drɪŋk] Getränk **I**
*to **drink** [drɪŋk] trinken **I**
*to **drive** [draɪv] fahren **I**
to drive s.o. crazy [ˌdraɪv ... 'kreɪzi] jdn. verrückt machen **II**
driver ['draɪvə] Fahrer/-in **I**
drooping ['dru:pɪŋ] nach unten zeigend, herunterhängend **IV U4,** 75
to **drop** [drɒp] fallen lassen **III**
to drop out ['drɒp ˌaʊt] abbrechen ⟨**IV U1,** 30⟩
in **droves** [ɪn 'drəʊvz] in Scharen ⟨**IV U1,** 21⟩
drug [drʌg] Droge, Rauschgift **III**
drum [drʌm] Trommel, *Plural* Schlagzeug **I**
dry [draɪ] trocken **IV U3,** 48
dumb [dʌm] blöde, dumm **IV U4,** 75
dungeon ['dʌndʒən] Verlies **II**
during ['djʊərɪŋ] während **II**
dusty ['dʌsti] staubig **IV U3,** 48
Dutch [dʌtʃ] holländisch, niederländisch; Holländisch, Niederländisch; Holländer/-in, Niederländer/-in **IV U1,** 18

English – German

DVD [ˌdi: vi: ˈdi:] DVD **I**
DVD player [ˌdi:vi:ˈdi: ˌpleɪə] DVD-Spieler, DVD-Player **II**

E

each [i:tʃ] jede/-r/-s **II**; je, jeweils **III**
each other [ˌi:tʃ ˈʌðə] sich (gegenseitig), einander **II**
ear [ɪə] Ohr **I**
early [ˈɜ:li] früh **II**
in the early 1600s [ɪn ði ˌɜ:li ˈsɪksti:n hʌndrədz] am Anfang/zu Beginn des 16. Jahrhunderts **IV ZI,** 12
to **earn** [ɜ:n] verdienen ⟨**IV U5,** 100⟩
earring [ˈɪərɪŋ] Ohrring **IV U2,** 34
Earth [ɜ:θ] Erde **IV U4,** 68
earthquake [ˈɜ:θkweɪk] Erdbeben **III**
east [i:st] Osten **I**
Easter [ˈi:stə] Ostern **III**
easy [ˈi:zi] einfach, leicht **I**
easy-going [ˌi:ziˈgəʊɪŋ] lässig ⟨**IV U5,** 100⟩
*to **eat** [i:t] essen **I**
eater [ˈi:tə] Esser/-in **II**
edge [edʒ] Rand, Kante; Grenze **IV U1,** 22
egg [eg] Ei **I**
not ... **either** [ˌnɒt ... ˈaɪðə] auch nicht **III**
elbow [ˈelbəʊ] Ellbogen **II**
to **elect** [ɪˈlekt] wählen **IV U2,** 40
election [ɪˈlekʃn] Wahl **IV U2,** 33
electrical [ɪˈlektrɪkl] elektrisch **IV U4,** 69
electricity [ˌelɪkˈtrɪsəti] Elektrizität, Strom **IV U4,** 72
electronics [ˌelekˈtrɒnɪks] Elektronik **IV U4,** 76
elementary [ˌelɪˈmentəri] einfach; elementar **III**
elephant [ˈelɪfənt] Elefant **II**
elevator *(AE)* [ˈelɪveɪtə] Aufzug **IV U1,** 15
else [els] sonst **III**
e-mail [ˈi:meɪl] E-Mail **I**
embarrassed [ɪmˈbærəst] verlegen **IV U1,** 20
embarrassing [ɪmˈbærəsɪŋ] peinlich **III**
empty [ˈemti] leer **II**
encyclopedia [ɪnˌsaɪkləˈpi:diə] Enzyklopädie (*Nachschlagewerk*) **III**
end [end] Ende **I**
to **end** [end] zu Ende gehen, enden; beenden **I**
ending [ˈendɪŋ] Schluss **II**
enemy [ˈenəmi] Feind/-in **II**
energy [ˈenədʒi] Energie **IV ZI,** 11
English [ˈɪŋglɪʃ] englisch, Englisch; Engländer/-in **I**
to **enjoy** [ɪnˈdʒɔɪ] genießen **II**
enjoyable [ɪnˈðʒɔɪəbl] angenehm; unterhaltsam **III**
enormous [ɪˈnɔ:məs] riesig, enorm, gewaltig **IV U4,** 76
enough [ɪˈnʌf] genug **II**
to **enter** [ˈentə] teilnehmen; eintreten **II**
entertainment [ˌentəˈteɪnmənt] Unterhaltung **IV U5,** 91
entrance [ˈentrənts] Eingang **II**
entry [ˈentri] Eintrag; Eingang **III**
equipment [ɪˈkwɪpmənt] Ausrüstung; Ausstattung **II**
to **escape** [ɪˈskeɪp] flüchten, entfliehen, entkommen **IV U1,** 18
especially [ɪˈspeʃəli] besonders, vor allem **IV U5,** 92
euro [ˈjʊərəʊ] Euro **II**
European [ˌjʊərəˈpi:ən] europäisch; Europäer/-in **I**
even [ˈi:vn] sogar **I**; noch **II**
evening [ˈi:vnɪŋ] Abend **I**
evening class [ˌi:vnɪŋ ˈklɑ:s] Abendkurs, Abendschule **II**
event [ɪˈvent] Veranstaltung **I**
ever [ˈevə] je, jemals **II**
ever since [ˌevə ˈsɪnts] seitdem **IV U4,** 75
every [ˈevri] jede/-r/-s **I**
everybody [ˈevriˌbɒdi] jede/-r/-s **I**
everybody else [ˈevribɒdi ˌels] jeder andere, jeden **IV U1,** 20
everyone [ˈevriwʌn] jeder, alle **II**
everything [ˈevriθɪŋ] alles **I**
everywhere [ˈevriweə] überall **I**
exactly [ɪgˈzæktli] genau **III**
exam [ɪgˈzæm] Examen, Prüfung **III**
example [ɪgˈzɑ:mpl] Beispiel **I**
for example [ˌfər‿ˈɪgzɑ:mpl] zum Beispiel **II**
except for [ɪkˈsept fɔ:] außer; ausgenommen **III**
exchange [ɪksˈtʃeɪndʒ] Austausch; Tausch, Umtausch **III**
to **exchange** [ɪksˈtʃeɪndʒ] umtauschen; tauschen **II**
excited [ɪkˈsaɪtɪd] aufgeregt **I**
exciting [ɪkˈsaɪtɪŋ] aufregend **I**
Excuse me. [ɪkˈskju:z mi] Entschuldigung!, Entschuldige!, Entschuldigen Sie! **I**
exercise [ˈeksəsaɪz] Übung **I**
exercise book [ˈeksəsaɪz ˌbʊk] Heft **I**
to **exercise** [ˈeksəsaɪz] Sport treiben; trainieren **II**
exhibition [ˌeksɪˈbɪʃn] Ausstellung **III**
to **expect** [ɪkˈspekt] erwarten **IV U5,** 91
expensive [ɪkˈspensɪv] teuer **I**
experience [ɪkˈspɪəriəns] Erfahrung, Erlebnis **II**
experiment [ɪkˈsperɪment] Experiment, Versuch **III**
to **explain (sth.)** [ɪkˈspleɪn] (etwas) erklären **II**
to **explode** [ɪkˈspləʊd] explodieren **IV U3,** 58
to **explore** [ɪkˈsplɔ:] erforschen, erkunden **II**
extra [ˈekstrə] extra, besonders **I**
eye [aɪ] Auge **I**
eyebrow [ˈaɪbraʊ] Augenbraue **III**

F

face [feɪs] Gesicht **I**
fact [fækt] Fakt, Tatsache **II**
factory [ˈfæktri] Fabrik **III**
factual text [ˈfæktʃʊəl ˌtekst] Sachtext **III**
fair [feə] Fest; Markt, Jahrmarkt **I**; Messe **IV U4,** 68
fair [feə] fair, gerecht **III**; hell, blond **III**
fall *(AE)* [fɔ:l] Herbst **IV U2,** 34
*to **fall** [fɔ:l] fallen **I**; stürzen, hinfallen **II**
to fall asleep [ˌfɔ:l əˈsli:p] einschlafen **I**
to fall back in with [fɔ:l ˌbæk ɪn ˈwɪð] sich wieder jdm. anschließen ⟨**IV U5,** 92⟩
to fall off [ˈfɔ:l‿ˈɒf] herunterfallen **III**
to fall over [fɔ:l‿ˈəʊvə] umfallen; (*Person*) hinfallen **I**
false [fɔ:ls] falsch **I**
fame [feɪm] Ruhm **IV U5,** 91
familiar [fəˈmɪliə] vertraut **IV U5,** 92
family [ˈfæməli] Familie **I**
family tree [ˌfæməli ˈtri:] Stammbaum **I**
famine [ˈfæmɪn] Hungersnot **IV U1,** 18
famous [ˈfeɪməs] berühmt, bekannt **I**
fan [fæn] Fan **II**
fantastic [fænˈtæstɪk] toll, fantastisch **II**
fantasy [ˈfæntəsi] Fantasie **II**
FAQs (= frequently asked questions) [ˌef eɪ ˈkju:z] häufig gestellte Fragen **IV U2,** 33
far [fɑ:] weit **III**
far away [ˌfɑ:r‿əˈweɪ] weit entfernt, weit weg **II**
farm [fɑ:m] Bauernhof **I**

farmer ['fɑ:mə] Bauer/Bäuerin, Landwirt/-in **I**
farther ['fɑ:ðə] weiter **IV U3,** 57
fast [fɑ:st] schnell **I**
fast food [ˌfɑ:st 'fu:d] Fastfood **II**
fat [fæt] Fett **II**
father ['fɑ:ðə] Vater **I**
faucet *(AE)* ['fɔ:sɪt] Wasserhahn **IV U4,** 72
favorite *(AE)* ['feɪvrɪt] Lieblings- **IV U1,** 17
favourite ['feɪvrɪt] Lieblings- **I**
feature ['fi:tʃə] Eigenschaft, Merkmal **IV U4,** 75
February ['febrʊri] Februar **I**
fee [fi:] Gebühr **IV ZI,** 13
*to **feed** [fi:d] füttern **I**
*to **feel** [fi:l] sich fühlen; empfinden **III**
to feel at home [ˌfi:l‿ət 'həʊm] sich wohl fühlen **III**
to feel homesick [ˌfi:l 'həʊmsɪk] Heimweh haben **II**
to feel sick [fi:l 'sɪk] Übelkeit verspüren **III**
to feel sorry for [fi:l 'sɒri ˌfə] (mit)fühlen mit, Mitgefühl haben **IV U1,** 20
to not feel well [ˌnɒt fi:l 'wel] sich schlecht fühlen **II**
feeling ['fi:lɪŋ] Gefühl **IV U1,** 20
female ['fi:meɪl] weiblich **III**
fence [fens] Zaun **III**
Ferris wheel ['ferɪs ˌwi:l] Riesenrad **III**
ferry ['feri] Fähre **III**
festival ['festɪvl] Festival; Fest **I**
a **few** [ə 'fju:] ein paar, einige **I**
field ['fi:ld] Sportfeld; Wiese; Feld **I**
fieldwork ['fi:ldwɜ:k] Feldforschung ⟨**IV U3,** 65⟩
fierce [fɪəs] wild **II**
fight [faɪt] Kampf; Streit **I**
*to **fight** [faɪt] kämpfen; (sich) streiten **I**
file [faɪl] Ordner **IV ZI,** 13
to **fill** [fɪl] füllen **III**
to fill in [fɪl 'ɪn] ausfüllen **I**
film [fɪlm] Film **I**
finally ['faɪnəli] endlich, schließlich **I**
*to **find** [faɪnd] finden **I**
to find out [faɪnd‿'aʊt] herausfinden **II**
fine [faɪn] Geldbuße, Geldstrafe **III**
fine [faɪn] gut **I**; in Ordnung; fein, schön **II**
finger ['fɪŋgə] Finger **II**
to **finish** ['fɪnɪʃ] beenden, fertig machen **I**
fire [faɪə] Feuer **II**
firefighter *(AE)* ['faɪəˌfaɪtə] Feuerwehrmann/-frau **IV U1,** 27
fireworks ['faɪəwɜ:ks] Feuerwerk **IV ZI,** 12
firm [fɜ:m] Firma, Unternehmen **III**
first [fɜ:st] zuerst; als Erste/-r/-s; erste/-r/-s **I**
first of all [ˌfɜ:st‿'ɒf‿'ɔ:l] zuerst **IV U4,** 83
first-footing [ˌfɜ:st 'fʊtɪŋ] *schott. Tradition* **III**
fish [fɪʃ] Fisch **II**
fit [fɪt] gesund, fit **II**
fitness ['fɪtnəs] Fitness, Kondition **III**
to **fix** [fɪks] reparieren, in Ordnung bringen **II**
flag [flæg] Flagge, Fahne **I**
flame [fleɪm] Flamme **IV U1,** 14
flat [flæt] Wohnung **I**
*to **flee** [fli:] fliehen, flüchten **II**
flight [flaɪt] Flug **III**
to **flip** [flɪp] *(Boot)* zum Kentern bringen; ausflippen **IV U3,** 58
to **float** [fləʊt] schweben; treiben **IV U4,** 70
floor [flɔ:] Boden **II**
flour [flaʊə] Mehl **I**
flower ['flaʊə] Blume **IV U1,** 22
fluid ['fluɪd] Flüssigkeit **IV U4,** 76
*to **fly** [flaɪ] fliegen **II**
fly fishing ['flaɪˌfɪʃɪŋ] Fliegenfischen **II**
fog [fɒg] Nebel **III**
foggy ['fɒgi] nebelig **III**
folder ['fəʊldə] Mappe, Hefter, Ordner **I**
to **follow** ['fɒləʊ] folgen **II**
food [fu:d] Essen; Lebensmittel **I**
food chain ['fu:d ˌtʃeɪn] Nahrungskette ⟨**IV U5,** 93⟩
fast **food** [ˌfɑ:st 'fu:d] Fastfood **II**
foot [fʊt] pl. **feet** [fi:t] Fuß **I**
foot, feet (ft) [fʊt, fi:t] Fuß (*Maßeinheit*) **III**
football ['fʊtbɔ:l] Fußball **I**
footstep ['fʊtstep] Schritt, Tritt **III**
for [fɔ:] für **I**; seit **III**
for … [fɔ:] … lang **III**
for example [ˌfər‿ɪg'zɑ:mpl] zum Beispiel **II**
for sale [ˌfɔ: 'seɪl] zu verkaufen **IV U2,** 34
foreground ['fɔ:graʊnd] Vordergrund **IV U1,** 15
foreign ['fɒrɪn] fremd, ausländisch **IV U4,** 83
forest ['fɒrɪst] Wald **II**
forever [fə'revə] für immer; ewig **IV U2,** 40
*to **forget** [fə'get] vergessen **I**
fork [fɔ:k] Gabel **II**
form [fɔ:m] Form **I**; Formular **II**
foul [faʊl] Foul, Regelverstoß **III**
to **found** [faʊnd] errichten, gründen **IV U1,** 18
fox [fɒks] Fuchs **II**
free [fri:] frei; kostenlos **I**
free climbing ['fri: ˌklaɪmɪŋ] Freiklettern **IV U3,** 54
freedom ['fri:dəm] Freiheit **IV ZI,** 12
French [frentʃ] französisch, Französisch **I**
French fries *(AE)* [ˌfrentʃ 'fraɪz] Pommes frites **IV U1,** 17
frequency ['fri:kwəntsi] Frequenz **IV U4,** 76
fresh [freʃ] frisch **II**
Friday ['fraɪdeɪ] Freitag **I**
Fridays ['fraɪdeɪz] freitags **I**
fried [fraɪd] gebraten **II**
friend [frend] Freund/-in **I**
friendly ['frendli] freundlich **III**
to give s.o. a **fright** [ˌgɪv … ə 'fraɪt] jdn. erschrecken **II**
from [frɒm] aus, von **I**
front page ['frʌnt ˌpeɪdʒ] Titelseite **II**
in **front of** [ˌɪn 'frʌnt‿əv] vor **II**
frost [frɒst] Frost ⟨**IV U5,** 100⟩
frozen ['frəʊzn] Tiefkühl-; gefroren **II**
fruit [fru:t] Obst, Frucht **II**
frustrated [frʌs'treɪtɪd] frustriert **III**
full [fʊl] voll **I**; ganz **III**
fun [fʌn] Spaß **I**
to **function** ['fʌnkʃn] funktionieren **IV U5,** 92
funny ['fʌni] lustig; komisch **I**
furniture ['fɜ:nɪtʃə] Möbel **I**
further ['fɜ:ðə] weiter **III**
fuse-box ['fju:z bɒks] Sicherungskasten **III**
fuss [fʌs] Aufregung, Wirbel **III**
future ['fju:tʃə] Futur; Zukunft **II**

G

Gaelic ['geɪlɪk] Gälisch **III**
to **gamble** ['gæmbl] (*Glücksspiele*) spielen **IV U3,** 48
game [geɪm] Spiel **I**
gang [gæŋ] Bande, Gang **IV U2,** 35
gangster movie ['gæŋkstə ˌmu:vi] Gangsterfilm **IV U5,** 84
garage ['gærɪdʒ] Garage; Autowerkstatt, Tankstelle **II**

English – German

garbage *(AE)* ['gɑ:bɪdʒ] Müll, Abfall **IV U3,** 50
garden ['gɑ:dn] Garten **I**
to **gasp** [gɑ:sp] erstaunt, nach Luft schnappen **II**
gate [geɪt] Tor **IV U1,** 21
GCSE (= General Certificate of Secondary Education) [ˌdʒi:si:es'i: = ˌdʒenrəl sə'tɪfɪkeɪt‿əv 'sekndri edʒʊ'keɪʃn] *Abschlussprüfung der Sekundarstufe mit 16 Jahren* **III**
geek [gi:k] Außenseiter/-in *(Umgangssprache)* **IV U2,** 39
gentleman ['dʒentlmən] Herr, Gentleman **IV U5,** 88
Geography [dʒi'ɒgrəfi] Erdkunde, Geographie **II**
German ['dʒ3:mən] Deutsch, deutsch; Deutsche/-r **I**
gerund ['dʒernd] Gerundium **IV U2,** 37
*to **get** [get] bekommen; werden **II**
Get out of here! [ˌget aʊt‿əv 'hɪə] Verschwinde/-t! **II**
to get divorced [ˌget dɪ'vɔ:sd] sich scheiden lassen **IV U5,** 84
to get drunk [get 'drʌŋk] sich betrinken **IV U5,** 92
to get fit [ˌget 'fɪt] fit werden **II**
to get into a state [get‿ɪntə‿ə 'steɪt] durchdrehen, (sich) verrückt machen **III**
to get lost [ˌget 'lɒst] sich verirren, sich verlaufen **I**
to get ready [ˌget 'redi] sich fertig machen **II**
to get to … ['get tʊ] zu/nach … kommen **I**
to get up [get‿'ʌp] aufstehen **I**
to get your kicks *(AE)* [get ˌjɔ:r 'kɪks] seinen Spaß haben ⟨**IV U3,** 61⟩
ghost [gəʊst] Geist **I**
gift shop ['gɪft ˌʃɒp] Geschenkladen, Souvenirshop **I**
girl [g3:l] Mädchen **I**
girlfriend ['g3:lfrend] Freundin *(in einer Paarbeziehung)* **III**
*to **give** [gɪv] geben **I**
to give away ['gɪv‿əweɪ] verschenken **IV U1,** 16
to give s.o. a fright [ˌgɪv … ə 'fraɪt] jdn. erschrecken **II**
to give thanks to s.o. [ˌgɪv 'θæŋks] sich bei jdm. bedanken **IV U1,** 21
to give up ['gɪv‿ʌp] aufgeben **II**
glad [glæd] froh **II**
glare [gleə] grelles Licht **III**
glass [glɑ:s] Glas **II**
glee [gli:] Entzücken **III**
to **glide** [glaɪd] gleiten, schweben ⟨**IV U4,** 77⟩
global ['gləʊbl] global ⟨**IV U1,** 30⟩
glove [glʌv] Handschuh **III**
to **glow** [gləʊ] leuchten, glühen **III**
*to **go** [gəʊ] gehen **I**
Go away! [ˌgəʊ ə'weɪ] Geh weg! **I**
to go away [ˌgəʊ ə'weɪ] verreisen, wegfahren; weggehen **II**
to go bananas [gəʊ 'bənɑ:nəz] verrückt werden, überschnappen **II**
to go camping [gəʊ 'kæmpɪŋ] zelten gehen, campen **II**
to go crazy about sth. [ˌgəʊ 'kreɪzi] nach etw. verrückt sein **IV U2,** 39
to go on [gəʊ 'ɒn] weitermachen **I**
to go out [gəʊ‿'aʊt] (hin)ausgehen; erlöschen **III**
to go shopping [gəʊ 'ʃɒpɪŋ] einkaufen gehen **I**
to go skiing [gəʊ 'ski:ɪŋ] Skilaufen gehen **IV U3,** 53
to go swimming [gəʊ 'swɪmɪŋ] schwimmen gehen **I**
to go to bed [ˌgəʊ tə 'bed] ins Bett gehen **I**
to go wrong [ˌgəʊ 'rɒŋ] schiefgehen, scheitern **III**
goal [gəʊl] Tor **III**
goal post ['gəʊl pəʊst] Torpfosten **III**
own goal [ˌəʊn 'gəʊl] Eigentor **III**
goalkeeper ['gəʊlˌki:pə] Torwart/-in **III**
goat [gəʊt] Ziege **I**
God [gɒd] Gott **IV U2,** 32
goggles pl. ['gɒglz] Schutzbrille; Taucherbrille, Schwimmbrille **III**
gold [gəʊld] Gold **IV U1,** 14
gone [gɒn] weg, fort **II**
gonna (= going to) ['gɒnə] werden *(Umgangssprache)* ⟨**IV U1,** 21⟩; ⟨**IV U4,** 77⟩
good [gʊd] gut **I**
good luck [ˌgʊd 'lʌk] viel Glück **II**
good morning [gʊd 'mɔ:nɪŋ] guten Morgen **I**
goodbye [gʊd'baɪ] tschüss, auf Wiedersehen; auf Wiederhören **I**
good-looking [ˌgʊd'lʊkɪŋ] gut aussehend **III**
goose [gu:s] pl. **geese** [gi:s] Gans **I**
gorge [gɔ:dʒ] Schlucht **IV U3,** 49
gossip ['gɒsɪp] Klatsch, Tratsch **IV U2,** 40
gotten *(AE)* ['gɒtn] *Past participle von 'to get' in AE* **IV U3,** 54
GPS (global positioning system) [ˌdʒi: pi: 'es] GPS *(ein satellitengestütztes Navigationssystem)* **IV U4,** 69
grade *(AE)* [greɪd] Klasse; Note **IV U2,** 33
graffiti [grə'fi:ti] Graffiti **III**
grain [greɪn] Getreide **IV U5,** 99
gram [græm] Gramm **I**
grammar ['græmə] Grammatik **I**
grammar school ['græmə ˌsku:l] Gymnasium **III**
grandad ['grændæd] Opa **I**
grandfather ['grænˌfɑ:ðə] Großvater **I**
grandma ['grænmɑ:] Oma **I**
grandmother ['grænˌmʌðə] Großmutter **I**
grandparents ['grænˌpeərnts] Großeltern **I**
graphics pl. ['græfɪks] Grafiken **IV U5,** 86
grass [grɑ:s] Gras **I**
gravity ['grævəti] Schwerkraft **IV U4,** 69
gray *(AE)* [greɪ] grau **IV U1,** 22
great [greɪt] großartig; toll **I**
Greek [gri:k] griechisch, Griechisch; Grieche/Griechin **I**
green [gri:n] grün **I**
greeting ['gri:tɪŋ] Gruß, Grußformel **II**
grey [greɪ] grau **I**
grid [grɪd] Tabelle, Gitter **I**
gritty ['grɪti] mutig, tapfer ⟨**IV U1,** 21⟩
ground [graʊnd] Boden, Erde **IV U1,** 27
group [gru:p] Klasse; Gruppe **I**
*to **grow** [grəʊ] wachsen **IV U3,** 51
to grow up [grəʊ‿'ʌp] aufwachsen, erwachsen werden **IV U5,** 88
gruesome ['gru:səm] grausig, schaurig **II**
guard [gɑ:d] Wärter/-in, Wache, Wächter/-in **II**
to **guess** [ges] raten, erraten **I**
Guess what! [ges 'wɒt] Rate mal! **I**
guest [gest] Gast **IV U4,** 73
guitar [gɪ'tɑ:] Gitarre **I**
guitarist [gɪ'tɑ:rɪst] Gitarrist/-in **III**
gun [gʌn] Schusswaffe, Pistole **III**
guy [gaɪ] Kerl **IV U1,** 20
guys [gaɪz] Leute **II**

H

to **hail from** [heɪl 'frəm] von … stammen ⟨**IV U1,** 21⟩
hair [heə] Haar **II**
hairdresser ['heəˌdresə] Friseur/-in **III**
hairdryer ['heəˌdraɪə] Fön **IV U4,** 72

half [hɑːf] pl. **halves** [hɑːvz] Hälfte **I**
half-sister ['hɑːfˌsɪstə] Halbschwester **I**
half past (two) [ˌhɑːf 'pɑːst] halb (drei) **I**
to meet **halfway** [miːt hɑːf'weɪ] sich (auf halbem Weg) entgegenkommen **IV U4,** 74
halfway down [hɑːfˌweɪ 'daʊn] auf halbem Wege nach unten **IV U3,** 58
hall [hɔːl] Aula, Saal; Flur **I**
ham [hæm] Schinken **I**
hand [hænd] Hand **II**
Hands off! [ˌhændz‿'ɒf] Finger weg! **II**
to **hand** [hænd] reichen, geben **II**
handbag ['hændbæg] Handtasche **III**
handout ['hændaʊt] Handout, Arbeitsblatt **IV U2,** 47
handsome ['hænsəm] attraktiv, gut aussehend **IV U5,** 84
*to **hang out** [hæŋ 'aʊt] rumhängen, sich treffen **III**
to **happen** ['hæpn] geschehen, passieren **I**
happiness ['hæpɪnəs] Glück **IV U3,** 64
happy ['hæpi] fröhlich; glücklich **I**
Happy Birthday! [ˌhæpi 'bɜːθdeɪ] Alles Gute zum Geburtstag! **I**
harbor *(AE)* ['hɑːbə] Hafen **IV U1,** 18
hard [hɑːd] hart, fest; schwierig, schwer **I**
harm [hɑːm] Schaden, Verletzung **III**
hat [hæt] Hut, Mütze **IV U3,** 49
to **hate** [heɪt] hassen **II**
to **have** [hæv] haben **I**
have/has been to … before [hæv/hæz biːn tʊ … bɪ'fɔː] sind/ist bereits in … gewesen **II**
have got/has got ['hæv gɒt/'hæz gɒt] haben, besitzen **I**
to have a fit [ˌhæv‿ə 'fɪt] einen Anfall bekommen; Zustände kriegen **III**
to have an argument [ˌhæv‿ən‿'ɑːgjəmənt] (sich) streiten **III**
to have to ['hæv tə] müssen **III**
he [hiː] er **I**
head [hed] Kopf **I**
headache ['hedeɪk] Kopfschmerzen ⟨**IV U5,** 100⟩
heading ['hedɪŋ] Überschrift **I**
headline ['hedlaɪn] Kopfzeile, Überschrift; Schlagzeile **IV U3,** 54
headphones ['hedfəʊnz] Kopfhörer **II**
headteacher [ˌhed'tiːtʃə] Schulleiter/-in **II**
headword ['hedwɜːd] Stichwort **III**
healthy ['helθi] gesund **II**
*to **hear** [hɪə] hören **I**
heart [hɑːt] Herz **IV U3,** 57
heartless ['hɑːtləs] herzlos **IV U3,** 64
heavy ['hevi] schwer **III**
heavy metal [ˌhevi 'metl] Heavy Metal *(Musikrichtung)* **III**
height [haɪt] Größe **III**
heir [eə] Erbe/Erbin **III**
helicopter ['helɪkɒptə] Hubschrauber **II**
hell [hel] Hölle **IV U1,** 21
hello [hel'əʊ] hallo **I**
helmet ['helmət] Helm **II**
help [help] Hilfe **I**
to **help** [help] helfen **I**
helpful ['helpfʊl] hilfreich **IV U3,** 58
helpless ['helpləs] hilflos **III**
her [hɜː] ihr/-e; sie; ihr **I**
Her Majesty [ˌhə 'mædʒəsti] Ihre Majestät **III**
here [hɪə] hier **I**
Here you are! ['hɪə jʊ‿ɑː] Bitte schön! **I**
hero ['hɪərəʊ] Held/-in **IV U1,** 27
hers [hɜːz] ihre/-r/-s **II**
herself [hɜː'self] sie/sich (selbst) **III**
Hey! [heɪ] He! **I**
Hi! [haɪ] Hi!, Hallo! **I**
*to **hide** [haɪd] sich verstecken; verstecken **II**
high [haɪ] hoch, groß **II**; high *(Stimmung nach dem Genuss von Drogen)* ⟨**IV U5,** 92⟩
high school ['haɪ ˌskuːl] High School *(weiterführende Schule in den USA, Oberstufe)* ⟨**IV U1,** 30⟩
high-tech [ˌhaɪ'tek] Hightech- **II**
to **highlight** ['haɪlaɪt] markieren **III**
highway *(AE)* ['haɪweɪ] Autobahn ⟨**IV U3,** 61⟩
hike [haɪk] Wanderung **II**
to take a hike [ˌteɪk‿ə 'haɪk] wandern, eine Wanderung machen **II**
hiking ['haɪkɪŋ] Wandern **IV U3,** 50
him [hɪm] ihn; ihm **I**
himself [hɪm'self] er/sich (selbst) **III**
hip [hɪp] cool, hip ⟨**IV U3,** 61⟩
hip hop ['hɪp hɒp] Hip-Hop *(Musikrichtung)* **III**
to **hire** [haɪə] einstellen; mieten **IV U5,** 92
his [hɪz] sein/-e **I**; seine/-r/-s; sein **II**
Hispanic [hɪ'spænɪk] hispanisch, lateinamerikanisch; Lateinamerikaner/-in **IV U5,** 99
History ['hɪstri] Geschichte **II**
hit [hɪt] Hit **III**
*to **hit** [hɪt] schlagen, treffen; stoßen **III**
hobby ['hɒbi] Hobby **I**
hockey ['hɒki] Hockey *(Sportart)* **III**
Hogmanay ['hɒgmənaɪ] *trad. schott. Neujahrsfest* **III**
*to **hold** [həʊld] halten, zuhalten **II**
to hold up [həʊld‿'ʌp] hochhalten **III**
hole [həʊl] Loch **IV U3,** 58
holiday ['hɒlədeɪ] Urlaub, Ferien **II**
holy ['həʊli] heilig ⟨**IV U1,** 22⟩
Holy mother [ˌhəʊli 'mʌðə] Heilige Mutter **IV U3,** 58
home [həʊm] zu Hause; Zuhause; Heim **I**
home page ['həʊm ˌpeɪdʒ] Homepage **IV U2,** 33
home-made [ˌhəʊm'meɪd] hausgemacht, selbstgemacht **III**
to feel **homesick** [ˌfiːl 'həʊmsɪk] Heimweh haben **II**
homework ['həʊmwɜːk] Hausaufgaben **I**
honest ['ɒnɪst] ehrlich ⟨**IV U2,** 41⟩
to **hope** [həʊp] hoffen **II**
horror ['hɒrə] Schrecken **II**
horse [hɔːs] Pferd **I**
horseriding ['hɔːs ˌraɪdɪŋ] Reiten **II**
hospital ['hɒspɪtl] Krankenhaus **III**
hostel ['hɒstl] Herberge **I**
hot [hɒt] heiß **II**
hot chocolate [ˌhɒt 'tʃɒklət] heiße Schokolade, Kakao **III**
hotel [həʊ'tel] Hotel **III**
hound [haʊnd] Jagdhund **III**
hour [aʊə] Stunde **I**
house [haʊs] Haus **I**
terraced house ['terɪst ˌhaʊs] Reihenhaus **II**
how [haʊ] wie **I**
How about … ? ['haʊ‿əˌbaʊt] Wie steht's mit … ?; Wie wär's mit … ? **I**
How are you? [ˌhaʊ‿'ɑː juː] Wie geht es dir/euch/Ihnen? **I**
How many … ? [haʊ 'meni] Wie viele … ? **I**
How much is/are … ? [haʊ 'mʌtʃ] Wie viel kostet/kosten … ? **I**
How old are you? [haʊ‿'əʊld‿ə ˌjuː] Wie alt bist du/sind Sie? **I**
however [haʊ'evə] allerdings, jedoch **IV U3,** 64
huge [hjuːdʒ] riesige/-r/-s, riesig **II**
hum [hʌm] Brummen, Summen **IV U4,** 76
hungry ['hʌŋgri] hungrig **I**
to **hunt** [hʌnt] jagen **II**
hurry ['hʌri] Eile **I**
Hurry up! [ˌhʌri‿'ʌp] Beeil dich!, Beeilt euch! **II**
*to **hurt** [hɜːt] weh tun; verletzen **II**

English – German

hustle-bustle [ˌhʌsl'bʌsl] hektisches Treiben ⟨**IV U5,** 100⟩

I

I [aɪ] ich **I**
I can't stand … [aɪ ˌkɑ:nt 'stænd] Ich kann … nicht ausstehen **IV U2,** 37
…, I guess. [aɪ 'ges] …, schätze ich. **IV U1,** 29
I would like (= I'd like) … [aɪ 'wʊd ˌlaɪk = 'aɪd laɪk] ich möchte gern …, ich hätte gern **I**
ice-cream [ˌaɪs'kri:m] Eis **I**
ice skating ['aɪs ˌskeɪtɪŋ] Schlittschuhlaufen **IV U2,** 37
ice skating rink (AE) ['aɪs skeɪtɪŋ ˌrɪŋk] Eislaufbahn **IV U2,** 37
icon ['aɪkɒn] Ikone **III**
idea [aɪ'dɪə] Idee, Einfall; Ahnung **I**
idiot ['ɪdiət] Idiot/-in, Dummkopf **I**
if [ɪf] wenn, falls; ob **II**
ill [ɪl] krank **I**
illegal [ɪ'li:gl] unerlaubt, illegal, gesetzwidrig ⟨**IV U1,** 30⟩
illegally [ɪ'li:gli] unerlaubt ⟨**IV U5,** 100⟩
illusion [ɪ'lu:ʒn] Illusion, Täuschung ⟨**IV U4,** 77⟩
image ['ɪmɪdʒ] Image; Bild **III**
to **imagine** [ɪ'mædʒɪn] sich ausdenken, sich vorstellen **III**
immigrant ['ɪmɪgrənt] Einwanderer/ Einwanderin **IV ZI,** 13
to **immigrate** ['ɪmɪgreɪt] einwandern **IV U1,** 18
immigration [ˌɪmɪ'greɪʃn] Einwanderung, Immigration **IV U1,** 18
important [ɪm'pɔ:tnt] wichtig, wichtige/-r/-s **II**
impression [ɪm'preʃn] Eindruck **II**
in [ɪn] in; hinein, herein **I**
in all [ɪn‿'ɔ:l] insgesamt **III**
in fact [ɪn 'fækt] tatsächlich **IV U4,** 83
in front of [ˌɪn 'frʌnt‿əv] vor **II**
inch [ɪntʃ] Zoll (*Maßeinheit*) **III**
independent [ˌɪndɪ'pendənt] unabhängig **III**
Indian ['ɪndiən] indisch; Inder/-in; Indianer/-in **II**
indivisible [ˌɪndɪ'vɪzəbl] unteilbar **IV U2,** 32
industry ['ɪndəstri] Industrie **III**
info ['ɪnfəʊ] *Abk.:* Information ⟨**IV U3,** 67⟩
information [ˌɪnfə'meɪʃn] Information(en); Auskunft **I**
tourist information centre [ˌtʊərɪst ɪnfə'meɪʃn sentə] Touristik-Information **I**
ingredient [ɪn'gri:diənt] Zutat **IV U1,** 16
inside [ˌɪn'saɪd] innen; drinnen **II**
instead of [ɪn'sted‿əv] statt, anstelle von **IV U3,** 49
instructions [ɪn'strʌkʃnz] Anweisungen **IV U1,** 17
instrument ['ɪnstrəmənt] (Musik-)Instrument **III**
intelligent [ɪn'telɪdʒnt] intelligent, klug **IV U4,** 72
interest ['ɪntrəst] Interesse **IV U4,** 82
interested ['ɪntrəstɪd] interessiert **I**
interesting ['ɪntrəstɪŋ] interessant **I**
international [ˌɪntə'næʃnl] international **III**
Internet ['ɪntənet] Internet **II**
interview ['ɪntəvju:] Interview **II**
to **interview** ['ɪntəvju:] interviewen, befragen **IV U5,** 87
into ['ɪntə] in; hinein **I**
to **introduce** [ˌɪntrə'dju:s] einführen; vorstellen **IV U5,** 86
introduction [ˌɪntrə'dʌkʃn] Einführung; Einleitung **III**
invader [ɪn'veɪdə] Eindringling **IV U4,** 75
invasion [ɪn'veɪʒn] Invasion, Einmarsch **IV U4,** 76
to **invent** [ɪn'vent] erfinden **III**
invention [ɪn'venʃn] Erfindung **IV U4,** 69
to **investigate** [ɪn'vestɪgeɪt] ermitteln, untersuchen **IV U4,** 76
invitation [ˌɪnvɪ'teɪʃn] Einladung **I**
to **invite** [ɪn'vaɪt] einladen **I**
I.Q. [ˌaɪ 'kju:] IQ (Intelligenzquotient) **IV U4,** 75
Irish ['aɪərɪʃ] irisch, Irisch; Ire/Irin **III**
irregular [ɪ'regjələ] unregelmäßig **I**
island ['aɪlənd] Insel **I**
it [ɪt] es **I**
Italian [ɪ'tæliən] italienisch, Italienisch; Italiener/-in **I**
its [ɪts] sein/-e, ihr/-e **I**

J

jacket ['dʒækɪt] Jacke **II**
Jamaican [dʒə'meɪkən] jamaikanisch; Jamaikaner/-in **III**
January ['dʒænjuri] Januar **I**
jazz [dʒæz] Jazz (*Musikrichtung*) **III**
jazz shoes ['dʒæz ˌʃu:z] *Tanzschuhe für Jazzdance* **III**
jealous ['dʒeləs] neidisch **IV U2,** 35
jeans pl. [dʒi:nz] Jeans **I**
jerk [dʒɜ:k] Idiot/-in, Blödmann *(Umgangssprache)* **IV U2,** 36
jet ski ['dʒet ˌski:] Wassermotorrad; Jet-Ski ⟨**IV U5,** 93⟩
jewelry *(AE)* ['dʒu:əlri] Schmuck **IV U2,** 34
job [dʒɒb] Arbeit, Beruf **II**
to **jog** [dʒɒg] joggen **II**
to **join** [dʒɔɪn] verbinden; Mitglied werden **II**
joke [dʒəʊk] Witz **I**
to **joke** [dʒəʊk] einen Witz machen **IV U2,** 40
journalist ['dʒɜ:nəlɪst] Journalist/-in **IV U5,** 87
journey ['dʒɜ:ni] Reise, Tour **IV ZI,** 10
joy [dʒɔɪ] Freude **IV U3,** 58
judge [dʒʌdʒ] Wettkampfrichter/-in **III**
judo ['dʒu:dəʊ] Judo **III**
juice [dʒu:s] Saft **I**
July [dʒʊ'laɪ] Juli **I**
jumbled ['dʒʌmbld] durcheinander geworfen **I**
to **jump** [dʒʌmp] springen **III**
June [dʒu:n] Juni **I**
junior ['dʒu:niə] Jugend-, Junioren- **III**
just [dʒʌst] nur **I**; gerade **II**
just in time [ˌdʒʌst‿ɪn 'taɪm] gerade rechtzeitig ⟨**IV U5,** 100⟩
justice ['dʒʌstɪs] Gerechtigkeit **IV U2,** 32

K

karaoke [ˌkæri'əʊki] Karaoke **IV U1,** 28
*to **keep** [ki:p] aufbewahren **II**; behalten **IV U1,** 16
to keep away [ˌki:p ə'weɪ] fernhalten; wegbleiben, sich fernhalten **II**
key [ki:] Erklärung, Legende; Schlüssel **I**
keyboard ['ki:bɔ:d] Keyboard **III**
keyword [ki:wɜ:d] Schlüsselwort **IV U1,** 28
khaki ['kɑ:ki] khakifarben **IV U2,** 35
kick [kɪk] Stoß, (Fuß-)Tritt; Schuss (*beim Fußball*) **III**
to **kick** [kɪk] kicken; treten **III**
kickboard ['kɪkbɔ:d] Kickboard, Tretroller **IV U1,** 15
kid [kɪd] Zicklein **I**; Kind **I**

to **kill** [kɪl] töten **III**
kilo (= kilogramme) ['kɪləʊ = 'kɪləʊgræm] Kilo(gramm) **II**
kilometre (= km) [kɪ'lɒmɪtə] Kilometer **III**
kind [kaɪnd] Art **I**; freundlich, nett **III**
kinda (= kind of) ['kaɪndə] irgendwie *(Umgangssprache)* ⟨**IV U5,** 93⟩
king [kɪŋ] König **II**
kiss [kɪs] Kuss **IV U2,** 36
to **kiss** [kɪs] küssen **IV U2,** 38
kit [kɪt] Ausrüstung, Zeug **II**
kitchen ['kɪtʃɪn] Küche **I**
knee [ni:] Knie **II**
knife [naɪf] pl. **knives** [naɪvz] Messer **II**
to **knock over** [ˌnɒk 'əʊvə] umstoßen **II**
*to **know** [nəʊ] wissen; kennen **I**

L

lady ['leɪdi] Dame **IV U3,** 54
lake [leɪk] See **II**
lamb [læm] Lamm **I**
lame [leɪm] lahm; schwach ⟨**IV U2,** 41⟩
lamp [læmp] Lampe **IV U4,** 73
land [lænd] Grundstück; Boden; Festland **IV U3,** 51
to **land** [lænd] landen **II**
landmark ['lændmɑ:k] Wahrzeichen **III**
landscape ['lændskeɪp] Landschaft **III**
language ['læŋgwɪdʒ] Sprache **I**
lantern ['læntən] Laterne **I**
laptop ['læptɒp] Laptop **II**
large [lɑ:dʒ] groß **I**
last [lɑ:st] letzte/-r/-s **I**
late [leɪt] zu spät, spät **I**
the late 1920s [ðə ˌleɪt ˌnaɪn'ti:nˌtwenti:z] die späten Zwanzigerjahre des 20. Jahrhunderts **IV U5,** 85
later ['leɪtə] später **I**
Latin ['lætɪn] lateinamerikanisch; Lateinamerikaner/-in **IV U1,** 21
to **laugh** [lɑ:f] lachen **I**
*to **lay the table** ['leɪ ðə ˌteɪbl] den Tisch decken **II**
lead [led] Blei **III**
leaf [li:f] pl. **leaves** [li:vz] Blatt **III**
leaflet ['li:flət] Flugblatt, Prospekt **III**
to **leak** [li:k] auslaufen, lecken **IV U4,** 72
*to **leap** [li:p] springen **IV U4,** 75
*to **learn** [lɜ:n] lernen **I**
least [li:st] am wenigsten **III**; geringste/-r/-s **IV U5,** 92
at least [ˌət 'li:st] mindestens, wenigstens **IV U1,** 20
leather ['leðə] Leder **III**
*to **leave** [li:v] abfahren; verlassen; lassen **I**
to leave a message [ˌli:v‿ə 'mesɪdʒ] eine Nachricht hinterlassen **III**
leek [li:k] Lauch **III**
left [left] links; linke/-r/-s **I**
on the left [ˌɒn ðə 'left] links **I**
leg [leg] Bein **II**
lemonade [ˌlemə'neɪd] Limonade **I**
*to **lend** [lend] leihen **II**
less [les] weniger **III**
lesson ['lesn] Unterrichtsstunde **I**
*to **let** [let] lassen **II**
Let it out! [ˌlet‿ɪt‿'aʊt] Lass(t) es raus! **III**
letter ['letə] Buchstabe; Brief **I**
letterbox ['letəˌbɒks] Briefkasten **II**
lettuce ['letɪs] Blattsalat **IV U1,** 17
level ['levl] Ebene **IV U1,** 14
liberty ['lɪbəti] Freiheit **IV U2,** 32
library ['laɪbrəri] Bibliothek, Bücherei **I**
license plate *(AE)* ['laɪsənsˌpleɪt] Nummernschild **IV ZI,** 13
life [laɪf] pl. **lives** [laɪvz] Leben **I**
lifestyle ['laɪfstaɪl] Lebensstil ⟨**IV U5,** 100⟩
to **lift** [lɪft] hochziehen, hochheben **III**
light [laɪt] Licht **II**
light bulb ['laɪt ˌbʌlb] Glühbirne **IV U4,** 73
lightning (no pl.) ['laɪtnɪŋ] Blitz **IV U3,** 58
like [laɪk] wie, ähnlich **I**
to **like** [laɪk] mögen; gern haben **I**
lime [laɪm] Limette, Limone **II**
limit ['lɪmɪt] Grenze, Begrenzung **IV U1,** 18
line [laɪn] Linie **I**; Zeile **IV U1,** 23
line *(AE)* [laɪn] Warteschlange **IV U1,** 25
lingua franca [ˌlɪŋgwə 'fræŋkə] Verkehrssprache, Lingua franca **II**
lion [laɪən] Löwe **II**
list [lɪst] Liste **I**
to **listen** ['lɪsn] zuhören; (an)hören **I**
listening ['lɪsnɪŋ] Hören; Hörübung **I**
listening skills [ˌlɪsənɪŋ 'skɪlz] Hörtechniken **I**
little [lɪtl] klein **I**
a little [ə 'lɪtl] ein bisschen **I**
live [laɪv] live **III**
to **live** [lɪv] wohnen, leben **I**
to live happily ever after [lɪv 'hæpɪli evə‿ɑ:ftə] glücklich und zufrieden bis ans Lebensende leben **IV U5,** 86
living room ['lɪvɪŋ rʊm] Wohnzimmer **I**
local ['ləʊkl] örtlich, lokal, ortsansässig **IV U5,** 99
loch [lɒx] See *(schottisch)* **III**
to **lock** [lɒk] abschließen; zuschließen **II**
locker ['lɒkə] Schließfach **II**
lonely ['ləʊnli] einsam **III**
long [lɒŋ] lang **I**
long form ['lɒŋ fɔ:m] Langform **I**
long jump ['lɒŋ ˌdʒʌmp] Weitsprung **I**
look [lʊk] Blick **IV U5,** 85
to **look** [lʊk] schauen, sehen; aussehen **I**
to look after ['lʊk ˌɑ:ftə] sich kümmern um, aufpassen auf **II**
to look at ['lʊk æt] ansehen, anschauen **I**
to look for ['lʊk fɔ:] suchen **I**
to look forward to [ˌlʊk 'fɔ:wəd tə] sich freuen auf **IV U3,** 50
to look up [lʊk‿'ʌp] nachschlagen, heraussuchen; aufblicken **II**
*to **lose** [lu:z] verlieren **II**
loser ['lu:zə] Verlierer/-in **III**
a **lot** [ə 'lɒt] sehr; viel **I**
a lot of [ə 'lɒt‿əv] viel/-e, eine Menge **I**
lots (of) [lɒts] viel **I**
Lots of love [ˌlɒts‿əv 'lʌv] Liebe Grüße *(am Briefende)* **III**
loud [laʊd] laut **I**
love [lʌv] Liebe **IV U1,** 22
to **love** [lʌv] lieben **I**
Love, ... [lʌv] Herzliche Grüße, ..., Liebe Grüße, ... **I**
lovely ['lʌvli] schön, herrlich **II**
luck [lʌk] Glück **III**
good luck [ˌgʊd 'lʌk] viel Glück **II**
it's **lucky** [ɪts 'lʌki] ein Glück, dass **III**
lucky him ['lʌki ˌhɪm] der Glückliche **III**
luggage ['lʌgɪdʒ] (Reise-)Gepäck **III**
lunch [lʌntʃ] Mittagessen **I**
lunchtime ['lʌntʃtaɪm] Mittagszeit **I**
lyrics pl. ['lɪrɪks] Liedtext **III**

M

machine [mə'ʃi:n] Automat; Maschine **II**
mad [mæd] verrückt **III**
to be mad [bɪ 'mæd] wütend sein, sauer sein **II**
magazine [ˌmægə'zi:n] Zeitschrift **I**
magic ['mædʒɪk] Zauber-, Zauberei, Magie **II**
magnetism ['mægnətɪzəm] Magnetismus, magnetische Kräfte ⟨**IV U4,** 77⟩
mail [meɪl] Post **II**
mailbox ['meɪlbɒks] Briefkasten, Mailbox ⟨**IV U3,** 65⟩
main [meɪn] Haupt-, wichtigste/-r/-s **II**

main course [ˌmeɪn ˈkɔːs] Hauptgericht, Hauptgang **II**
*to **make** [meɪk] bilden; machen, tun **I**
to make ends meet [meɪk ˈendz ˌmiːt] mit seinem Geld auskommen ⟨**IV U1,** 22⟩
to make it [ˈmeɪk ˌɪt] es schaffen **IV U3,** 58
to make notes [ˌmeɪk ˈnəʊts] Notizen machen **III**
to make sure [ˌmeɪk ˈʃɔː] sich vergewissern, sichergehen **II**
make-up [ˈmeɪkʌp] Schminke, Make-up **II**
man [mæn] pl. **men** [men] Mann **I**
man [mæn] Mann *(Ausruf)* ⟨**IV U1,** 30⟩
manager [ˈmænɪdʒə] Geschäftsführer/-in **I**
mango [ˈmæŋgəʊ] Mango **II**
maniac [ˈmeɪniæk] Fanatiker/-in **II**
many [ˈmeni] viele **I**
map [mæp] Stadtplan, Landkarte **I**
maple [ˈmeɪpl] Ahorn **IV U1,** 17
marathon [ˈmærəθn] Marathon **IV U3,** 51
March [mɑːtʃ] März **I**
to **march** [mɑːtʃ] marschieren **IV U3,** 58
mark [mɑːk] Fleck; Note **II**
market [ˈmɑːkɪt] Markt **III**
married [ˈmærid] verheiratet **I**
to **marry** [ˈmæri] heiraten **III**
master [ˈmɑːstə] Meister **II**
match [mætʃ] Spiel, Match **II**
to **match** [mætʃ] zuordnen **I**; zusammenfügen; passen **III**
material [məˈtɪəriəl] materiell ⟨**IV U5,** 93⟩
Math *(AE)* [mæθ] Mathe **IV U2,** 33
Maths [mæθs] Mathe **II**
May [meɪ] Mai **I**
may [meɪ] dürfen **I**; könnte(n) vielleicht **IV U2,** 40
It may be … [ɪt ˈmeɪ biː] Es ist vielleicht … **II**
maybe [ˈmeɪbi] vielleicht **I**
mayonnaise [ˌmeɪəˈneɪz] Majonäse **IV U2,** 39
me [miː] mich; mir **I**
meal [miːl] Mahlzeit, Essen **II**
*to **mean** [miːn] bedeuten; meinen **I**
meaning [ˈmiːnɪŋ] Bedeutung **I**
mechanic [mɪˈkænɪk] Mechaniker/-in **IV U4,** 69
media [ˈmiːdiə] Medien **II**
medium [ˈmiːdiəm] mittel **I**
*to **meet** [miːt] sich treffen, treffen **I**
to meet halfway [miːt hɑːfˈweɪ] sich (auf halbem Weg) entgegenkommen **IV U4,** 74

meeting [ˈmiːtɪŋ] Treffen; Besprechung ⟨**IV U3,** 67⟩
member [ˈmembə] Mitglied **III**
to **mend** [mend] reparieren, ausbessern **IV U1,** 21
to **mention** [ˈmenʃn] erwähnen **IV U3,** 64
menu [ˈmenjuː] Speiseplan, Speisekarte **II**
Meow! [miːˈaʊ] Miau! **I**
merit [ˈmerɪt] Auszeichnung **II**
mess [mes] Unordnung, Durcheinander **I**
message [ˈmesɪdʒ] Nachricht **II**
text message [ˈtekst ˌmesɪdʒ] SMS **I**
to leave a message [ˌliːv‿ə ˈmesɪdʒ] eine Nachricht hinterlassen **III**
to **mess up** [ˈmes‿ʌp] durcheinanderbringen **III**
metre [ˈmiːtə] Meter **II**
Mexican [ˈmeksɪkən] mexikanisch; Mexikaner/-in ⟨**IV U5,** 100⟩
microphone [ˈmaɪkrəfəʊn] Mikrofon **II**
microscope [ˈmaɪkrəskəʊp] Mikroskop **IV U2,** 32
microwave [ˈmaɪkrəweɪv] Mikrowelle **IV U4,** 72
midday [ˌmɪdˈdeɪ] Mittag ⟨**IV U5,** 100⟩
middle [ˈmɪdl] Mitte **II**
Middle-Eastern [ˌmɪdl ˈiːstən] aus dem Nahen Osten **IV U1,** 21
middle school [ˈmɪdl ˌskuːl] *Schulform zwischen Grundschule und weiterführender Schule* **IV ZI,** 11
might [maɪt] könnte(n) **IV U3,** 57
mighty [ˈmaɪti] mächtig, gewaltig ⟨**IV U3,** 61⟩
migrant worker [ˌmaɪgrnt ˈwɜːkə] Wanderarbeiter/-in, Gastarbeiter/-in ⟨**IV U5,** 100⟩
mile [maɪl] Meile **II**
milk [mɪlk] Milch **I**
to **milk** [mɪlk] melken **I**
milkshake [ˈmɪlkˌʃeɪk] Milkshake **IV U1,** 17
millennium [mɪˈleniəm] Jahrtausend; das Jahr 2000 **III**
million [ˈmɪljən] Million **II**
mind [maɪnd] Meinung, Ansicht **III**
mind map [ˈmaɪnd mæp] Wörternetz *(eine Art Schaubild)* **I**
to **mind s.th.** [maɪnd] etw. ausmachen **IV U1,** 29
mine [maɪn] meins, meine/-r **II**; Bergwerk **III**
mineral water [ˈmɪnrl ˌwɔːtə] Mineralwasser **II**
minestrone [ˌmɪnɪˈstrəʊni] Minestrone, Gemüsesuppe **II**

mini [ˈmɪni] Mini- **I**
minibus [ˈmɪnɪbʌs] Kleinbus ⟨**IV U3,** 65⟩
minute [ˈmɪnɪt] Minute **I**
mirror [ˈmɪrə] Spiegel **III**
to **miss** [mɪs] verpassen; vermissen **II**
missing [ˈmɪsɪŋ] fehlend **I**
mistake [mɪˈsteɪk] Fehler **II**
mixed [mɪkst] gemischt **IV U1,** 27
mobile [ˈməʊbaɪl] Handy **I**
modal [ˈməʊdl] Modalverb **II**
model [ˈmɒdl] Modell **III**
modern [ˈmɒdn] modern **II**
mom *(AE)* [mɒm] Mama **IV U1,** 21
moment [ˈməʊmənt] Augenblick **IV U3,** 58
at the moment [ˌæt ðə ˈməʊmənt] im Augenblick, momentan **I**
monastery [ˈmɒnəstri] Kloster **III**
Monday [ˈmʌndeɪ] Montag **I**
on Mondays [ˌɒn ˈmʌndeɪz] montags **I**
money [ˈmʌni] Geld **I**
monster [ˈmɒnstə] Monster **IV U1,** 16
month [mʌnθ] Monat **I**
moon [muːn] Mond **II**
moor [mɔː] Hochmoor **III**
more [mɔː] mehr; weitere **I**
more and more [ˌmɔː‿ən‿ˈmɔː] immer (mehr) **III**
more and more popular [ˌmɔː‿ən‿mɔː ˈpɒpjələ] immer beliebter **III**
morning [ˈmɔːnɪŋ] Morgen; Vormittag **I**
most [məʊst] am meisten, am liebsten **III**
most … [məʊst] die meisten … **III**
motel [məʊˈtel] Motel **IV U4,** 73
mother [ˈmʌðə] Mutter **I**
motor [ˈməʊtə] Motor **IV U4,** 76
to **motor** [ˈməʊtə] fahren ⟨**IV U3,** 61⟩
motorcycle [ˈməʊtəˌsaɪkl] Motorrad **IV U3,** 49
mountain [ˈmaʊntɪn] Berg **III**
mouse [maʊs] pl. **mice** [maɪs] Maus **I**
mousetrap [ˈmaʊstræp] Mausefalle **II**
mouth [maʊθ] Mund **II**
to **move** [muːv] bewegen **II**; umziehen **III**
to move along [muːv əˈlɒŋ] weitergehen **III**
movie *(AE)* [ˈmuːvi] Film **IV ZI,** 13
movie theater *(AE)* [ˌmuːvi ˈθɪətə] Kino **IV U5,** 87
the movies *(AE)* [ˈmuːviz] das Kino **IV U2,** 36
MP3 player [ˌempiːˈθriː ˌpleɪə] MP3-Spieler, MP3-Player **II**
Mr [ˈmɪstə] Herr **I**

Mrs ['mɪsɪz] Frau **I**
much [mʌtʃ] viel **I**
mum [mʌm] Mutti, Mama **I**
to **murder** ['mɜ:də] ermorden **III**
museum [mju:'zi:əm] Museum **I**
music ['mju:zɪk] Musik **I**
music stand ['mju:zɪk ˌstænd] Notenständer **III**
musical ['mju:zɪkəl] Musical **IV ZI,** 13
musician [mju:'zɪʃn] Musiker/-in **III**
must [mʌst] müssen **I**
mustn't ['mʌsnt] nicht dürfen **II**
my [maɪ] mein/-e **I**
myself [maɪ'self] ich/mir/mich (selbst) **III**
mystery ['mɪstəri] Geheimnis, Rätsel **III**

N

name [neɪm] Name **I**
to **name** [neɪm] nennen **IV U1,** 18
napkin ['næpkɪn] Serviette **II**
narrator [nə'reɪtə] Erzähler/-in **IV U4,** 76
narrow ['nærəʊ] eng, schmal **IV U3,** 58
nasty ['nɑ:sti] schlimm; böse, gemein; gefährlich **IV U3,** 57
national ['næʃnl] national **III**
national park [ˌnæʃnl 'pɑ:k] Nationalpark, Naturpark **IV U3,** 49
Native American [ˌneɪtɪv ə'merɪkən] *Ureinwohner/-in von Amerika,* Indianer/-in **IV ZI,** 11
naturally ['nætʃrəli] natürlich, selbstverständlich **IV U4,** 75
nature ['neɪtʃə] Natur **IV U3,** 50
near [nɪə] in der Nähe von; nahe **I**
neat [ni:t] klasse, prima; ordentlich, sauber **II**
neck [nek] Hals, Nacken **II**
to **need** [ni:d] brauchen **I**
needn't ['ni:dnt] nicht müssen, nicht brauchen **I**
negation [nɪ'geɪʃn] Verneinung **II**
negative ['negətɪv] negativ **IV U4,** 74
neighborhood *(AE)* ['neɪbəhʊd] Gegend, Viertel; Nachbarschaft **IV U1,** 15
neighbour ['neɪbə] Nachbar/-in **III**
nephew ['nefju:] Neffe **III**
nervous ['nɜ:vəs] nervös **II**
net [net] Netz **III**
never ['nevə] nie **I**
Never mind. [ˌnevə 'maɪnd] Macht nichts. **III**
new [nju:] neu **I**
news [nju:z] Nachricht(en) **III**
newsagent ['nju:zˌeɪdʒnt] Zeitungsladen **I**
newspaper ['nju:sˌpeɪpə] Zeitung **I**
next [nekst] als nächste/-r/-s **I**; nächste/-r/-s **I**
next door [ˌnekst 'dɔ:] nebenan; neben **II**
next to ['nekst tʊ] neben **I**
nice [naɪs] nett; schön **I**; gut **II**
nickel ['nɪkl] *amerik. Geldeinheit* **IV U1,** 17
night [naɪt] Nacht **I**
nightclub ['naɪtklʌb] Disko, Nachtklub **IV U5,** 91
nil [nɪl] Null *(in Sportergebnissen)* **III**
no [nəʊ] nein; kein/-e **I**
no one ['nəʊ wʌn] niemand, keiner **II**
no way [ˌnəʊ 'weɪ] auf keinen Fall **IV U3,** 57
No way! [ˌnəʊ 'weɪ] Gibt's nicht! **III**
nobody ['nəʊbədi] niemand **II**
noise [nɔɪz] Lärm, Krach; Geräusch **II**
noodle ['nu:dl] Nudel **II**
normal ['nɔ:ml] normal **III**
north [nɔ:θ] Norden **I**
nose [nəʊz] Nase **I**
not [nɒt] nicht; kein/-e **I**
not at all [ˌnɒt‿ət‿'ɔ:l] gar nicht, überhaupt nicht **II**
not … either [ˌnɒt … 'aɪðə] auch nicht **III**
not … nor [nɔ:] weder … noch **IV U4,** 76
not … yet [nɒt … 'jet] noch nicht **II**
notes [nəʊt(s)] Notiz(en) **II**
to make notes [ˌmeɪk 'nəʊts] Notizen machen **III**
to take notes [ˌteɪk 'nəʊts] Notizen machen **II**
nothing ['nʌθɪŋ] nichts **II**
to **notice** ['nəʊtɪs] bemerken **III**
notice board ['nəʊtɪs bɔ:d] Anschlagbrett, Schwarzes Brett **III**
novel ['nɒvl] Roman **IV U3,** 57
November [nəʊ'vembə] November **I**
now [naʊ] jetzt, nun **I**
number ['nʌmbə] Zahl, Nummer **I**
number plate *(BE)* ['nʌmbə ˌpleɪt] Nummernschild **IV ZI,** 13

O

object ['ɒbdʒɪkt] Objekt **II**
observatory [əb'zɜ:vətri] Observatorium, Sternwarte **III**
o'clock [ə'klɒk] Uhr **I**
October [ɒk'təʊbə] Oktober **I**
odd [ɒd] merkwürdig, seltsam **II**
odd one out [ˌɒd wʌn 'aʊt] Element, das nicht dazugehört; Element, das aus der Reihe fällt **II**
of [ɒv] von **I**
of course [ˌəv 'kɔ:s] selbstverständlich, natürlich **I**
to **offer** ['ɒfə] anbieten **III**
office ['ɒfɪs] Büro **IV U2,** 38
officer ['ɒfɪsə] Beamter/Beamtin **III**
official [ə'fɪʃl] offiziell, amtlich **II**; Beamter/Beamtin **IV U1,** 18
often ['ɒfn] oft **I**
Oh dear. [əʊ 'dɪə] Oje. **II**
oil platform ['ɔɪl ˌplætfɔ:m] Ölbohrinsel **II**
OK [əʊ'keɪ] o.k., okay **I**
old [əʊld] alt **I**
old-fashioned [ˌəʊld 'fæʃnd] altmodisch **IV U5,** 90
ollie ['ɒli] *Skateboardtrick* **III**
Olympic [ə'lɪmpɪk] olympisch **III**
on [ɒn] auf; am **I**
on foot [ˌɒn 'fʊt] zu Fuß **I**
on Mondays [ˌɒn 'mʌndeɪz] montags **I**
on the left [ˌɒn ðə 'left] links **I**
on the right [ˌɒn ðə 'raɪt] rechts **I**
once [wʌns] einmal **II**
Once upon a time … [wʌns‿ə'pɒn‿ə ˌtaɪm] Es war einmal … **II**
one(s) [wʌn(z)] *Platzhalter für ein Nomen* **III**
one and a half [ˌwʌn‿ən‿ə 'hɑ:f] eineinhalb, anderthalb **III**
one another [ˌwʌn‿ə'nʌðə] einander **III**
one way ['wʌn weɪ] einfach **II**
online [ˌɒn'laɪn] online **IV U2,** 46
only ['əʊnli] einzige/-r/-s; nur; erst; bloß **I**
only child ['əʊnli ˌtʃaɪld] Einzelkind **I**
onto ['ɒntu:] auf **II**
open ['əʊpn] offen **II**
to **open** ['əʊpn] öffnen, aufmachen **I**
opening night ['əʊpnɪŋ ˌnaɪt] Premiere **I**
opening time ['əʊpnɪŋ ˌtaɪm] Öffnungszeit **I**
opera ['ɒprə] Oper **III**
opinion [ə'pɪnjən] Meinung **IV U3,** 53
opposite ['ɒpəzɪt] gegenüber **I**; Gegenteil, Gegensatz **II**
oppression [ə'preʃn] Unterdrückung **IV U1,** 18
or [ɔ:] oder **I**
orange ['ɒrɪndʒ] orange(farben) **I**; Orange **II**

English – German

orchestra ['ɔ:kɪstrə] Orchester **III**
order ['ɔ:də] Reihenfolge **I**
to **order** ['ɔ:də] bestellen **II**
ordinal number ['ɔ:dɪnl ˌnʌmbə] Ordnungszahl **I**
organization [ˌɔ:gənaɪ'zeɪʃn] Organization ⟨**IV U1,** 30⟩
to **organize** ['ɔ:gənaɪz] organisieren **I**
organizer ['ɔ:gənaɪzə] Organisator/-in; Veranstalter/-in ⟨**IV U1,** 30⟩
other ['ʌðə] andere/-/r/-s **I**
ought to [ɔ:t] sollen **IV U2,** 34
our [aʊə] unser/-e **I**
ours [aʊəz] unsere/-r/-s **II**
ourselves [ˌaʊə'selvz] wir/uns (selbst) **III**
out and about ['aʊt‿nd‿ə'baʊt] unterwegs **III**
outdoor [ˌaʊt'dɔ:] Freiluft-; Outdoor- **IV U3,** 50
outer space [ˌaʊtə 'speɪs] Weltraum, Weltall ⟨**IV U4,** 77⟩
outside [ˌaʊt'saɪd] draußen; nach draußen **I**; vor; außerhalb **II**
over ['əʊvə] über; vorbei **I**
over the moon [ˌəʊvə ðə 'mu:n] überglücklich **II**
over there [ˌəʊvə 'ðeə] da drüben **I**
to **overdo sth.** [ˌəʊvə'du:] etw. übertreiben **IV U2,** 36
overhead projector [ˌəʊvəhed prə'dʒektə] Tageslichtprojektor, Overheadprojektor **III**
overnight [ˌəʊvə'naɪt] über Nacht **IV U5,** 91
overwhelmed [ˌəʊvə'welmd] überwältigt **IV U5,** 84
own [əʊn] eigene/-r/-s **I**
own goal [ˌəʊn 'gəʊl] Eigentor **III**
owner ['əʊnə] Besitzer/-in **III**

P

pacemaker ['peɪsˌmeɪkə] Herzschrittmacher **IV U4,** 69
to **pack** [pæk] packen **I**
packet ['pækɪt] Päckchen, Packung **I**
page [peɪdʒ] Seite **I**
front page ['frʌnt ˌpeɪdʒ] Titelseite **II**
to be a **pain** [ˌbi: ə 'peɪn] jdm. auf den Geist gehen (*Umgangssprache*) **I**
painful ['peɪnfʊl] schmerzhaft **IV U5,** 92
paint [peɪnt] Lack; Farbe **II**
to **paint** [peɪnt] streichen; malen **I**
painter ['peɪntə] Maler/-in **II**
painting ['peɪntɪŋ] Gemälde **III**
pair [peə] Paar **I**
palace ['pælɪs] Palast **III**
pancake ['pænkeɪk] Pfannkuchen **III**
Pancake Day ['pænkeɪk ˌdeɪ] Fastnachtsdienstag **III**
OK, don't **panic.** ['pænɪk] OK, nur keine Panik. **II**
pants *(AE)* [pænts] Hose **IV U2,** 34
paper ['peɪpə] Papier **III**
parade [pə'reɪd] Umzug (*bei Festen, Karneval*) **III**
paragraph ['pærəgrɑ:f] Absatz, Abschnitt **III**
parents ['peərənts] Eltern **I**
park [pɑ:k] Park **I**
to **park** [pɑ:k] parken **I**
part [pɑ:t] Rolle **I**; Teil **I**
partner ['pɑ:tnə] Partner/-in **I**
party ['pɑ:ti] Party, Feier **I**
to **pass** [pɑ:s] durchgehen **IV U1,** 21; weitergeben **IV U2,** 32
passenger ['pæsndʒə] Passagier/-in **IV U1,** 29
passive voice [ˌpæsɪv 'vɔɪs] Passiv (*Grammatik*) **IV U4,** 72
passport ['pɑ:spɔ:t] Pass, Reisepass **III**
Passport Control [ˌpɑ:spɔ:t kən'trəʊl] Passkontrolle **III**
past [pɑ:st] nach (*bei Uhrzeiten*) **I**; Vergangenheit **II**
past progressive [ˌpɑ:st prə'gresɪv] Verlaufsform der Vergangenheit **II**
past tense [ˌpɑ:st 'tens] Vergangenheit **II**
simple past [ˌsɪmpl 'pɑ:st] einfache Vergangenheit **II**
past … [pɑ:st] an … vorbei, an … vorüber **II**
pasta ['pæstə] Nudeln **II**
pastrami *(AE)* [pæs'trɑ:mi] geräuchertes Rindfleisch **IV U1,** 17
to **pat** [pæt] tätscheln **I**
path [pɑ:θ] Weg; Pfad **II**
to **pave** [peɪv] pflastern **IV U5,** 99
*to **pay** [peɪ] (be)zahlen **II**
PC [ˌpi:'si:] PC **II**
PE (= Physical Education) [ˌpi:'i: = ˌfɪzɪkl‿edʒʊ'keɪʃn] Sport **II**
pen [pen] Füller **I**
penalty ['penlti] Elfmeter **III**
pencil ['pensl] Bleistift **I**
pencil case ['pensl ˌkeɪs] Federmäppchen **I**
penny ['peni] pl. **pence (p)** [pens] Penny, *Plural* Pence (*britisches Geld*) **I**
pen-pal ['penˌpæl] Brieffreund/-in **II**
people ['pi:pl] Leute **I**
per [pɜ:] pro **IV U5,** 99
per cent [pə'sent] Prozent **IV U4,** 83
perfect ['pɜ:fɪkt] perfekt **II**
present perfect [ˌpreznt 'pɜ:fɪkt] Perfekt **II**
to **perform** [pə'fɔ:m] aufführen, auftreten **III**
performance [pə'fɔ:məns] Aufführung, Vorstellung **III**
period ['pɪəriəd] Unterrichtsstunde **II**
permanent home ['pɜ:mənənt ˌhəʊm] fester Wohnsitz ⟨**IV U5,** 100⟩
person ['pɜ:sn] Person **I**
personal ['pɜ:sənl] persönlich **III**
pet [pet] Haustier **I**
pets corner [ˌpets 'kɔ:nə] Streichelzoo **I**
phone (= telephone) [fəʊn = 'telɪfəʊn] Telefon **I**
phone number ['fəʊn ˌnʌmbə] Telefonnummer **I**
to **phone** [fəʊn] anrufen **I**
photo ['fəʊtəʊ] Foto **I**
to **photograph** ['fəʊtəgrɑ:f] fotografieren **IV U5,** 91
photographer [fə'tɒgrəfə] Fotograf/-in **IV U5,** 91
photography [fə'tɒgrəfi] Fotografie **IV U5,** 86
phrasal verb [ˌfreɪzl 'vɜ:b] Phrasal Verb (*Verb mit Präposition oder Partikel*) **IV U2,** 43
phrase [freɪz] Ausdruck; Redewendung **I**
PE (= Physical Education) [ˌpi:'i: = ˌfɪzɪkl‿edʒʊ'keɪʃn] Sport **II**
Physics ['fɪzɪks] Physik **II**
piano [pɪ'ænəʊ] Klavier **III**
to **pick** [pɪk] pflücken ⟨**IV U5,** 100⟩
to pick up ['pɪk‿ˌʌp] aufheben; abholen **II**
picker ['pɪkə] (Obst)pflücker/-in ⟨**IV U5,** 100⟩
pickpocket ['pɪkˌpɒkɪt] Taschendieb/-in **III**
picnic ['pɪknɪk] Picknick **I**
picture ['pɪktʃə] Bild **I**
pie [paɪ] Pastete **II**
piece [pi:s] Stück; Teil **I**
pier [pɪə] Pier, Hafendamm **III**
to **pierce** [pɪəs] durchstechen, piercen **III**
pig [pɪg] Schwein **I**
pigeon ['pɪdʒən] Taube **II**
pilot ['paɪlət] Pilot/-in **II**

pine [paɪn] Tanne **IV U3,** 51
pineapple ['paɪnˌæpl] Ananas **IV U5,** 99
pink [pɪŋk] rosa, pink **I**
pipe [paɪp] Pfeife **III**
pirate ['paɪrət] Pirat/-in **I**
pitch [pɪtʃ] Spielfeld **III**
(that's a) **pity** [ˌðæts ə 'pɪti] (Das ist) schade **IV U2,** 37
pizza ['pi:tsə] Pizza **I**
place [pleɪs] Platz, Ort, Stelle **I**
plan [plæn] Plan **I**
to **plan** [plæn] planen **II**
plane [pleɪn] Flugzeug **II**
planet ['plænɪt] Planet **IV U4,** 71
plank [plæŋk] Planke; Brett **I**
planner ['plænə] Jahresplaner **I**
plant [plɑ:nt] Pflanze **IV U3,** 49
plastic ['plæstɪk] Plastik **III**
plate [pleɪt] Teller **II**
platform ['plætfɔ:m] Plattform, Tribüne; Bahnsteig **III**
play [pleɪ] Theaterstück **I**
to **play** [pleɪ] spielen **I**
player ['pleɪə] Spieler/-in **II**
playground ['pleɪgraʊnd] Schulhof; Spielplatz **I**
please [pli:z] bitte **I**
to **pledge** [pledʒ] geloben **IV U2,** 33
plenty ['plenti] genug, ausreichend **I**
plug [plʌg] Stöpsel; Stecker **IV U4,** 72
plural ['plʊərl] Plural, Mehrzahl **I**
pm [ˌpi:'em] nachmittags **I**
poacher ['pəʊtʃə] Wilderer **IV U3,** 64
back **pocket** [ˌbæk 'pɒkɪt] hintere Hosentasche **II**
pocket money ['pɒkɪt ˌmʌni] Taschengeld **II**
poem ['pəʊɪm] Gedicht **I**
poet ['pəʊɪt] Dichter/-in, Poet/-in **III**
poetry ['pəʊətri] Dichtung; Gedichte **III**
poetry slam ['pəʊətri ˌslæm] Gedichtewettbewerb **III**
point [pɔɪnt] Punkt **II**
to **point** [pɔɪnt] zeigen **I**
to point to ... [pɔɪnt 'tə] auf ... zeigen **II**
pointed ['pɔɪntɪd] spitz zulaufend **IV U4,** 75
polar bear ['pəʊlə ˌbeə] Eisbär **IV U3,** 64
police [pə'li:s] Polizei **II**
policewoman [pə'li:sˌwʊmən] Polizistin **II**
Polish ['pəʊlɪʃ] polnisch, Polnisch; Pole/Polin **IV U1,** 16
polite [pə'laɪt] höflich **I**
pompom ['pɒmpɒm] Pompom (*bunte Quaste*) **IV U2,** 32
poor [pɔ:] arm **III**
pop [pɒp] Popmusik **II**
pop concert ['pɒp ˌkɒnsət] Popkonzert **II**
popular ['pɒpjələ] beliebt, populär **II**
more and more popular [ˌmɔ:‿ən‿mɔ: 'pɒpjələ] immer beliebter **III**
population [ˌpɒpjə'leɪʃn] Bevölkerung **IV U5,** 99
pork [pɔ:k] Schweinefleisch **II**
positive ['pɒzətɪv] positiv **IV U1,** 23
possessive pronoun [pəˌzesɪv 'prəʊnaʊn] Possessivpronomen **II**
possible ['pɒsəbl] möglich **III**
post office ['pəʊst ˌɒfɪs] Postamt **II**
postcard ['pəʊstkɑ:d] Postkarte **I**
poster ['pəʊstə] Poster **I**
potato [pə'teɪtəʊ] pl. **potatoes** [pə'teɪtəʊz] Kartoffel **II**
pound [paʊnd] Pfund **I**
pound (lb) [paʊnd] Pfund (*Gewichtseinheit*) **III**
to **pound** [paʊnd] hämmern, schlagen **II**
poverty ['pɒvəti] Armut **IV U1,** 18
powder ['paʊdə] Puder, Pulver **III**
powerful ['paʊəfl] stark, mächtig **III**
practice ['præktɪs] Übung; Probe; Training **I**
to **practice** *(AE)* ['præktɪs] üben **IV U4,** 69
to **practise** ['præktɪs] üben **I**
pre-listening [ˌpri:'lɪsnɪŋ] vor dem Hören **II**
predictable [prɪ'dɪktəbl] vorhersehbar, voraussagbar **IV U3,** 64
to **prefer** [prə'fɜ:] vorziehen, bevorzugen **IV U2,** 35
premiere ['premieə] Premiere, Uraufführung **IV U5,** 91
preposition [ˌprepə'zɪʃn] Präposition **I**
present ['preznt] Gegenwart **I**; Geschenk **I**
present perfect [ˌpreznt 'pɜ:fɪkt] Perfekt **II**
present progressive [ˌpreznt prə'gresɪv] Verlaufsform der Gegenwart **I**
to **present** [prɪ'zent] vorstellen, präsentieren **II**
presentation [ˌprezn'teɪʃn] Präsentation **III**
president ['prezɪdnt] Präsident/-in **IV ZI,** 12
pretty ['prɪti] hübsch, nett; ziemlich **IV U1,** 21
price [praɪs] Preis **I**
primary school ['praɪməri ˌsku:l] Grundschule **III**
prince [prɪns] Prinz **III**
principal *(AE)* ['prɪntsəpl] Schulleiter/-in **IV U2,** 34
to **print** [prɪnt] drucken **II**
prison ['prɪzn] Gefängnis **II**
private ['praɪvɪt] privat **IV U5,** 91
prize [praɪz] Preis **I**
probably ['prɒbəbli] wahrscheinlich **II**
problem ['prɒbləm] Problem **I**; schwierige Aufgabe **II**
procession [prə'seʃn] Umzug **I**
profile ['prəʊfaɪl] Profil **III**
program *(AE)* ['prəʊgræm] Programm; Sendung **IV U3,** 50
programme ['prəʊgræm] Programm **I**
past **progressive** [ˌpɑ:st prə'gresɪv] Verlaufsform der Vergangenheit **II**
present **progressive** [ˌpreznt prə'gresɪv] Verlaufsform der Gegenwart **I**
project ['prɒdʒekt] Projekt **I**
to **promise** ['prɒmɪs] versprechen **II**
prompt [prɒmt] Stichwort **IV U3,** 56
pronoun ['prəʊnaʊn] Pronomen, Fürwort **I**
possessive pronoun [pəˌzesɪv 'prəʊnaʊn] Possessivpronomen **II**
pros and cons pl. [ˌprəʊz‿n 'kɒnz] Pro und Kontra, Für und Wider **IV U1,** 19
to **protect** [prə'tekt] (be)schützen **III**
proud [praʊd] stolz **IV U5,** 84
to **provide** [prəʊ'vaɪd] zur Verfügung stellen **IV U1,** 21
public ['pʌblɪk] öffentlich; Öffentlichkeit **IV U3,** 56
pudding ['pʊdɪŋ] Nachtisch **II**
rice pudding [raɪs 'pʊdɪŋ] Milchreis **II**
to **pull** [pʊl] ziehen **IV U3,** 58
pullover ['pʊləʊvə] Pullover **I**
pupil ['pju:pl] Schüler/-in **I**
purple ['pɜ:pl] lila **I**
purse [pɜ:s] Geldbeutel, Portmonnee **III**
to **push** [pʊʃ] stoßen, schieben, drücken, drängeln **III**
*to **put** [pʊt] legen, setzen, stellen, tun **I**
to put away [pʊt‿ə'weɪ] aufräumen **III**
to put in [pʊt‿'ɪn] einsetzen **I**
to put on [ˌpʊt‿'ɒn] anziehen **II**
puzzle ['pʌzl] Rätsel **I**

Q

quarter ['kwɔ:tə] Viertel **I**; *amerik. Geldeinheit* **IV U1,** 17
queen [kwi:n] Königin **III**
the Queen [ðə 'kwi:n] die Königin **II**
question ['kwestʃən] Frage **I**
question tag ['kwestʃən ˌtæg] Frageanhängsel **II**
questionnaire [ˌkwestʃə'neə] Fragebogen **II**
queue [kju:] Warteschlange **II**
to **queue** [kju:] anstehen, sich anstellen **III**
quick [kwɪk] schnell **I**
quiet ['kwaɪət] ruhig, still **I**; leise **II**
*to **quit** [kwɪt] aufhören; aufgeben **IV U3,** 57
quite [kwaɪt] ziemlich; ganz, völlig **III**
quiz [kwɪz] Quiz, Ratespiel **I**
quota ['kwəʊtə] Anteil; zugelassene Einwanderungsquote **IV U1,** 18

R

race [reɪs] Rennen, Lauf **I**
racket ['rækɪt] Schläger **III**
radio ['reɪdiəʊ] Radio **I**
raft [rɑ:ft] Floß **IV U3,** 57
rain [reɪn] Regen **III**
to **rain** [reɪn] regnen **I**
ramp [ræmp] Sprungrampe; Rampe **III**
ranch *(AE)* [ræntʃ] Ranch **IV U5,** 99
ranger ['reɪndʒə] Aufseher/-in, Ranger/-in **IV U3,** 50
rap [ræp] Rap **I**
rapids (pl.) ['ræpɪdz] Stromschnellen **IV U3,** 57
rapper ['ræpə] Rapper (*Rapsänger/-in*) **III**
rating ['reɪtɪŋ] Bewertung **IV U3,** 64
raven ['reɪvn] Rabe **II**
RE (= Religious Education) [ˌɑ:r'i: = rɪˌlɪdʒəs‿edʒʊ'keɪʃn] Religion **II**
to **react** [ri'ækt] reagieren **IV U1,** 29
*to **read** [ri:d] lesen **I**
readable ['ri:dəbl] lesbar **III**
ready ['redi] fertig, bereit **II**
to get ready [ˌget 'redi] sich fertig machen **II**
real [rɪəl] echt **I**
real talk [ˌrɪəl 'tɔ:k] echtes Alltagsenglisch **I**
real estate *(AE)* ['rɪəl ɪˌsteɪt] Immobilien **IV U5,** 99
reality [ri'æləti] Realität, Wirklichkeit **IV U4,** 69
to **realize** ['rɪəlaɪz] begreifen, erkennen **IV U3,** 58
really ['rɪəli] wirklich **I**
reason ['ri:zn] Grund **II**
to **receive** [rɪ'si:v] bekommen, empfangen **IV U2,** 33
reception [rɪ'sepʃn] Rezeption, Empfang **IV U4,** 73
recipe ['resɪpi] Rezept **I**
to **recognize** ['rekəgnaɪz] wiedererkennen, erkennen **II**
to **recommend** [ˌrekə'mend] empfehlen **IV U5,** 90
record ['rekɔ:d] Schallplatte **III**
to **record** [rɪ'kɔ:d] aufnehmen **IV U1,** 23
recorder [rɪ'kɔ:də] Blockflöte **III**
red [red] rot **I**
referee (= ref) [ˌrefr'i:] Schiedsrichter/-in **III**
reflexive pronoun [rɪˌfleksɪv 'prəʊnaʊn] Reflexivpronomen **III**
refrigerator [rɪ'frɪdʒəreɪtə] Kühlschrank **IV U4,** 72
reggae ['regeɪ] Reggae (*Musikrichtung*) **III**
region ['ri:dʒn] Region, Gebiet **III**
register ['redʒɪstə] Klassenbuch **II**; Register, Sprachebene **IV U2,** 38
regular ['regjələ] regelmäßig **I**
rehabilitation [ˌri:həˌbɪlɪ'teɪʃn] Rehabilitation, Drogenentzug ⟨**IV U5,** 92⟩
rehabilitation program [ˌri:həˌbɪlɪ'teɪʃn ˌprəʊgræm] Entziehungskur ⟨**IV U5,** 92⟩
to **reject** [ri:'dʒekt] ablehnen, zurückweisen, abweisen **IV U1,** 21
to **relate to (s.o./sth.)** [rɪ'leɪt‿tə] eine Beziehung/Zugang zu jdm./etw. finden ⟨**IV U5,** 91⟩
to **relax** [rɪ'læks] (sich) entspannen, sich erholen **III**
religion [rɪ'lɪdʒn] Religion **III**
RE (= Religious Education) [ˌɑ:r'i: = rɪˌlɪdʒəs‿edʒʊ'keɪʃn] Religion **II**
to **remember** [rɪ'membə] denken an, nicht vergessen; sich erinnern an **I**
to **remind s.o. of s.th.** [rɪ'maɪnd] jdn. an etw. erinnern **IV U4,** 75
remote control [rɪ'məʊt 'kəntrəʊl] Fernbedienung **IV U4,** 69
to **repair** [rɪ'peə] reparieren, ausbessern **IV U4,** 69
to **repeat** [rɪ'pi:t] wiederholen **I**
to **reply** [rɪ'plaɪ] antworten **IV U2,** 40
report [rɪ'pɔ:t] Bericht **II**
report card (AE) [rɪ'pɔ:t ˌkɑ:d] Zeugnis **IV U2,** 33
to **report** [rɪ'pɔ:t] berichten **III**
reported speech [rɪˌpɔ:tɪd 'spi:tʃ] indirekte Rede **IV U5,** 89
reporter [rɪ'pɔ:tə] Reporter/-in **III**
republic [rɪ'pʌblɪk] Republik **IV U2,** 32
to **rescue** ['reskju:] retten **IV U3,** 58
research [rɪ'sɜ:tʃ] Forschung ⟨**IV U3,** 65⟩
reservation [ˌrezə'veɪʃn] Reservat ⟨**IV U3,** 67⟩
respect [rɪ'spekt] Respekt **III**
response [rɪ'spɒns] Reaktion, Antwort **III**
responsible [rɪ'spɒnsəbl] verantwortlich **II**
rest [rest] Rest **II**
to **rest** [rest] sich ausruhen, eine Pause machen **III**
restaurant ['restrɒnt] Restaurant **II**
restroom *(AE)* ['restru:m] Toilette **IV U1,** 25
result [rɪ'zʌlt] Ergebnis, Resultat **IV U4,** 83
return [rɪ'tɜ:n] hin und zurück **II**
to **return** [rɪ'tɜ:n] zurückgeben; zurückkommen **II**
revision [rɪ'vɪʒn] Wiederholung **I**
*to **rewrite** [ˌri:'raɪt] umschreiben, neu schreiben **II**
rhyme [raɪm] Reim **I**
rice [raɪs] Reis **II**
rice pudding [raɪs 'pʊdɪŋ] Milchreis **II**
rich [rɪtʃ] reich **IV U3,** 63
ride [raɪd] Ritt **I**
*to **ride** [raɪd] fahren; reiten **I**
right [raɪt] richtig; rechts; rechte/-r/-s **I**
on the right [ˌɒn ðə 'raɪt] rechts **I**
right away ['raɪt əˌweɪ] sofort **II**
right from the start ['raɪt frəm ðə ˌstɑ:t] von Anfang an ⟨**IV U5,** 92⟩
right here [ˌraɪt 'hɪə] genau hier **II**
right now ['raɪt ˌnaʊ] jetzt gerade **I**
rim [rɪm] Radkranz, Rahmen **III**
*to **ring** [rɪŋ] läuten; klingeln **I**
to **rip** [rɪp] zerreißen; reißen **II**
*to **rise** [raɪz] steigen,aufgehen; wachsen, zunehmen **III**
river ['rɪvə] Fluss **I**
road [rəʊd] Straße **I**
to **rob** [rɒb] rauben, ausrauben **III**
robot ['rəʊbɒt] Roboter **IV U4,** 69
rock [rɒk] Rock (*Musikrichtung*) **III**; Fels; Stein; Gestein **IV ZI,** 11
rocket ['rɒkɪt] Rakete **IV U4,** 70
role [rəʊl] Rolle **I**

role play ['rəʊl pleɪ] Rollenspiel **I**
romance [rəʊ'mænts] Liebesfilm; Romanze **IV U5,** 86
romantic [rə'mæntɪk] romantisch **IV U5,** 84
room [ru:m] Zimmer, Raum; Platz **I**
rope [rəʊp] Seil **IV U3,** 58
round [raʊnd] Runde **III**
round ... [raʊnd] um ... herum **I**
row [rəʊ] Reihe **IV U4,** 69
to **row** [rəʊ] rudern **IV U3,** 57
royal ['rɔɪəl] königlich **III**
royal family [ˌrɔɪəl 'fæməli] königliche Familie **III**
RSVP [ˌɑ:r‿es vi:'pi:] Um Antwort wird gebeten. **I**
rubber ['rʌbə] Radiergummi **I**
rubbish ['rʌbɪʃ] Abfall, Abfälle, Müll **III**
rucksack ['rʌksæk] Rucksack **III**
rude [ru:d] unhöflich **III**
rugby ['rʌgbi] Rugby (*Sportart*) **III**
rule [ru:l] Regel **I**
ruler ['ru:lə] Lineal **I**
*to **run** [rʌn] rennen, laufen **I**
to run away [rʌn‿ə'weɪ] wegrennen, weglaufen **I**
Russian ['rʌʃn] russisch, Russisch; Russe/Russin **I**

S

sacred ['seɪkrɪd] heilig ⟨**IV U3,** 66⟩
sad [sæd] traurig; bedauerlich **III**
saddle ['sædl] Sattel **II**
safari [sə'fɑ:ri] Safari **I**
safari ride [sə'fɑ:ri ˌraɪd] Safarifahrt **I**
safe [seɪf] sicher **III**
safely ['seɪfli] sicher **II**
to **sail** [seɪl] segeln **I**
salad ['sæləd] Salat **II**
for **sale** [ˌfɔ: 'seɪl] zu verkaufen **IV U2,** 34
the **same** [seɪm] derselbe/dieselbe/dasselbe **I**
sandwich ['sænwɪdʒ] belegtes Brot, Sandwich **I**
satellite ['sætəlaɪt] Satellit **IV U4,** 69
Saturday ['sætədeɪ] Samstag, Sonnabend **I**
sauce [sɔ:s] Soße, Sauce **II**
sausage ['sɒsɪdʒ] Wurst, Würstchen **II**
to **save** [seɪv] sparen; retten; speichern **II**
*to **say** [seɪ] sagen **I**
scan [skæn] Ultraschall(untersuchung) **IV U4,** 69
to **scan** [skæn] durchsuchen **III**
to **scare** [skeə] erschrecken, Angst einjagen **I**
scarf [skɑ:f] pl. **scarves** [skɑ:vz] Schal **II**
scary ['skeəri] unheimlich, gruselig **I**
scene [si:n] Kulisse **I**; Szene **II**
scenery ['si:nəri] Bühnenbild **I**; Landschaft **IV ZI,** 11
schedule *(AE)* ['skedʒu:l] Stundenplan **IV U2,** 33
school [sku:l] Schule **I**
school bag ['sku:l bæg] Schultasche, Schulranzen **I**
Science [saɪəns] Naturwissenschaft(en) **II**
science fiction [ˌsaɪəns 'fɪkʃn] Science-Fiction **IV U4,** 75
scientist ['saɪəntɪst] Wissenschaftler/-in **III**
scone [skɒn] *brötchenartiges Gebäck* **I**
to **score** [skɔ:] schießen, erzielen **III**
scorer ['skɔ:rə] Torschütze/Torschützin; Punktezähler/-in **III**
Scottish ['skɒtɪʃ] schottisch **II**
to **scout** [skaʊt] auskundschaften **IV U3,** 57
scratch [skrætʃ] Kratzer **II**
to **scratch** [skrætʃ] zerkratzen; kratzen **II**
to **scream** [skri:m] schreien **IV U5,** 86
screen [skri:n] Bildschirm **III**
screenplay ['skri:npleɪ] Drehbuch **IV U3,** 64
sea [si:] Meer **I**
search engine ['sɜ:tʃ ˌendʒɪn] Suchmaschine **IV U2,** 46
to **search for sth.** [sɜ:tʃ] nach etw. suchen ⟨**IV U5,** 93⟩; ⟨**IV U5,** 100⟩
search term ['sɜ:tʃ ˌtɜ:m] Suchbegriff **IV U2,** 46
seasick ['si:sɪk] seekrank **IV U1,** 18
season ['si:zn] Jahreszeit **I**
seat [si:t] Sitz; Platz **II**
second ['seknd] Sekunde **I**; zweite/-r/-s **I**
secondly ['sekndli] zweitens **IV U4,** 83
secret ['si:krət] Geheimnis **I**
secretary ['sekrətri] Sekretär/-in **III**
*to **see** [si:] sehen; treffen **I**
See you. ['si: ju:] Bis dann., Bis bald. **I**
See you around! [ˌsi: jə ə'raʊnd] Man sieht sich! *(Umgangssprache)* **IV U2,** 36
seeker ['si:kə] Suchende/-r; Jäger/-in **IV U5,** 91
to **seem** [si:m] (er)scheinen **II**
*to **sell** [sel] verkaufen **I**
semester *(AE)* [sɪ'mestə] Semester **IV U2,** 34
*to **send** [send] schicken, senden **I**
to send off [send 'ɒf] abschicken **II**; vom Platz verweisen **III**
senior citizens [ˌsi:niə 'sɪtɪznz] Senioren **III**
sensation [sen'seɪʃn] Sensation **IV U5,** 91
sentence ['sentəns] Satz **I**
September [sep'tembə] September **I**
serious ['sɪəriəs] ernst **IV U2,** 32
servant ['sɜ:vnt] Diener/-in **III**
service ['sɜ:vɪs] Dienst **IV U3,** 64
setting ['setɪŋ] Rahmen, Schauplatz **IV U4,** 76
several ['sevrəl] einige, mehrere, verschiedene **IV U5,** 99
shades of gray [ˌʃeɪdz‿əv 'greɪ] Grautöne ⟨**IV U1,** 22⟩
*to **shake** [ʃeɪk] zittern, beben; schütteln **III**
shall [ʃæl] sollen **III**
shape [ʃeɪp] Gestalt; Form **II**
to **share** [ʃeə] teilen **II**
sharply ['ʃɑ:pli] scharf **IV U4,** 75
she [ʃi:] sie **I**
shed [ʃed] Schuppen **I**
sheep [ʃi:p] pl. **sheep** [ʃi:p] Schaf **I**
sheet [ʃi:t] Blatt **III**
shelf [ʃelf] pl. **shelves** [ʃelvz] Brett **II**
shell [ʃel] Muschel; Panzer **III**
ship [ʃɪp] Schiff **I**
shirt [ʃɜ:t] Trikot, Shirt; Hemd **II**
shit [ʃɪt] Scheiße ⟨**IV U5,** 92⟩
to **shock** [ʃɒk] schockieren; schocken **IV U3,** 59
shocking ['ʃɒkɪŋ] schockierend **IV U3,** 58
shoe [ʃu:] Schuh **I**
*to **shoot** [ʃu:t] schießen **III**; *(Film)* drehen **IV U5,** 85
shop [ʃɒp] Geschäft, Laden **I**
shopping ['ʃɒpɪŋ] Einkaufen; Einkäufe **I**
shopping list ['ʃɒpɪŋ ˌlɪst] Einkaufsliste, Einkaufszettel **I**
shopping trolley ['ʃɒpɪŋ ˌtrɒli] Einkaufswagen **II**
to go **shopping** [gəʊ 'ʃɒpɪŋ] einkaufen gehen **I**
short [ʃɔ:t] kurz **I**; zu wenig **IV U4,** 76
short for [ˌʃɔ:t 'fə] Kurzform von **IV U1,** 16
short form ['ʃɔ:t fɔ:m] Kurzform **I**
should [ʃʊd] sollen **II**
shoulder ['ʃəʊldə] Schulter **IV U3,** 58

to shout [ʃaʊt] schreien, rufen **I**
show [ʃəʊ] Show, Schau, Darbietung **III**
show-business ['ʃəʊ ˌbɪznɪs] Showgeschäft **IV U5, 91**
*to **show** [ʃəʊ] zeigen **I**
shower ['ʃaʊə] Dusche ⟨**IV U3, 66**⟩
shuttle ['ʃʌtl] Raumfähre **IV U2, 35**
sick [sɪk] krank **IV U1, 18**
to feel sick [fi:l 'sɪk] Übelkeit verspüren **III**
side [saɪd] Seite **III**
side street ['saɪd ˌstri:t] Seitenstraße **IV U1, 29**
sight [saɪt] Sehenswürdigkeit **I**
sign [saɪn] Schild; Zeichen **II**
to **sign** [saɪn] unterschreiben **II**
signal ['sɪgnl] Signal, Zeichen **IV U4, 68**
silent ['saɪlənt] stumm **IV U5, 85**
silently ['saɪləntli] lautlos, leise ⟨**IV U4, 77**⟩
silly ['sɪli] dumm; albern **I**; Dummkopf **IV U2, 40**
similar ['sɪmilə] ähnlich **IV U2, 46**
simple past [ˌsɪmpl 'pɑ:st] einfache Vergangenheit **II**
simple present [ˌsɪmpl 'preznt] Präsens **I**
since [sɪns] seit, seitdem **III**
ever since [ˌevə 'sɪnts] seitdem **IV U4, 75**
*to **sing** [sɪŋ] singen **I**
singer ['sɪŋə] Sänger/-in **III**
single ['sɪŋgl] einfach **II**; Single **III**
sink [sɪŋk] Waschbecken, Spülbecken **IV U4, 72**
Sir [sɜ:] Sir (*Anrede für einen Adeligen oder Ritter*) **III**
sister ['sɪstə] Schwester **I**
*to **sit** [sɪt] sich setzen; sitzen **I**
situation [ˌsɪtju'eɪʃn] Situation **I**
size [saɪz] Größe **I**
skateboard ['skeɪtbɔ:d] Skateboard **I**
to **skateboard** ['skeɪtbɔ:d] Skateboard fahren **II**
skateboarder ['skeɪtbɔ:də] Skateboarder/-in **III**
skatepark ['skeɪtpɑ:k] Skatepark **III**
skates [skeɪts] Rollschuhe, Inlineskates **I**
skeleton ['skelɪtn] Skelett **III**
skeptical ['skeptɪkl] skeptisch ⟨**IV U5, 100**⟩
ski [ski:] Ski **IV U3, 56**
skiing ['ski:ɪŋ] Skifahren **IV U3, 53**
skill [skɪl] Fertigkeit, Fähigkeit **I**
to **skim** [skɪm] überfliegen **III**
skin [skɪn] Haut ⟨**IV U5, 101**⟩
skirt [skɜ:t] Rock **I**
sky [skaɪ] Himmel **III**
skyscraper ['skaɪˌskreɪpə] Wolkenkratzer **IV ZI, 13**
to **slam the door** [ˌslæm ðə 'dɔ:] die Tür zuknallen **IV U4, 75**
slamster ['slæmstə] Teilnehmer/-in bei einem Gedichtewettbewerb **III**
*to **sleep** [sli:p] schlafen **I**
slice [slaɪs] Stück; Scheibe **II**
slide [slaɪd] Folie, Dia **IV U2, 46**
*to **slide off s.th.** [ˌslaɪd‿'ɒf] von etw. rutschen **IV U4, 76**
slot [slɒt] Schlitz **IV U3, 58**
slow [sləʊ] langsam **II**
small [smɔ:l] klein **I**
small talk ['smɔ:l ˌtɔ:k] oberflächliche Konversation, Smalltalk **IV U3, 56**
smart [smɑ:t] schlau, klug **IV U4, 68**
*to **smell** [smel] riechen **III**
to **smile** [smaɪl] lächeln **I**
smiley ['smaɪli] Smiley **II**
smoke [sməʊk] Rauch **III**
to **smoke** [sməʊk] rauchen **III**
smuggler ['smʌglə] Schmuggler/-in **III**
snack [snæk] Snack, Imbiss **I**
snack bar ['snæk ˌbɑ:] Schnellimbiss **II**
to **sneer** [snɪə] spotten; spöttisch grinsen **IV U3, 58**
to **sniff** [snɪf] schnüffeln, schnuppern **III**
to **snort** [snɔ:t] schnupfen (*Kokain usw.*) ⟨**IV U5, 92**⟩
so [səʊ] also; so **I**
so far [ˌsəʊ 'fɑ:] bis jetzt **IV U3, 58**
so that [səʊ 'ðæt] sodass **IV U4, 72**
to **soar** [sɔ:] in die Höhe schnellen **IV U4, 75**
sober ['səʊbə] nüchtern **IV U5, 92**
sofa ['səʊfə] Sofa **I**
softball ['sɒftbɔ:l] Softball (*Variante von Baseball*) **III**
software ['sɒftweə] Software ⟨**IV U1, 30**⟩
solo ['səʊləʊ] Solo-; allein **III**
solvable ['sɒlvəbl] lösbar **III**
to **solve** [sɒlv] lösen **III**
some [sʌm] einige, ein paar, etwas **I**
somebody ['sʌmbədi] (irgend)jemand **III**
someone ['sʌmwʌn] (irgend)jemand **II**
something ['sʌmθɪŋ] etwas, irgendetwas **I**
sometimes ['sʌmtaɪmz] manchmal **I**
somewhere ['sʌmweə] irgendwo **II**
son [sʌn] Sohn **I**
song [sɒŋ] Lied **I**
songwriter ['sɒŋraɪtə] Texter/-in, Komponist/-in, Liedermacher/-in **III**
sore [sɔ:] schmerzhaft, wund **III**
Sorry! ['sɒri] Entschuldigung!, Verzeihung! **I**
I'm **sorry.** [ˌaɪm 'sɒri] Es tut mir leid. **III**
to **sort** [sɔ:t] sortieren **I**
to sort out [sɔ:t 'aʊt] klären, lösen; in Ordnung bringen **I**
sound [saʊnd] Laut; Ton; Geräusch **I**
to **sound** [saʊnd] sich anhören, klingen **III**
sound file ['saʊnd ˌfaɪl] Audiodatei **IV U1, 23**
soup [su:p] Suppe **II**
sweet and **sour** [ˌswi:t ən 'saʊə] süßsauer **II**
south [saʊθ] Süden **I**
southbound ['saʊθbaʊnd] in Richtung Süden **III**
space [speɪs] Weltraum; Raum **IV U4, 68**
space ship ['speɪs ˌʃɪp] Raumschiff **IV U5, 87**
space station ['speɪs ˌsteɪʃn] Raumstation **IV U4, 69**
outer space [ˌaʊtə 'speɪs] Weltraum, Weltall ⟨**IV U4, 77**⟩
spaghetti [spə'geti] Spaghetti **II**
spaghetti bolognaise [spəˌgeti bɒlə'neɪz] Spaghetti Bolognese **II**
Spanish ['spænɪʃ] spanisch, Spanisch; Spanier/-in **IV U5, 99**
spare [speə] Ersatz- **III**
*to **speak** [spi:k] sprechen **I**
speaker ['spi:kə] Sprecher/-in **II**
special ['speʃl] besondere/-r/-s **I**; Spezialität **IV U1, 16**
special effects [ˌspeʃl ɪ'fekts] Spezialeffekte (*von Computern erzeugter Bild- oder Toneffekt*) **IV U5, 86**
speech [spi:tʃ] Rede, Vortrag; Sprache **IV U4, 75**
reported speech [rɪˌpɔ:tɪd 'spi:tʃ] indirekte Rede **IV U5, 89**
*to **spell** [spel] buchstabieren **I**
*to **spend** [spend] verbringen; ausgeben **II**
spicy ['spaɪsi] würzig, scharf **II**
spider ['spaɪdə] Spinne **II**
*to **split apart** [ˌsplɪt‿ə'pɑ:t] auseinanderbrechen **IV U4, 76**
*to **split up** [ˌsplɪt‿'ʌp] sich trennen **III**
sponge [spʌndʒ] Schwamm **IV U5, 94**
spooky ['spu:ki] gespenstisch, gruselig **I**
spoon [spu:n] Löffel **II**
sport [spɔ:t] Sport **I**
sports day ['spɔ:ts deɪ] Sportfest **I**

sports hall ['spɔ:ts ˌhɔ:l] Sporthalle **I**
spot [spɒt] Platz ⟨**IV U1,** 22⟩
spring [sprɪŋ] Frühling, Frühjahr **I**
to **squint** [skwɪnt] blinzeln; schielen **IV U4,** 75
St David's Day [snt 'deɪvɪdz ˌdeɪ] *walisischer Nationalfeiertag* **III**
stadium ['steɪdiəm] Stadion **III**
stage [steɪdʒ] Bühne **I**
stain [steɪn] Fleck; Verfärbung **IV U2,** 39
stairs [steəz] Treppe **II**
stall [stɔ:l] Stand **I**
stamp [stæmp] Briefmarke **II**
stand [stænd] Tribüne **IV U4,** 75
*to **stand** [stænd] stehen **I**
I can't stand … . [aɪ ˌkɑ:nt 'stænd] Ich kann … nicht ausstehen. **IV U2,** 37
to stand up to s.o. [stænd‿'ʌp tə] sich jdm. gegenüber behaupten **IV U3,** 58
star [stɑ:] Stern **II**; Star **III**
start [stɑ:t] Anfang, Beginn **IV U2,** 33
to **start** [stɑ:t] anfangen, beginnen **I**
Start like this … [ˌstɑ:t laɪk 'ðɪs] Beginne so … **I**
starter ['stɑ:tə] Vorspeise **II**
state [steɪt] Staat, Land; ein Bundesstaat in den USA **IV ZI,** 10
station ['steɪʃn] Bahnhof **II**; Station, Posten **IV U1,** 18
statistics pl. [stə'tɪstɪks] Statistik **IV U4,** 82
statue ['stætʃu:] Statue, Standbild **IV U1,** 15
to **stay** [steɪ] übernachten; bleiben **I**
to stay away [ˌsteɪ‿ə'weɪ] wegbleiben **IV U3,** 52
*to **steal** [sti:l] stehlen **II**
steel [sti:l] Stahl **III**
steel band [ˌsti:l 'bænd] Steelband (*Band mit Trommeln aus Stahlblech*) **III**
step [step] Stufe **II**; Schritt **III**
stepfather ['stepˌfɑ:ðə] Stiefvater **I**
still [stɪl] noch, immer noch **I**
stomach ['stʌmək] Magen, Bauch **II**
stone [stəʊn] *brit. Gewichtseinheit* **III**; Stein **III**
Stone Age ['stəʊn ˌeɪdʒ] Steinzeit **III**
stop [stɒp] Haltestelle **III**
to **stop** [stɒp] aufhören; anhalten **I**
store *(AE)* [stɔ:] Laden; Geschäft **IV U1,** 15
storm [stɔ:m] Sturm **II**
stormy ['stɔ:mi] stürmisch **II**
story ['stɔ:ri] Geschichte **I**
story *(AE)* ['stɔ:ri] Stockwerk **IV U1,** 15
straight [streɪt] gerade **I**
strange [streɪndʒ] seltsam, merkwürdig **II**
strawberry ['strɔ:bri] Erdbeere **IV U1,** 17
street [stri:t] Straße **I**
stress [stres] Stress; Betonung **III**
strict [strɪkt] streng **II**
stripe [straɪp] Streifen **IV ZI,** 11
stroke [strəʊk] Schlag(anfall) **III**
strong [strɒŋ] stark **II**
student *(AE)* ['stu:dnt] Schüler/-in **IV U3,** 33
student ['stju:dnt] Student/-in **III**
student council [ˌstju:dnt 'kaʊnsl] Schülervertretung **IV U2,** 34
studio ['stju:diəʊ] Studio **IV U5,** 87
stuff [stʌf] Zeug, Sachen **II**
stupid ['stju:pɪd] dumm, blöd **III**
style [staɪl] Stil **I**
subject ['sʌbdʒɪkt] Fach **II**; Betreff **III**; Thema **IV U2,** 40
to **substitute** ['sʌbstɪtju:t] ersetzen, austauschen **III**
success [sək'ses] Erfolg ⟨**IV U5,** 100⟩
successful [sək'sesfl] erfolgreich **III**
such [sʌtʃ] solch **III**
sudden ['sʌdn] plötzlich; plötzliche/-r/-s **III**
suddenly ['sʌdnli] plötzlich **I**
sugar ['ʃʊgə] Zucker **I**
to **suggest** [sə'dʒest] vorschlagen **II**
suggestion [sə'dʒestʃn] Vorschlag **II**
suitcase ['su:tkeɪs] Koffer **III**
summary ['sʌməri] Zusammenfassung **III**
summer ['sʌmə] Sommer **I**
summer camp ['sʌmə ˌkæmp] Sommerlager **IV U3,** 52
sun [sʌn] Sonne **I**
Sunday ['sʌndeɪ] Sonntag **I**
sunglasses pl. ['sʌnˌglɑ:sɪz] Sonnenbrille **I**
sunny ['sʌni] sonnig **I**
sunshine ['sʌnʃaɪn] Sonnenschein **IV U1,** 22
super ['su:pə] super, toll **I**
superlative [su:'pɜ:lətɪv] Superlativ **III**
supermarket ['su:pəˌmɑ:kɪt] Supermarkt **I**
superstar ['su:pəstɑ:] Superstar ⟨**IV U5,** 93⟩
supper ['sʌpə] Abendessen **II**
to **support** [sə'pɔ:t] unterstützen **IV U2,** 33
to **suppose** [sə'pəʊz] denken, annehmen **II**
sure [ʃɔ:] sicher **II**
to **surf** [sɜ:f] surfen **II**
surface mail ['sɜ:fɪs ˌmeɪl] Post auf dem Landweg/Seeweg **II**
surfer ['sɜ:fə] Wellenreiter/-in, Surfer/-in **III**
surprise [sə'praɪz] Überraschung **I**
to **surprise** [sə'praɪz] überraschen **II**
surprised [sə'praɪzd] überrascht **III**
surroundings [sə'raʊndɪŋz] Umgebung **IV U5,** 92
survey ['sɜ:veɪ] Umfrage, Untersuchung **II**
*to **swear** [sweə] schwören ⟨**IV U4,** 77⟩; fluchen; schwören **IV U5,** 92
sweatshirt ['swetʃɜ:t] Sweatshirt **I**
sweet [swi:t] Bonbon **I**; süß; niedlich **I**
sweet and sour [ˌswi:t ən 'saʊə] süßsauer **II**
to **swerve** [swɜ:v] ausweichen, ausscheren **III**
*to **swim** [swɪm] schwimmen **I**
swimming cap ['swɪmɪŋ ˌkæp] Bademütze, Badekappe **III**
swimming pool ['swɪmɪŋ ˌpu:l] Schwimmbad; Swimmingpool **II**
to go **swimming** [gəʊ 'swɪmɪŋ] schwimmen gehen **I**
to **switch off** [ˌswɪtʃ 'ɒf] ausschalten **IV U4,** 72
to **switch on** [ˌswɪtʃ‿'ɒn] anschalten, einschalten **II**
symbol ['sɪmbl] Symbol **III**
sympathetic [ˌsɪmpə'θetɪk] mitfühlend, verständnisvoll **IV U1,** 20
syrup ['sɪrəp] Sirup **IV U1,** 17
system ['sɪstəm] System **III**

T

table ['teɪbl] Tisch **I**
table tennis ['teɪbl ˌtenɪs] Tischtennis **III**
tackle ['tækl] Zweikampf; Angriff **III**
to **tackle** ['tækl] angreifen **III**
tail [teɪl] Schwanz, Schweif **I**
*to **take** [teɪk] nehmen; bringen; dauern, (Zeit) brauchen **I**
to take a hike [ˌteɪk‿ə 'haɪk] wandern, eine Wanderung machen **II**
to take notes [ˌteɪk 'nəʊts] Notizen machen **II**
to take off [teɪk‿'ɒf] ausziehen; starten, abheben **III**
to take part [teɪk 'pɑ:t] teilnehmen **III**
to take pictures [teɪk 'pɪktʃəz] Fotos machen, fotografieren **II**
to take place [ˌteɪk 'pleɪs] stattfinden **III**
to take the dog for a walk [teɪk ðə 'dɒg fɔ:r‿ə ˌwɔ:k] den Hund ausführen **I**
to take your chance [ˌteɪk jɔ: 'tʃɑ:ns] etwas wagen, etwas riskieren **III**

takeaway ['teɪkəweɪ] Restaurant mit Straßenverkauf; Essen zum Mitnehmen **II**
take-off ['teɪk‿ɒf] Start **IV U2,** 35
talk [tɔ:k] Unterhaltung, Gespräch **I**; Vortrag **IV U1,** 15
small talk ['smɔ:l ˌtɔ:k] oberflächliche Konversation, Smalltalk **IV U3,** 56
talk show ['tɔ:k ˌʃəʊ] Talkshow **IV U5,** 91
to **talk** [tɔ:k] sprechen, reden **I**
tall [tɔ:l] hoch; groß **IV U1,** 15
tape [teɪp] Band; Klebeband **III**
to **taste** [teɪst] schmecken; (Essen, Trinken) probieren **II**
tasty ['teɪsti] lecker **II**
tattoo [tæt'u:] Tätowierung **III**
taxi ['tæksi] Taxi **I**
tea [ti:] Tee **I**
*to **teach** [ti:tʃ] unterrichten, lehren; beibringen **II**
teacher ['ti:tʃə] Lehrer/-in **I**
team [ti:m] Team, Mannschaft **I**
technology [tek'nɒlədʒi] Technik **II**; Technologie **IV U4,** 68
teen [ti:n] Teenager; Jugendliche/-r **IV U2,** 38
teenage ['ti:neɪdʒ] jugendlich **III**
teenager ['ti:neɪdʒə] Teenager/-in, Jugendliche/Jugendlicher **III**
*to **tell** [tel] sagen; erzählen **I**
ten mill (= ten million) [ten 'mɪl] zehn Millionen *(Umgangssprache)* ⟨**IV U5,** 93⟩
tennis ['tenɪs] Tennis **III**
tense [tens] Zeit(form) **II**
past tense [ˌpɑ:st 'tens] Vergangenheit **II**
term [tɜ:m] Semester, Trimester **III**
terraced house ['terɪst ˌhaʊs] Reihenhaus **II**
terrible ['terəbl] schrecklich, furchtbar **II**
terribly ['terəbli] schrecklich **III**
terrorist ['terərɪst] Terrorist/-in **IV U1,** 15
test [test] Klassenarbeit, Prüfung, Test; Untersuchung **III**
text [tekst] Text **I**
text message ['tekst ˌmesɪdʒ] SMS **I**
to **text** [tekst] Textnachricht (SMS) schicken **III**
than [ðæn] als **II**
to **thank** [θæŋk] danken, sich bedanken **III**
thank you ['θæŋk ju:] danke (schön) **I**
to thank your lucky stars [ˌθæŋk jɔ:r 'lʌki stɑ:s] seinem Schutzengel danken ⟨**IV U5,** 92⟩
thanks [θæŋks] danke **I**
to give thanks [ˌgɪv 'θæŋks] sich bedanken **IV U1,** 21
that [ðæt] das **I**; dass **II**; der, die, das *(Relativpronomen)* **III**
(that's a) pity [ˌðæts ə 'pɪti] (Das ist) schade **IV U2,** 37
the [ðə] der, die *(auch Plural)*, das **I**
theater *(AE)* ['θɪətə] Theater **IV U1,** 29
movie theater *(AE)* [ˌmu:vi 'θɪətə] Kino **IV U5,** 87
theatre ['θɪətə] Theater **III**
their [ðeə] ihr/-e **I**
theirs [ðeəz] ihre/-r/-s **II**
them [ðem] sie/ihnen **I**
themselves [ðem'selvz] sie/sich (selbst) **III**
then [ðen] dann **I**
there [ðeə] da, dort **I**
these [ði:z] diese (hier) **I**
they [ðeɪ] sie *(Plural)* **I**
They all lived happily ever after. [ðeɪ ɔ:l lɪvd 'hæpəli evə ˌɑ:ftə] Und wenn sie nicht gestorben sind, dann leben sie noch heute. **II**
thief [θi:f] pl. **thieves** [θi:vz] Dieb/-in **II**
thin [θɪn] dünne/-r/-s, dünn **II**
thing [θɪŋ] Ding, Sache **I**
*to **think** [θɪŋk] denken; glauben **I**
third [θɜ:d] dritte/-r/-s **I**
third-grader [ˌθɜ:d 'greɪdə] Drittklässler **IV U5,** 91
thirsty ['θɜ:sti] durstig **III**
this [ðɪs] das; dies; diese/-r/-s **I**
those [ðəʊz] diese (da), die (da); jene **I**
thousand ['θaʊznd] tausend **II**
thread [θred] Faden **II**
three G's (= three grand) [ˌθri: 'dʒi:z] dreitausend (Dollar) *(Umgangssprache)* ⟨**IV U1,** 22⟩
through [θru:] durch **I**; über **III**
*to **throw** [θrəʊ] werfen **I**
to throw away [ˌθrəʊ ə'weɪ] wegwerfen **II**
thunder (no pl.) ['θʌndə] Donner **IV U3,** 58
Thursday ['θɜ:zdeɪ] Donnerstag **I**
tick [tɪk] Häkchen **III**
to **tick** [tɪk] abhaken, mit einem Haken versehen **II**; ticken **IV U1,** 22
ticket ['tɪkɪt] Eintrittskarte; Fahrkarte **I**; Verweis; Ticket; Strafzettel **II**
ticket office ['tɪkɪt ˌɒfɪs] Kartenverkaufsstelle; Fahrkartenschalter **III**
tidy ['taɪdi] ordentlich; aufgeräumt **II**
to **tidy** ['taɪdi] aufräumen **II**
time [taɪm] Zeit; Mal **I**; Uhrzeit **I**
time line ['taɪm laɪn] Zeitleiste **I**
timely ['taɪmli] rechtzeitig ⟨**IV U3,** 61⟩
timetable ['taɪmˌteɪbl] Stundenplan; Fahrplan **II**
tiny ['taɪni] winzig **I**
tip [tɪp] Tipp **I**; Trinkgeld **IV U1,** 16
tired [taɪəd] müde **I**
tiring ['taɪrɪŋ] anstrengend, ermüdend **III**
title ['taɪtl] Überschrift; Titel **I**
to [tʊ] an; zu; nach **I**
to go [tə 'gəʊ] zum Mitnehmen **IV U1,** 17
toast [təʊst] Toast, Toastbrot **IV U1,** 17
today [tə'deɪ] heute **I**
toe [təʊ] Zeh **II**
together [tə'geðə] zusammen, miteinander **I**
toilet ['tɔɪlət] Toilette **II**
tomato [tə'mɑ:təʊ] pl. **tomatoes** [tə'mɑ:təʊz] Tomate **II**
tomorrow [tə'mɒrəʊ] morgen **II**
ton [tʌn] Tonne *(Gewicht)* **III**
tongue [tʌŋ] Zunge **III**
tonight [tə'naɪt] heute Abend; heute Nacht **I**
too [tu:] auch **I**; zu **I**
top [tɒp] Spitze; oberer Teil, oberes Ende; Oberteil; ganz oben **II**
topic ['tɒpɪk] Thema **II**
top-up card ['tɒpʌp ˌkɑ:d] Aufladekarte, Guthabenkarte **II**
torch [tɔ:tʃ] Fackel **IV U1,** 15
tortoise ['tɔ:təs] Schildkröte **III**
to **touch** [tʌtʃ] berühren, antippen **III**
tour [tʊə] Besichtigung, Rundgang, Rundfahrt **II**; Tour **III**
tourist ['tʊərɪst] Tourist/-in **I**
tourist information centre [ˌtʊərɪst ɪnfə'meɪʃn sentə] Touristik-Information **I**
towards [tə'wɔ:dz] in Richtung, auf … zu, darauf zu **III**
tower ['taʊə] Turm **II**
clock tower ['klɒk ˌtaʊə] Uhrturm **II**
town [taʊn] Stadt **I**
track [træk] Spur; Pfad, Weg; Gleis **IV U3,** 52
tractor ['træktə] Traktor **I**
tradition [trə'dɪʃn] Tradition **III**
traditional [trə'dɪʃənl] traditionell **IV ZI,** 11

traffic ['træfɪk] Verkehr **IV U1,** 29
traffic lights ['træfɪk ˌlaɪts] Verkehrsampel **III**
trail [treɪl] Weg, Pfad **IV U3,** 54
train [treɪn] Zug **I**
to **train** [treɪn] trainieren **III**
trainer ['treɪnə] Turnschuh **I**
training ['treɪnɪŋ] Training **III**
to **transform** [ˌtræns'fɔ:m] sich verwandeln **IV U4,** 76
translation [trænz'leɪʃn] Übersetzung **II**
to **transmit** [trænz'mɪt] funken, senden **IV U4,** 69
transmitter [ˌtrænz'mɪtə] Sendegerät, Funkgerät **IV U4,** 76
transparency [træn'spærntsi] Overheadfolie **III**
transport ['trænspɔ:t] Verkehrsmittel **I**
trash *(AE)* [træʃ] Müll, Abfall **IV U1,** 25
to **travel** ['trævl] reisen, fahren **II**
treasure ['treʒə] Schatz **I**
tree [tri:] Baum **I**
trend [trend] Trend, Mode **III**
trendy ['trendi] modisch **II**
triangle ['traɪæŋgl] Dreieck **IV U2,** 42
tribal ['traɪbl] Stammes- ⟨**IV U3,** 66⟩
tribe [traɪb] Stamm **IV U3,** 51
trick [trɪk] Kunststück, Trick **III**
to **trick** [trɪk] hereinlegen, täuschen **II**
trip [trɪp] Ausflug **I**
to **trip** [trɪp] stolpern **II**
to trip over … [ˌtrɪp 'əʊvə] über … stolpern **II**
trolley ['trɒli] Gepäckwagen; Einkaufswagen; Handkarren **III**
trouble ['trʌbl] Schwierigkeiten **I**; Mühe, Ärger **III**
trousers pl. ['traʊzəz] Hose **I**
truck *(AE)* [trʌk] Lastwagen **IV U3,** 48
true [tru:] wahr, richtig **I**
to **trust** [trʌst] vertrauen **III**
truth [tru:θ] Wahrheit **IV U5,** 92
to **try** [traɪ] versuchen, probieren **I**
to try hard [traɪ 'hɑ:d] sich sehr bemühen **III**
to try on [traɪ‿'ɒn] anprobieren **I**
try-out *(AE)* ['traɪaʊt] Aufnahmetest für die Mannschaft **IV U2,** 45
T-shirt ['ti:ʃɜ:t] T-Shirt **I**
Tuesday ['tju:zdeɪ] Dienstag **I**
to **tug** [tʌg] ziehen, zupfen **III**
tuna ['tju:nə] Thunfisch **II**
tune [tju:n] Melodie **III**
tunnel ['tʌnl] Tunnel **I**
turkey ['tɜ:ki] Pute, Truthahn **IV U1,** 17
it is s.o.'s **turn** [tɜ:n] jd. ist an der Reihe **II**
to **turn** [tɜ:n] einbiegen, abbiegen; drehen, wenden; sich umdrehen **I**
to turn round [ˌtɜ:n‿'raʊnd] sich umdrehen **IV U4,** 75
to turn into ['tɜ:n‿ˌɪntʊ] sich verwandeln in **II**
to turn off ['tɜ:n‿ˌɒf] ausschalten, abschalten; zudrehen **II**
to turn on ['tɜ:n‿ˌɒn] anschalten, einschalten; aufdrehen **II**
to turn to … ['tɜ:n ˌtə] … aufschlagen **I**
tutor ['tju:tə] Klassenlehrer/-in **I**
tutor group ['tju:tə ˌgru:p] Klasse *(in einer englischen Schule)* **I**
TV (= television) [ˌti: 'vi: = 'telɪvɪʒn] Fernseher; Fernsehen **I**
twice [twaɪs] zweimal **III**
twin [twɪn] Zwilling **IV U1,** 15
type [taɪp] Typ, Art **IV U4,** 83
to **type** [taɪp] tippen **II**
Typical! ['tɪpɪkl] Typisch! **II**

U

UFO ['ju: ef 'əʊ] UFO **IV U4,** 80
umbrella [ʌm'brelə] Regenschirm **II**
umpire ['ʌmpaɪə] Schiedsrichter/-in *(beim Tennis)* **III**
uncle ['ʌŋkl] Onkel **I**
under ['ʌndə] unter **I**
to **underline** [ˌʌndə'laɪn] unterstreichen **III**
*to **understand** [ˌʌndə'stænd] verstehen **I**
unfair [ʌn'feə] ungerecht, unfair **III**
unforgettable [ˌʌnfə'getəbl] unvergesslich **III**
unhappy [ʌn'hæpi] unglücklich **II**
unhealthy [ʌn'helθi] ungesund **II**
uniform ['ju:nɪfɔ:m] Uniform **I**
unit ['ju:nɪt] Kapitel; Lektion **I**
university [ˌju:nɪ'vɜ:səti] Universität **III**
unplayable [ʌn'pleɪəbl] nicht spielbar **III**
unrecognizable [ʌn'rekəgnaɪzəbl] nicht wiederzuerkennen **III**
untidy [ʌn'taɪdi] unordentlich, unaufgeräumt **III**
until [ʌn'tɪl] bis **II**
not until [nɒt ʌn'tɪl] erst **II**
up [ʌp] nach oben, hinauf, herauf **I**
upstairs [ʌp'steəz] oben *(im Gebäude)* **I**
us [ʌs] uns **I**
use [ju:s] Verwendung, Gebrauch, Benutzung **II**
to **use** [ju:z] verwenden; benutzen **I**
to be used to [bi:‿'ju:st tə] gewöhnt sein **IV U3,** 50
useful ['ju:sfl] nützlich **I**
useful phrase ['ju:sfl ˌfreɪz] nützlicher Ausdruck **I**
usually ['ju:ʒəli] gewöhnlich, normalerweise **I**

V

vacation *(AE)* [və'keɪʃn] Urlaub, Ferien **IV U1,** 16
valuable ['væljuəbl] wertvoll **III**
van [væn] Lieferwagen, Kleintransporter **II**
vase [vɑ:z] Vase **III**
vegetable ['vedʒtəbl] Gemüse **II**
verb [vɜ:b] Verb **I**
version ['vɜ:ʃn] Version **III**
very ['veri] sehr **I**
vest [vest] Unterhemd **III**
video ['vɪdiəʊ] Video **I**
view [vju:] Sicht; Blick **II**
village ['vɪlɪdʒ] Dorf **II**
violence (no pl.) ['vaɪəlns] Gewalt, Gewalttätigkeit **IV U3,** 58
violent ['vaɪəlnt] gewaltsam, gewaltig **IV U3,** 58
virtual ['vɜ:tʃuəl] virtuell **III**
to **visit** ['vɪzɪt] besuchen **I**
visitor ['vɪzɪtə] Besucher/-in **I**
vitamin ['vɪtəmɪn] Vitamin **II**
vocabulary [və'kæbjəlri] Wortschatz, Vokabular **I**
vocals ['vəʊklz] Gesang **III**
voice [vɔɪs] Stimme **I**
voice mail ['vɔɪs meɪl] Voicemail *(System zur Speicherung und Weiterleitung mündlicher Nachrichten)* **III**
volleyball ['vɒlibɔ:l] Volleyball **I**
to **vote** [vəʊt] abstimmen, wählen **IV U2,** 34
vs. (= versus) ['vɜ:səs] gegen, gegenüber **II**

W

to **wait** [weɪt] warten **I**
to wait for ['weɪt fɔ:] warten auf **I**
waiter ['weɪtə] Kellner **IV U1,** 17
waitress ['weɪtrəs] Kellnerin **II**
*to **wake up** [ˌweɪk‿'ʌp] aufwachen **I**
walk [wɔ:k] Spaziergang; Wanderung **I**

to take the dog for a walk [teɪk ðə ˈdɒg fɔːr‿ə ˌwɔːk] den Hund ausführen **I**
to **walk** [wɔːk] (zu Fuß) gehen, laufen **I**
to walk the plank [ˌwɔːk ðə ˈplæŋk] über eine Schiffsplanke ins Wasser getrieben werden (*alte Strafe für Seeleute*) **I**
wall [wɔːl] Wand; Mauer **I**
wallet [ˈwɒlɪt] Brieftasche, Geldbeutel, Portmonnee **II**
to **want** [wɒnt] wollen **I**
war [wɔː] Krieg **IV U1,** 18
wardrobe [ˈwɔːdrəʊb] Kleiderschrank **I**
warm [wɔːm] warm **I**
to **warm up** [ˌwɔːm ˈʌp] (sich) aufwärmen **III**
to **wash** [wɒʃ] waschen **I**
washing up [ˌwɒʃɪŋ ˈʌp] Abwasch **II**
watch [wɒtʃ] Armbanduhr **IV U1,** 22
to **watch** [wɒtʃ] (zu)schauen, gucken **I**
Watch it! [ˈwɒtʃ ˌɪt] Pass auf! **IV U4,** 75
water [ˈwɔːtə] Wasser **I**
mineral water [ˈmɪnrl ˌwɔːtə] Mineralwasser **II**
wave [weɪv] Welle **III**
to **wave** [weɪv] winken **I**
waxwork [ˈwæksw3ːk] Wachsfigur **III**
way [weɪ] Weg **I**; Art und Weise, Weise **IV U1,** 24
one way [ˈwʌn weɪ] einfach **II**
we [wiː] wir **I**
weak [wiːk] schwach **III**
*to **wear** [weə] tragen **I**
to wear off [weər‿ˈɒf] nachlassen **IV U5,** 92
weather [ˈweðə] Wetter **I**
weatherman [ˈweðəmæn] Wettermann, Meteorologe **II**
weather report [ˈweðə ˌrɪpɔːt] Wetterbericht **II**
weather station [ˈweðə ˌsteɪʃn] Wetterstation **II**
web [web] Netz **II**; Web-, Internet- **IV ZI,** 10
webcam [ˈwebkæm] Webcam **II**
website [ˈwebsaɪt] Website **II**
Wednesday [ˈwenzdeɪ] Mittwoch **I**
week [wiːk] Woche **I**
weekend [ˌwiːkˈend] Wochenende **I**
to **weigh** [weɪ] wiegen **II**
weight [weɪt] Gewicht **III**
weird [wɪəd] seltsam, komisch **IV U4,** 76
Welcome ... [ˈwelkəm] Willkommen ... **II**
well [wel] na ja, also **I**; gut **II**
welly [ˈweli] Gummistiefel **I**
Welsh [welʃ] walisisch; Waliser/-in **III**
west [west] Westen **I**
western [ˈwestən] Western (*Filmart*) **IV ZI,** 11
wet [wet] nass **I**
what [wɒt] was **I**
What about ... ? [ˌwɒt‿əˈbaʊt] Was ist mit ... ? **I**
what else [wɒt ˈels] was noch **II**
What the heck ... ? [ˌwɒt ðə ˈhek] Was zum Teufel ... ? **III**
What time is it? [ˌwɒt ˈtaɪm ɪz‿ɪt] Wie viel Uhr ist es?, Wie spät ist es? **I**
What's ... got to do with it? [ˈwɒts ... ˌgɒt‿tə duː wɪð‿ɪt] Was hat ... damit zu tun? **III**
What's the matter? [ˌwɒts ðə ˈmætə] Was ist los? **III**
What's up? [wɒts‿ˈʌp] Wie geht's? (*Umgangssprache*) **IV U2,** 38
What's your name? [ˌwɒts jə ˈneɪm] Wie heißt du/heißen Sie? **I**
wheat [wiːt] Weizen **IV ZI,** 12
wheel [wiːl] Steuerrad, Lenkrad; Rad **I**
when [wen] wann **I**; wenn; als **II**
where [weə] wo; wohin **I**
Where are you from? [ˌweər‿ə jə ˈfrɒm] Woher kommst du/kommt ihr/kommen Sie? **I**
wherever [weəˈrevə] egal wo, wo (auch) immer **IV U1,** 21
whether [ˈweðə] ob **IV U4,** 75
which [wɪtʃ] welche/-r/-s **I**; der, die, das (*Relativpronomen*) **III**
while [waɪl] während **II**
to **whip** [wɪp] schlagen; peitschen **IV U5,** 88
to **whisper** [ˈwɪspə] flüstern **I**
white [waɪt] weiß **I**
white water rafting [ˌwaɪt ˈwɔːtə ˈrɑːftɪŋ] Wildwasser-Rafting **IV U3,** 52
who [huː] wer; wem, wen **I**; der, die, das (*Relativpronomen*) **III**
whole [həʊl] ganz **IV U3,** 58
whom [huːm] den, dem **III**
with whom [wɪð ˈhuːm] mit der/dem **III**
whose [huːz] wessen **II**; dessen, deren **III**
why [waɪ] warum **I**
wicked [ˈwɪkɪd] spitze, geil (*Umgangssprache*); böse **II**
wife [waɪf] pl. **wives** [waɪvz] Ehefrau **II**
wig [wɪg] Perücke **II**
wild [waɪld] wild **IV U5,** 88
wilderness [ˈwɪldənəs] Wildnis ⟨**IV U5,** 100⟩
wildlife [ˈwaɪldlaɪf] Tierwelt **III**
will [wɪl] werden **II**
will-future [ˌwɪl ˈfjuːtʃə] will-Futur **III**
*to **win** [wɪn] gewinnen **I**
wind [wɪnd] Wind **I**
to **wind** [waɪnd] sich winden, sich schlängeln ⟨**IV U3,** 61⟩
window [ˈwɪndəʊ] Fenster **I**
windsock [ˈwɪndsɒk] Windsack, Luftsack ⟨**IV U3,** 65⟩
windy [ˈwɪndi] windig **I**
wing [wɪŋ] Flügel **II**
winner [ˈwɪnə] Gewinner/-in **II**
winter [ˈwɪntə] Winter **I**
with [wɪð] mit; bei **I**
within [wɪˈðɪn] innerhalb **III**
without [wɪˈðaʊt] ohne **I**
wizard [ˈwɪzəd] Zauberer **II**
apprentice wizard [əˌprentɪs ˈwɪzəd] Zauberlehrling **II**
woman [ˈwʊmən] pl. **women** [ˈwɪmɪn] Frau **I**
to **wonder** [ˈwʌndə] sich wundern, sich fragen **II**
wonderful [ˈwʌndəfl] wunderbar **IV U5,** 92
won't [wəʊnt] wird/werden nicht ... **II**
wood [wʊd] Holz; Wald **II**
wooden [ˈwʊdn] hölzern, Holz- **IV U4,** 76
word [w3ːd] Wort **I**
work [w3ːk] Arbeit **I**
to **work** [w3ːk] arbeiten; funktionieren **I**
worker [ˈw3ːkə] Arbeiter/-in **II**
workshop [ˈw3ːkʃɒp] Workshop, Arbeitsgruppe **III**
world [w3ːld] Welt **I**
from all round the world [frɒm ɔːl ˌraʊnd ðə ˈw3ːld] aus der ganzen Welt **I**
worry [ˈwʌri] Sorge **II**
Don't worry! [ˌdəʊnt ˈwʌri] Mach dir keine Sorgen! **II**
to **worry** [ˈwʌri] sich Sorgen machen **II**
worse [w3ːs] schlechter **II**
worse and worse [ˌw3ːs‿ən ˈw3ːs] immer schlechter **III**
the **worst** [ðə ˈw3ːst] schlechteste/-r/-s, schlimmste/-r/-s; am schlechtesten, am schlimmsten **II**
was **worth it** [wɒz ˈw3ːθ‿ɪt] hat sich gelohnt **II**
wouldn't [ˈwʊdnt] sich weigern, nicht wollen **III**

wreck [rek] Wrack **III**
*to **write** [raɪt] schreiben **I**
to write down [ˌraɪt ˈdaʊn] aufschreiben **IV U1,** 16
wrong [rɒŋ] falsch **I**
to go wrong [ˌɡəʊ ˈrɒŋ] schiefgehen, scheitern **III**

Y

yacht [jɒt] Jacht ⟨**IV U5,** 93⟩
yard [jɑːd] amerik./brit. Längenmaß, ca. 91,5 cm **IV U4,** 75
to **yawn** [jɔːn] gähnen **II**
Yeah! [jeə] Ja! (*Umgangssprache*) **I**
year [jɪə] Klasse; Jahr **I**
yellow [ˈjeləʊ] gelb **I**
yep [jep] ja (*Umgangssprache*) **IV ZI,** 10
yes [jes] ja **I**
yesterday [ˈjestədeɪ] gestern **II**
yet [jet] schon **II**
yet another [jet əˈnʌðə] noch ein/-e **IV U5,** 92
yoghurt [ˈjɒɡət] Jogurt **II**
you [juː] du, ihr, Sie **I**
you'd better [juːd ˈbetə] du solltest lieber **III**
You're welcome. [jɔː ˈwelkəm] Bitte (schön). **I**
young [jʌŋ] jung **I**
your [jɔː] dein/-e, euer/eure, Ihr/-e **I**
yours [jɔːz] deine/-r/-s, eure/-r/-s **II**
Yours, [jɔːz] Mit freundlichen Grüßen, (*am Briefende*) ⟨**IV U3,** 66⟩
yourself [jɔːˈself] du/dir/dich/Sie/sich (selbst) **III**
yourselves [jɔːˈselvz] ihr/euch/Sie/sich (selbst) **III**
youth [juːθ] Jugend- **III**
youth club [ˈjuːθ ˌklʌb] Jugendklub, Jugendzentrum **II**
youth hostel [ˈjuːθ ˌhɒstl] Jugendherberge ⟨**IV U3,** 65⟩

Z

zero [ˈzɪərəʊ] Null **I**
zone [zəʊn] Zone **IV ZI,** 13
to **zoom** [zuːm] rasen **IV U4,** 75
to zoom-in [ˌzuːmˈɪn] heranzoomen, nahe herangehen **IV ZI,** 10

Boys' names

Adam [ˈædəm] **III**
Al [æl] **IV U3,** 57
Alf [ælf] **II**
Andrew [ˈændruː] **III**
Ben [ben] **I**
Benny [ˈbeni] **III**
Bill [bɪl] **IV U4,** 76
Björn [bjɔːn] **III**
Bob [bɒb] **II**
Bruce [bruːs] **II**
Charles [tʃɑːlz] **III**
Cody [ˈkəʊdi] **IV U2,** 39
Cubby [ˈkʌbi] **IV U3,** 64
Daniel [ˈdænjəl] **III**
David [ˈdeɪvɪd] **I**
Diego [diˈeɪɡəʊ] **IV U1,** 16
Eddie [ˈedi] **IV U5,** 85
Elvis [ˈelvɪs] **III**
Frank [fræŋk] **II**
Freddy [ˈfredi] **IV U3,** 57
Greg [ɡreɡ] **III**
Harry [ˈhæri] **III**
Hector [ˈhektə] **II**
Henry [ˈhenri] **III**
Jamal [dʒəˈmɑːl] **III**
James [dʒeɪmz] **I**
Jody [ˈdʒəʊdi] **IV U2,** 44
Joe [dʒəʊ] ⟨**IV U5,** 100⟩
John [dʒɒn] **III**
José [həʊˈzeɪ] **IV U1,** 16
Joshua [ˈdʒɒʃjuə] **IV U2,** 39
Kadar [ˈkədɑː] **I**
Kevin [ˈkevɪn] **III**
Kyle [kaɪl] **IV U5,** 85
Leroy [ˈliːrɔɪ] **III**
Leslie [ˈlezli] **II**
Luis [ˈluːɪs] ⟨**IV U1,** 31⟩
Marco [ˈmɑːkəʊ] **I**
Matt [mæt] **IV U1,** 20
Max [mæks] **IV U3,** 63
Mehmet [ˈmemet] **I**
Paul [pɔːl] **III**
Perry [ˈperi] **IV U3,** 64
Peter [ˈpiːtə] **I**
Phil [fɪl] **I**
Pug [pʌɡ] **IV U3,** 57
Ray [reɪ] **III**
Reece [riːs] **III**
Reg [redʒ] **III**
Richard [ˈrɪtʃəd] **I**
Rob [rɒb] **I**
Robert [ˈrɒbət] **II**
Rodger [ˈrɒdʒə] **III**
Ronnie [ˈrɒni] **II**
Rory [ˈrɔːri] ⟨**IV U3,** 66⟩
Ross [rɒs] **II**
Roy [rɔɪ] **IV U4,** 75
Sam [sæm] **I**
Scott [skɒt] **II**
Sean [ʃɔːn] **IV U3,** 64
Shane [ʃɑːn] **IV U5,** 85
Steve [stiːv] **II**
Ted [ted] **I**
Terry [ˈteri] **I**
Thomas [ˈtɒməs] **I**
Tim [tɪm] **I**
Tom [tɒm] **I**
Tony [ˈtəʊni] **I**
Troy [trɔɪ] **IV U3,** 57

Girls' names

Abby [ˌæbi] **IV U3,** 52
Agnetha [ˈænjetə] **III**
Alexandra [ˌælɪɡˈzɑːndrə] **I**
Alison [ˈælɪsən] **I**
Ann [æn] **III**
Anna [ˈænə] **III**
Anni-Frid [ˈænifriːd] **III**
Brittany [ˈbrɪtəni] **IV U2,** 39
Carol [ˈkærəl] **II**
Carrie [ˈkæri] **III**
Cathy [ˈkæθi] **II**
Cristina [krɪˈstiːnə] **IV U5,** 85
Daedia [ˈdeɪdɪə] **IV U5,** 99
Daisy [ˈdeɪzɪ] **III**
Darcy [ˈdɑːsi] **IV U2,** 38
Dorothy [ˈdɒrəθi] **II**
Edith [ˈiːdɪθ] **II**
Elena [ˈelɪnə] **I**
Emily [ˈemɪli] **III**
Emma [ˈemə] **I**
Farah [ˈfɑːrə] **I**
Fiona [fɪˈəʊnə] **I**
Grace [ɡreɪs] **I**
Jade [dʒeɪd] **I**
Jane [dʒeɪn] **II**
Janice [ˈdʒænɪs] **II**
Jessie [ˈdʒesi] **IV U3,** 57
Joanie [ˈdʒəʊni] **IV U2,** 38
Julia [ˈdʒuːliə] **III**
Julie [ˈdʒuːli] **II**
Kate [keɪt] **II**
Kelsey [ˈkelsi] **IV ZI,** 10
Kerry [ˈkeri] **IV U2,** 40
Kim [kɪm] **III**
Kimberly [ˈkimbəli] **II**
Kitt [kɪt] **IV U2,** 38
Laura [ˈlɔːrə] **II**

Lauren ['lɔ:rən] **III**
Lindy ['lɪndi] **IV U3,** 50
Lisa ['li:sə] **I**
Louisa [li'i:zə] ⟨**IV U3,** 67⟩
Louise [lu'i:z] **III**
Lucy ['lu:si] **I**
Lynn [lɪn] **IV U3,** 52
Marge [mɑ:dʒ] **III**
Marie [mə'ri:] **IV U5,** 88
Marlene ['mɑ:rli:n] ⟨**IV U5,** 100⟩
Mary ['meəri] **III**
Michelle [mɪ'ʃel] ⟨**IV U5,** 101⟩
Nasreen [nʌs'ri:n] **I**
Nina ['ni:nə] **I**
Nyla ['naɪlə] **III**
Polly ['pɒli] **I**
Rachel ['reɪtʃl] **I**
Rita ['ri:tə] **IV U3,** 57
Rosa ['rəʊzə] ⟨**IV U1,** 31⟩
Rosanne [rəʊ'zæn] **IV U2,** 38
Sarah ['seərə] **I**
Shania [ˌʃə'naɪə] **II**
Sharon ['ʃærən] **II**
Shelley [ʃeli] ⟨**IV U1,** 30⟩
Shirin ['ʃɪrɪn] **III**
Sita ['sɪtə] **III**
Star [stɑ:] **IV U3,** 57
Sue [su:] **I**
Susan ['su:zn] **I**
Suzanne [su:'zæn] **I**
Tamara [tə'mɑ:rə] **I**
Tess [tes] **I**
Tiffany ['tɪfəni] **IV U2,** 39
Tilly ['tɪli] **I**
Tracy ['treɪsi] **I**
Wendy ['wendi] **II**

Surnames

Akodu [ə'kəʊdʊ] **III**
Barnes [bɑ:nz] **III**
Barnfield ['bɑ:nfi:ld] **III**
Barrymore ['bærɪmɔ:] **III**
Baskerville ['bæskəvɪl] **III**
Bell [bel] **II**
Blake [bleɪk] **II**
Branson ['brænsn] **II**
Brook [brʊk] **I**
Brown [braʊn] **I**
Carter ['kɑ:tə] **I**
Clarke [klɑ:k] **III**
Davenport ['dævnpɔ:t] **IV U2,** 38
Deacon ['di:kən] **III**
Dust [dʌst] **II**
Dwight [dwaɪt] **IV U4,** 75
Easton ['i:stən] **II**
Glenn [glen] **III**
Goodman ['gʊdmən] **IV U1,** 20
Green [gri:n] **I**
Jackson ['dʒæksn] **I**
Jones [dʒəʊnz] **II**
Kolden ['kɒldn] **IV U2,** 39
Lopez ['ləʊpez] **IV U2,** 33
Lumière ['lu:mieə] **IV U5,** 86
Marks [mɑ:ks] **III**
Marley ['mɑ:li] **III**
Martin ['mɑ:tɪn] **II**
Mason ['meɪsn] **II**
Monte ['mɒnteɪ] **I**
Negrete ['ni:grət] **IV U5,** 99
Newman ['nju:mən] **I**
Nosey ['nəʊzi] **III**
Presley ['prezli] **III**
Quasala ['kwəˌsɑ:lə] ⟨**IV U3,** 66⟩
Redman ['redmən] **III**
Rodrigo [rɒd'ri:gəʊ] **IV U5,** 85
Rose [rəʊz] **IV U4,** 80
Ross [rɒs] **II**
Sanchez ['sæntʃez] ⟨**IV U1,** 31⟩
Smart [smɑ:t] **III**
Smith [smɪθ] **I**
Spencer [spen'sə] **I**
Stapleton ['steɪpltən] **III**
Taylor ['teɪlə] **I**
Tiny ['taɪni] **I**
Turner ['tɜ:nə] **IV U3,** 50
Warner ['wɔ:nə] **IV U5,** 85
Wilkins ['wɪlkɪnz] **III**
Wilson ['wɪlsn] **III**

Place names

Aberdeen [ˌæbə'di:n] **II**
Africa ['æfrɪkə] **III**
Alaska [ə'læskə] **IV ZI,** 13
Amarillo [ˌæmər'ləʊ] ⟨**IV U3,** 61⟩
America [ə'merɪkə] **II**
Arizona [ˌærɪ'zəʊnə] **IV ZI,** 11
Athens ['æθənz] **I**
Australia [ɒs'treɪliə] **II**
Ayrshire ['eəʃə] **II**
Barstow ['bɑ:stəʊ] ⟨**IV U3,** 61⟩
Birmingham ['bɜ:mɪŋəm] **II**
Blackheath [ˌblæk'hi:θ] **I**
Bombay [ˌbɒm'beɪ] **IV U5,** 86
Boston ['bɒstən] **IV ZI,** 12
Brazil [brə'zɪl] **II**
Brighton ['braɪtn] **II**
Bristol ['brɪstl] **I**
Britain ['brɪtn] **I**
The **British Isles** [ðə ˌbrɪtɪʃ 'aɪlz] **III**
the **Bronx** [də 'brɒŋks] **IV U1,** 15
Brooklyn ['brʊklɪn] **IV U1,** 15
Calais ['kæleɪ] **III**
California [ˌkælɪ'fɔ:niə] **III**
Canada ['kænədə] **III**
Cardiff ['kɑ:dɪf] **I**
Chicago [ʃɪ'kɑ:gəʊ] **III**
China ['tʃaɪnə] **II**
Chinatown ['tʃaɪnətaʊn] **IV U1,** 15
Colorado [ˌkɒlə'rɑ:dəʊ] **IV U3,** 49
Cornwall ['kɔ:nwɔ:l] **III**
Cotswold ['kɒtswəʊld] **I**
Crystal Rapids ['krɪstl ˌræpɪdz] **IV U3,** 58
Dartmoor ['dɑ:tmɔ:] **III**
Detroit [də'trɔɪt] **IV U2,** 46
Dover ['dəʊvə] **III**
Dumfries [dʌm'fri:s] **II**
Dundee [dʌn'di:] **II**
Edinburgh ['edɪnbrə] **II**
Ellis Island [ˌelɪs 'aɪlənd] **IV U1,** 18
England ['ɪŋglənd] **I**
Europe ['jʊərəp] **III**
Flagstaff ['flægstɑ:f] ⟨**IV U3,** 61⟩
Florida ['flɒrɪdə] **IV U2,** 35
Folkestone ['fəʊkstən] **III**
Forest Springs [ˌfɒrɪst 'sprɪŋz] **IV U3,** 52
France [frɑ:ns] **I**
Gallup ['gæləp] ⟨**IV U3,** 61⟩
Germany ['dʒɜ:məni] **I**
The **Grand Canyon** [ðə ˌgrænd 'kænjən] **IV U3,** 49
Grange-over-Sands [ˌgreɪndʒ 'əʊvə ˌsændz] **II**
Granite Falls ['grænɪt ˌfɔ:lz] **IV U3,** 57
Greece [gri:s] **I**
Greensburg ['gri:nzˌbɜ:g] **IV U4,** 75
Greenwich ['grenɪdʒ] **I**
Greenwich Village [ˌgrenɪdʒ 'vɪlɪdʒ] **IV U1,** 26
Harlem ['hɑ:ləm] ⟨**IV U1,** 21⟩
Hawaii [hə'wai:] **IV ZI,** 13
Hermit Rapids ['hɜ:mɪt ˌræpɪdz] **IV U3,** 58
the **Highlands** [ˌðə 'haɪləndz] **II**
Hollywood ['hɒliwʊd] **IV U5,** 84
India ['ɪndiə] **II**
Iowa ['aɪəʊə] **IV U1,** 20
Istanbul [ˌɪstæn'bʊl] **I**
Italy ['ɪtəli] **I**
Jamaica [dʒə'meɪkə] **III**
Joplin ['dʒɒplɪn] ⟨**IV U3,** 61⟩
Kansas ['kænsəs] **IV ZI,** 12
Kingman ['kɪŋmn] ⟨**IV U3,** 61⟩
Lake District ['leɪk ˌdɪstrɪkt] **II**
Las Vegas [ˌlæs 'veɪgəs] **IV U3,** 49

Leicester ['lestə] **I**
Liberty Island [ˌlɪbəti 'aɪlənd] **IV U1,** 26
Little Italy [ˌlɪtl 'ɪtəli] **IV U1,** 26
Little Oyster Island [ˌlɪtl ɔɪstə 'aɪlənd] **IV U1,** 18
Liverpool ['livəpu:l] **III**
London ['lʌndən] **I**
Los Angeles [lɒs 'ændʒəli:z] **IV ZI,** 10
Louisiana [luˌi:zi'ænə] ⟨**IV U5,** 100⟩
Manhattan [mæn'hætn] **IV U1,** 14
Mersey ['mɜ:zi] **III**
Mesquite [mes'ki:t] **IV U2,** 34
Mexico ['meksɪkəʊ] **IV U1,** 18
Midwest [ˌmɪd'west] **IV ZI,** 12
Missouri [mɪ'zʊəri] ⟨**IV U3,** 61⟩; ⟨**IV U5,** 100⟩
Monument Valley [ˌmɒnjəmənt 'væli] **IV ZI,** 11
Moscow ['mɒskəʊ] **III**
Mumbai [ˌmʌm'baɪ] **IV U5,** 86
Nevada [nə'vɑ:də] **IV U3,** 49
New Amsterdam [ˌnju: 'æmstədæm] **IV U1,** 18
New England [ˌnju: 'ɪŋglənd] **IV ZI,** 12
New Mexico [ˌnju: 'meksɪkəʊ] **IV U3,** 49
New Orleans [ˌnju: 'ɔ:liənz] **IV U2,** 46
New York City (NYC) [ˌnju: jɔ:k 'sɪti] **IV ZI,** 12
North Sea [ˌnɔ:θ 'si:] **II**
Northern Ireland [ˌnɔ:ðn 'aɪələnd] **III**
Notting Hill [ˌnɒtɪŋ 'hɪl] **III**
Ohio [əʊ'haɪəʊ] **IV ZI,** 12
Okehampton [əʊk'hæmptn] **III**
Oklahoma [ˌəʊklə'həʊmə] **IV U3,** 49
Paris ['pærɪs] **I**
Peach Springs [ˌpi:tʃ 'sprɪŋz] ⟨**IV U3,** 66⟩
Queens [kwi:nz] **IV U1,** 15
Republic of Ireland [rɪˌpʌblɪk‿əv‿'aɪələnd] **III**
Rome [rəʊm] **I**
Route 66 [ˌru:t ˌsɪkstisɪks] **IV U3,** 49
Russia ['rʌʃə] **I**
Saint Louis [ˌseɪnt 'lu:i] ⟨**IV U3,** 61⟩
San Bernardino [ˌsæn 'bɜ:nədi:nəʊ] ⟨**IV U3,** 61⟩
San Diego [ˌsæn di'eɪgəʊ] **IV U5,** 99
San Francisco [ˌsæn frən'sɪskəʊ] **IV ZI,** 10
Scotland ['skɒtlənd] **II**
Seattle [si'ætl] **IV U2,** 46
Shanghai [ˌʃæŋ'haɪ] **I**
Shoreditch ['ʃɔ:dɪtʃ] **III**
Silicon Valley [ˌsɪlɪkən 'væli] **IV ZI,** 10
Snowdon ['snəʊdn] **III**
South Africa [ˌsaʊθ 'æfrɪkə] **II**
Spain [speɪn] **III**
Staten Island [ˌstætn 'aɪlənd] **IV U1,** 15
Swansea ['swɒnzi] **III**
Sweden ['swi:dn] **III**
Texas ['teksəs] **IV ZI,** 11
Thames ['temz] **I**
Turkey ['tɜ:ki] **I**
the **UK** [ðə ˌju:'keɪ] **II**
UK (= United Kingdom) [ˌju:'keɪ] **III**
Ulverston ['ʌlvəstən] **II**
United States of America [ju:ˌnaɪtɪd 'steɪts əv 'əmerɪkə] **IV U2,** 33
Upper West (Side) ['ʌpə ˌwest (saɪd)] ⟨**IV U1,** 21⟩
US [ˌju:'es] **IV ZI,** 10
Utah [ˌju:tɑ:] **IV U3,** 63
Virginia [və'dʒɪnjə] ⟨**IV U5,** 100⟩
Wales [weɪlz] **III**
Washington ['wɒʃɪŋtən] ⟨**IV U5,** 100⟩
Washington D.C. [ˌwɒʃɪŋtən ˌdi: 'si:] **IV ZI,** 12
Wenatchee Valley [wen'ætʃi ˌvæli] ⟨**IV U5,** 100⟩
Westminster [west'mɪnstə] **III**
Winona [wɪ'nəʊnə] ⟨**IV U3,** 61⟩

Other names

The **39 steps** [ðə ˌθɜ:tinaɪn 'steps] **III**
Abba ['æbə] **III**
Airbus ['eəbʌs] **III**
Damon **Albarn** [ˌdeɪmən 'ɔ:lbɑ:n] **III**
Apple [ˌæpl] **III**
Arctic Monkeys [ˌɑ:ktɪk 'mʌŋki:z] **III**
Arsenal ['ɑ:snl] **II**
Asterix ['æstərɪks] **III**
Baker Street ['beɪkə ˌstri:t] **III**
Bakerloo Line [ˌbeɪkəlu: 'laɪn] **III**
Barker ['bɑ:kə] **I**
Jake **Barnes** [ˌdʒeɪk 'bɑ:nz] **IV U3,** 64
Drew **Barrymore** [ˌdru: 'bærɪmɔ:] **IV U5,** 85
Baskerville Hall [ˌbæskəvɪl 'hɑ:l] **III**
the **Battery** [ðə 'bætərɪ] ⟨**IV U1,** 21⟩
BBC [ˌbi:bi:'si:] **III**
Beastie Boys ['bi:sti ˌbɔɪz] **IV U1,** 21
Beatlemania ['bi:tlˌmeɪnɪə] **III**
The **Beatles** [ˌðə 'bi:tlz] **III**
Beefeater ['bi:fˌi:tə] **II**
Beethoven ['beɪthəʊvn] **II**
Dirk **Benedict** [ˌdɜ:k 'benɪdɪkt] **IV U3,** 64
Halle **Berry** [ˌhæl 'beri] **IV U5,** 88
Berry Middle School ['beri mɪdl ˌsku:l] **IV U2,** 34
Pete **Best** [ˌpi:t 'best] **III**
Big Ben [ˌbɪg 'ben] **II**
Black Tower ['blæk ˌtaʊə] **II**
Blur [blɜ:] **III**
Bollywood ['bɒliwʊd] **IV U5,** 86
Bono ['bəʊnəʊ] **III**
Broadway ['brɔ:dweɪ] **IV U1,** 29
Buckingham Palace [ˌbʌkɪŋəm 'pælɪs] **III**
Buzz [bʌz] **I**
Camden Market [ˌkæmdən 'mɑ:kɪt] **III**
Canarsie High School [ˌkænɑ:zi 'haɪ sku:l] ⟨**IV U1,** 30⟩
Capital Radio [ˌkæpɪtl 'reɪdɪəʊ] **III**
Casino Royale [kə'si:nəʊ ˌrɔɪɑ:l] **III**
Celtic ['seltɪk] **III**
Central Park [ˌsentrəl 'pɑ:k] **IV U1,** 14
Ray **Charles** [ˌreɪ 'tʃɑ:lz] **IV U5,** 88
Chelsea ['tʃelsi] **II**
Circle Line [ˌsɜ:kl 'laɪn] **III**
Adam **Clayton** [ˌædəm 'kleɪtn] **III**
Covent Garden [ˌkɒvnt 'gɑ:dn] **III**
Crawford Park [ˌkrɔ:fəd 'pɑ:k] **III**
Crazy Horse ['kreɪzi ˌhɔ:s] **IV U3,** 60
Cutty Sark [ˌkʌti 'sɑ:k] **I**
Matt **Damon** [ˌmæt 'deɪmən] **IV U3,** 53
Destiny's Child ['destɪni:z ˌtʃaɪld] **III**
Detroit Red Wings ['detrɔɪt ˌred wɪŋz] **IV U2,** 46
Dick Whittington [ˌdɪk 'wɪtɪŋtən] **I**
Docklands Light Railway (= DLR) ['dɒkləndz ˌlaɪt 'reɪlweɪ] **I**
Downriver [daʊn'rɪvə] **IV U3,** 57
Dynamo Moscow [ˌdaɪnəməʊ 'mɒskəʊ] **III**
Linda **Eastman** [ˌlɪndə ˌi:stmn] **III**
the **Edge** [ðɪ: 'edʒ] **III**
Samuel **Ellis** [ˌsæmjʊəl 'elɪs] **IV U1,** 18
Empire State Building [ˌempaɪə 'steɪt ˌbɪldɪŋ] **IV ZI,** 13
E.T. (= The Extra-Terrestrial) [ˌi: 'ti: = ði: ˌekstrə tə'restriəl] **IV U5,** 87
FA Cup [ˌefeɪ 'kʌp] **II**
Fifth Avenue [ˌfɪfθ 'ævənju:] **IV U1,** 20
For auld lang syne [fə əʊld læŋ 'saɪn] **III**
Jamie **Foxx** [ˌdʒeɪmi 'fɒks] **IV U5,** 84
Elina **Furman** [ˌelɪnə 'fɜ:mən] **IV U5,** 92
Leah **Furman** [ˌli:ə ˌfɜ:mən] **IV U5,** 92
Evelyn **Glennie** [ˌevəlɪn 'gleni] **III**
Carlos **Gomez** [ˌkɑ:lɒs 'gəʊmez] **IV U5,** 99
Gone with the wind ['gɒn wɪð ðə 'wɪnd] **IV U5,** 86
Gorillaz [gə'rɪləz] **III**
Grammy ['græmi] ⟨**IV U5,** 93⟩
the **Grand Concourse** [ðə ˌgrænd 'kɒŋkɔ:s] ⟨**IV U1,** 21⟩
Greenwich Mean Time (= GMT) [ˌgrenɪdʒ 'mi:n taɪm] **I**

English – German

The **Greenwich Foot Tunnel** [ðə 'grenɪdʒ fʊt ˌtʌnl] **I**
The **Growl** [ðə 'graʊl] **IV U2,** 34
Happy Feet [ˌhæpi 'fi:t] **III**
Louise Amanda **Harman** [ˌlii:z əmændə 'hɑ:mn] **III**
George **Harrison** [ˌdʒɔ:dʒ 'hærɪsn] **III**
Heathrow Airport [ˌhi:θrəʊ 'eəpɔ:t] **III**
Charlton **Heston** [ˌtʃɑ:ltn 'hestn] **IV U3,** 64
High Bridge [ˌhaɪ 'brɪdʒ] ⟨**IV U1,** 21⟩
High Noon [ˌhaɪ 'nu:n] **IV U5,** 95
Will **Hobbs** [ˌwɪl 'hɒbz] **IV U3,** 58
Sherlock **Holmes** [ˌʃɜ:lɒk 'həʊmz] **III**
Hot Chocolate [ˌhɒt 'tʃɒklət] ⟨**IV U4,** 77⟩
Houses of Parliament [ˌhaʊzɪz‿əv 'pɑ:ləmənt] **III**
Hualapai ['wɔ:ləpaɪ] **IV U3,** 51
Hyde Park [ˌhaɪd 'pɑ:k] **II**
Independence Day [ɪndɪ'pendənts ˌdeɪ] **IV ZI,** 12
International Space Station (ISS) ['ɪntənæʃnl speɪs ˌsteɪʃn = ˌaɪ es 'es] **IV U4,** 70
Shirlyn **Jackson** [ˌʃi:rlɪn 'dʒæksn] **IV U5,** 99
Elton **John** [ˌeltn 'dʒɒn] **III**
John F. Kennedy Space Center [ˌdʒɒn 'ef kenədi 'speɪs ˌsentə] **IV U2,** 35
King Kong ['kɪŋ ˌkɒŋ] **IV U5,** 95
Kingsdale Comprehensive School ['kɪŋzdeɪl kɒmprɪhensɪv 'sku:l] **III**
Beyoncé **Knowles** [ˌbi:ɒnsɑ: 'nəʊlz] **III**
Lady Sovereign [ˌleɪdi 'sɒvrɪn] **III**
John **Lennon** [ˌdʒɒn 'lenən] **III**
The **Lion King** [ðə 'laɪən ˌkɪŋ] **IV U1,** 29
Liverpool Institute for Performing Arts (LIPA) [livəpu:l ˌɪnstɪtju:t fɔ: 'pəfɔ:mɪŋ ɑ:ts (lɪpə)] **III**
London Bridge [ˌlʌndən 'brɪdʒ] **II**
The **London Dungeon** [ðə 'lʌndən ˌdʌndʒn] **II**
The **London Eye** [ðə ˌlʌndən 'aɪ] **II**
Londoner ['lʌndənə] **II**
Lord of the Rings ['lɔ:s‿əv ðə ˌrɪŋz] **IV U5,** 87
MED-Theatre ['emi:di: ˌθɪətə] **III**
Madonna [mə'dɒnə] **III**
Main Street ['meɪn ˌstri:t] **IV U4,** 75
Manchester United ['mæntʃɪstə ju:naɪtɪd] **II**
Maranello ['mærəˌneləʊ] ⟨**IV U5,** 93⟩
Marble Arch ['mɑ:bl ˌɑ:tʃ] **III**
Paul **McCartney** [ˌpɔ:l mə'kɑ:tni] **III**
Georges **Méliès** [ˌʒɔɪrʒ 'meliəs] **IV U5,** 86
Meridian Line [mə'rɪdiən ˌlaɪn] **I**
Mill Hill High ['mɪl hɪl ˌhaɪ] **III**
Monument ['mɒnjəmənt] **III**
Larry **Mullen** [ˌlæri 'mʌlən] **III**
Andy **Murray** [ˌændi 'mʌri] **III**
Myspace ['maɪspeɪs] **III**
NASA ['næsə] **IV U4,** 69
Natural History Museum [ˌnætʃrl hɪstri 'mju:zi:əm] **III**
Naturally 7 ['nætʃrəli ˌsevn] **IV U1,** 22
Nestor Company ['nestɔ: ˌkʌmpəni] **IV U5,** 99
New Yorker [ˌnju: 'jɔ:kə] **IV U1,** 15
Newtech ['nju:tek] ⟨**IV U3,** 66⟩
Oaklands Skatepark ['əʊkləndz ˌskeɪtpɑ:k] **III**
Obelix ['ɒbəlɪks] **III**
Yoko **Ono** [ˌjəʊkəʊ 'əʊnəʊ] **III**
Oscar ['ɒskə] **IV U5,** 84
Oxford Street ['ɒksfəd ˌstri:t] **II**
Piccadilly Circus [ˌpɪkədɪli 'sɜ:kəs] **II**
Pluto ['plu:təʊ] **IV U4,** 76
Pondelsbury Road [ˌpɒndlzbri 'rəʊd] **III**
The **Quarrymen** [ˌdə 'krɒrimən] **III**
Queen Elizabeth I [kwi:n ˌɪlɪzəbəθ ðə 'fɜ:st] **II**
Rock Circus ['rɒk ˌsɜ:kəs] **III**
The **Rolling Stones** [ˌðə rəʊlɪŋ 'stəʊnz] **III**
Rowntree Park Skatepark ['raʊntri: pɑ:k ˌskeɪtpɑ:k] **III**
Royal Observatory [ˌrɔɪəl əb'zɜ:vətri] **I**
Run-up [ˌrʌn‿'ʌp] **IV U1,** 14
Shakespeare ['ʃeɪkspɪə] **II**
the **Skywalk** [ðə 'skaɪwɔ:k] **IV U3,** 49
Marc **Smith** [ˌmɑ:k 'smɪθ] **III**
Steven **Spielberg** [ˌsti:vn 'spi:lbɜ:g] **IV U5,** 87
Spock [spɒk] **IV U4,** 75
Star Trek ['stɑ: ˌtrk] **IV U4,** 75
Ringo **Starr** [ˌrɪŋgəʊ 'stɑ:] **III**
The **Statue of Liberty** [ðə 'stætʃu: əv ˌlɪbəti] **IV U1,** 15
St. James's Park [snt 'dʒeɪmzɪz ˌpɑ:k] **III**
St. Paul's Cathedral [snt 'pɔ:lz ˌkə'θi:drl] **III**
Stonehenge [ˌstəʊn'hendʒ] **III**
Summer of Love [ˌsʌmər‿əv 'lʌv] **III**
Bryn **Terfel** [ˌbrɪn 'tɜ:fl] **III**
Thomas Tallis School [ˌtɒməs 'tælɪs sku:l] **I**
The **Tower of London** [ðə ˌtaʊə əv 'lʌndən] **II**
Tron [trɒn] **IV U5,** 86
the **Tube** [ðə 'tju:b] **II**
U2 [ˌju: 'tu:] **III**
the **Underground** [ðɪ 'ʌndəˌgraʊnd] **I**
Volkswagen ['fɒlksˌvɑ:gən] ⟨**IV U5,** 100⟩
The **Wailers** [ˌdə 'weɪləz] **III**
Walk of Fame [ˌwɔ:k‿əv 'feɪm] **IV ZI,** 10
Water Park ['wɑ:tə ˌpɑ:k] **II**
West Side Story ['west saɪd ˌstɔ:ri] **IV ZI,** 13
The **White House** ['waɪt ˌhaʊs] **IV ZI,** 12
White Tower ['waɪt ˌtaʊə] **II**
White Hart Lane [waɪt 'hɑ:t leɪn] **III**
Harvey Henderson **Wilcox** [hɑ:vi ˌhendəsn 'wɪlkɒks] **IV U5,** 99
Robbie **Williams** [ˌrɒbi 'wɪljəmz] **III**
Wimbledon ['wɪmbldn] **III**
The **Wizard of Oz** [ðə ˌwɪzəd‿əv 'ɒz] **II**
World Trade Center [ˌwɜ:ld 'treɪd sentə] **IV U1,** 15
Peter **Yared** [ˌpi:tə 'jærɪd] **IV U4,** 76
Zargon ['zɑ:gɒn] **IV U4,** 76

A

abbiegen to turn [tɜ:n]
abbrechen to drop out ['drɒp ˌaʊt]
Abend evening ['i:vnɪŋ]
Abendessen supper ['sʌpə]; dinner ['dɪnə]
Abendschule evening class [ˌi:vnɪŋ 'klɑ:s]
Abenteuer adventure [əd'ventʃə]
aber but [bʌt]
abfahren to leave [li:v]
Abfall trash *(AE)* [træʃ]; garbage *(AE)* ['gɑ:bɪdʒ]; rubbish ['rʌbɪʃ]
abhaken to tick [tɪk]
Abhängigkeit addiction [ə'dɪkʃn]
abheben to take off [teɪk‿'ɒf]
abholen to pick up ['pɪk‿ʌp]; to collect [kə'lekt]
Abitur A-Level (= Advanced Level) ['eɪlevl = ˌədvɑ:nst 'levl]
ablehnen to reject [ri:'dʒekt]
Abmachung arrangement [ə'reɪndʒmənt]
abmalen to copy ['kɒpi]
Absatz paragraph ['pærəgrɑ:f]
abschalten to turn off ['tɜ:n‿ɒf]
abschicken to send off [send 'ɒf]
abschließen to lock [lɒk]
abschneiden to cut off [ˌkʌt 'ɒf]
Abschnitt paragraph ['pærəgrɑ:f]
abschreiben to copy ['kɒpi]
abstellen to cut off [ˌkʌt 'ɒf]
abstimmen to vote [vəʊt]
abstürzen to crash [kræʃ]; to break down ['breɪk daʊn]
abtrennen to cut off [ˌkʌt 'ɒf]
Abwasch washing up [ˌwɒʃɪŋ 'ʌp]
abweisen to reject [ri:'dʒekt]
achte/-r/-s eighth [eɪtθ]
Actionfilm action movie ['ækʃn ˌmu:vi]
addieren to add [æd]
Adjektiv adjective ['ædʒɪktɪv]
Adrenalin adrenaline [ə'drenəlɪn]
Adresse address [ə'dres]
Adverb adverb ['ædvɜ:b]
Aftershave aftershave ['ɑ:ftəʃeɪv]
Agentur agency ['eɪdʒntsi]
ähnlich similar ['sɪmilə]; like [laɪk]
Ahnung idea [aɪ'dɪə]
Ahorn maple ['meɪpl]
Akku battery ['bætri]
aktiv active ['æktɪv]
Aktivität activity [æk'tɪvəti]
Akzent accent ['æksnt]
akzeptieren to accept [ək'sept]
albern silly ['sɪli]
Album album ['ælbəm]
Alkohol alcohol (no pl) ['ælkəhɒl]
alle all [ɔ:l]; everyone ['evriwʌn]
allein alone [ə'ləʊn]; solo ['səʊləʊ]
allerdings however [haʊ'evə]
alles everything ['evriθɪŋ]
Alles Gute zum Geburtstag! Happy Birthday! [ˌhæpi 'bɜ:θdeɪ]
Alphabet alphabet ['ælfəbet]
als than [ðæn]; when [wen]
als Erste/-r/-s first [fɜ:st]
als nächste/-r/-s next [nekst]
als ob as if [æz‿'ɪf]
also well [wel]; so [səʊ]
alt ancient ['eɪnʃnt]; old [əʊld]
Alter age [eɪdʒ]
altmodisch old-fashioned [ˌəʊld 'fæʃnd]
am on [ɒn]
Amerikaner/-in American [ə'merɪkən]
amerikanisch American [ə'merɪkən]
amtlich official [ə'fɪʃl]
an at [æt; ət]; to [tʊ]
an ... vorbei past ... [pɑ:st]
Ananas pineapple ['paɪnˌæpl]
anbieten to offer ['ɒfə]
andere/-r/-s other ['ʌðə]; different ['dɪfrnt]
eine **andere/-r/-s** another [ə'nʌðə]
ändern to change [tʃeɪndʒ]
anders different ['dɪfrnt]
anderthalb one and a half [ˌwʌn‿ən‿ə 'hɑ:f]
Änderung change [tʃeɪndʒ]
einen **Anfall bekommen** to have a fit [ˌhæv‿ə 'fɪt]
Anfang beginning [bɪ'gɪnɪŋ]; start [stɑ:t]
anfangen to begin [bɪ'gɪn]; to start [stɑ:t]
Angaben directions [dɪ'rekʃnz]
angeben to brag (to s.o. about sth.) [bræg]
angehören to belong [bɪ'lɒŋ ˌtə]
angenehm enjoyable [ɪn'dʒɔɪəbl]
angreifen to tackle ['tækl]
Angriff tackle ['tækl]
Angst einjagen to scare [skeə]
Angst haben to be afraid of [ˌbi: ə'freɪd əv]; to be frightened [bi: 'fraɪtnd]; to be scared [ˌbi: 'skeəd]
anhalten to stop [stɒp]
anhören to listen ['lɪsn]
sich **anhören** to sound [saʊnd]
Animation animation [ˌænɪ'meɪʃn]
ankommen to arrive [ə'raɪv]
Ankündigung announcement [ə'naʊnsmənt]
anmalen to colour ['kʌlə]
sich **anmelden** to check into [ˌtʃek 'ɪntə]
annehmen to accept [ək'sept]; to suppose [sə'pəʊz]
anprobieren to try on [traɪ‿'ɒn]
Anruf call [kɔ:l]
Anrufbeantworter answering machine ['ɑ:nsrɪŋ məˌʃi:n]
anrufen to call [kɔ:l]; to phone [fəʊn]
anschalten to turn on ['tɜ:n‿ɒn]; to switch on [ˌswɪtʃ‿'ɒn]
ansehen to look at ['lʊk æt]
Anschlagbrett notice board ['nəʊtɪs bɔ:d]
Anschrift address [ə'dres]
ansehen to look at ['lʊk æt]
Ansicht mind [maɪnd]
anstehen to queue [kju:]
anstelle von instead of [ɪn'sted‿əv]
sich **anstellen** to queue [kju:]
anstrengend tiring ['taɪrɪŋ]
Anteil quota ['kwəʊtə]
Antenne antenna [æn'tenə]
antik ancient ['eɪnʃnt]
antippen to touch [tʌtʃ]
Antwort response [rɪ'spɒns]; answer ['ɑ:nsə]
antworten to reply [rɪ'plaɪ]; to answer ['ɑ:nsə]
Anweisungen instructions [ɪn'strʌkʃnz]; directions [dɪ'rekʃnz]
anziehen to put on [ˌpʊt‿'ɒn]
Apfel apple ['æpl]
Appetit appetite ['æpɪtaɪt]
April April ['eɪprəl]
Arbeit work [wɜ:k]; job [dʒɒb]
arbeiten to work [wɜ:k]
Arbeiter/-in worker ['wɜ:kə]
Arbeitsblatt handout ['hændaʊt]
Arbeitsgruppe workshop ['wɜ:kʃɒp]
Architekt/-in architect ['ɑ:kɪtekt]
Ärger trouble ['trʌbl]
Argument argument ['ɑ:gjəmənt]
arm poor [pɔ:]
Arm arm [ɑ:m]
Armbanduhr watch [wɒtʃ]
Armee army ['ɑ:mi]
Armut poverty ['pɒvəti]
Art type [taɪp]; kind [kaɪnd]
Artikel article ['ɑ:tɪkl]
Arzt/Ärztin doctor ['dɒktə]
Asiat/-in Asian ['eɪʒn]
asiatisch Asian ['eɪʒn]
Assistent/-in assistant [ə'sɪstnt]
Astronaut/-in astronaut ['æstrənɔ:t]
attraktiv handsome ['hænsəm]; attractive [ə'træktɪv]
auch also ['ɔ:lsəʊ]; too [tu:]

German – English

auch nicht not … either [ˌnɒt … ˈaɪðə]
Audiodatei sound file [ˈsaʊnd ˌfaɪl]
auf at [æt; ət]; onto [ˈɒntuː]; on [ɒn]
auf … zu towards [təˈwɔːdz]
auf der anderen Seite von across [əˈkrɒs]
auf Wiederhören goodbye [gʊdˈbaɪ]
auf Wiedersehen goodbye [gʊdˈbaɪ]
aufbauen to build [bɪld]
aufbewahren to keep [kiːp]
aufblicken to look up [lʊk‿ˈʌp]
aufdrehen to turn on [ˈtɜːn‿ɒn]
aufführen to perform [pəˈfɔːm]
Aufführung performance [pəˈfɔːməns]
aufgeben to quit [kwɪt]; to give up [ˈgɪv‿ʌp]
aufgehen to rise [raɪz]
aufgeräumt tidy [ˈtaɪdi]
aufgeregt excited [ɪkˈsaɪtɪd]
aufgeteilt divided [dɪˈvaɪdɪd]
aufheben to pick up [ˈpɪk‿ʌp]
aufhören to quit [kwɪt]; to stop [stɒp]
Aufladekarte top-up card [ˈtɒpʌp ˌkɑːd]
aufmachen to open [ˈəʊpn]
aufnehmen to record [rɪˈkɔːd]
aufpassen auf to look after [ˈlʊk ˌɑːftə]
aufräumen to tidy [ˈtaɪdi]; to clean [kliːn]; to put away [pʊt‿əˈweɪ]
aufregend exciting [ɪkˈsaɪtɪŋ]
Aufregung fuss [fʌs]
aufschieben to delay [dɪˈleɪ]
… aufschlagen to turn to … [ˈtɜːn ˌtə]
aufschreiben to write down [ˌraɪt ˈdaʊn]
Aufseher/-in ranger [ˈreɪndʒə]
aufstehen to get up [get‿ˈʌp]
Aufstieg climb [klaɪm]
auftauchen to appear [əˈpɪə]
auftreten to perform [pəˈfɔːm]
aufwachen to wake up [ˌweɪk‿ˈʌp]
aufwachsen to grow up [grəʊ‿ˈʌp]
(sich) **aufwärmen** to warm up [ˌwɔːm ˈʌp]
Aufzug elevator *(AE)* [ˈelɪveɪtə]
Auge eye [aɪ]
Augenblick moment [ˈməʊmənt]
im **Augenblick** at the moment [ˌæt ðə ˈməʊmənt]
Augenbraue eyebrow [ˈaɪbraʊ]
August August [ˈɔːgəst]
Aula hall [hɔːl]
aus from [frɒm]
ausbessern to repair [rɪˈpeə]; to mend [mend]
auschecken to check-out [ˈtʃekaʊt]
sich **ausdenken** to imagine [ɪˈmædʒɪn]
Ausdruck phrase [freɪz]
auseinanderbrechen to split apart [ˌsplɪt‿əˈpɑːt]
sich **auseinandersetzen** to argue [ˈɑːgjuː]
Auseinandersetzung argument [ˈɑːgjəmənt]
ausflippen to flip [flɪp]
Ausflug trip [trɪp]
ausfüllen to fill in [fɪl ˈɪn]
Ausgangssperre curfew [ˈkɜːfjuː]
ausgeben to spend [spend]
ausgehen to go out [gəʊ‿ˈaʊt]
ausgenommen except for [ɪkˈsept fɔː]
auskundschaften to scout [skaʊt]
Auskunft information [ˌɪnfəˈmeɪʃn]
ausländisch foreign [ˈfɒrɪn]
auslaufen to leak [liːk]
ausleihen to borrow [ˈbɒrəʊ]
ausliefern to deliver [dɪˈlɪvə]
etw. **ausmachen** to mind s.th. [maɪnd]
ausmalen to colour [ˈkʌlə]
ausrauben to rob [rɒb]
ausreichend plenty [ˈplenti]
sich **ausruhen** to rest [rest]
Ausrüstung kit [kɪt]; equipment [ɪˈkwɪpmənt]
ausschalten to switch off [ˌswɪtʃ ˈɒf]; to turn off [ˈtɜːn‿ɒf]
ausscheren to swerve [swɜːv]
ausschneiden to cut out [ˌkʌt ˈaʊt]
Ausschnitt clip [klɪp]
aussehen to look [lʊk]
Außenseiter/-in geek [giːk]
außer except for [ɪkˈsept fɔː]
außerhalb outside [ˌaʊtˈsaɪd]
Außerirdische/-r alien [ˈeɪliən]
Ausstattung equipment [ɪˈkwɪpmənt]
Ausstellung exhibition [ˌeksɪˈbɪʃn]
aussuchen to choose [tʃuːz]
Austausch exchange [ɪksˈtʃeɪndʒ]
austauschen to substitute [ˈsʌbstɪtjuːt]
Auswahl choice [tʃɔɪs]
(aus)wählen to choose [tʃuːz]
auswechseln to change [tʃeɪndʒ]
ausweichen to swerve [swɜːv]
Auszeichnung award [əˈwɔːd]; merit [ˈmerɪt]
ausziehen to take off [teɪk‿ˈɒf]
Auszubildende/-r apprentice [əˈprentɪs]
Auto car [kɑː]
Autobahn highway *(AE)* [ˈhaɪweɪ]
Autogramm autograph [ˈɔːtəgrɑːf]
Automat machine [məˈʃiːn]
Autorität authority [ɔːˈθɒrəti]
Autowerkstatt garage [ˈgærɪdʒ]

B

Baby baby [ˈbeɪbi]
Badekappe swimming cap [ˈswɪmɪŋ ˌkæp]
Badminton badminton [ˈbædmɪntən]
Bahnhof station [ˈsteɪʃn]
Bahnsteig platform [ˈplætfɔːm]
Ball dance [dɑːns]; ball [bɔːl]
Banane banana [bəˈnɑːnə]
Band tape [teɪp]; band [bænd]
Bande gang [gæŋ]
Bank bench [bentʃ]
Bart beard [bɪəd]
Baseball baseball [ˈbeɪsbɔːl]
Basketball basketball [ˈbɑːskɪtbɔːl]
Bass bass [beɪs]
Batterie battery [ˈbætri]
Bauch stomach [ˈstʌmək]
bauen to build [bɪld]
Bauer/Bäuerin farmer [ˈfɑːmə]
Bauernhof farm [fɑːm]
Baum tree [triː]
Beamter/Beamtin official [əˈfɪʃl]; officer [ˈɒfɪsə]
beantworten to answer [ˈɑːnsə]
bearbeitet adapted [əˈdæptɪd]
beben to shake [ʃeɪk]
sich **bedanken** to give thanks [ˌgɪv ˈθæŋks]
bedanken to thank [θæŋk]
bedauerlich sad [sæd]
bedeuten to mean [miːn]
Bedeutung meaning [ˈmiːnɪŋ]
Bedingungs- conditional [kədˈdɪʃnl]
Beeil dich! Hurry up! [ˌhʌri‿ˈʌp]
beenden to end [end]; to finish [ˈfɪnɪʃ]
befragen to interview [ˈɪntəvjuː]
Beginn start [stɑːt]
beginnen to begin [bɪˈgɪn]; to start [stɑːt]
begreifen to realize [ˈrɪəlaɪz]
Begrenzung limit [ˈlɪmɪt]
behalten to keep [kiːp]
Behörde agency [ˈeɪdʒntsi]
bei at [æt; ət]; with [wɪð]
beibringen to teach [tiːtʃ]
beide both [bəʊθ]
Bein leg [leg]
beinahe nearly [ˈnɪəli]; almost [ˈɔːlməʊst]
zum **Beispiel** for example [ˌfər‿ˈɪgzɑːmpl]
bekannt famous [ˈfeɪməs]
Bekanntgabe announcement [əˈnaʊnsmənt]
Bekleidungsvorschriften dress code [ˌdres ˈkəʊd]
bekommen to receive [rɪˈsiːv]; to get [get]

belästigen to bother ['bɒðə]
belebt busy ['bɪzi]
belegtes Brot sandwich ['sænwɪdʒ]
beliebt popular ['pɒpjələ]
bellen to bark [bɑ:k]
Bellen bark [bɑ:k]
bemerken to notice ['nəʊtɪs]
Benehmen behaviour [bɪ'heɪvjə]
sich **benehmen** to act [ækt]
benutzen to use [ju:z]
Benutzung use [ju:s]
bereit ready ['redi]
bereits already [ɔ:l'redi]
Berg mountain ['maʊntɪn]
Bergwerk mine [maɪn]
Bericht report [rɪ'pɔ:t]
berichten to report [rɪ'pɔ:t]
Beruf job [dʒɒb]
berühmt famous ['feɪməs]
berühren to touch [tʌtʃ]
beschädigen to damage ['dæmɪdʒ]
beschäftigt busy ['bɪzi]
beschließen to decide [dɪ'saɪd]
beschreiben to describe [dɪ'skraɪb]
(be)schützen to protect [prə'tekt]
sich **beschweren** to complain [kəm'pleɪn]
Besichtigung tour [tʊə]
besitzen have got/has got ['hæv gɒt/ 'hæz gɒt]
Besitzer/-in owner ['əʊnə]
besondere/-r/-s special ['speʃl]
besonders especially [ɪ'speʃəli]; extra ['ekstrə]
besorgt sein to be worried [ˌbi: 'wʌrid]
Besprechung meeting ['mi:tɪŋ]
besser better ['betə]
beste/-r/-s best [best]
besteigen to climb [klaɪm]
bestellen to order ['ɔ:də]
besuchen to visit ['vɪzɪt]
Besucher/-in visitor ['vɪzɪtə]
Beton concrete ['kɒŋkri:t]
Betonung stress [stres]
Betreff subject ['sʌbdʒekt]
sich **betrinken** to get drunk [get 'drʌŋk]
Bett bed [bed]
ins Bett gehen to go to bed [ˌgəʊ tə 'bed]
beunruhigt sein to be worried [ˌbi: 'wʌrid]
Bevölkerung population [ˌpɒpjə'leɪʃn]
bevor before [bɪ'fɔ:]
bevorzugen to prefer [prə'fɜ:]
bewegen to move [mu:v]
Bewerbungsformular application form [ˌæplɪ'keɪʃn ˌfɔ:m]
Bewertung rating ['reɪtɪŋ]
(be)zahlen to pay [peɪ]
Bezirk borough ['bʌrə]
Bibliothek library ['laɪbrəri]
Bier beer [bɪə]
Bild image ['ɪmɪdʒ]; picture ['pɪktʃə]
bilden to make [meɪk]
Bildschirm screen [skri:n]
billig cheap [tʃi:p]
bin am [əm]
Bindewort conjunction [kən'dʒʌŋkʃn]
Biografie biography [baɪ'ɒgrəfi]
Biologie Biology [baɪ'ɒlədʒi]
bis until [ʌn'tɪl]; by [baɪ]
Bis bald. See you. ['si: ˌju:]
ein **bisschen** a little [ə 'lɪtl]
bitte please [pli:z]
Bitte (schön). You're welcome. [jɔ: 'welkəm]
Bitte schön! Here you are! ['hɪə jʊ‿ɑ:]
Blatt sheet [ʃi:t]; leaf [li:f]
Blattsalat lettuce ['letɪs]
Blei lead [led]
bleiben to stay [steɪ]
Bleistift pencil ['pensl]
Blick look [lʊk]; view [vju:]
blind blind [blaɪnd]
blinzeln to squint [skwɪnt]
Blitz lightning (no pl.) ['laɪtnɪŋ]
Blockflöte recorder [rɪ'kɔ:də]
blöd stupid ['stju:pɪd]
blöde dumb [dʌm]
Blödmann jerk [dʒɜ:k]
Blog blog [blɒg]
blond fair [feə]
bloß only ['əʊnli]
Blume flower ['flaʊə]
Boden land [lænd]; ground [graʊnd]; floor [flɔ:]
bohren to drill [drɪl]
Bombe bomb [bɒm]
Bonbon sweet [swi:t]
Boot boat [bəʊt]
böse nasty ['nɑ:sti]; wicked ['wɪkɪd]
Boulevard boulevard ['bu:ləvɑ:d]
Branche business ['bɪznɪs]
brauchen to need [ni:d]
braun brown [braʊn]
Brett shelf [ʃelf]; plank [plæŋk]; board [bɔ:d]
Brief letter ['letə]
Brieffreund/-in pen-pal ['penˌpæl]
Briefkasten letterbox ['letəˌbɒks]; mailbox ['meɪlbɒks]
Briefmarke stamp [stæmp]
Brieftasche wallet ['wɒlɪt]
bringen to bring [brɪŋ]; to take [teɪk]
britisch British ['brɪtɪʃ]
Broschüre brochure ['brəʊʃə]
Brot bread [bred]
Brücke bridge [brɪdʒ]
Bruder brother ['brʌðə]
Brummen hum [hʌm]
brutal brutal ['bru:tl]
Buch book [bʊk]
Bücherei library ['laɪbrəri]
Buchhandlung bookshop ['bʊkʃɒp]
Buchstabe letter ['letə]
buchstabieren to spell [spel]
Bucht bay [beɪ]
Bühne stage [steɪdʒ]
Bühnenbild scenery ['si:nəri]
bunt colourful ['kʌləfl]
Burg castle ['kɑ:sl]
Burger burger ['bɜ:gə]
Büro office ['ɒfɪs]
Bus bus [bʌs]
Busch bush [bʊʃ]
Bushaltestelle bus stop ['bʌs ˌstɒp]

C

Café café ['kæfeɪ]
Cafeteria cafeteria [ˌkæfə'tɪəriə]
campen to go camping [gəʊ 'kæmpɪŋ]
Camper/-in camper ['kæmpə]
Campingplatz campsite ['kæmpsaɪt]
Canyon canyon ['kænjən]
Cartoon cartoon [kɑ:'tu:n]
CD CD [ˌsi:'di:]
CD-ROM CD-Rom [ˌsi:di:'rɒm]
Charakter character ['kærəktə]
Chat chat [tʃæt]
Checkliste checklist ['tʃeklɪst]
Cheerleader/-in cheerleader ['tʃɪəˌli:də]
Cheerleading cheerleading ['tʃɪəli:dɪŋ]
Chemie Chemistry ['kemɪstri]
Chinese/Chinesin Chinese [tʃaɪ'ni:z]
chinesisch Chinese [tʃaɪ'ni:z]
Chor choir [kwaɪə]
Clip clip [klɪp]
Clique crowd [kraʊd]
Coach coach [kəʊtʃ]
Cola coke [kəʊk]
College college ['kɒlɪdʒ]
Comic(heft) comic ['kɒmɪk]
Computer computer [kəm'pju:tə]
cool hip [hɪp]; cool [ku:l]
Cousin/-e cousin ['kʌzn]
Cowboy cowboy ['kaʊbɔɪ]

German – English

Creme cream [kri:m]
Curry(gericht) curry ['kʌri]

D

da because [bɪ'kɒz]; there [ðeə]
da drüben over there [ˌəʊvə 'ðeə]
Dachboden attic ['ætɪk]
Dame lady ['leɪdi]
danach after that ['ɑ:ftə ˌðæt]
danke (schön) thank you ['θæŋk ju:]
danken to thank [θæŋk]
seinem Schutzengel danken to thank your lucky stars [ˌθæŋk jɔ:r 'lʌki stɑ:s]
dann then [ðen]
darauf zu towards [tə'wɔ:dz]
Darbietung show [ʃəʊ]
das who [hu:]; which [wɪtʃ]; that [ðæt]; the [ðə]; this [ðɪs]
dass that [ðæt]
Date date [deɪt]
Datum date [deɪt]
dauern to take [teɪk]
definieren to define [dɪ'faɪn]
dein/-e your [jɔ:]
deine/-r/-s yours [jɔ:z]
dem whom [hu:m]
den whom [hu:m]
denken to suppose [sə'pəʊz]; to think [θɪŋk]
denken an to remember [rɪ'membə]
der who [hu:]; which [wɪtʃ]; the [ðə]
deren whose [hu:z]
derselbe/dieselbe/dasselbe the same [seɪm]
dessen whose [hu:z]
Detektiv/-in detective [dɪ'tektɪv]
deutlich clear [klɪə]
deutsch German ['dʒɜ:mən]
Dezember December [dɪ'sembə]
Dia slide [slaɪd]
Dialog dialogue ['daɪəlɒg]
Diamantring diamond ring ['daɪəmənd ˌrɪŋ]
Diät diet [daɪət]
Dichter/-in poet ['pəʊɪt]
Dichtung poetry ['pəʊətri]
die who [hu:]; which [wɪtʃ]; that [ðæt]; the [ðə]
die (da) those [ðəʊz]
Dieb/-in thief [θi:f]
Diener/-in servant ['sɜ:vnt]
Dienst service ['sɜ:vɪs]
Dienstag Tuesday ['tju:zdeɪ]
dies this [ðɪs]
diese/-r/-s this [ðɪs]
diese (da) those [ðəʊz]
diese (hier) these [ði:z]
digital digital ['dɪdʒɪtl]
Ding thing [θɪŋ]
Dinosaurier dinosaur ['daɪnəsɔ:]
direkt direct [dɪ'rekt]
Disko disco ['dɪskəʊ]; nightclub ['naɪtklʌb]
diskutieren to argue ['ɑ:gju:]
DJ DJ [ˌdi:'dʒeɪ]
Dollar dollar ['dɒlə]
Dom cathedral [kə'θi:drl]
Donner thunder (no pl.) ['θʌndə]
Donnerstag Thursday ['θɜ:zdeɪ]
Doppel- double ['dʌbl]
Doppeldeckerbus double-decker bus [ˌdʌbldekə 'bʌs]
Dorf village ['vɪlɪdʒ]
dort there [ðeə]
downloaden to download [ˌdaʊn'ləʊd]
Drache dragon ['drægn]
drängeln to push [pʊʃ]
draußen outside [ˌaʊt'saɪd]
dreckig dirty ['dɜ:ti]
Drehbuch screenplay ['skri:npleɪ]
(Film) **drehen** to shoot [ʃu:t]
drehen to turn [tɜ:n]
Dreieck triangle ['traɪæŋgl]
drinnen inside [ˌɪn'saɪd]
dritte/-r/-s third [θɜ:d]
Drittklässler third-grader [ˌθɜ:d 'greɪdə]
Droge drug [drʌg]
Drogenentzug rehabilitation [ˌri:həˌbɪlɪ'teɪʃn]
drucken to print [prɪnt]
drücken to push [pʊʃ]
du you [ju:]
dumm dumb [dʌm]; stupid ['stju:pɪd]; silly ['sɪli]
Dummkopf idiot ['ɪdiət]; silly ['sɪli]
dunkel dark [dɑ:k]
Dunkelheit dark [dɑ:k]
dünn thin [θɪn]
dünne/-r/-s thin [θɪn]
durch through [θru:]
durchdrehen to get into a state [getˌɪntəˌə 'steɪt]
Durcheinander confusion [kən'fju:ʒn]; mess [mes]
durcheinander geworfen jumbled ['dʒʌmbld]
durcheinanderbringen to mess up ['mesˌʌp]
durchgehen to pass [pɑ:s]
durchsichtig clear [klɪə]
durchstechen to pierce [pɪəs]
durchsuchen to scan [skæn]
dürfen to be allowed to [bi: ə'laʊd tʊ]; may [meɪ]
durstig thirsty ['θɜ:sti]
Dusche shower ['ʃaʊə]
DVD DVD [ˌdi: vi: 'di:]
DVD-Spieler DVD player [ˌdi:vi:'di: ˌpleɪə]

E

Ebene level ['levl]
echt real [rɪəl]
egal wo wherever [weə'revə]
Ehefrau wife [waɪf]
Ehrfurcht gebietend awesome ['ɔ:səm]
ehrlich honest ['ɒnɪst]
Ei egg [eg]
eigene/-r/-s own [əʊn]
Eigenschaft feature ['fi:tʃə]
Eigenschaftswort adjective ['ædʒɪktɪv]
eigentlich actually [ˌæktʃʊəli]
Eigentor own goal [ˌəʊn 'gəʊl]
ein/-e a [ə], an [ən]; one [wʌn]
einander one another [ˌwʌnˌə'nʌðə]; each other [ˌi:tʃ 'ʌðə]
Einband cover ['kʌvə]
einbiegen to turn [tɜ:n]
Einbrecher/-in burglar ['bɜ:glə]
einchecken to check-in ['tʃekɪn]
Eindringling invader [ɪn'veɪdə]
Eindruck impression [ɪm'preʃn]
eineinhalb one and a half [ˌwʌnˌənˌə 'hɑ:f]
einfach elementary [ˌelɪ'mentəri]; one way ['wʌn weɪ]; single ['sɪŋgl]; easy ['i:zi]
Einfall idea [aɪ'dɪə]
einführen to introduce [ˌɪntrə'dju:s]
Einführung introduction [ˌɪntrə'dʌkʃn]
Eingang entry ['entri]; entrance ['entrənts]
Eingangsstufe doorstep ['dɔ:step]
einige several ['sevrəl]; a few [ə 'fju:]; some [sʌm]
Einkäufe shopping ['ʃɒpɪŋ]
Einkaufen shopping ['ʃɒpɪŋ]
einkaufen gehen to go shopping [gəʊ 'ʃɒpɪŋ]
Einkaufsliste shopping list ['ʃɒpɪŋ ˌlɪst]
Einkaufswagen shopping trolley ['ʃɒpɪŋ ˌtrɒli]

Einkaufszettel shopping list ['ʃɒpɪŋ ˌlɪst]
einladen to invite [ɪn'vaɪt]
Einladung invitation [ˌɪnvɪ'teɪʃn]
Einlass admission [əd'mɪʃn]
Einleitung introduction [ˌɪntrə'dʌkʃn]
einmal once [wʌns]
Einmarsch invasion [ɪn'veɪʒn]
einsam lonely ['ləʊnli]
einsammeln to collect [kə'lekt]
einschalten to turn on ['tɜːn‿ˌɒn]; to switch on [ˌswɪtʃ‿'ɒn]
einschlafen to fall asleep [ˌfɔːl ə'sliːp]
einsetzen to put in [pʊt‿'ɪn]
einstellen to hire [haɪə]
Eintrag entry ['entri]
eintreffen to arrive [ə'raɪv]
eintreten to enter ['entə]
Eintritt admission [əd'mɪʃn]
Eintrittskarte ticket ['tɪkɪt]
Einwanderer/Einwanderin immigrant ['ɪmɪgrənt]
einwandern to immigrate ['ɪmɪgreɪt]
Einwanderung immigration [ˌɪmɪ'greɪʃn]
Einzelkind only child ['əʊnli ˌtʃaɪld]
einzige/-r/-s only ['əʊnli]
Eis ice-cream [ˌaɪs'kriːm]
Eisbär polar bear ['pəʊlə ˌbeə]
Eislaufbahn ice skating rink *(AE)* ['aɪs skeɪtɪŋ ˌrɪŋk]
Elefant elephant ['elɪfənt]
elektrisch electrical [ɪ'lektrɪkl]
Elektrizität electricity [ˌelɪk'trɪsəti]
Elektronik electronics [ˌelek'trɒnɪks]
elementar elementary [ˌelɪ'mentəri]
Elfmeter penalty ['penlti]
Ellbogen elbow ['elbəʊ]
Eltern parents ['peərənts]
E-Mail e-mail ['iːmeɪl]
Empfang reception [rɪ'sepʃn]
empfangen to receive [rɪ'siːv]
empfehlen to recommend [ˌrekə'mend]
empfinden to feel [fiːl]
Ende end [end]
enden to end [end]
endlich finally ['faɪnəli]
Energie energy ['enədʒi]
eng narrow ['nærəʊ]
englisch English ['ɪŋglɪʃ]
enorm enormous [ɪ'nɔːməs]
entdecken to discover [dɪ'skʌvə]
entfliehen to escape [ɪ'skeɪp]
sich (auf halbem Weg) **entgegenkommen** to meet halfway [miːt hɑːf'weɪ]
entkommen to escape [ɪ'skeɪp]
entlang down [daʊn]
entscheiden to decide [dɪ'saɪd]
sich **entschuldigen** to apologize [ə'pɒlədʒaɪz]
Entschuldigung! Excuse me. [ɪk'skjuːz mi]; Sorry! ['sɒri]
(sich) **entspannen** to relax [rɪ'læks]
enttäuscht sein to be disappointed [ˌbiː dɪsə'pɔɪntɪd]
entwerfen to design [dɪ'zaɪn]
Entziehungskur rehabilitation programm [ˌriːhəˌbɪlɪ'teɪʃn ˌprəʊgræm]
Entzücken glee [gliː]
Enzyklopädie encyclopedia [ɪnˌsaɪklə'piːdiə]
er he [hiː]
Erbe/Erbin heir [eə]
Erdbeben earthquake ['ɜːθkweɪk]
Erdbeere strawberry ['strɔːbri]
Erde Earth [ɜːθ]; ground [graʊnd]
Erdkunde Geography [dʒi'ɒgrəfi]
Erfahrung experience [ɪk'spɪəriəns]
erfinden to create [kriː'eɪt]; to invent [ɪn'vent]
Erfindung invention [ɪn'venʃn]
Erfolg success [sək'ses]
erfolgreich successful [sək'sesfl]
erforschen to explore [ɪk'splɔː]
ergänzen to complete [kəm'pliːt]
Ergebnis result [rɪ'zʌlt]
sich **erholen** to relax [rɪ'læks]
jdn. an etw. **erinnern** to remind s.o. of s.th. [rɪ'maɪnd]
sich **erinnern an** to remember [rɪ'membə]
erkennen to realize ['rɪəlaɪz]; to recognize ['rekəgnaɪz]
(etwas) **erklären** to explain (sth.) [ɪk'spleɪn]
Erklärung key [kiː]
erkunden to explore [ɪk'splɔː]
Erlebnis experience [ɪk'spɪəriəns]
erlöschen to go out [gəʊ‿'aʊt]
ermitteln to investigate [ɪn'vestɪgeɪt]
ermorden to murder ['mɜːdə]
ermüdend tiring ['taɪrɪŋ]
ernst serious ['sɪəriəs]
erraten to guess [ges]
erreichen to catch [kætʃ]
errichten to found [faʊnd]
Ersatz- spare [speə]
erscheinen to appear [ə'pɪə]; to seem [siːm]
erschrecken to scare [skeə]
jdn. **erschrecken** to give s.o. a fright [ˌgɪv … ə 'fraɪt]
ersetzen to substitute ['sʌbstɪtjuːt]
erst only ['əʊnli]; not until [nɒt ʌn'tɪl]
erstaunlich amazing [ə'meɪzɪŋ]
erstaunt to gasp [gɑːsp]
erste/-r/-s first [fɜːst]
zu **ersticken drohen** to choke [tʃəʊk]
erwachsen werden to grow up [grəʊ‿'ʌp]
Erwachsene/-r adult ['ædʌlt]
erwähnen to mention ['menʃn]
erwarten to expect [ɪk'spekt]
erzählen to tell [tel]
Erzähler/-in narrator [nə'reɪtə]
erzielen to score [skɔː]
es it [ɪt]
Es war einmal … Once upon a time … [wʌns‿ə'pɒn‿ə ˌtaɪm]
essen to eat [iːt]
Essen meal [miːl]; food [fuːd]
Essen zum Mitnehmen takeaway ['teɪkəweɪ]
Esser/-in eater ['iːtə]
Esszimmer dining room ['daɪnɪŋ rʊm]
etwa about [ə'baʊt]
etwas something ['sʌmθɪŋ]; some [sʌm]
euer/eure your [jɔː]
eure/-r/-s yours [jɔːz]
Euro euro ['jʊərəʊ]
Europäer/-in European [ˌjʊərə'piːən]
europäisch European [ˌjʊərə'piːən]
ewig forever [fə'revə]
Examen exam [ɪg'zæm]
Exemplar copy ['kɒpi]
Experiment experiment [ɪk'sperɪment]
explodieren to explode [ɪk'spləʊd]
extra extra ['ekstrə]

F

Fabrik factory ['fæktri]
Fach subject ['sʌbdʒɪkt]
Fackel torch [tɔːtʃ]
Faden thread [θred]
fähig sein to be able to [biː 'eɪbl tʊ]
Fähigkeit skill [skɪl]
Fahne banner ['bænə]; flag [flæg]
Fähre ferry ['feri]
fahren to motor ['məʊtə]; to drive [draɪv]; to travel ['trævl]; to ride [raɪd]
Fahrrad fahren to cycle ['saɪkl]
Fahrer/-in driver ['draɪvə]
Fahrkarte ticket ['tɪkɪt]
Fahrkartenschalter ticket office ['tɪkɪt ˌɒfɪs]

German – English

grau gray *(AE)* [greɪ]; grey [greɪ]
grausig gruesome ['gru:səm]
Grautöne shades of gray [ˌʃeɪdz‿əv 'greɪ]
grelles Licht glare [gleə]
Grenze edge [edʒ]; limit ['lɪmɪt]
griechisch Greek [gri:k]
groß high [haɪ]; big [bɪg]; large [lɑ:dʒ]; tall [tɔ:l]
großartig great [greɪt]
Großbuchstabe capital letter [ˌkæpɪtl 'letə]
Größe height [haɪt]; size [saɪz]
Großeltern grandparents ['græn,peərnts]
Großmutter grandmother ['græn,mʌðə]
(Groß-)Stadt city ['sɪti]
Großvater grandfather ['græn,fɑ:ðə]
grün green [gri:n]
Grund reason ['ri:zn]
gründen to found [faʊnd]
Grundschule primary school ['praɪməri ˌsku:l]
Grundstück land [lænd]
Gruppe group [gru:p]
gruselig scary ['skeəri]; spooky ['spu:ki]
Gruß greeting ['gri:tɪŋ]
gucken to watch [wɒtʃ]
Gummistiefel welly ['weli]
gut well [wel]; fine [faɪn]; nicely ['naɪsli]; good [gʊd]
gut können to be good at … [ˌbi: 'gʊd‿ət]
gut aussehend handsome ['hænsəm]; good-looking [ˌgʊd'lʊkɪŋ]
gut sein in … to be good at … [ˌbi: 'gʊd‿ət]
Guten Appetit! Enjoy your meal! ['ɪndʒɔɪ jɔ: ˌmi:l]
guten Morgen good morning [gʊd 'mɔ:nɪŋ]
Guthabenkarte top-up card ['tɒpʌp ˌkɑ:d]
Gymnasium grammar school ['græmə ˌsku:l]

H

Haar hair [heə]
haben have/has [hæv/hæz]; have got/has got ['hæv gɒt/'hæz gɒt]
Hafen harbor *(AE)* ['hɑ:bə]
Hafendamm pier [pɪə]
Hähnchen chicken ['tʃɪkɪn]
Häkchen tick [tɪk]
mit einem **Haken versehen** to tick [tɪk]
halb half [hɑ:f]
halb (drei) half past (two) [ˌhɑ:f 'pɑ:st]
Hälfte half [hɑ:f]
hallo hello [hel'əʊ]; hi [haɪ]
Hals neck [nek]
halten to hold [həʊld]
Haltestelle stop [stɒp]
hämmern to pound [paʊnd]
Hand hand [hænd]
Handel deal [di:l]
Handkarren trolley ['trɒli]
Handlung action ['ækʃn]
Handout handout ['hændaʊt]
Handschuh glove [glʌv]
Handtasche handbag ['hændbæg]
Handy cell phone *(AE)* ['sel ˌfəʊn]
hängen bleiben to be stuck [ˌbi: 'stʌk]
hart hard [hɑ:d]
hassen to hate [heɪt]
Haupt- main [meɪn]
Hauptgang main course [ˌmeɪn 'kɔ:s]
Hauptgericht main course [ˌmeɪn 'kɔ:s]
Hauptstadt capital ['kæpɪtl]
Hausaufgaben homework ['həʊmwɜ:k]
hausgemacht home-made [ˌhəʊm'meɪd]
Hausmeister/-in caretaker ['keəˌteɪkə]
Haustier pet [pet]
Haut skin [skɪn]
Heavy Metal heavy metal [ˌhevi 'metl]
Hecktür back door [ˌbæk 'dɔ:]
Heft exercise book ['eksəsaɪz ˌbʊk]
Hefter folder ['fəʊldə]
heilig sacred ['seɪkrɪd]; holy ['həʊli]
Heilige Mutter Holy mother [ˌhəʊli 'mʌðə]
Heim home [həʊm]
Heimweh haben to feel homesick [ˌfi:l 'həʊmsɪk]
heiraten to marry ['mæri]
heiß hot [hɒt]
heiße Schokolade hot chocolate [ˌhɒt 'tʃɒklət]
Held/-in hero ['hɪərəʊ]
helfen to help [help]
hell fair [feə]; bright [braɪt]
Helm helmet ['helmət]
Hemd shirt [ʃɜ:t]
heranzoomen to zoom-in [ˌzu:m‿'ɪn]
herauf up [ʌp]
herausfinden to find out [faɪnd‿'aʊt]
heraussuchen to look up [lʊk‿'ʌp]
Herberge hostel ['hɒstl]
Herbst fall *(AE)* [fɔ:l]; autumn ['ɔ:təm]
herein in [ɪn]
hereinlegen to trick [trɪk]
Herr Mr ['mɪstə]; gentleman ['dʒentlmən]
herrlich lovely ['lʌvli]
herüberkommen to come over [ˌkʌm‿'əʊvə]
herunter down [daʊn]
herunterfallen to fall off ['fɔ:l‿'ɒf]
herunterhängend drooping ['dru:pɪŋ]
herunterladen to download [ˌdaʊn'ləʊd]
hervorragend brilliant ['brɪliənt]
Herz heart [hɑ:t]
Herzliche Grüße, … Love, … [lʌv]
herzlos heartless ['hɑ:tləs]
Herzschrittmacher pacemaker ['peɪsˌmeɪkə]
heute today [tə'deɪ]
heute Abend tonight [tə'naɪt]
heute Nacht tonight [tə'naɪt]
hier here [hɪə]
high *(Stimmung nach dem Genuss von Drogen)* high [haɪ]
Hightech- high-tech [ˌhaɪ'tek]
Hilfe help [help]
hilflos helpless ['helpləs]
hilfreich helpful ['helpfʊl]
Himmel sky [skaɪ]
hin und zurück return [rɪ'tɜ:n]
hinauf up [ʌp]
(hin)ausgehen to go out [gəʊ‿'aʊt]
hinauszögern to delay [dɪ'leɪ]
hinein in [ɪn]; into ['ɪntə]
hinfallen to fall [fɔ:l]
(Person) hinfallen to fall over [fɔ:l‿'əʊvə]
hinten im Buch at the back of the book [æt ðə 'bæk‿əv ðə ˌbʊk]
hinter behind [bɪ'haɪnd]
hintere Hosentasche back pocket [ˌbæk 'pɒkɪt]
Hintergrund background ['bækgraʊnd]
hinterherrennen to chase [tʃeɪs]
Hintertür back door [ˌbæk 'dɔ:]
hinunter down [daʊn]
Hinweis clue [klu:]
hinzufügen to add [æd]
Hip-Hop hip hop ['hɪp hɒp]
hispanisch Hispanic [hɪ'spænɪk]
Hit hit [hɪt]
Hobby hobby ['hɒbi]

Einkaufszettel shopping list [ˈʃɒpɪŋ ˌlɪst]
einladen to invite [ɪnˈvaɪt]
Einladung invitation [ˌɪnvɪˈteɪʃn]
Einlass admission [ədˈmɪʃn]
Einleitung introduction [ˌɪntrəˈdʌkʃn]
einmal once [wʌns]
Einmarsch invasion [ɪnˈveɪʒn]
einsam lonely [ˈləʊnli]
einsammeln to collect [kəˈlekt]
einschalten to turn on [ˈtɜ:n‿ɒn]; to switch on [ˌswɪtʃ‿ˈɒn]
einschlafen to fall asleep [ˌfɔ:l əˈsli:p]
einsetzen to put in [pʊt‿ˈɪn]
einstellen to hire [haɪə]
Eintrag entry [ˈentri]
eintreffen to arrive [əˈraɪv]
eintreten to enter [ˈentə]
Eintritt admission [ədˈmɪʃn]
Eintrittskarte ticket [ˈtɪkɪt]
Einwanderer/Einwanderin immigrant [ˈɪmɪgrənt]
einwandern to immigrate [ˈɪmɪgreɪt]
Einwanderung immigration [ˌɪmɪˈgreɪʃn]
Einzelkind only child [ˈəʊnli ˌtʃaɪld]
einzige/-r/-s only [ˈəʊnli]
Eis ice-cream [ˌaɪsˈkri:m]
Eisbär polar bear [ˈpəʊlə ˌbeə]
Eislaufbahn ice skating rink *(AE)* [ˈaɪs skeɪtɪŋ ˌrɪŋk]
Elefant elephant [ˈelɪfənt]
elektrisch electrical [ɪˈlektrɪkl]
Elektrizität electricity [ˌelɪkˈtrɪsəti]
Elektronik electronics [ˌelekˈtrɒnɪks]
elementar elementary [ˌelɪˈmentəri]
Elfmeter penalty [ˈpenlti]
Ellbogen elbow [ˈelbəʊ]
Eltern parents [ˈpeərənts]
E-Mail e-mail [ˈi:meɪl]
Empfang reception [rɪˈsepʃn]
empfangen to receive [rɪˈsi:v]
empfehlen to recommend [ˌrekəˈmend]
empfinden to feel [fi:l]
Ende end [end]
enden to end [end]
endlich finally [ˈfaɪnəli]
Energie energy [ˈenədʒi]
eng narrow [ˈnærəʊ]
englisch English [ˈɪŋglɪʃ]
enorm enormous [ɪˈnɔ:məs]
entdecken to discover [dɪˈskʌvə]
entfliehen to escape [ɪˈskeɪp]
sich (auf halbem Weg) **entgegenkommen** to meet halfway [mi:t hɑ:fˈweɪ]
entkommen to escape [ɪˈskeɪp]
entlang down [daʊn]
entscheiden to decide [dɪˈsaɪd]
sich **entschuldigen** to apologize [əˈpɒlədʒaɪz]
Entschuldigung! Excuse me. [ɪkˈskju:z mi]; Sorry! [ˈsɒri]
(sich) **entspannen** to relax [rɪˈlæks]
enttäuscht sein to be disappointed [ˌbi: dɪsəˈpɔɪntɪd]
entwerfen to design [dɪˈzaɪn]
Entziehungskur rehabilitation programm [ˌri:həˌbɪlɪˈteɪʃn ˌprəʊgræm]
Entzücken glee [gli:]
Enzyklopädie encyclopedia [ɪnˌsaɪkləˈpi:diə]
er he [hi:]
Erbe/Erbin heir [eə]
Erdbeben earthquake [ˈɜ:θkweɪk]
Erdbeere strawberry [ˈstrɔ:bri]
Erde Earth [ɜ:θ]; ground [graʊnd]
Erdkunde Geography [dʒiˈɒgrəfi]
Erfahrung experience [ɪkˈspɪəriəns]
erfinden to create [kri:ˈeɪt]; to invent [ɪnˈvent]
Erfindung invention [ɪnˈvenʃn]
Erfolg success [səkˈses]
erfolgreich successful [səkˈsesfl]
erforschen to explore [ɪkˈsplɔ:]
ergänzen to complete [kəmˈpli:t]
Ergebnis result [rɪˈzʌlt]
sich **erholen** to relax [rɪˈlæks]
jdn. an etw. **erinnern** to remind s.o. of s.th. [rɪˈmaɪnd]
sich **erinnern an** to remember [rɪˈmembə]
erkennen to realize [ˈrɪəlaɪz]; to recognize [ˈrekəgnaɪz]
(etwas) **erklären** to explain (sth.) [ɪkˈspleɪn]
Erklärung key [ki:]
erkunden to explore [ɪkˈsplɔ:]
Erlebnis experience [ɪkˈspɪəriəns]
erlöschen to go out [gəʊ‿ˈaʊt]
ermitteln to investigate [ɪnˈvestɪgeɪt]
ermorden to murder [ˈmɜ:də]
ermüdend tiring [ˈtaɪrɪŋ]
ernst serious [ˈsɪəriəs]
erraten to guess [ges]
erreichen to catch [kætʃ]
errichten to found [faʊnd]
Ersatz- spare [speə]
erscheinen to appear [əˈpɪə]; to seem [si:m]
erschrecken to scare [skeə]
jdn. **erschrecken** to give s.o. a fright [ˌgɪv … ə ˈfraɪt]
ersetzen to substitute [ˈsʌbstɪtju:t]
erst only [ˈəʊnli]; not until [nɒt ʌnˈtɪl]
erstaunlich amazing [əˈmeɪzɪŋ]
erstaunt to gasp [gɑ:sp]
erste/-r/-s first [fɜ:st]
zu **ersticken drohen** to choke [tʃəʊk]
erwachsen werden to grow up [grəʊ‿ˈʌp]
Erwachsene/-r adult [ˈædʌlt]
erwähnen to mention [ˈmenʃn]
erwarten to expect [ɪkˈspekt]
erzählen to tell [tel]
Erzähler/-in narrator [nəˈreɪtə]
erzielen to score [skɔ:]
es it [ɪt]
Es war einmal … Once upon a time … [wʌns‿əˈpɒn‿ə ˌtaɪm]
essen to eat [i:t]
Essen meal [mi:l]; food [fu:d]
Essen zum Mitnehmen takeaway [ˈteɪkəweɪ]
Esser/-in eater [ˈi:tə]
Esszimmer dining room [ˈdaɪnɪŋ rʊm]
etwa about [əˈbaʊt]
etwas something [ˈsʌmθɪŋ]; some [sʌm]
euer/eure your [jɔ:]
eure/-r/-s yours [jɔ:z]
Euro euro [ˈjʊərəʊ]
Europäer/-in European [ˌjʊərəˈpi:ən]
europäisch European [ˌjʊərəˈpi:ən]
ewig forever [fəˈrevə]
Examen exam [ɪgˈzæm]
Exemplar copy [ˈkɒpi]
Experiment experiment [ɪkˈsperɪment]
explodieren to explode [ɪkˈspləʊd]
extra extra [ˈekstrə]

F

Fabrik factory [ˈfæktri]
Fach subject [ˈsʌbdʒɪkt]
Fackel torch [tɔ:tʃ]
Faden thread [θred]
fähig sein to be able to [bi: ˈeɪbl tʊ]
Fähigkeit skill [skɪl]
Fahne banner [ˈbænə]; flag [flæg]
Fähre ferry [ˈferi]
fahren to motor [ˈməʊtə]; to drive [draɪv]; to travel [ˈtrævl]; to ride [raɪd]
Fahrrad fahren to cycle [ˈsaɪkl]
Fahrer/-in driver [ˈdraɪvə]
Fahrkarte ticket [ˈtɪkɪt]
Fahrkartenschalter ticket office [ˈtɪkɪt ˌɒfɪs]

German – English

Fahrplan timetable ['taɪmˌteɪbl]
Fahrrad bike [baɪk]
Fahrrad fahren to cycle ['saɪkl]
Fahrradschuppen bike shed [ˌbaɪk 'ʃed]
Fahrradtour bike ride [baɪk 'raɪd]
fair fair [feə]
Fakt fact [fækt]
fallen to fall [fɔːl]
fallen lassen to drop [drɒp]
falls if [ɪf]
falsch false [fɔːls]; wrong [rɒŋ]
Familie family ['fæməli]
Fan fan [fæn]
Fanatiker/-in maniac ['meɪniæk]
fangen to catch [kætʃ]
Fantasie fantasy ['fæntəsi]
fantastisch fantastic [fæn'tæstɪk]; brilliant ['brɪliənt]
Farbe color *(AE)* ['kʌlə]; colour ['kʌlə]; paint [peɪnt]
Farmtierpark farm park ['fɑːm ˌpɑːk]
fast nearly ['nɪəli]; almost ['ɔːlməʊst]
Fastfood fast food [ˌfɑːst 'fuːd]
Februar February ['febrʊri]
Federball badminton ['bædmɪntən]
Federmäppchen pencil case ['pensl ˌkeɪs]
fehlend missing ['mɪsɪŋ]
Fehler mistake [mɪ'steɪk]
Feier party ['pɑːti]
feiern to celebrate ['seləbreɪt]
fein fine [faɪn]
Feind/-in enemy ['enəmi]
Feinkostgeschäft deli (= delicatessen) ['deli (= ˌdelɪkə'tesn)]
Feld field ['fiːld]
Feldforschung fieldwork ['fiːldwɜːk]
Fels rock [rɒk]; cliff [klɪf]
Felsblock boulder ['bəʊldə]
Felsbrocken boulder ['bəʊldə]
Felsenschlucht canyon ['kænjən]
Fenster window ['wɪndəʊ]
Ferien vacation *(AE)* [və'keɪʃn]; holiday ['hɒlədeɪ]
Fernbedienung remote control [rɪ'məʊt 'kəntrəʊl]
sich **fernhalten** to keep away [ˌkiːp ə'weɪ]
Fernsehen TV (= television) [ˌtiː 'viː = 'telɪvɪʒn]
Fernseher TV (= television) [ˌtiː 'viː = 'telɪvɪʒn]
fertig ready ['redi]
fertig machen to finish ['fɪnɪʃ]
sich fertig machen to get ready [ˌget 'redi]

Fertigkeit skill [skɪl]
fertig stellen to complete [kəm'pliːt]
fest hard [hɑːd]
Fest fair [feə]; festival ['festɪvl]
fester Wohnsitz permanent home ['pɜːmənənt ˌhəʊm]
festhalten to catch [kætʃ]
Festival festival ['festɪvl]
Festland land [lænd]
festnehmen to catch [kætʃ]; to arrest [ə'rest]
Fett fat [fæt]
Feuer fire [faɪə]
Feuerwehrmann/-frau firefighter *(AE)* ['faɪəˌfaɪtə]
Feuerwerk fireworks ['faɪəwɜːks]
Film movie *(AE)* ['muːvi]; film [fɪlm]
finden to find [faɪnd]
Finger finger ['fɪŋgə]
Finger weg! Hands off! [ˌhændz‿'ɒf]
Firma company ['kʌmpəni]; firm [fɜːm]
Fisch fish [fɪʃ]
fit fit [fɪt]
fit werden to get fit [ˌget 'fɪt]
Fitness fitness ['fɪtnəs]
Flagge flag [flæg]
Flamme flame [fleɪm]
Flasche bottle ['bɒtl]
Fleck mark [mɑːk]; stain [steɪn]
fliegen to fly [flaɪ]
fliehen to flee [fliː]
Floß raft [rɑːft]
fluchen to swear [sweə]; to curse [kɜːs]
flüchten to escape [ɪ'skeɪp]; to flee [fliː]
Flug flight [flaɪt]
Flugblatt leaflet ['liːflət]
Flügel wing [wɪŋ]
Flughafen airport ['eəpɔːt]
Flugzeug plane [pleɪn]
Flur hall [hɔːl]
Fluss river ['rɪvə]
flussabwärts downriver [daʊn'rɪvə]
Flüssigkeit fluid ['fluɪd]
flüstern to whisper ['wɪspə]
folgen to follow ['fɒləʊ]
Folie slide [slaɪd]
Fön hairdryer ['heəˌdraɪə]
Form shape [ʃeɪp]; form [fɔːm]
Formular form [fɔːm]
Forschung research [rɪ'sɜːtʃ]
fort gone [gɒn]; away [ə'weɪ]
Foto photo ['fəʊtəʊ]
Fotoapparat camera ['kæmrə]
Fotografie photography [fə'tɒgrəfi]

fotografieren to photograph ['fəʊtəgrɑːf]; to take pictures [teɪk 'pɪktʃəz]
Fotograf/-in photographer [fə'tɒgrəfə]
Fotos machen to take pictures [teɪk 'pɪktʃəz]
Foul foul [faʊl]
Frage question ['kwestʃən]
Frageanhängsel question tag ['kwestʃən ˌtæg]
Fragebogen questionnaire [ˌkwestʃə'neə]
fragen to ask [ɑːsk]
sich fragen to wonder ['wʌndə]
französisch French [frentʃ]
Frau woman ['wʊmən]; Mrs ['mɪsɪz]
frei free [friː]
Freiheit liberty ['lɪbəti]; freedom ['friːdəm]
Freiklettern free climbing ['friː ˌklaɪmɪŋ]
Freiluft- outdoor [ˌaʊt'dɔː]
Freitag Friday ['fraɪdeɪ]
freitags Fridays ['fraɪdeɪz]
fremd foreign ['fɒrɪn]
Frequenz frequency ['friːkwəntsi]
Freude joy [dʒɔɪ]
sich **freuen auf** to look forward [ˌlʊk 'fɔːwəd tə]
Freund/-in friend [frend]
freundlich friendly ['frendli]; kind [kaɪnd]
frisch fresh [freʃ]
Frischkäse cream cheese [ˌkriːm 'tʃiːz]
Friseur/-in hairdresser ['heəˌdresə]
froh glad [glæd]
froh sein to be glad [ˌbiː 'glæd]
fröhlich happy ['hæpi]
Frost frost [frɒst]
Frucht fruit [fruːt]
früh early ['ɜːli]
Frühling spring [sprɪŋ]
Frühstück breakfast ['brekfəst]
Frühstückscerealien cereal ['sɪəriəl]
frustriert frustrated [frʌs'treɪtɪd]
Fuchs fox [fɒks]
(mit)**fühlen mit** to feel sorry for [fiːl 'sɒri ˌfə]
sich **fühlen** to feel [fiːl]
füllen to fill [fɪl]
Füller pen [pen]
fünfte/-r/-s fifth [fɪfθ]
funken to transmit [trænz'mɪt]
Funkgerät transmitter [ˌtrænz'mɪtə]
funktionieren to function ['fʌnkʃn]; to work [wɜːk]

für for [fɔː]
für immer forever [fəˈrevə]
furchtbar terrible [ˈterəbl]
Fürwort pronoun [ˈprəʊnaʊn]
Fuß foot [fʊt] pl. feet [fiːt]
Fuß (Maßeinheit) foot, feet (ft) [fʊt, fiːt]
(Fuß-)Tritt kick [kɪk]
Fußball football [ˈfʊtbɔːl]
füttern to feed [fiːd]
Futur future [ˈfjuːtʃə]

G

Gabel fork [fɔːk]
gähnen to yawn [jɔːn]
Gälisch Gaelic [ˈgeɪlɪk]
Gang gang [gæŋ]
Gangsterfilm gangster movie [ˈgæŋkstə ˌmuːvi]
Gans goose [guːs] pl. geese [giːs]
ganz whole [həʊl]; full [fʊl]; all [ɔːl]; quite [kwaɪt]
ganz oben top [tɒp]
ganze/-r/-s complete [kəmˈpliːt]
gar nicht not at all [ˌnɒt‿ət‿ˈɔːl]
Garage garage [ˈgærɪdʒ]
Gast guest [gest]
Gastarbeiter/-in migrant worker [ˌmaɪgrnt ˈwɜːkə]
Gebäude building [ˈbɪldɪŋ]
geben to hand [hænd]; to give [gɪv]
Gebiet region [ˈriːdʒn]; area [ˈeəriə]
geboren born [bɔːn]
gebraten fried [fraɪd]
Gebrauch use [juːs]
Gebühr fee [fiː]
Geburt birth [bɜːθ]
Geburtstag birthday [ˈbɜːθdeɪ]
Alles Gute zum Geburtstag! Happy Birthday! [ˌhæpi ˈbɜːθdeɪ]
Gedicht poem [ˈpəʊɪm]
Gedichte poetry [ˈpəʊətri]
Gedichtewettbewerb poetry slam [ˈpəʊətri ˌslæm]
Gefahr danger [ˈdeɪndʒə]
gefährlich nasty [ˈnɑːsti]; dangerous [ˈdeɪndʒrəs]
Gefängnis prison [ˈprɪzn]
gefroren frozen [ˈfrəʊzn]
Gefühl feeling [ˈfiːlɪŋ]
gegen vs. (= versus) [ˈvɜːsəs]; against [əˈgenst]
Gegend neighborhood *(AE)* [ˈneɪbəhʊd]; area [ˈeəriə]
Gegensatz opposite [ˈɒpəzɪt]

sich **(gegenseitig)** each other [ˌiːtʃˈʌðə]
Gegenstand article [ˈɑːtɪkl]
Gegenteil opposite [ˈɒpəzɪt]
gegenüber vs. (= versus) [ˈvɜːsəs]; opposite [ˈɒpəzɪt]
Gegenwart present [ˈpreznt]
Geheimnis mystery [ˈmɪstəri]; secret [ˈsiːkrət]
gehen to go [gəʊ]
(zu Fuß) gehen to walk [wɔːk]
gehören to belong [bɪˈlɒŋ ˌtə]
geil wicked [ˈwɪkɪd]
Geist ghost [gəʊst]
Geld money [ˈmʌni]
Geldbeutel purse [pɜːs]; wallet [ˈwɒlɪt]
Geldschein bill *(AE)* [bɪl]
Geldstrafe fine [faɪn]
geloben to pledge [pledʒ]
Gemälde painting [ˈpeɪntɪŋ]
gemein nasty [ˈnɑːsti]
Gemeinde community [kəmˈjuːnəti]
Gemeinderat council [ˈkaʊnsl]
Gemüse vegetable [ˈvedʒtəbl]
Gemüsesuppe minestrone [ˌmɪnɪˈstrəʊni]
genau exactly [ɪgˈzæktli]
genau hier right here [ˌraɪt ˈhɪə]
(genau)so ... wie as ... as [əz ... əz]
genießen to enjoy [ɪnˈdʒɔɪ]
genug enough [ɪˈnʌf]; plenty [ˈplenti]
von etw. **genug haben** to be sick of s.th. [ˈsɪk‿əv]
Geographie Geography [dʒiˈɒgrəfi]
(Reise-)**Gepäck** luggage [ˈlʌgɪdʒ]
Gepäckwagen trolley [ˈtrɒli]
gepflastert paved [ˈpeɪvd]
Geplauder chat [tʃæt]
gerade just [dʒʌst]; straight [streɪt]
Gerät device [dɪˈvaɪs]
Geräusch noise [nɔɪz]; sound [saʊnd]
gerecht fair [feə]
Gerechtigkeit justice [ˈdʒʌstɪs]
geringste/-r/-s least [liːst]
gern haben to like [laɪk]
Gerundium gerund [ˈdʒernd]
Gesamtschule comprehensive school [kɒmprɪˈhensɪv ˌskuːl]
Gesang vocals [ˈvəʊklz]
Geschäft business [ˈbɪznɪs]; deal [diːl]; shop [ʃɒp]; store [stɔː]
Geschäftsführer/-in manager [ˈmænɪdʒə]
geschehen to happen [ˈhæpn]
Geschenk present [ˈpreznt]
Geschenkladen gift shop [ˈgɪft ˌʃɒp]

Geschichte History [ˈhɪstri]; story [ˈstɔːri]
geschieden divorced [dɪˈvɔːst]
Geschöpf creature [ˈkriːtʃə]
gesetzwidrig illegal [ɪˈliːgl]
Gesicht face [feɪs]
gespenstisch spooky [ˈspuːki]
Gespräch conversation [ˌkɒnvəˈseɪʃn]; talk [tɔːk]; dialogue [ˈdaɪəlɒg]
Gesprächstechniken communication skills [ˌkəmjuːnɪkeɪʃn ˈskɪlz]
Gestalt shape [ʃeɪp]
Gestein rock [rɒk]
gestern yesterday [ˈjestədeɪ]
gesund healthy [ˈhelθi]; fit [fɪt]
Getränk drink [drɪŋk]
Getreide grain [greɪn]
Getreideflakes cereal [ˈsɪəriəl]
Gewalt violence (no pl.) [ˈvaɪəlns]
Gewalttätigkeit violence [ˈvaɪəlns]
gewaltig enormous [ɪˈnɔːməs]; mighty [ˈmaɪti]; violent [ˈvaɪəlnt]
gewaltsam violent [ˈvaɪəlnt]
Gewicht weight [weɪt]
gewinnen to win [wɪn]
Gewinner/-in winner [ˈwɪnə]
gewohnt sein to be used to *(+ gerund)* [biː‿ˈjuːst tə]
gewöhnlich usually [ˈjuːʒəli]
Gitarre guitar [gɪˈtɑː]
Gitarrist/-in guitarist [gɪˈtɑːrɪst]
Gitter grid [grɪd]
Glas glass [glɑːs]
glauben to think [θɪŋk]; to believe [bɪˈliːv]
Gleis track [træk]
gleiten to glide [glaɪd]
global global [ˈgləʊbl]
Glocke bell [bel]
Glück happiness [ˈhæpɪnəs]; luck [lʌk]
Glück haben to be lucky [ˌbiː ˈlʌki]
glücklich happy [ˈhæpi]
(Glücksspiele) spielen to gamble [ˈgæmbl]
Glühbirne light bulb [ˈlaɪt ˌbʌlb]
glühen to glow [gləʊ]
Gold gold [gəʊld]
Gondel capsule [ˈkæpsjuːl]
Gott God [gɒd]
GPS *(ein satellitengestütztes Navigationssystem)* GPS (global positioning system) [ˌdʒiː piː ˈes]
Graffiti graffiti [grəˈfiːti]
Grafiken graphics pl. [ˈgræfɪks]
Gramm gram [græm]
Grammatik grammar [ˈgræmə]
Gras grass [grɑːs]

grau gray *(AE)* [greɪ]; grey [greɪ]
grausig gruesome ['gru:səm]
Grautöne shades of gray [ˌʃeɪdz‿əv 'greɪ]
grelles Licht glare [gleə]
Grenze edge [edʒ]; limit ['lɪmɪt]
griechisch Greek [gri:k]
groß high [haɪ]; big [bɪg]; large [lɑ:dʒ]; tall [tɔ:l]
großartig great [greɪt]
Großbuchstabe capital letter [ˌkæpɪtl 'letə]
Größe height [haɪt]; size [saɪz]
Großeltern grandparents ['græn͵peərnts]
Großmutter grandmother ['græn͵mʌðə]
(Groß-)Stadt city ['sɪti]
Großvater grandfather ['græn͵fɑ:ðə]
grün green [gri:n]
Grund reason ['ri:zn]
gründen to found [faʊnd]
Grundschule primary school ['praɪməri ͵sku:l]
Grundstück land [lænd]
Gruppe group [gru:p]
gruselig scary ['skeəri]; spooky ['spu:ki]
Gruß greeting ['gri:tɪŋ]
gucken to watch [wɒtʃ]
Gummistiefel welly ['weli]
gut well [wel]; fine [faɪn]; nicely ['naɪsli]; good [gʊd]
gut können to be good at … [ˌbi: 'gʊd‿ət]
gut aussehend handsome ['hænsəm]; good-looking [ˌgʊd'lʊkɪŋ]
gut sein in … to be good at … [ˌbi: 'gʊd‿ət]
Guten Appetit! Enjoy your meal! ['ɪndʒɔɪ jɔ: ͵mi:l]
guten Morgen good morning [gʊd 'mɔ:nɪŋ]
Guthabenkarte top-up card ['tɒpʌp ͵kɑ:d]
Gymnasium grammar school ['græmə ͵sku:l]

H

Haar hair [heə]
haben have/has [hæv/hæz]; have got/has got ['hæv gɒt/'hæz gɒt]
Hafen harbor *(AE)* ['hɑ:bə]
Hafendamm pier [pɪə]
Hähnchen chicken ['tʃɪkɪn]
Häkchen tick [tɪk]
mit einem **Haken versehen** to tick [tɪk]
halb half [hɑ:f]
halb (drei) half past (two) [ˌhɑ:f 'pɑ:st]
Hälfte half [hɑ:f]
hallo hello [hel'əʊ]; hi [haɪ]
Hals neck [nek]
halten to hold [həʊld]
Haltestelle stop [stɒp]
hämmern to pound [paʊnd]
Hand hand [hænd]
Handel deal [di:l]
Handkarren trolley ['trɒli]
Handlung action ['ækʃn]
Handout handout ['hændaʊt]
Handschuh glove [glʌv]
Handtasche handbag ['hændbæg]
Handy cell phone *(AE)* ['sel ͵fəʊn]
hängen bleiben to be stuck [ˌbi: 'stʌk]
hart hard [hɑ:d]
hassen to hate [heɪt]
Haupt- main [meɪn]
Hauptgang main course [ˌmeɪn 'kɔ:s]
Hauptgericht main course [ˌmeɪn 'kɔ:s]
Hauptstadt capital ['kæpɪtl]
Hausaufgaben homework ['həʊmwɜ:k]
hausgemacht home-made [ˌhəʊm'meɪd]
Hausmeister/-in caretaker ['keə͵teɪkə]
Haustier pet [pet]
Haut skin [skɪn]
Heavy Metal heavy metal [ˌhevi 'metl]
Hecktür back door [ˌbæk 'dɔ:]
Heft exercise book ['eksəsaɪz ͵bʊk]
Hefter folder ['fəʊldə]
heilig sacred ['seɪkrɪd]; holy ['həʊli]
Heilige Mutter Holy mother [ˌhəʊli 'mʌðə]
Heim home [həʊm]
Heimweh haben to feel homesick [ˌfi:l 'həʊmsɪk]
heiraten to marry ['mæri]
heiß hot [hɒt]
heiße Schokolade hot chocolate [ˌhɒt 'tʃɒklət]
Held/-in hero ['hɪərəʊ]
helfen to help [help]
hell fair [feə]; bright [braɪt]
Helm helmet ['helmət]
Hemd shirt [ʃɜ:t]
heranzoomen to zoom-in [ˌzu:m‿'ɪn]
herauf up [ʌp]
herausfinden to find out [faɪnd‿'aʊt]
heraussuchen to look up [lʊk‿'ʌp]
Herberge hostel ['hɒstl]
Herbst fall *(AE)* [fɔ:l]; autumn ['ɔ:təm]
herein in [ɪn]
hereinlegen to trick [trɪk]
Herr Mr ['mɪstə]; gentleman ['dʒentlmən]
herrlich lovely ['lʌvli]
herüberkommen to come over [ˌkʌm‿'əʊvə]
herunter down [daʊn]
herunterfallen to fall off ['fɔ:l‿'ɒf]
herunterhängend drooping ['dru:pɪŋ]
herunterladen to download [ˌdaʊn'ləʊd]
hervorragend brilliant ['brɪliənt]
Herz heart [hɑ:t]
Herzliche Grüße, … Love, … [lʌv]
herzlos heartless ['hɑ:tləs]
Herzschrittmacher pacemaker ['peɪs͵meɪkə]
heute today [tə'deɪ]
heute Abend tonight [tə'naɪt]
heute Nacht tonight [tə'naɪt]
hier here [hɪə]
high *(Stimmung nach dem Genuss von Drogen)* high [haɪ]
Hightech- high-tech [ˌhaɪ'tek]
Hilfe help [help]
hilflos helpless ['helpləs]
hilfreich helpful ['helpfʊl]
Himmel sky [skaɪ]
hin und zurück return [rɪ'tɜ:n]
hinauf up [ʌp]
(hin)ausgehen to go out [gəʊ‿'aʊt]
hinauszögern to delay [dɪ'leɪ]
hinein in [ɪn]; into ['ɪntə]
hinfallen to fall [fɔ:l]
(Person) hinfallen to fall over [fɔ:l‿'əʊvə]
hinten im Buch at the back of the book [æt ðə 'bæk‿əv ðə ͵bʊk]
hinter behind [bɪ'haɪnd]
hintere Hosentasche back pocket [ˌbæk 'pɒkɪt]
Hintergrund background ['bækgraʊnd]
hinterherrennen to chase [tʃeɪs]
Hintertür back door [ˌbæk 'dɔ:]
hinunter down [daʊn]
Hinweis clue [klu:]
hinzufügen to add [æd]
Hip-Hop hip hop ['hɪp hɒp]
hispanisch Hispanic [hɪ'spænɪk]
Hit hit [hɪt]
Hobby hobby ['hɒbi]

hoch tall [tɔ:l]; high [haɪ]
hochhalten to hold up [həʊld‿'ʌp]
hochheben to lift [lɪft]
Hochmoor moor [mɔ:]
hochziehen to lift [lɪft]
Hockey *(Sportart)* hockey ['hɒki]
hoffen to hope [həʊp]
höflich polite [pə'laɪt]
in die **Höhe schnellen** to soar [sɔ:]
Höhle cave [keɪv]
holländisch Dutch [dʌtʃ]
Hölle hell [hel]
Holz wood [wʊd]
Holz- wooden ['wʊdn]
hölzern wooden ['wʊdn]
hölzerne Uferpromenade (am Strand) boardwalk ['bɔ:dwɔ:k]
Homepage home page ['həʊm ˌpeɪdʒ]
hören to hear [hɪə]; to listen ['lɪsn]
Hose pants *(AE)* [pænts]; trousers pl. ['traʊzəz]
Hotel hotel [həʊ'tel]
hübsch pretty ['prɪti]
Hubschrauber helicopter ['helɪkɒptə]
Huhn chicken ['tʃɪkɪn]
den **Hund ausführen** to take the dog for a walk [teɪk ðə 'dɒg fɔ:r‿ə ˌwɔ:k]
Hund dog [dɒg]
hundert one hundred [wʌn 'hʌndrəd]
Hungersnot famine ['fæmɪn]
hungrig hungry ['hʌŋgri]
Hut hat [hæt]
Hütte cabin ['kæbɪn]

I

ich I [aɪ]
Idee idea [aɪ'dɪə]
Idiot/-in idiot ['ɪdiət]; jerk [dʒɜ:k]
ihm him [hɪm]
ihn him [hɪm]
ihnen them [ðem]
ihr you [ju:]; her [hɜ:]
Ihr/-e your [jɔ:]
ihr/-e their [ðeə]; its [ɪts]; her [hɜ:]
ihre/-r/-s hers [hɜ:z]; theirs [ðeəz]
Ikone icon ['aɪkɒn]
illegal illegal [ɪ'li:gl]
Illusion illusion [ɪ'lu:ʒn]
Image image ['ɪmɪdʒ]
Imbiss snack [snæk]; deli ['deli]
immer always ['ɔ:lweɪz]
immer (mehr) more and more [ˌmɔ:‿ən‿'mɔ:]
immer noch still [stɪl]
Immigration immigration [ˌɪmɪ'greɪʃn]
Immobilien real estate *(AE)* ['rɪəl ɪˌsteɪt]
in at [æt; ət]; in [ɪn]; into ['ɪntə]
in der Nähe von near [nɪə]
in Ordnung fine [faɪn]
in Ordnung bringen to sort out [sɔ:t 'aʊt]
in Richtung towards [tə'wɔ:dz]
Inder/-in Indian ['ɪndiən]
Indianer/-in Indian ['ɪndiən]; Native American [ˌneɪtɪv ə'merɪkən]
indirekte Rede reported speech [rɪˌpɔ:tɪd 'spi:tʃ]
indisch Indian ['ɪndiən]
Industrie industry ['ɪndəstri]
Information(en) information [ˌɪnfə'meɪʃn]; info ['ɪnfəʊ]
Inhalt content ['kɒntent]
Inlineskates skates [skeɪts]
innen inside [ˌɪn'saɪd]
in der **Innenstadt** downtown *(AE)* [ˌdaʊn'taʊn]
innerhalb within [wɪ'ðɪn]
ins Bett gehen to go to bed [ˌgəʊ tə 'bed]
Insel island ['aɪlənd]
insgesamt in all [ɪn‿'ɔ:l]
Institut college ['kɒlɪdʒ]
intelligent intelligent [ɪn'telɪdʒnt]
Intensivkurs crash course ['kræʃ ˌkɔ:s]
interessant interesting ['ɪntrəstɪŋ]
Interesse interest ['ɪntrəst]
sich **interessieren** to care [keə]
interessiert interested ['ɪntrəstɪd]
international international [ˌɪntə'næʃnl]
Internet web [web]; Internet ['ɪntənet]
Internettagebuch blog [blɒg]
Interview interview ['ɪntəvju:]
interviewen to interview ['ɪntəvju:]
Invasion invasion [ɪn'veɪʒn]
IQ (Intelligenzquotient) I.Q. [ˌaɪ 'kju:]
Ire/Irin Irish ['aɪərɪʃ]
irgendetwas something ['sʌmθɪŋ]
(irgend)etwas anything ['eniθɪŋ]
irgendjemand anybody ['enibɒdi]
(irgend)jemand somebody ['sʌmbədi]; someone ['sʌmwʌn]
(irgend)welche any ['eni]
irgendwo somewhere ['sʌmweə]; anywhere ['eniweə]
irisch Irish ['aɪərɪʃ]
ist is [ɪz]
italienisch Italian [ɪ'tæliən]

J

ja yes [jes]; yep [jep]
Jacht yacht [jɒt]
Jacke jacket ['dʒækɪt]
Jagdhund hound [haʊnd]
jagen to hunt [hʌnt]; to chase [tʃeɪs]
Jäger/-in seeker ['si:kə]
Jahr year [jɪə]
Jahresplaner planner ['plænə]
Jahreszeit season ['si:zn]
Jahrhundert century ['sentʃəri]
Jahrmarkt fair [feə]
Jahrtausend millennium [mɪ'leniəm]
jamaikanisch Jamaican [dʒə'meɪkən]
Januar January ['dʒænjuri]
Jazz jazz [dʒæz]
je each [i:tʃ]; ever ['evə]
Jeans jeans pl. [dʒi:nz]
jede/-r/-s any ['eni]; each [i:tʃ]; everybody ['evriˌbɒdi]; every ['evri]
jeden everybody else ['evribɒdi ˌels]
jeder everyone ['evriwʌn]
jeder andere everybody else ['evribɒdi ˌels]
jedoch however [haʊ'evə]
jemals ever ['evə]
(irgend)jemand anyone ['eniwʌn]
jene those [ðəʊz]
Jet-Ski jet ski ['dʒet ˌski:]
jetzt now [naʊ]
jetzt gerade right now ['raɪt ˌnaʊ]
jeweils each [i:tʃ]
joggen to jog [dʒɒg]
Jogurt yoghurt ['jɒgət]
Journalist/-in journalist ['dʒɜ:nəlɪst]
jubeln to cheer [tʃɪə]
Judo judo ['dʒu:dəʊ]
Jugend- junior ['dʒu:niə]; youth [ju:θ]
Jugendherberge youth hostel ['ju:θ ˌhɒstl]
Jugendklub youth club ['ju:θ ˌklʌb]
jugendlich teenage ['ti:neɪdʒ]
Jugendliche/Jugendlicher teenager ['ti:neɪdʒə]
Jugendliche/-r teen [ti:n]
Jugendzentrum activity centre [ˌæktɪvəti 'sentə]; youth club ['ju:θ ˌklʌb]
Juli July [dʒʊ'laɪ]
jung young [jʌŋ]
Junge boy [bɔɪ]
Juni June [dʒu:n]
Junioren- junior ['dʒu:niə]

German – English

K

Kabelfernsehen cable-TV [ˌkeɪbl ˈtiːviː]
Kabine cabin [ˈkæbɪn]
Kaffee coffee [ˈkɒfi]
Kakao hot chocolate [ˌhɒt ˈtʃɒklət]
Kalender calendar [ˈkæləndə]
kalt cold [kəʊld]
Kamera camera [ˈkæmrə]
Kampf fight [faɪt]; battle [ˈbætl]
kämpfen to fight [faɪt]
Kanadier/-in Canadian [kəˈneɪdiən]
kanadisch Canadian [kəˈneɪdiən]
Kanal channel [ˈtʃænl]
kann/-st nicht cannot [ˈkænɒt]
Kante edge [edʒ]
Kapitän captain [ˈkæptɪn]
Kapitel unit [ˈjuːnɪt]
Kappe cap [kæp]
Kapsel capsule [ˈkæpsjuːl]
kaputt broken [ˈbrəʊkn]
kaputt machen to destroy [dɪˈstrɔɪ]; to break [breɪk]
Karaoke karaoke [ˌkæriˈəʊki]
Karneval carnival [ˈkɑːnɪvl]
Karriere career [kəˈrɪə]
Karte card [kɑːd]
Kartenverkaufsstelle ticket office [ˈtɪkɪt ˌɒfɪs]
Kartoffel potato [pəˈteɪtəʊ]
Kartoffelchip crisp [krɪsp]
Karton box [bɒks]
Kasino casino [kəˈsiːnəʊ]
Kassierer/-in cashier [kæˈʃɪə]
Katastrophe disaster [dɪˈzɑːstə]
Katze cat [kæt]
kaufen to buy [baɪ]
Kaufhaus department store [dɪˈpɑːtmənt ˌstɔː]
kein/-e not [nɒt]; no [nəʊ]
keiner no one [ˈnəʊ wʌn]
Keks biscuit [ˈbɪskɪt]
Kellergeschoss basement [ˈbeɪsmənt]
Kellner waiter [ˈweɪtə]
Kellnerin waitress [ˈweɪtrəs]
kennen to know [nəʊ]
Kerl guy [gaɪ]; bloke [bləʊk]
Kerze candle [ˈkændl]
Kette chain [tʃeɪn]
Keyboard keyboard [ˈkiːbɔːd]
khakifarben khaki [ˈkɑːki]
Kickboard kickboard [ˈkɪkbɔːd]
kicken to kick [kɪk]
Kilo(gramm) kilo (= kilogramme) [ˈkɪləʊ = ˈkɪləʊgræm]
Kilometer kilometre (= km) [kɪˈlɒmɪtə]
Kind child [tʃaɪld]; kid [kɪd]
Kino movie theater *(AE)* [ˌmuːvi ˈθɪətə]; cinema [ˈsɪnəmə]; the movies *(AE)* [ˈmuːviz]
Kirche church [tʃɜːtʃ]
Kirsche cherry [ˈtʃeri]
Kiste box [bɒks]
klar clear [klɪə]
klären to sort out [sɔːt ˈaʊt]
klasse neat [niːt]; cool [kuːl]
Klasse grade *(AE)* [greɪd]; year [jɪə]; class [klɑːs]; group [gruːp]
Klasse (in einer englischen Schule) tutor group [ˈtjuːtə ˌgruːp]
Klassenarbeit test [test]
Klassenbuch register [ˈredʒɪstə]
Klassenkamerad/-in classmate [ˈklɑːsmeɪt]
Klassenlehrer/-in tutor [ˈtjuːtə]
Klassenzimmer classroom [ˈklɑːsruːm]
Klassik classical music [ˌklæsɪkl ˈmjuːzɪk]
Klassiker classic [ˈklæsɪk]
Klatsch gossip [ˈgɒsɪp]
klatschen to clap [klæp]
Klavier piano [pɪˈænəʊ]
Klebeband tape [teɪp]
Kleid dress [dres]
Kleider clothes pl. [kləʊðz]
Kleiderordnung dress code [ˌdres ˈkəʊd]
Kleiderschrank wardrobe [ˈwɔːdrəʊb]
Kleidung dress [dres]; clothes pl. [kləʊðz]
klein small [smɔːl]; little [lɪtl]
Kleinbus minibus [ˈmɪnɪbʌs]
Kleingeld change [tʃeɪndʒ]
Kleintransporter van [væn]
klettern to climb [klaɪm]
klicken to click [klɪk]
Klima climate [ˈklaɪmət]
Klingel bell [bel]
klingeln to ring [rɪŋ]
klingen to sound [saʊnd]
Klippe cliff [klɪf]
Kloster monastery [ˈmɒnəstri]
Klub club [klʌb]
Klubhaus clubhouse [ˈklʌbhaʊs]
klug intelligent [ɪnˈtelɪdʒnt]; smart [smɑːt]; clever [ˈklevə]
Knall bang [bæŋ]
Knie knee [niː]
Knochen bone [bəʊn]
Knopf button [ˈbʌtn]
Koch/Köchin chef [ʃef]
kochen to cook [kʊk]
Koffer suitcase [ˈsuːtkeɪs]
Kohle coal [kəʊl]
Kohlenbergwerk coal mine [ˈkəʊl maɪn]
Kokain cocaine (no pl.) [kəˈkeɪn]
komisch weird [wɪəd]; funny [ˈfʌni]
kommen to come [kʌm]
Kommunikation communication [kəˌmjuːnɪˈkeɪʃn]
Komödie *(Filmart)* comedy [ˈkɒmədi]
kompakt compact [ˈkɒmpækt]
Komparativ comparative [kəmˈpærətɪv]
Komponist/-in songwriter [ˈsɒŋraɪtə]
Kondition fitness [ˈfɪtnəs]
Konditional- conditional [kənˈdɪʃnl]
König king [kɪŋ]
Königin queen [kwiːn]
königlich royal [ˈrɔɪəl]
Konjunktion conjunction [kənˈdʒʌŋkʃn]
können to be able to [biː ˈeɪbl tʊ]; can [kæn]
könnte/-n could [kʊd]
könnte(n) might [maɪt]
könnte(n) vielleicht may [meɪ]
könntest could [kʊd]
Kontrolle control [kənˈtrəʊl]
kontrollieren to check [tʃek]
Kontrollliste checklist [ˈtʃeklɪst]
Konversation conversation [ˌkɒnvəˈseɪʃn]
Konzert concert [ˈkɒnsət]
Kopf head [hed]
Kopfhörer headphones [ˈhedfəʊnz]
Kopfschmerzen headache [ˈhedeɪk]
Kopfzeile headline [ˈhedlaɪn]
Kopie copy [ˈkɒpi]
kopieren to copy [ˈkɒpi]
Korb basket [ˈbɑːskɪt]
Körper body [ˈbɒdi]
korrigieren to correct [kəˈrekt]
kosten to cost [kɒst]
kostenlos free [friː]
köstlich delicious [dɪˈlɪʃəs]
Kostüm costume [ˈkɒstjuːm]
Krach noise [nɔɪz]
Kragen collar [ˈkɒlə]
krank sick [sɪk]; ill [ɪl]
Krankenhaus hospital [ˈhɒspɪtl]
kratzen to scratch [skrætʃ]
Kratzer scratch [skrætʃ]
Kreatur creature [ˈkriːtʃə]
kreieren to create [kriːˈeɪt]
Kreis circle [ˈsɜːkl]
Kreuz cross [krɒs]
kreuzen to cross [krɒs]
Kricket cricket [ˈkrɪkɪt]
Krieg war [wɔː]
Krone crown [kraʊn]

Kronjuwelen crown jewels [ˌkraʊn ˈdʒuːəlz]
Küche kitchen [ˈkɪtʃɪn]
Kuchen cake [keɪk]
Kuh cow [kaʊ]
Kühlschrank refrigerator [rɪˈfrɪdʒəreɪtə]
Kulisse scene [siːn]
Kultur culture [ˈkʌltʃə]
sich kümmern to care [keə]
sich kümmern um to look after [ˈlʊk ˌɑːftə]
Kunde/Kundin customer [ˈkʌstəmə]
Kunst Art [ɑːt]
Kunststück trick [trɪk]
Kurier courier [ˈkʊriə]
Kurs course [kɔːs]
Kurve curve [kɜːv]
kurz short [ʃɔːt]
Kurzform short form [ˈʃɔːt fɔːm]
Kurzform von short for [ˌʃɔːt ˈfə]
Kuss kiss [kɪs]
küssen to kiss [kɪs]
Küste coast [kəʊst]
Küstenlinie coastline [ˈkəʊstlaɪn]

L

lächeln to smile [smaɪl]
lachen to laugh [lɑːf]
Lack paint [peɪnt]
Laden store *(AE)* [stɔː]; shop [ʃɒp]
Lagerfeuer campfire [ˈkæmpfaɪə]
lahm lame [leɪm]
Lamm lamb [læm]
Lampe lamp [læmp]
Land country [ˈkʌntri]; state [steɪt]
landen to land [lænd]
kleines **Landhaus** cottage [ˈkɒtɪdʒ]
Landkarte map [mæp]
Landschaft scenery [ˈsiːnəri]
Landschaft landscape [ˈlændskeɪp]
Landwirt/-in farmer [ˈfɑːmə]
lang long [lɒŋ]
Langform long form [ˈlɒŋ fɔːm]
langsam slow [sləʊ]
sich **langweilen** to be bored [biː ˈbɔːd]
langweilig boring [ˈbɔːrɪŋ]
Laptop laptop [ˈlæptɒp]
Lärm noise [nɔɪz]
lassen to leave [liːv]; to let [let]
lass(t) uns ... let's ... [lets]
lässig easy-going [ˌiːziˈgəʊɪŋ]; casual [ˈkæʒjuəl]
Lastwagen truck *(AE)* [trʌk]
lateinamerikanisch Hispanic [hɪˈspænɪk]; Latin [ˈlætɪn]
Laterne lantern [ˈlæntən]
Lauch leek [liːk]
Lauf race [reɪs]
laufen to walk [wɔːk]; to run [rʌn]
laut loud [laʊd]
Laut sound [saʊnd]
läuten to ring [rɪŋ]
lautlos silently [ˈsaɪləntli]
leben to live [lɪv]
Leben life [laɪf]
lebendig alive [əˈlaɪv]
Lebensgeschichte biography [baɪˈɒgrəfi]
Lebensmittel food [fuːd]
Lebensstil lifestyle [ˈlaɪfstaɪl]
lecken to leak [liːk]
lecker delicious [dɪˈlɪʃəs]; tasty [ˈteɪsti]
Leder leather [ˈleðə]
leer dead [ded]; empty [ˈemti]
legen to put [pʊt]
Legende key [kiː]
lehren to teach [tiːtʃ]
Lehrer/-in teacher [ˈtiːtʃə]
Lehrerpult desk [desk]
Lehrgang course [kɔːs]
Lehrling apprentice [əˈprentɪs]
leicht easy [ˈiːzi]
(Leicht-)Athletik athletics [æθˈletɪks]
Es tut mir **leid.** I'm sorry. [ˌaɪm ˈsɒri]
leihen to lend [lend]
leise quiet [ˈkwaɪət]; silently [ˈsaɪləntli]
Lektion unit [ˈjuːnɪt]
Lenkrad wheel [wiːl]
lernen to learn [lɜːn]
lesbar readable [ˈriːdəbl]
lesen to read [riːd]
letzte/-r/-s last [lɑːst]
leuchten to glow [gləʊ]
Leute guys [gaɪz]; people [ˈpiːpl]
Licht light [laɪt]
Liebe love [lʌv]
Liebe/-r ... Dear ... [dɪə]
Liebe Grüße, ... Love, ... [lʌv]
lieben to love [lʌv]
Liebesfilm romance [rəʊˈmænts]
Lieblings- favorite *(AE)* [ˈfeɪvrɪt]; favourite [ˈfeɪvrɪt]
am **liebsten** most [məʊst]
Lied song [sɒŋ]
Liedermacher/-in songwriter [ˈsɒŋraɪtə]
Liedtext lyrics pl. [ˈlɪrɪks]
liefern to deliver [dɪˈlɪvə]
Lieferwagen van [væn]
lila purple [ˈpɜːpl]
Limette lime [laɪm]
Limonade lemonade [ˌleməˈneɪd]
Limone lime [laɪm]
Lineal ruler [ˈruːlə]
Lingua franca lingua franca [ˌlɪŋgwə ˈfræŋkə]
Linie line [laɪn]
linke/-r/-s left [left]
links left [left]; on the left [ˌɒn ðə ˈleft]
Liste list [lɪst]
live live [laɪv]
Loch hole [həʊl]
Löffel spoon [spuːn]
lokal local [ˈləʊkl]
lösbar solvable [ˈsɒlvəbl]
löschen to delete [dɪˈliːt]
lösen to solve [sɒlv]; to sort out [sɔːt ˈaʊt]
Löwe lion [laɪən]
Luft air [eə]
nach **Luft schnappen** to gasp [gɑːsp]
Luftballon balloon [bəˈluːn]
Luftpost air mail [ˈeə meɪl]
Luftsack windsock [ˈwɪndsɒk]
lustig funny [ˈfʌni]

M

machen to do [duː]; to make [meɪk]
Macht nichts. Never mind. [ˌnevə ˈmaɪnd]
mächtig mighty [ˈmaɪti]; powerful [ˈpaʊəfl]
Mädchen girl [gɜːl]
Magen stomach [ˈstʌmək]
Magie magic [ˈmædʒɪk]
magnetische Kräfte magnetism [ˈmægnətɪzəm]
Mahlzeit meal [miːl]
Mai May [meɪ]
Mailbox mailbox [ˈmeɪlbɒks]
Mais corn [kɔːn]
Majonäse mayonnaise [ˌmeɪəˈneɪz]
Make-up make-up [ˈmeɪkʌp]
Mal time [taɪm]
malen to colour [ˈkʌlə]; to draw [drɔː]; to paint [peɪnt]
Maler/-in painter [ˈpeɪntə]
Mama mum [mʌm]; mom *(AE)* [mɒm]
manchmal sometimes [ˈsʌmtaɪmz]
Mango mango [ˈmæŋgəʊ]
Mann man [mæn]
Mannschaft team [tiːm]
Mantel coat [kəʊt]
Mappe folder [ˈfəʊldə]

German – English

Marathon marathon ['mærəθn]
markieren to highlight ['haɪlaɪt]
Markt market ['mɑ:kɪt]; fair [feə]
marschieren to march [mɑ:tʃ]
März March [mɑ:tʃ]
Maschine machine [mə'ʃi:n]
Match match [mætʃ]
materiell material [mə'tɪəriəl]
Mathe Math *(AE)* [mæθ]; Maths [mæθs]
Mauer wall [wɔ:l]
Maus mouse [maʊs]
Mausefalle mousetrap ['maʊstræp]
Mechaniker/-in mechanic [mɪ'kænɪk]
Medien media ['mi:diə]
Meer sea [si:]
Mehl flour [flaʊə]
mehr more [mɔ:]
mehrere several ['sevrəl]
Mehrzahl plural ['plʊərl]
Meile mile [maɪl]
mein/-e my [maɪ]
meine/-r mine [maɪn]
meinen to mean [mi:n]
meins mine [maɪn]
Meinung opinion [ə'pɪnjən]; mind [maɪnd]
am **meisten** most [məʊst]
Meister master ['mɑ:stə]
meistverkauft best-selling [ˌbest 'selɪŋ]
melken to milk [mɪlk]
Melodie tune [tju:n]
eine **Menge** a lot of [ə 'lɒt‿əv]
Menschenmenge crowd [kraʊd]
Merkmal feature ['fi:tʃə]
merkwürdig odd [ɒd]; strange [streɪndʒ]
Messe fair [feə]
Messer knife [naɪf]
Meteorologe weatherman ['weðəmæn]
Meter metre ['mi:tə]
Mexikaner/-in Mexican ['meksɪkən]
mexikanisch Mexican ['meksɪkən]
mich me [mi:]
mieten to hire [haɪə]
Mikrofon microphone ['maɪkrəfəʊn]
Mikroskop microscope ['maɪkrəskəʊp]
Mikrowelle microwave ['maɪkrəweɪv]
Milch milk [mɪlk]
Milchreis rice pudding [raɪs 'pʊdɪŋ]
Milkshake milkshake ['mɪlkˌʃeɪk]
Milliarde billion ['bɪliən]
Million million ['mɪljən]
mindestens at least [ˌət 'li:st]
Mineralwasser mineral water ['mɪnrl ˌwɔ:tə]
Minestrone minestrone [ˌmɪnɪ'strəʊni]
Mini- mini ['mɪni]
Minute minute ['mɪnɪt]
mir me [mi:]
mit by [baɪ]; with [wɪð]
Mit freundlichen Grüßen, *(am Briefende)* Yours, [jɔ:z]
mitbringen to bring [brɪŋ]
miteinander together [tə'geðə]
mitfühlend sympathetic [ˌsɪmpə'θetɪk]
Mitgefühl haben to feel sorry for [fi:l 'sɒri ˌfə]
Mitglied member ['membə]
Mitglied werden to join [dʒɔɪn]
zum **Mitnehmen** to go [tə 'gəʊ]
Mitschüler/-in classmate ['klɑ:smeɪt]
Mittag midday [ˌmɪd'deɪ]
Mittagessen lunch [lʌntʃ]; dinner ['dɪnə]
Mittagszeit lunchtime ['lʌntʃtaɪm]
Mitte middle ['mɪdl]; centre ['sentə]
mittel medium ['mi:diəm]
Mittwoch Wednesday ['wenzdeɪ]
Möbel furniture ['fɜ:nɪtʃə]
Modalverb modal ['məʊdl]
Mode trend [trend]
Modell model ['mɒdl]
modern modern ['mɒdn]
modisch trendy ['trendi]
mögen to like [laɪk]
möglich possible ['pɒsəbl]
Möglichkeit chance [tʃɑ:ns]
momentan at the moment [ˌæt ðə 'məʊmənt]
Monat month [mʌnθ]
Mond moon [mu:n]
Monster monster ['mɒnstə]
Montag Monday ['mʌndeɪ]
montags on Mondays [ˌɒn 'mʌndeɪz]
morgen tomorrow [tə'mɒrəʊ]
Morgen morning ['mɔ:nɪŋ]
Motel motel [məʊ'tel]
Motor motor ['məʊtə]
Motorrad motorcycle ['məʊtəˌsaɪkl]
MP3-Spieler MP3 player [ˌempi:'θri: ˌpleɪə]
müde tired [taɪəd]
Mühe trouble ['trʌbl]
Müll trash *(AE)* [træʃ]; garbage *(AE)* ['gɑ:bɪdʒ]; rubbish ['rʌbɪʃ]
Mund mouth [maʊθ]
Muschel shell [ʃel]
Museum museum [mju:'zi:əm]
Musical musical ['mju:zɪkəl]
Musik music ['mju:zɪk]
Musiker/-in musician [mju:'zɪʃn]
(Musik-)Instrument instrument ['ɪnstrəmənt]
müssen must [mʌst]; to have to ['hæv tə]
mutig gritty ['grɪti]; brave [breɪv]
Mutti mum [mʌm]
Mütze hat [hæt]

N

na ja well [wel]
nach after ['ɑ:ftə]; to [tʊ]; past [pɑ:st]
nach draußen outside [ˌaʊt'saɪd]
nach oben up [ʌp]
nach unten down [daʊn]
Nachbar/-in neighbour ['neɪbə]
Nachbarschaft neighborhood *(AE)* ['neɪbəhʊd]
nachlassen to wear off [weər‿'ɒf]
Nachmittag afternoon [ˌɑ:ftə'nu:n]
nachmittags pm [ˌpi:'em]
Nachricht message ['mesɪdʒ]
eine **Nachricht hinterlassen** to leave a message [ˌli:v‿ə 'mesɪdʒ]
Nachricht(en) news [nju:z]
nachschlagen to look up [lʊk‿'ʌp]
Nachsitzen detention [dɪ'tentʃn]
nächste/-r/-s next [nekst]
Nacht night [naɪt]
Nachtisch pudding ['pʊdɪŋ]; dessert [dɪ'zɜ:t]
Nachtklub nightclub ['naɪtklʌb]
Nacken neck [nek]
nahe herangehen to zoom-in [ˌzu:m‿'ɪn]
nahe near [nɪə]
in der **Nähe von** close to [ˌkləʊs‿'tʊ]
Nahrungskette food chain ['fu:d ˌtʃeɪn]
Name name [neɪm]
Napf bowl [bəʊl]
Narzisse daffodil ['dæfədɪl]
Nase nose [nəʊz]
nass wet [wet]
national national ['næʃnl]
Nationalpark national park [ˌnæʃnl 'pɑ:k]
Natur nature ['neɪtʃə]
natürlich naturally ['nætʃrəli]; of course [ˌəv 'kɔ:s]
Naturpark national park [ˌnæʃnl 'pɑ:k]
Naturwissenschaft(en) Science [saɪəns]
Nebel fog [fɒg]
nebelig foggy ['fɒgi]

neben beside [bɪ'saɪd]; next door [ˌnekst 'dɔ:]; next to ['nekst tʊ]
nebenan next door [ˌnekst 'dɔ:]
Neffe nephew ['nefju:]
negativ negative ['negətɪv]
nehmen to take [teɪk]
neidisch jealous ['dʒeləs]
nein no [nəʊ]
nennen to name [neɪm]; to call [kɔ:l]
(Nerven)zusammenbruch breakdown ['breɪkdaʊn]
nervös nervous ['nɜ:vəs]
nett pretty ['prɪti]; kind [kaɪnd]; nicely ['naɪsli]; nice [naɪs]
Netz net [net]; web [web]
neu new [nju:]
neu schreiben to rewrite [ˌri:'rait]
neunte/-r/-s ninth [naɪnθ]
nicht not [nɒt]
nichts nothing ['nʌθɪŋ]
nie never ['nevə]
niederländisch Dutch [dʌtʃ]
niedlich cute [kju:t]; sweet [swi:t]
niemand no one ['nəʊ wʌn]; nobody ['nəʊbədi]
noch still [stɪl]; even ['i:vn]
noch ein/e/-r another [ə'nʌðə]; yet another [jet ə'nʌðə]
noch einmal again [ə'gen]
noch nicht not … yet [nɒt … 'jet]
Norden north [nɔ:θ]
normal normal ['nɔ:ml]
normalerweise usually ['ju:ʒəli]
Note mark [mɑ:k]; grade *(AE)* [greɪd]
Notenständer music stand ['mju:zɪk ˌstænd]
Notiz(en) note(s) [nəʊt(s)]
Notizen machen to make notes [ˌmeɪk 'nəʊts]; to take notes [ˌteɪk 'nəʊts]
November November [nəʊ'vembə]
nüchtern sober ['səʊbə]
Nudel noodle ['nu:dl]
Nudeln pasta ['pæstə]
Null *(in Sportergebnissen)* nil [nɪl]; zero ['zɪərəʊ]
Nummer number ['nʌmbə]
Nummernschild license plate *(AE)* ['laɪsəns ˌpleɪt]; number plate *(BE)* ['nʌmbə ˌpleɪt]
nun now [naʊ]
nur only ['əʊnli]; just [dʒʌst]
nützlich useful ['ju:sfl]

O

ob if [ɪf]; whether ['weðə]
oben above [ə'bʌv]; upstairs [ʌp'steəz]
oberer Teil top [tɒp]
oberes Ende top [tɒp]
oberflächliche Konversation small talk ['smɔ:l ˌtɔ:k]
oberhalb above [ə'bʌv]
Oberteil top [tɒp]
Objekt object ['ɒbdʒɪkt]
Observatorium observatory [əb'zɜ:vətri]
Obst fruit [fru:t]
Obstpflücker/-in picker ['pɪkə]
obwohl although [ɔ:l'ðəʊ]
oder or [ɔ:]
offen open ['əʊpn]
öffentlich public ['pʌblɪk]
Öffentlichkeit public ['pʌblɪk]
offiziell official [ə'fɪʃl]
öffnen to open ['əʊpn]
Öffnungszeit opening time ['əʊpnɪŋ ˌtaɪm]
oft often ['ɒfn]
ohne without [wɪ'ðaʊt]
Ohr ear [ɪə]
Ohrring earring ['ɪərɪŋ]
o.k. OK [əʊ'keɪ]
okay OK [əʊ'keɪ]
Oktober October [ɒk'təʊbə]
Ölbohrinsel oil platform ['ɔɪl ˌplætfɔ:m]
olympisch Olympic [ə'lɪmpɪk]
online online [ˌɒn'laɪn]
Opa grandad ['grændæd]
Oper opera ['ɒprə]
Orange orange ['ɒrɪndʒ]
orange(farben) orange ['ɒrɪndʒ]
Orchester orchestra ['ɔ:kɪstrə]
ordentlich neatly ['ni:tli]; neat [ni:t]; tidy ['taɪdi]
Ordner file [faɪl]; folder ['fəʊldə]
in **Ordnung bringen** to fix [fɪks]
Ordnungszahl ordinal number ['ɔ:dɪnl ˌnʌmbə]
Organisator/-in organizer ['ɔ:gənaɪzə]
organisieren to arrange [ə'reɪndʒ]; to organize ['ɔ:gənaɪz]
Organisation organization [ˌɔ:gənaɪ'zeɪʃn]
original original [ə'rɪdʒənl]
Ort place [pleɪs]
örtlich local ['ləʊkl]
ortsansässig local ['ləʊkl]
(Orts-)Vorwahl area code ['eəriə ˌkəʊd]
Osten east [i:st]
Osterglocke daffodil ['dæfədɪl]
Ostern Easter ['i:stə]
Outdoor- outdoor [ˌaʊt'dɔ:]
Overheadfolie transparency [træn'spærntsi]
Overheadprojektor overhead projector [ˌəʊvəhed prə'dʒektə]

P

ein **paar** a few [ə 'fju:]; some [sʌm]
Paar pair [peə]
Päckchen packet ['pækɪt]
packen to pack [pæk]
Packung packet ['pækɪt]
Palast palace ['pælɪs]
Panzer shell [ʃel]
Papa dad [dæd]
Papier paper ['peɪpə]
parken to park [pɑ:k]
Partner/-in partner ['pɑ:tnə]
Party party ['pɑ:ti]
Pass passport ['pɑ:spɔ:t]
Pass auf! Watch it! ['wɒtʃ ˌɪt]
Passagier/-in passenger ['pæsndʒə]
passen to match [mætʃ]
passieren to happen ['hæpn]
Passiv *(Grammatik)* passive voice [ˌpæsɪv 'vɔɪs]
Passkontrolle Passport Control [ˌpɑ:spɔ:t kən'trəʊl]
Pastete pie [paɪ]
Pause break [breɪk]
eine **Pause machen** to rest [rest]
PC PC [ˌpi:'si:]
peinlich embarrassing [ɪm'bærəsɪŋ]
peitschen to whip [wɪp]
Penny penny ['peni]
perfekt perfect ['pɜ:fɪkt]
Perfekt present perfect [ˌpreznt 'pɜ:fɪkt]
Person character ['kærəktə]; person ['pɜ:sn]
persönlich personal ['pɜ:sənl]
Perücke wig [wɪg]
Pfad track [træk]; trail [treɪl]; path [pɑ:θ]
Pfannkuchen pancake ['pænkeɪk]
Pfeife pipe [paɪp]
Pferd horse [hɔ:s]
Pflanze plant [plɑ:nt]
pflücken to pick [pɪk]
Pfund pound [paʊnd]
Phrasal Verb *(Verb mit Präposition oder Partikel)* phrasal verb [ˌfreɪzl 'vɜ:b]

German – English

Physik Physics ['fɪzɪks]
Picknick picnic ['pɪknɪk]
Pier pier [pɪə]
piercen to pierce [pɪəs]
Pilot/-in pilot ['paɪlət]
pink pink [pɪŋk]
Pirat/-in pirate ['paɪrət]
Pistole gun [gʌn]
Pizza pizza ['piːtsə]
Plan plan [plæn]
planen to plan [plæn]
Planet planet ['plænɪt]
Planke plank [plæŋk]
Plastik plastic ['plæstɪk]
Plattform platform ['plætfɔːm]
Platz spot [spɒt]; seat [siːt]; room [ruːm]; place [pleɪs]
vom **Platz verweisen** to send off [send 'ɒf]
plaudern to chat [tʃæt]
plötzlich sudden ['sʌdn]; suddenly ['sʌdnli]
plötzliche(r/s) sudden ['sʌdn]
Plundergebäck Danish ['deɪnɪʃ]
Plural plural ['plʊərl]
Poet/-in poet ['pəʊɪt]
Polizei police [pə'liːs]
Polizist/-in cop *(AE)* [kɒp]
Polizistin policewoman [pə'liːsˌwʊmən]
polnisch Polish ['pəʊlɪʃ]
Pommes frites French fries *(AE)* [ˌfrentʃ 'fraɪz]; chips [tʃɪps]
Pompom *(bunte Quaste)* pompom ['pɒmpɒm]
Popkonzert pop concert ['pɒp ˌkɒnsət]
Popmusik pop [pɒp]
populär popular ['pɒpjələ]
Portmonnee wallet ['wɒlɪt]; purse [pɜːs]
positiv positive ['pɒzətɪv]
Possessivpronomen possessive pronoun [pəˌzesɪv 'prəʊnaʊn]
Post mail [meɪl]
Post auf dem Landweg/Seeweg surface mail ['sɜːfɪs ˌmeɪl]
Postamt post office ['pəʊst ˌɒfɪs]
Posten station ['steɪʃn]
Poster poster ['pəʊstə]
Postkarte postcard ['pəʊstkɑːd]
prahlen to brag (to s.o. about s.th.) [bræg]
Präposition preposition [ˌprepə'zɪʃn]
Präsens simple present [ˌsɪmpl 'preznt]
Präsentation presentation [ˌprezn'teɪʃn]
präsentieren to present [prɪ'zent]
Präsident/-in president ['prezɪdnt]
Preis charge [tʃɑːdʒ]; prize [praɪz]; price [praɪs]
preiswert cheap [tʃiːp]
Premiere premiere ['premieə]; opening night ['əʊpnɪŋ ˌnaɪt]
prima neat [niːt]
Prinz prince [prɪns]
privat private ['praɪvɪt]
pro per [pɜː]
Probe practice ['præktɪs]
probieren to try [traɪ]
(Essen, Trinken) probieren to taste [teɪst]
Problem problem ['prɒbləm]
Profil profile ['prəʊfaɪl]
Programm channel ['tʃænl]; programme ['prəʊgræm]; program *(AE)* ['prəʊgræm]
Projekt project ['prɒdʒekt]
Pronomen pronoun ['prəʊnaʊn]
Prospekt leaflet ['liːflət]
Prozent per cent [pə'sent]
Prüfung exam [ɪg'zæm]; test [test]
Publikum audience ['ɔːdiəns]
Puder powder ['paʊdə]
Pullover pullover ['pʊləʊvə]
Pulver powder ['paʊdə]
Punkt point [pɔɪnt]
Punktezähler/-in scorer ['skɔːrə]
Pute turkey ['tɜːki]
putzen to clean [kliːn]

Q

Quiz quiz [kwɪz]

R

Rabe raven ['reɪvn]
Rad wheel [wiːl]
radeln to cycle ['saɪkl]
Radiergummi rubber ['rʌbə]
Radio radio ['reɪdiəʊ]
Radiowecker clock radio ['klɒk ˌreɪdiəʊ]
Radkranz rim [rɪm]
Rahmen setting ['setɪŋ]; rim [rɪm]
Rakete rocket ['rɒkɪt]
Rampe ramp [ræmp]
Ranch ranch *(AE)* [ræntʃ]
an den **Rand** to the brink [tə ðə 'brɪŋk]
Rand edge [edʒ]
Ranger/-in ranger ['reɪndʒə]
Rap rap [ræp]
Rapper *(Rapsänger/-in)* rapper ['ræpə]
rasen to zoom [zuːm]
Rasierwasser aftershave ['ɑːftəʃeɪv]
Rat advice [əd'vaɪs]
Rate mal! Guess what! [ges 'wɒt]
raten to guess [ges]
Ratespiel quiz [kwɪz]
Ratschlag advice [əd'vaɪs]
Rätsel mystery ['mɪstəri]; puzzle ['pʌzl]
rauben to rob [rɒb]
Rauch smoke [sməʊk]
rauchen to smoke [sməʊk]
Raum space [speɪs]; room [ruːm]
Raumfähre shuttle ['ʃʌtl]
Raumschiff space ship ['speɪs ˌʃɪp]
Raumstation space station ['speɪs ˌsteɪʃn]
Rauschgift drug [drʌg]
rausspringen to come off [kʌm‿'ɒf]
reagieren to react [ri'ækt]
Reaktion response [rɪ'spɒns]
Realität reality [ri'æləti]
Rechnung check *(AE)* [tʃek]; bill [bɪl]
rechte/-r/-s right [raɪt]
rechts right [raɪt]; on the right [ˌɒn ðə 'raɪt]
rechtzeitig timely ['taɪmli]
gerade **rechtzeitig** just in time [ˌdʒʌst‿ɪn 'taɪm]
Rede speech [spiːtʃ]
reden to talk [tɔːk]
Redewendung phrase [freɪz]
Reflexivpronomen reflexive pronoun [rɪˌfleksɪv 'prəʊnaʊn]
Regel rule [ruːl]
regelmäßig regular ['regjələ]
eine **Regel brechen** to break a rule [ˌbreɪk‿ə 'ruːl]
Regelverstoß foul [faʊl]
Regen rain [reɪn]
Regenschirm umbrella [ʌm'brelə]
Reggae reggae ['regeɪ]
Regie führen to direct [dɪ'rekt]
Region region ['riːdʒn]
Regisseur/-in director [dɪ'rektə]
Register register ['redʒɪstə]
regnen to rain [reɪn]
Rehabilitation rehabilitation [ˌriːhəˌbɪlɪ'teɪʃn]
reich rich [rɪtʃ]
reichen to hand [hænd]
Reihe row [rəʊ]
an der Reihe turn [tɜːn]
jd. ist an der Reihe it is s.o.'s turn [tɜːn]
Reihenfolge order ['ɔːdə]

Reihenhaus terraced house ['terɪst ˌhaʊs]
Reis rice [raɪs]
Reise journey ['dʒɜ:ni]
Reisebus coach [kəʊtʃ]
reisen to travel ['trævl]
Reisepass passport ['pɑ:spɔ:t]
reißen to rip [rɪp]
reiten to ride [raɪd]
Reiten horseriding ['hɔ:s ˌraɪdɪŋ]
Religion religion [rɪ'lɪdʒn]; RE (= Religious Education) [ˌɑ:r'i: = rɪˌlɪdʒəs‿edʒʊ'keɪʃn]
rennen to run [rʌn]
Rennen race [reɪs]
reparieren to repair [rɪ'peə]; to mend [mend]; to fix [fɪks]
Reporter/-in reporter [rɪ'pɔ:tə]
Republik republic [rɪ'pʌblɪk]
Reservat reservation [ˌrezə'veɪʃn]
Respekt respect [rɪ'spekt]
Rest rest [rest]
Restaurant restaurant ['restrɒnt]
Resultat result [rɪ'zʌlt]
retten to rescue ['reskju:]; to save [seɪv]
Rezept recipe ['resɪpi]
Rezeption reception [rɪ'sepʃn]
rhythmisch rufen to chant [tʃɑ:nt]
richtig right [raɪt]; true [tru:]; correct [kə'rekt]
riechen to smell [smel]
Riesenrad Ferris wheel ['ferɪs ˌwi:l]
riesig enormous [ɪ'nɔ:məs]; huge [hju:dʒ]
etwas **riskieren** to take your chance [ˌteɪk jɔ: 'tʃɑ:ns]
Ritt ride [raɪd]
Roboter robot ['rəʊbɒt]
Rock skirt [skɜ:t]; rock [rɒk]
Rodeo-Reiter bronc rider ['brɒŋk ˌraɪdə]
Rolle part [pɑ:t]
Rollenspiel role play ['rəʊl pleɪ]
Rollschuhe skates [skeɪts]
Roman novel ['nɒvl]
romantisch romantic [rə'mæntɪk]
Romanze romance [rəʊ'mænts]
rosa pink [pɪŋk]
rot red [red]
Rücken back [bæk]
Rucksack backpack *(AE)* ['bækpæk]; rucksack ['rʌksæk]
rudern to row [rəʊ]
rufen to call [kɔ:l]; to cry [kraɪ]; to shout [ʃaʊt]
Rugby *(Sportart)* rugby ['rʌgbi]
ruhig calm [kɑ:m]; quiet ['kwaɪət]
Ruhm fame [feɪm]
rumhängen to hang out [hæŋ 'aʊt]
Runde round [raʊnd]
Rundfahrt tour [tʊə]
Rundgang tour [tʊə]
russisch Russian ['rʌʃn]
von etw. **rutschen** to slide off s.th. [ˌslaɪd‿'ɒf]

S

Saal hall [hɔ:l]
Sache thing [θɪŋ]
Sachen stuff [stʌf]
Sachtext factual text ['fæktʃʊəl ˌtekst]
Safari safari [sə'fɑ:ri]
Safarifahrt safari ride [sə'fɑ:ri ˌraɪd]
Saft juice [dʒu:s]
sagen to say [seɪ]; to tell [tel]
Sahne cream [kri:m]
sahnig creamy ['kri:mi]
Salat salad ['sæləd]
sammeln to collect [kə'lekt]
Sammler/-in collector [kə'lektə]
Samstag Saturday ['sætədeɪ]
Sandwich sandwich ['sænwɪdʒ]
Sänger/-in singer ['sɪŋə]
Satellit satellite ['sætəlaɪt]
Sattel saddle ['sædl]
Satz sentence ['sentəns]
sauber neatly ['ni:tli]; neat [ni:t]; clean [kli:n]
sauber machen to clean [kli:n]
Sauce sauce [sɔ:s]
sauer sein to be mad [bɪ 'mæd]
Schach chess [tʃes]
Schachtel box [bɒks]
(Das ist) schade (that's a) pity [ˌðæts ə 'pɪti]
Schaden harm [hɑ:m]
Schaf sheep [ʃi:p]
es **schaffen** to make it ['meɪk ˌɪt]; to create [kri:'eɪt]
Schal scarf [skɑ:f]
Schale bowl [bəʊl]
Schallplatte record ['rekɔ:d]
in **Scharen** in droves [ɪn 'drəʊvz]
scharf sharply ['ʃɑ:pli]; spicy ['spaɪsi]
Schatz treasure ['treʒə]
Schau show [ʃəʊ]
schauen to look [lʊk]
Schauplatz setting ['setɪŋ]
schaurig gruesome ['gru:səm]
Schauspiel drama ['drɑ:mə]
Schauspieler actor ['æktə]
Schauspielerin actress ['æktrəs]
Scheibe slice [slaɪs]
sich **scheiden lassen** to get divorced [ˌget dɪ'vɔ:sd]
Scheiße shit [ʃɪt]
scheitern to go wrong [ˌgəʊ 'rɒŋ]
Scheune barn [bɑ:n]
schicken to send [send]
schieben to push [pʊʃ]
Schiedsrichter/-in referee (= ref) [ˌrefr'i:]; umpire ['ʌmpaɪə]
schiefgehen to to go wrong [ˌgəʊ 'rɒŋ]
schielen to squint [skwɪnt]
schießen to score [skɔ:]; to shoot [ʃu:t]
Schiff ship [ʃɪp]
Schild sign [saɪn]
Schildkröte tortoise ['tɔ:təs]
Schinken ham [hæm]
Schirmmütze cap [kæp]
Schlacht battle ['bætl]
schlafen to sleep [sli:p]
Schlafzimmer bedroom ['bedrʊm]
Schlag(anfall) stroke [strəʊk]
schlagen to beat [bi:t]; to hit [hɪt]; to pound [paʊnd]; to whip [wɪp]
Schläger racket ['rækɪt]
Schlagzeile headline ['hedlaɪn]
Schlagzeug drum [drʌm]
sich **schlängeln** to wind [waɪnd]
schlau smart [smɑ:t]; clever ['klevə]
schlecht bad [bæd]
sich schlecht fühlen to not feel well [ˌnɒt fi:l 'wel]
schlechter worse [wɜ:s]
am **schlechtesten** the worst [ðə 'wɜ:st]
schlechteste/-r/-s the worst [ðə 'wɜ:st]
schließen to close [kləʊz]
Schließfach locker ['lɒkə]
schließlich finally ['faɪnəli]
schlimm nasty ['nɑ:sti]
am **schlimmsten** the worst [ðə 'wɜ:st]
schlimmste/-r/-s the worst [ðə 'wɜ:st]
Schlittschuhlaufen ice skating ['aɪs ˌskeɪtɪŋ]
Schlitz slot [slɒt]
Schloss castle ['kɑ:sl]
Schlucht gorge [gɔ:dʒ]
Schluss ending ['endɪŋ]
Schlüssel key [ki:]
Schlüsselwort keyword ['ki:wɜ:d]
schmal narrow ['nærəʊ]
schmecken to taste [teɪst]
schmerzhaft painful ['peɪnfʊl]; sore [sɔ:]
Schminke make-up ['meɪkʌp]
Schmuck jewelry *(AE)* ['dʒu:əlri]

Schmuggler/-in smuggler ['smʌglə]
schmutzig dirty ['dɜ:ti]
schneiden to cut [kʌt]
schnell quickly ['kwɪkli]; fast [fɑ:st]; quick [kwɪk]
schneller faster ['fɑ:stə]
Schnellimbiss snack bar ['snæk ˌbɑ:]
schnüffeln to sniff [snɪf]
schnupfen *(Kokain usw.)* to snort [snɔ:t]
schnuppern to sniff [snɪf]
schocken to shock [ʃɒk]
schockieren to shock [ʃɒk]
schockierend shocking ['ʃɒkɪŋ]
Schokocrossie chocolate crispie [ˌtʃɒklət 'krɪspi]
Schokolade chocolate ['tʃɒklət]
schon yet [jet]; already [ɔ:l'redi]
schön fine [faɪn]; beautiful ['bju:tɪfʊl]; lovely ['lʌvli]; nice [naɪs]
schottisch Scottish ['skɒtɪʃ]
Schrank cupboard ['kʌbəd]
Schrecken horror ['hɒrə]
schrecklich terribly ['terəbli]; terrible ['terəbl]; awful ['ɔ:fl]
schreiben to write [raɪt]
Schreibtisch desk [desk]
schreien to scream [skri:m]; to cry [kraɪ]; to shout [ʃaʊt]
Schritt footstep ['fʊtstep]; step [step]
Schuh shoe [ʃu:]
Schule school [sku:l]
Schüler/-in pupil ['pju:pl]; student *(AE)* ['stu:dnt]
Schülervertretung student council [ˌstju:dnt 'kaʊnsl]
Schulhof playground ['pleɪgraʊnd]
Schulleiter/-in headteacher [ˌhed'ti:tʃə]; principal *(AE)* ['prɪntsəpl]
Schulranzen school bag ['sku:l bæg]
Schultasche school bag ['sku:l bæg]
Schulter shoulder ['ʃəʊldə]
Schulversammlung assembly [ə'sembli]
Schuppen shed [ʃed]
Schuss *(Fußball)* kick [kɪk]
Schüssel bowl [bəʊl]
Schusswaffe gun [gʌn]
schütteln to shake [ʃeɪk]
Schutzbrille goggles pl. ['gɒglz]
schützen to protect [prə'tekt]
(Schutz-)Hülle cover ['kʌvə]
schwach lame [leɪm]; weak [wi:k]
Schwamm sponge [spʌndʒ]
Schwanz tail [teɪl]
schwarz black [blæk]
Schwarzes Brett notice board ['nəʊtɪs bɔ:d]
schweben to glide [glaɪd]; to float [fləʊt]
Schweif tail [teɪl]
Schwein pig [pɪg]
Schweinefleisch pork [pɔ:k]
schwer heavy ['hevi]; difficult ['dɪfɪklt]; hard [hɑ:d]
Schwerkraft gravity ['grævəti]
schwierig difficult ['dɪfɪklt]; hard [hɑ:d]
schwierige Aufgabe problem ['prɒbləm]
Schwimmbad swimming pool ['swɪmɪŋ ˌpu:l]
Schwimmbrille goggles pl. ['gɒglz]
schwimmen to swim [swɪm]
schwimmen gehen to go swimming [gəʊ 'swɪmɪŋ]
schwindelig dizzy ['dɪzi]
schwören to swear [sweə]
Science-Fiction science fiction [ˌsaɪəns 'fɪkʃn]
sechste/-r/-s sixth [sɪksθ]
See lake [leɪk]
seekrank seasick ['si:sɪk]
segeln to sail [seɪl]
sehen to look [lʊk]; to see [si:]
Sehenswürdigkeit attraction [ə'trækʃn]; sight [saɪt]
sehr a lot [ə 'lɒt]; very ['veri]
sich **sehr bemühen** to try hard [traɪ 'hɑ:d]
Sei vorsichtig! Be careful! [ˌbi: 'keəfl]
Seil rope [rəʊp]
sein to be [bi:]
sein/-e his [hɪz]; its [ɪts]
seine/-r/-s his [hɪz]
seit since [sɪns]; for [fɔ:]
seitdem ever since [ˌevə 'sɪnts]; since [sɪns]
Seite side [saɪd]; page [peɪdʒ]
Seitenstraße side street ['saɪd ˌstri:t]
Sekretär/-in secretary ['sekrətri]
Sekunde second ['seknd]
selbstgemacht home-made [ˌhəʊm'meɪd]
selbstverständlich naturally ['nætʃrəli]; of course [ˌəv 'kɔ:s]
seltsam weird [wɪəd]; odd [ɒd]; strange [streɪndʒ]
Semester semester *(AE)* [sɪ'mestə]; term [tɜ:m]
Sendegerät transmitter [ˌtrænz'mɪtə]
senden to send [send]; to transmit [trænz'mɪt]
Sendung program *(AE)* ['prəʊgræm]
Senioren senior citizens [ˌsi:niə 'sɪtɪznz]
Sensation sensation [sen'seɪʃn]
September September [sep'tembə]
Serviette napkin ['næpkɪn]
setzen to put [pʊt]
sich setzen to sit [sɪt]
Shirt shirt [ʃɜ:t]
Show show [ʃəʊ]
Showgeschäft show-business ['ʃəʊ ˌbɪznɪs]
sicher safe [seɪf]; safely ['seɪfli]; sure [ʃɔ:]
sichergehen to make sure [ˌmeɪk 'ʃɔ:]
Sicherungskasten fuse-box ['fju:z bɒks]
Sicht view [vju:]
sie she [ʃi:]; them [ðem]; her [hɜ:]; they [ðeɪ]
Sie you [ju:]
siebte/-r/-s seventh ['sevnθ]
Signal signal ['sɪgnl]
singen to sing [sɪŋ]
Single single ['sɪŋgl]
Sir *(Anrede für einen Adeligen oder Ritter)* Sir [sɜ:]
Sirup syrup ['sɪrəp]
Situation situation [ˌsɪtju'eɪʃn]
Sitz seat [si:t]
sitzen to sit [sɪt]
Skateboard skateboard ['skeɪtbɔ:d]
Skateboard fahren to skateboard ['skeɪtbɔ:d]
Skateboarder/-in skateboarder ['skeɪtbɔ:də]
Skatepark skatepark ['skeɪtpɑ:k]
Skelett skeleton ['skelɪtn]
skeptisch skeptical ['skeptɪkl]
Ski ski [ski:]
Skifahren skiing ['ski:ɪŋ]
Skilaufen gehen to go skiing [gəʊ 'ski:ɪŋ]
Smalltalk small talk ['smɔ:l ˌtɔ:k]
Smiley smiley ['smaɪli]
SMS text message ['tekst ˌmesɪdʒ]
Snack snack [snæk]
so so [səʊ]
sobald as soon as [əz 'su:n‿əz]
sodass so that [səʊ 'ðæt]
sofort right away ['raɪt ˌəweɪ]
Softball softball ['sɒftbɔ:l]
Software software ['sɒftweə]
sogar even ['i:vn]
Sohn son [sʌn]
solange as long as [əz 'lɒŋ‿əz]
solch such [sʌtʃ]
sollen shall [ʃæl]; should [ʃʊd]; ought to [ɔ:t]
Solo- solo ['səʊlə]
Sommer summer ['sʌmə]

Sommerlager summer camp ['sʌmə ˌkæmp]
Sonnabend Saturday ['sætədeɪ]
Sonne sun [sʌn]
Sonnenbrille sunglasses pl. ['sʌnˌglɑ:sɪz]
Sonnenschein sunshine ['sʌnʃaɪn]
sonnig sunny ['sʌni]
Sonntag Sunday ['sʌndeɪ]
sonst else [els]
Sorge worry ['wʌri]
sich **Sorgen machen** to worry ['wʌri]
sortieren to sort [sɔ:t]
Soße sauce [sɔ:s]
Souvenirshop gift shop ['gɪft ˌʃɒp]
sowieso anyway ['eniweɪ]
sowohl ... als auch both ... and [bəʊθ]
Spaghetti spaghetti [spə'geti]
spanisch Spanish ['spænɪʃ]
sparen to save [seɪv]
Spaß fun [fʌn]
spät late [leɪt]
Spaziergang walk [wɔ:k]
Spezialeffekte *(von Computern erzeugter Bild- oder Toneffekt)* special effects [ˌspeʃl ɪ'fekts]
Speck bacon ['beɪkn]
Speicher attic ['ætɪk]
speichern to save [seɪv]
Speisekarte menu ['menju:]
Sperrstunde curfew ['kɜ:fju:]
Spezialität special ['speʃl]
Spiegel mirror ['mɪrə]
Spiel match [mætʃ]; game [geɪm]
spielen to act [ækt]; to play [pleɪ]
fair spielen to play fairly [ˌpleɪ 'feəli]
Spieler/-in player ['pleɪə]
Spielfeld pitch [pɪtʃ]
Spielkarte card [kɑ:d]
Spielplatz playground ['pleɪgraʊnd]
Spinne spider ['spaɪdə]
spitz zulaufend pointed ['pɔɪntɪd]
spitze wicked ['wɪkɪd]
Spitze top [tɒp]
Sport PE (= Physical Education) [ˌpi:'i: = ˌfɪzɪkl‿edʒʊ'keɪʃn]; sport [spɔ:t]
Sport treiben to exercise ['eksəsaɪz]
Sportfeld field ['fi:ld]
Sportfest sports day ['spɔ:ts deɪ]
Sporthalle sports hall ['spɔ:ts ˌhɔ:l]
spotten to sneer [snɪə]
spöttisch grinsen to sneer [snɪə]
Sprache speech [spi:tʃ]; language ['læŋgwɪdʒ]
Sprachebene register ['redʒɪstə]
Sprechchor chant [tʃɑ:nt]
sprechen to speak [spi:k]; to talk [tɔ:k]
Sprecher/-in speaker ['spi:kə]
Sprechgesang chant [tʃɑ:nt]
springen to leap [li:p]; to jump [dʒʌmp]
Sprungrampe ramp [ræmp]
Spülbecken sink [sɪŋk]
Spur track [træk]
Staat state [steɪt]
Stadion stadium ['steɪdiəm]
Stadt town [taʊn]
Stadtgemeinde borough ['bʌrə]
Stadtplan map [mæp]
Stadtrat council ['kaʊnsl]
im **Stadtzentrum** downtown *(AE)* [ˌdaʊn'taʊn]
Stahl steel [sti:l]
Stall barn [bɑ:n]
Stamm tribe [traɪb]
Stammbaum family tree [ˌfæməli 'tri:]
von ... **stammen** to hail from [heɪl 'frəm]
Stammes- tribal ['traɪbl]
Stand stall [stɔ:l]
Standbild statue ['stætʃu:]
Star star [stɑ:]
stark powerful ['paʊəfl]; strong [strɒŋ]
Start take-off ['teɪk‿ɒf]
starten to take off [teɪk‿'ɒf]
Station station ['steɪʃn]
Statistik statistics *(pl)* [stə'tɪstɪks]
statt instead of [ɪn'sted‿əv]
stattfinden to take place [ˌteɪk 'pleɪs]
Statue statue ['stætʃu:]
staubig dusty ['dʌsti]
Stecker plug [plʌg]
Steelband *(Band mit Trommeln aus Stahlblech)* steel band [ˌsti:l 'bænd]
stehen to stand [stænd]
stehlen to steal [sti:l]
steigen to climb [klaɪm]; to rise [raɪz]
Stein rock [rɒk]; stone [stəʊn]
Steinzeit Stone Age ['stəʊn ˌeɪdʒ]
Stelle place [pleɪs]
stellen to put [pʊt]
(eine Frage) **stellen** to ask [ɑ:sk]
sterben to die [daɪ]
Stern star [stɑ:]
Sternwarte observatory [əb'zɜ:vətri]
Steuerrad wheel [wi:l]
Stichwort prompt [prɒmt]; headword ['hedwɜ:d]
Stiefel boot [bu:t]
Stil style [staɪl]
still quiet ['kwaɪət]
Stimme voice [vɔɪs]
Stockwerk story *(AE)* ['stɔ:ri]
stolpern to trip [trɪp]
stolz proud [praʊd]
Stöpsel plug [plʌg]
stören to bother ['bɒðə]
Stoß kick [kɪk]
stoßen to push [pʊʃ]; to hit [hɪt]
Strafzettel ticket ['tɪkɪt]
Strand beach [bi:tʃ]
Straße street [stri:t]
Straßenbahn cable car ['keɪbl ˌkɑ:]
Streichelzoo pets corner [ˌpets 'kɔ:nə]
streichen to delete [dɪ'li:t]; to paint [peɪnt]
Streifen stripe [straɪp]
Streit fight [faɪt]; argument ['ɑ:gjəmənt]
(sich) **streiten** to have an argument [ˌhæv‿ən‿'ɑ:gjəmənt]; to fight [faɪt]; to argue ['ɑ:gju:]
streng strict [strɪkt]
Stress stress [stres]
Strom electricity [ˌelɪk'trɪsəti]
stromabwärts downriver [daʊn'rɪvə]
Stromausfall blackout ['blækaʊt]
Stromschnellen rapids pl. ['ræpɪdz]
Strömung current ['kʌrnt]
Stück slice [slaɪs]; piece [pi:s]
Student/-in student ['stju:dnt]
Studio studio ['stju:diəʊ]
Stufe step [step]
Stuhl chair [tʃeə]
stumm silent ['saɪlənt]
Stunde hour [aʊə]
Stundenplan schedule *(AE)* ['skedʒu:l]; timetable ['taɪmˌteɪbl]
Sturm storm [stɔ:m]
stürmisch stormy ['stɔ:mi]
stürzen to fall [fɔ:l]
Suchbegriff search term ['sɜ:tʃ ˌtɜ:m]
suchen to search [sɜ:tʃ]; to look for ['lʊk fɔ:]
Suchende/-r seeker ['si:kə]
Suchmaschine search engine ['sɜ:tʃ ˌendʒɪn]
Sucht addiction [ə'dɪkʃn]
süchtig nach ... sein to be addicted to ... [bi ə'dɪktɪd‿tʊ]
Süden south [saʊθ]
Summen hum [hʌm]
super super ['su:pə]; awesome ['ɔ:səm]
Superlativ superlative [su:'pɜ:lətɪv]
Supermarkt supermarket ['su:pəˌmɑ:kɪt]

German – English

Superstar superstar ['su:pəstɑ:]
Suppe soup [su:p]
surfen to surf [sɜ:f]
Surfer/-in surfer ['sɜ:fə]
süß cute [kju:t]; sweet [swi:t]
süßsauer sweet and sour [ˌswi:t ən 'saʊə]
Sweatshirt sweatshirt ['swetʃɜ:t]
Swimmingpool swimming pool ['swɪmɪŋ ˌpu:l]
Symbol symbol ['sɪmbl]
System system ['sɪstəm]
Szene scene [si:n]

T

Tabelle chart [tʃɑ:t]; grid [grɪd]
Tafel bar [bɑ:]; board [bɔ:d]
Tag day [deɪ]
Tagebuch diary ['daɪəri]
Tageslichtprojektor overhead projector [ˌəʊvəhed prə'dʒektə]
Talkshow talk show ['tɔ:k ˌʃəʊ]
Tankstelle garage ['gærɪdʒ]
Tanne pine [paɪn]
Tante aunt [ɑ:nt]
Tanz dance [dɑ:ns]
tanzen to dance [dɑ:ns]
Tänzer/-in dancer ['dɑ:nsə]
Tanz(veranstaltung) dance [dɑ:ns]
tapfer gritty ['grɪti]; brave [breɪv]
Tasche bag [bæg]
Taschendieb/-in pickpocket ['pɪkˌpɒkɪt]
Taschengeld pocket money ['pɒkɪt ˌmʌni]
Tasse cup [kʌp]
tätig active ['æktɪv]
Tätowierung tattoo [tæt'u:]
Tatsache fact [fækt]
tatsächlich in fact [ɪn 'fækt]
tätscheln to pat [pæt]
taub deaf [def]
Taube pigeon ['pɪdʒən]
Taucherbrille goggles ['gɒglz]
Tausch exchange [ɪks'tʃeɪndʒ]
tauschen to exchange [ɪks'tʃeɪndʒ]; to change [tʃeɪndʒ]
täuschen to trick [trɪk]
Täuschung illusion [ɪ'lu:ʒn]
tausend thousand ['θaʊznd]
Taxi cab *(AE)* [kæb]; taxi ['tæksi]
Team team [ti:m]
Technik technology [tek'nɒlədʒi]
Technologie technology [tek'nɒlədʒi]
Tee tea [ti:]
Teenager/-in teenager ['ti:neɪdʒə]
Teil piece [pi:s]; part [pɑ:t]
teilen to share [ʃeə]
teilnehmen to take part [teɪk 'pɑ:t]; to enter ['entə]
Telefon phone (= telephone) [fəʊn = 'telɪfəʊn]
Telefonnummer phone number ['fəʊn ˌnʌmbə]
Teller plate [pleɪt]
Tennis tennis ['tenɪs]
Terminkalender diary ['daɪəri]
Terrorist/-in terrorist ['terərɪst]
Test test [test]
teuer expensive [ɪk'spensɪv]
Text text [tekst]
Texter/-in songwriter ['sɒŋraɪtə]
Textnachricht (SMS) schicken to text [tekst]
Theater theater *(AE)* ['θɪətə]; theatre ['θɪətə]
Theaterklub Drama Club ['drɑ:mə ˌklʌb]
Theaterstück play [pleɪ]
Theke counter ['kaʊntə]
Thema subject ['sʌbdʒekt]; topic ['tɒpɪk]
Thunfisch tuna ['tju:nə]
ticken to tick [tɪk]
Ticket ticket ['tɪkɪt]
tief deep [di:p]
Tiefkühl- frozen ['frəʊzn]
Tier animal ['ænɪml]
Tierfutter animal snacks ['ænɪml ˌsnæks]
Tierwelt wildlife ['waɪldlaɪf]
Tipp tip [tɪp]
tippen to type [taɪp]
Tisch table ['teɪbl]
den **Tisch decken** to lay the table ['leɪ ðə ˌteɪbl]
Tischtennis table tennis ['teɪbl ˌtenɪs]
Titel title ['taɪtl]
Titelseite front page ['frʌnt ˌpeɪdʒ]
Toast toast [təʊst]
Toastbrot toast [təʊst]
Tochter daughter ['dɔ:tə]
Tod death [deθ]
Toilette restroom *(AE)* ['restru:m]; toilet ['tɔɪlət]
toll amazing [ə'meɪzɪŋ]; fantastic [fæn'tæstɪk]; super ['su:pə]; great [greɪt]; awesome ['ɔ:səm]
Tomate tomato [tə'mɑ:təʊ]
Ton sound [saʊnd]
Tonne *(Gewicht)* ton [tʌn]
Tor gate [geɪt]; goal [gəʊl]
Torpfosten goal post ['gəʊl pəʊst]
Torschütze/Torschützin scorer ['skɔ:rə]
Torwart/-in goalkeeper ['gəʊlˌki:pə]
tot dead [ded]
töten to kill [kɪl]
Tour tour [tʊə]; journey ['dʒɜ:ni]
Tourist/-in tourist ['tʊərɪst]
Touristik-Information tourist information centre [ˌtʊərɪst ɪnfə'meɪʃn sentə]
Tradition tradition [trə'dɪʃn]
traditionell traditional [trə'dɪʃənl]
tragen to carry ['kæri]; to wear [weə]
Trainer/-in coach [kəʊtʃ]
trainieren to train [treɪn]; to exercise ['eksəsaɪz]
Training training ['treɪnɪŋ]; practice ['præktɪs]
Traktor tractor ['træktə]
Tratsch gossip ['gɒsɪp]
Traum dream [dri:m]
träumen to dream [dri:m]
traurig sad [sæd]
treffen to meet [mi:t]; to see [si:]; to hit [hɪt]
sich treffen to hang out [hæŋ 'aʊt]; to meet [mi:t]
Treffen meeting ['mi:tɪŋ]
treiben to float [fləʊt]
Trend trend [trend]
sich **trennen** to split up [ˌsplɪt‿'ʌp]
Treppe stairs [steəz]
treten to kick [kɪk]
Tretroller kickboard ['kɪkbɔ:d]
Treue allegiance [ə'li:dʒənts]
Tribüne stand [stænd]; platform ['plætfɔ:m]
Trick trick [trɪk]
Trikot shirt [ʃɜ:t]
Trimester term [tɜ:m]
trinken to drink [drɪŋk]
Trinkgeld tip [tɪp]
Tritt footstep ['fʊtstep]
trocken dry [draɪ]
Trommel drum [drʌm]
Trottel jerk [dʒɜ:k]
Truthahn turkey ['tɜ:ki]
tschüss goodbye [gʊd'baɪ]; Bye! [baɪ]
T-Shirt T-shirt ['ti:ʃɜ:t]
tun to put [pʊt]; to do [du:]; to make [meɪk]
Tunnel tunnel ['tʌnl]
Tür door [dɔ:]
türkisch Turkish ['tɜ:kɪʃ]
Türklingel doorbell ['dɔ:bel]
Turm tower ['taʊə]

Turnschuh trainer ['treɪnə]
Tüte bag [bæg]
Typ type [taɪp]; bloke [bləʊk]
Typisch! Typical! ['tɪpɪkl]

U

Übelkeit verspüren to feel sick [fi:l 'sɪk]
üben to practise ['præktɪs]; to practice *(AE)* ['præktɪs]
über through [θru:]; across [ə'krɒs]; above [ə'bʌv]; over ['əʊvə]
über Nacht overnight [ˌəʊvə'naɪt]
überall everywhere ['evriweə]
überfliegen to skim [skɪm]
überglücklich over the moon [ˌəʊvə ðə 'mu:n]
überhaupt at all [æt 'ɔ:l]
überhaupt nicht not at all [ˌnɒt‿ət‿'ɔ:l]
übernachten to stay [steɪ]
überprüfen to check [tʃek]
überqueren to cross [krɒs]
überraschen to surprise [sə'praɪz]
überrascht surprised [sə'praɪzd]
Überraschung surprise [sə'praɪz]
überschnappen to go bananas [gəʊ 'bənɑ:nəz]
Überschrift headline ['hedlaɪn]; heading ['hedɪŋ]; title ['taɪtl]
Übersetzung translation [trænz'leɪʃn]
etw. **übertreiben** to overdo sth. [ˌəʊvə'du:]
überwältigt overwhelmed [ˌəʊvə'welmd]
übrigens actually [ˌæktʃʊəli]; by the way [ˌbaɪ ðə 'weɪ]
Übung practice ['præktɪs]; exercise ['eksəsaɪz]
UFO UFO ['ju: ef 'əʊ]
Uhr clock [klɒk]; o'clock [ə'klɒk]
Uhrturm clock tower ['klɒk ˌtaʊə]
Uhrzeit time [taɪm]
Ultraschall(untersuchung) scan [skæn]
um at [æt; ət]
um … herum round … [raʊnd]; around … [ə'raʊnd]
Um Antwort wird gebeten. RSVP [ˌɑ:r‿es vi:'pi:]
sich **umdrehen** to turn round [ˌtɜ:n‿'raʊnd]; to turn [tɜ:n]
umfallen to fall over [fɔ:l‿'əʊvə]
Umfrage survey ['sɜ:veɪ]
Umgebung surroundings [sə'raʊndɪŋz]
umher about [ə'baʊt]
umringt sein/werden to be mobbed [bi 'mɒbd]
umringt sein von to be surrounded [ˌbi: sə'raʊndɪd]
Umschlag cover ['kʌvə]
umschreiben to rewrite [ˌri:'rait]
Umstandswort adverb ['ædvɜ:b]
umsteigen to change [tʃeɪndʒ]
umstoßen to knock over [ˌnɒk 'əʊvə]
Umtausch exchange [ɪks'tʃeɪndʒ]
umtauschen to exchange [ɪks'tʃeɪndʒ]
umziehen to move [mu:v]
sich umziehen to change [tʃeɪndʒ]
Umzug *(bei Festen, Karneval)* parade [pə'reɪd]; procession [prə'seʃn]
unabhängig independent [ˌɪndɪ'pendənt]
unaufgeräumt untidy [ʌn'taɪdi]
und and [ænd; ən]
unerlaubt illegally [ɪ'li:gli]; illegal [ɪ'li:gl]
unfair unfair [ʌn'feə]
Unfall accident ['æksɪdnt]
ungefähr about [ə'baʊt]
ungerecht unfair [ʌn'feə]
ungesund unhealthy [ʌn'helθi]
unglaublich amazing [ə'meɪzɪŋ]
unglücklich unhappy [ʌn'hæpi]
unheimlich scary ['skeəri]
unhöflich rude [ru:d]
Uniform uniform ['ju:nɪfɔ:m]
Universität university [ˌju:nɪ'vɜ:səti]
unordentlich untidy [ʌn'taɪdi]
Unordnung mess [mes]
unregelmäßig irregular [ɪ'regjələ]
uns us [ʌs]
unser/-e our [aʊə]
unsere/-r/-s ours [aʊəz]
unteilbar indivisible [ˌɪndɪ'vɪzəbl]
unten below [bɪ'ləʊ]; downstairs [ˌdaʊn'steəz]
bis ganz unten to the bottom [tə ðe 'bɒtəm]
ganz unten at the bottom [æt ðə 'bɒtəm]
nach **unten zeigend** drooping ['dru:pɪŋ]
unter under ['ʌndə]; below [bɪ'ləʊ]
Unterdrückung oppression [ə'preʃn]
Untergeschoss basement ['beɪsmənt]
sich **unterhalten** to chat [tʃæt]
unterhaltsam enjoyable [ɪn'ðʒɔɪəbl]
Unterhaltung entertainment [ˌentə'teɪnmənt]; talk [tɔ:k]
Unterhemd vest [vest]
Unternehmen company ['kʌmpəni]; firm [fɜ:m]
unterrichten to teach [ti:tʃ]
Unterrichtsstunde period ['pɪəriəd]; lesson ['lesn]; class [klɑ:s]
Unterschied difference ['dɪfrənts]
unterschiedlich different ['dɪfrnt]
unterschreiben to sign [saɪn]
unterstreichen to underline [ˌʌndə'laɪn]
unterstützen to support [sə'pɔ:t]
untersuchen to investigate [ɪn'vestɪgeɪt]
Untersuchung test [test]; survey ['sɜ:veɪ]
unterwegs out and about ['aʊt‿nd‿ə'baʊt]
unvergesslich unforgettable [ˌʌnfə'getəbl]
Uraufführung premiere ['premieə]
Urlaub vacation *(AE)* [və'keɪʃn]; holiday ['hɒlədeɪ]

V

Vase vase [vɑ:z]
Vater father ['fɑ:ðə]
Vati dad [dæd]
verabreden to arrange [ə'reɪndʒ]
sich verabreden to date [deɪt]
Verabredung date [deɪt]
(sich) **verändern** to change [tʃeɪndʒ]
Veränderung change [tʃeɪndʒ]
Veranstalter/-in organizer ['ɔ:gənaɪzə]
Veranstaltung event [ɪ'vent]
verantwortlich responsible [rɪ'spɒnsəbl]
verärgert angry ['æŋgri]
Verb verb [vɜ:b]
verbinden to join [dʒɔɪn]; to connect [kə'nekt]
(sich mit jdm.) in **Verbindung setzen** to contact (s.o.) ['kɒntækt]
Verbrechen crime [kraɪm]
verbringen to spend [spend]
verdienen to earn [ɜ:n]
Verein club [klʌb]
Vereinbarung arrangement [ə'reɪndʒmənt]
Verfärbung stain [steɪn]
verfolgen to chase [tʃeɪs]
zur **Verfügung stellen** to provide [prəʊ'vaɪd]
Vergangenheit past [pɑ:st]; past tense [ˌpɑ:st 'tens]

einfache **Vergangenheit** simple past [ˌsɪmpl ˈpɑːst]
vergessen to forget [fəˈget]
sich **vergewissern** to make sure [ˌmeɪk ˈʃɔː]
vergleichen to compare [kəmˈpeə]
verhaften to arrest [əˈrest]
sich **verhalten** to act [ækt]
Verhalten behaviour [bɪˈheɪvjə]
verheiratet married [ˈmærid]
sich **verirren** to get lost [ˌget ˈlɒst]
verkaufen to sell [sel]
zu **verkaufen** for sale [ˌfɔː ˈseɪl]
Verkäufer/-in assistant [əˈsɪstnt]
Verkehr traffic [ˈtræfɪk]
Verkehrsampel traffic lights [ˈtræfɪk ˌlaɪts]
Verkehrsmittel transport [ˈtrænspɔːt]
verkehrsreich busy [ˈbɪzi]
Verkehrssprache lingua franca [ˌlɪŋgwə ˈfræŋkə]
verlassen to leave [liːv]
sich **verlaufen** to get lost [ˌget ˈlɒst]
verlegen embarrassed [ɪmˈbærəst]
verletzen to hurt [hɜːt]
Verletzung harm [hɑːm]
verlieren to lose [luːz]
Verlierer/-in loser [ˈluːzə]
Verlies dungeon [ˈdʌndʒən]
vermischen to blend [blend]
vermissen to miss [mɪs]
Vermittlung communication [kəˌmjuːnɪˈkeɪʃn]
Verneinung negation [nɪˈgeɪʃn]
vernichten to destroy [dɪˈstrɔɪ]
verpassen to miss [mɪs]
verreisen to go away [ˌgəʊ əˈweɪ]
verrückt mad [mæd]; crazy [ˈkreɪzi]
(sich) verrückt machen to get into a state [get‿ɪntə‿ə ˈsteɪt]
jdn. verrückt machen to drive s.o. crazy [ˌdraɪv … ˈkreɪzi]
verrückt sein nach to be mad about … [biː ˈmæd‿əˌbaʊt]; to be crazy about [biː ˈkreɪzi əˌbaʊt]
verrückt werden to go crazy [ˌgəʊ ˈkreɪzi]; to go bananas [gəʊ ˈbənɑːnəz]
verschenken to give away [ˈgɪv‿əweɪ]
verschieden different [ˈdɪfrnt]
verschiedene several [ˈsevrəl]
Verschwinde/-t! Get out of here! [ˌget aʊt‿əv ˈhɪə]
Version version [ˈvɜːʃn]
versprechen to promise [ˈprɒmɪs]
Verständigung communication [kəˌmjuːnɪˈkeɪʃn]
Verständnis comprehension [ˌkɒmprɪˈhentʃn]
verständnisvoll sympathetic [ˌsɪmpəˈθetɪk]
Verstärker booster [ˈbuːstə]
verstecken to hide [haɪd]
sich verstecken to hide [haɪd]
verstehen to understand [ˌʌndəˈstænd]
Versuch experiment [ɪkˈsperɪment]
versuchen to try [traɪ]
vertrauen to trust [trʌst]
vertraut familiar [fəˈmɪliə]
sich **verwandeln** to transform [ˌtrænsˈfɔːm]
sich verwandeln in to turn into [ˈtɜːn‿ɪntʊ]
Verweis ticket [ˈtɪkɪt]
verwenden to use [juːz]
Verwendung use [juːs]
Verwirrung confusion [kənˈfjuːʒn]
Verzeihung! Sorry! [ˈsɒri]
Video video [ˈvɪdiəʊ]
viel a lot [ə ˈlɒt]; lots (of) [lɒts]; much [mʌtʃ]
viel/-e a lot of [ə ˈlɒt‿əv]
viel Glück good luck [ˌgʊd ˈlʌk]
viele many [ˈmeni]
Viele Grüße (am Briefende) Best wishes, [ˌbest ˈwɪʃɪz]
vielleicht maybe [ˈmeɪbi]
Viertel neighborhood *(AE)* [ˈneɪbəhʊd]; quarter [ˈkwɔːtə]
vierte/-r/-s fourth [fɔːθ]
virtuell virtual [ˈvɜːtʃuəl]
Vitamin vitamin [ˈvɪtəmɪn]
Vogel bird [bɜːd]
Vokabular vocabulary [vəˈkæbjəlri]
voll full [fʊl]
Volleyball volleyball [ˈvɒlibɔːl]
völlig quite [kwaɪt]
von of [ɒv]; from [frɒm]; by [baɪ]
von Anfang an right from the start [ˈraɪt frəm ðə ˌstɑːt]
vor before [bɪˈfɔː]; outside [ˌaʊtˈsaɪd]; in front of [ˌɪn ˈfrʌnt‿əv]
vor … … ago [əˈgəʊ]
vor allem especially [ɪˈspeʃəli]
vor langer Zeit a long time ago [ə lɒŋ ˈtaɪm ˌəgəʊ]
voraussagbar predictable [prɪˈdɪktəbl]
vorbei over [ˈəʊvə]
vorbeikommen to come along [ˌkʌm‿əˈlɒŋ]
Vordergrund foreground [ˈfɔːgraʊnd]
Vorfahr ancestor [ˈænsestə]
Vorhang curtain [ˈkɜːtn]
vorher before [bɪˈfɔː]
vorhersehbar predictable [prɪˈdɪktəbl]
Vormittag morning [ˈmɔːnɪŋ]
vormittags am [ˌeɪˈem]
Vorrichtung device [dɪˈvaɪs]
Vorschlag suggestion [səˈdʒestʃn]
vorschlagen to suggest [səˈdʒest]
vorsichtig careful [ˈkeəfl]
Vorsingen audition [ɔːˈdɪʃn]
Vorspeise starter [ˈstɑːtə]
Vorspielen audition [ɔːˈdɪʃn]
Vorsprechen audition [ɔːˈdɪʃn]
vorstellen to introduce [ˌɪntrəˈdjuːs]; to present [prɪˈzent]
sich vorstellen to imagine [ɪˈmædʒɪn]
Vorstellung performance [pəˈfɔːməns]
Vortanzen audition [ɔːˈdɪʃn]
Vorteil advantage [ədˈvɑːntɪdʒ]
Vortrag speech [spiːtʃ]; talk [tɔːk]
vorziehen to prefer [prəˈfɜː]

W

wach awake [əˈweɪk]
Wache guard [gɑːd]
wachsen to grow [grəʊ]; to rise [raɪz]
Wachsfigur waxwork [ˈwækswɜːk]
Wächter/-in guard [gɑːd]
etwas **wagen** to take your chance [ˌteɪk jɔː ˈtʃɑːns]
Wahl election [ɪˈlekʃn]
Wahlmöglichkeit choice [tʃɔɪs]
wählen to elect [ɪˈlekt]; to vote [vəʊt]
wahr true [truː]
wahr werden to come true [kʌm ˈtruː]
während while [waɪl]; during [ˈdjʊərɪŋ]
Wahrheit truth [truːθ]
wahrscheinlich probably [ˈprɒbəbli]
Wahrzeichen landmark [ˈlændmɑːk]
Wald wood [wʊd]; forest [ˈfɒrɪst]
Waliser/-in Welsh [welʃ]
walisisch Welsh [welʃ]
Wand wall [wɔːl]
Wanderarbeiter/-in migrant worker [ˌmaɪgrnt ˈwɜːkə]
wandern to take a hike [ˌteɪk‿ə ˈhaɪk]
Wandern hiking [ˈhaɪkɪŋ]
Wanderung hike [haɪk]; walk [wɔːk]
eine Wanderung machen to take a hike [ˌteɪk‿ə ˈhaɪk]
wann when [wen]
Warenhaus department store [dɪˈpɑːtmənt ˌstɔː]

warm warm [wɔ:m]
warten to wait [weɪt]
Warteschlange line *(AE)* [laɪn]; queue [kju:]
Wärter/-in guard [gɑ:d]
warum why [waɪ]
was what [wɒt]
Waschbecken sink [sɪŋk]
waschen to wash [wɒʃ]
Wasser water ['wɔ:tə]
Wasserhahn faucet *(AE)* ['fɔ:sɪt]
Wassermotorrad jet ski ['dʒet ˌski:]
Web- web [web]
Webcam webcam ['webkæm]
Website website ['websaɪt]
Wechselgeld change [tʃeɪndʒ]
Wecker alarm clock [ə'lɑ:m ˌklɒk]
weder ... noch not ... nor [nɔ:]
weg gone [gɒn]; away [ə'weɪ]
Weg track [træk]; trail [treɪl]; path [pɑ:θ]; way [weɪ]
wegbleiben to keep away [ˌki:p ə'weɪ]; to stay away [ˌsteɪ‿ə'weɪ]
wegfahren to go away [ˌgəʊ ə'weɪ]
weggehen to go away [ˌgəʊ ə'weɪ]
weglaufen to run away [rʌn‿ə'weɪ]
wegrennen to run away [rʌn‿ə'weɪ]
wegwerfen to throw away [ˌθrəʊ ə'weɪ]
wegen about [ə'baʊt]
weh tun to hurt [hɜ:t]
weiblich female ['fi:meɪl]
sich **weigern** wouldn't ['wʊdnt]
weinen to cry [kraɪ]
Weise way [weɪ]
weit far [fɑ:]
weit entfernt far away [ˌfɑ:r‿ə'weɪ]
weit weg far away [ˌfɑ:r‿ə'weɪ]
weiter further ['fɜ:ðə]; farther ['fɑ:ðə]
weitere more [mɔ:]
ein(e) weitere(-r/-s) another [ə'nʌðə]
weitergeben to pass [pɑ:s]
weitergehen to move along [mu:v ə'lɒŋ]
weitermachen to go on [gəʊ 'ɒn]
Weitsprung long jump ['lɒŋ ˌdʒʌmp]
Weizen wheat [wi:t]
welche/-r/-s which [wɪtʃ]
Welle wave [weɪv]
Wellenreiter/-in surfer ['sɜ:fə]
Welt world [wɜ:ld]
Weltall outer space [ˌaʊtə 'speɪs]
Weltraum outer space [ˌaʊtə 'speɪs]; space [speɪs]
wem who [hu:]
wen who [hu:]
wenden to turn [tɜ:n]
zu **wenig** short [ʃɔ:t]
weniger less [les]; fewer ['fju:ə]
wenigstens at least [ˌət 'li:st]
wenn if [ɪf]; when [wen]
wer who [hu:]
werden to become [bɪ'kʌm]; will [wɪl]
werfen to throw [θrəʊ]
wertvoll valuable ['væljuəbl]
wessen whose [hu:z]
Westen west [west]
Western *(Filmart)* western ['westən]
Wettbewerb competition [ˌkɒmpə'tɪʃn]
wetten to bet [bet]
Wetter weather ['weðə]
Wetterbericht weather report ['weðə ˌrɪpɔ:t]
Wetterstation weather station ['weðə ˌsteɪʃn]
Wettkampf competition [ˌkɒmpə'tɪʃn]
Wettkampfrichter/-in judge [dʒʌdʒ]
wichtig important [ɪm'pɔ:tnt]
wichtig nehmen to care [keə]
wider con [kɒn]
widmen to dedicate ['dedɪkeɪt]
wie as [æz]; how [haʊ]; like [laɪk]
wieder again [ə'gen]
wiedererkennen to recognize ['rekəgnaɪz]
wiederholen to repeat [rɪ'pi:t]
Wiederholung revision [rɪ'vɪʒn]
wiegen to weigh [weɪ]
Wiese field ['fi:ld]
wild wild [waɪld]; fierce [fɪəs]
Wilderer poacher ['pəʊtʃə]
Wildnis wilderness ['wɪldənəs]
Wildwasser-Rafting white water rafting [ˌwaɪt 'wɔ:tə 'ra:ftɪŋ]
Willkommen ... Welcome ... ['welkəm]
Wind wind [wɪnd]
sich **winden** to wind [waɪnd]
windig windy ['wɪndi]
Windsack windsock ['wɪndsɒk]
winken to wave [weɪv]
Winter winter ['wɪntə]
winzig tiny ['taɪni]
wir we [wi:]
Wirbel fuss [fʌs]
wird/werden nicht ... won't [wəʊnt]
wirklich really ['rɪəli]
Wirklichkeit reality [ri'æləti]
wissen to know [nəʊ]
Wissenschaftler/-in scientist ['saɪəntɪst]
Witz joke [dʒəʊk]
einen **Witz machen** to joke [dʒəʊk]
wo where [weə]
wo (auch) immer wherever [weə'revə]
wohin where [weə]
sich **wohl fühlen** to feel at home [ˌfi:l‿ət 'həʊm]
Wohltätigkeitsverein charity ['tʃærɪti]
wohnen to live [lɪv]
Wohnung apartment *(AE)* [ə'pɑ:tmənt]; flat [flæt]
Wohnzimmer living room ['lɪvɪŋ rʊm]
Wolke cloud [klaʊd]
Wolkenkratzer skyscraper ['skaɪˌskreɪpə]
wollen to want [wɒnt]
nicht wollen wouldn't ['wʊdnt]
Workshop workshop ['wɜ:kʃɒp]
Wort word [wɜ:d]
Wörterbuch dictionary ['dɪkʃənri]
Wortschatz vocabulary [və'kæbjəlri]
Wrack wreck [rek]
wund sore [sɔ:]
wunderbar wonderful ['wʌndəfl]
sich **wundern** to wonder ['wʌndə]
wunderschön beautiful ['bju:tɪfʊl]
wundervoll beautiful ['bju:tɪfʊl]
Wurst sausage ['sɒsɪdʒ]
Würstchen sausage ['sɒsɪdʒ]
würzig spicy ['spaɪsi]
Wüste desert ['dezət]
wütend angry ['æŋgri]
wütend sein to be mad [bɪ 'mæd]

Z

Zahl number ['nʌmbə]
zählen to count [kaʊnt]
Zauber- magic ['mædʒɪk]
Zauberei magic ['mædʒɪk]
Zauberer wizard ['wɪzəd]
Zauberkasten magic kit ['mædʒɪ‿kɪt]
Zauberlehrling apprentice wizard [əˌprentɪs 'wɪzəd]
Zaun fence [fens]
Zeche coal mine ['kəʊl maɪn]
Zeh toe [təʊ]
zehnte/-r/-s tenth [tenθ]
Zeichen signal ['sɪgnl]; sign [saɪn]
zeichnen to draw [drɔ:]
zeigen to show [ʃəʊ]; to point [pɔɪnt]
auf ... zeigen to point to ... [pɔɪnt 'tə]
Zeit time [taɪm]
Zeit(form) tense [tens]
Zeitleiste time line ['taɪm laɪn]
Zeitung newspaper ['nju:sˌpeɪpə]
Zeitungsladen newsagent ['nju:zˌeɪdʒnt]
zelten gehen to go camping [gəʊ 'kæmpɪŋ]

German – English

Zelten camping ['kæmpɪŋ]
Zeltplatz campsite ['kæmpsaɪt]
Zentrum center *(AE)* ['sentə]; centre ['sentə]
(zer)brechen to break [breɪk]
zerbrechlich breakable ['breɪkəbl]
Zeremonie ceremony ['serɪməni]
zerkratzen to scratch [skrætʃ]
zerreißen to rip [rɪp]
zerstören to destroy [dɪ'strɔɪ]
Zeug kit [kɪt]; stuff [stʌf]
Zeugnis report card *(AE)* [rɪ'pɔ:t ˌkɑ:d]
Zicklein kid [kɪd]
Ziege goat [gəʊt]
ziehen to pull [pʊl]; to tug [tʌg]
ziemlich pretty ['prɪti]; quite [kwaɪt]
Zimmer room [ru:m]
zittern to shake [ʃeɪk]
Zoll Customs pl. ['kʌstəmz]
Zoll *(Maßeinheit)* inch [ɪntʃ]
Zone zone [zəʊn]
zu too [tu:]; to [tʊ]
zu/nach ... kommen to get to ... ['get tʊ]
zu Ende gehen to end [end]
zu Fuß on foot [ˌɒn 'fʊt]
zu Hause home [həʊm]
zu spät late [leɪt]
Zucker sugar ['ʃʊgə]
zudrehen to turn off ['tɜ:n‿ɒf]
zuerst first [fɜ:st]; first of all [ˌfɜ:st‿'ɒf‿'ɔ:l]
Zufall chance [tʃɑ:ns]
Zug train [treɪn]
zugeben to admit [əd'mɪt]
zuhalten to hold [həʊld]
Zuhause home [həʊm]
zuhören to listen ['lɪsn]
die Tür **zuknallen** to slam the door [ˌslæm ðə 'dɔ:]
Zukunft future ['fju:tʃə]
zum Beispiel for example [ˌfər‿'ɪgzɑ:mpl]
zumachen to close [kləʊz]
zunehmen to rise [raɪz]
Zunge tongue [tʌŋ]
zuordnen to match [mætʃ]
zupfen to tug [tʌg]
zurück back [bæk]
jdn. zurückrufen to call s.o. back [ˌkɔ:l 'bæk]
zurückgeben to return [rɪ'tɜ:n]
zurückkommen to return [rɪ'tɜ:n]
zurückweisen to reject [ri:'dʒekt]
zusammen together [tə'geðə]
zusammenbrechen to break down ['breɪk daʊn]
zusammenfügen to match [mætʃ]
zusammengesetztes Wort compound ['kɒmpaʊnd]
Zusammenfassung summary ['sʌməri]
zuschauen to watch [wɒtʃ]
zuschließen to lock [lɒk]
Zustände kriegen to have a fit [ˌhæv‿ə 'fɪt]
zustimmen to agree [ə'gri:]
nicht zustimmen to disagree [ˌdɪsə'gri:]
Zutat ingredient [ɪn'gri:diənt]
Zutritt admission [əd'mɪʃn]
zwanzigste/-r/-s twentieth ['twentiɪθ]
Zweifel doubt [daʊt]
Zweikampf tackle ['tækl]
zweimal twice [twaɪs]; double ['dʌbl]
zweite/-r/-s second ['seknd]
zweitens secondly ['sekndli]
Zwilling twin [twɪn]
zwischen between [bɪ'twi:n]

In the classroom

You

Problems!

I can't find my pencil.	Ich finde meinen Bleistift nicht.
Have you got a pen that I can borrow?	Hast du einen Stift für mich?
Mr … , Tobias has taken my bag.	Herr …, Tobias hat meine Tasche genommen.
Mrs … / Miss … , I've forgotten my PE kit.	Frau …, ich habe meine Sportsachen vergessen.
Should I ask … about the homework?	Soll ich … fragen was wir aufhaben?
I don't understand this exercise.	Ich verstehe diese Übung nicht.
Wait, I'll help you.	Augenblick, ich helfe dir / Ihnen.
I'm not feeling well.	Ich fühle mich nicht gut.

Questions

What subjects do you teach?	Welche Fächer unterrichten Sie?
Who have you got for Maths / … ?	Wen hast du / habt ihr in Mathe / … ?
When does the next lesson start?	Wann fängt die nächste Unterrichtsstunde an?
How do you say 'Tasche' in English / … ?	Wie heißt „Tasche" auf Englisch / … ?
What are we doing in the lesson tomorrow?	Was machen wir morgen im Unterricht?
What do we have to do?	Was müssen wir machen?

Sorry!

I'm sorry about my homework / … .	Es tut mir leid wegen meiner Hausaufgaben.
I'm sorry I'm late.	Tut mir leid, dass ich mich verspätet habe.

Your teacher

Instructions

Do this exercise for homework.	Mach(t) diese Übung als Hausaufgabe.
Make a 'grammar card'.	Mach dir / Macht euch eine Grammatikkarte.
Make notes.	Mach dir / Macht euch Notizen.
Take notes.	Mach dir / Macht euch Notizen.
Read the definitions.	Lies / Lest die Definitionen.
Look on the Internet for more information.	Such(t) weitere Informationen im Internet.
Sort it out with him / her!	Klär(t) es mit ihm / ihr!
Don't send text messages in class.	Versende(t) keine SMS im Unterricht.
Come to the board, please.	Komm(t) bitte an die Tafel.
Ask your parents to sign the form, please.	Deine / Eure Eltern sollen die Formulare bitte unterschreiben.

Questions

What subjects have you got after lunch?	Welche Fächer hast du / habt ihr nach dem Mittagessen?
What have you done with your book?	Wo ist dein Buch?
Who would like to read?	Wer möchte (vor)lesen?
How did you do that?	Wie hast du / habt ihr das denn geschafft?
Can you find the mistakes?	Kannst du / Könnt ihr die Fehler entdecken?
What did I tell you yesterday?	Was habe ich dir / euch gestern gesagt?

List of irregular verbs

infinitive	simple past	past participle	German
be [bi:]	was, were [wɒz, wɜ:]	been [bi:n]	sein
beat [bi:t]	beat [bi:t]	beaten ['bi:tn]	schlagen
become [bɪ'kʌm]	became [bɪ'keɪm]	become [bɪ'kʌm]	werden
begin [bɪ'gɪn]	began [bɪ'gæn]	begun [bɪ'gʌn]	anfangen, beginnen
bet [bet]	bet [bet]	bet [bet]	wetten
break [breɪk]	broke [brəʊk]	broken ['brəʊkn]	kaputt machen, zerbrechen
bring [brɪŋ]	brought [brɔ:t]	brought [brɔ:t]	mitbringen, bringen
build [bɪld]	built [bɪlt]	built [bɪlt]	bauen, aufbauen
buy [baɪ]	bought [bɔ:t]	bought [bɔ:t]	kaufen
catch [kætʃ]	caught [kɔ:t]	caught [kɔ:t]	fangen
choose [tʃu:z]	chose [tʃəʊz]	chosen ['tʃəʊzn]	aussuchen, (aus)wählen
come [kʌm]	came [keɪm]	come [kʌm]	kommen
cost [kɒst]	cost [kɒst]	cost [kɒst]	kosten
cut [kʌt]	cut [kʌt]	cut [kʌt]	schneiden
do [du:]	did [dɪd]	done [dʌn]	machen, tun
draw [drɔ:]	drew [dru:]	drawn [drɔ:n]	zeichnen, malen
dream [dri:m]	dreamed/dreamt [dremt]	dreamed/dreamt [dremt]	träumen
drink [drɪŋk]	drank [dræŋk]	drunk [drʌŋk]	trinken
drive [draɪv]	drove [drəʊv]	driven ['drɪvn]	fahren
eat [i:t]	ate [eɪt]	eaten ['i:tn]	essen
fall [fɔ:l]	fell [fel]	fallen ['fɔ:ln]	fallen
feed [fi:d]	fed [fed]	fed [fed]	füttern
feel [fi:l]	felt [felt]	felt [felt]	(sich) fühlen, empfinden
fight [faɪt]	fought [fɔ:t]	fought [fɔ:t]	kämpfen, (sich) streiten
find [faɪnd]	found [faʊnd]	found [faʊnd]	finden
flee [fli:]	fled [fled]	fled [fled]	fliehen, flüchten
fly [flaɪ]	flew [flu:]	flown [fləʊn]	fliegen
forget [fə'get]	forgot [fə'gɒt]	forgotten [fə'gotn]	vergessen
get [get]	got [gɒt]	got [gɒt]	bekommen
give [gɪv]	gave [geɪv]	given ['gɪvn]	geben
go [gəʊ]	went [went]	gone [gɒn]	gehen
grow [grəʊ]	grew [gru:]	grown [grəʊn]	wachsen
hang [hæŋ]	hung [hʌŋ]	hung [hʌŋ]	hängen
have [hæv]	had [hæd]	had [hæd]	haben
hear [hɪə]	heard [hɜ:d]	heard [hɜ:d]	hören
hide [haɪd]	hid [hɪd]	hidden ['hɪdn]	(sich) verstecken
hit [hɪt]	hit [hɪt]	hit [hɪt]	schlagen, treffen, stoßen
hold [həʊld]	held [held]	held [held]	halten
hurt [hɜ:t]	hurt [hɜ:t]	hurt [hɜ:t]	verletzen, weh tun
keep [ki:p]	kept [kept]	kept [kept]	aufbewahren, behalten
know [nəʊ]	knew [nju:]	known [nəʊn]	wissen, kennen
leap [li:p]	leaped/leapt [lept]	leaped/leapt [lept]	springen
learn [lɜ:n]	learned/learnt [lɜ:nt]	learned/learnt [lɜ:nt]	lernen
leave [li:v]	left [left]	left [left]	abfahren; verlassen, lassen
lose [lu:z]	lost [lɒst]	lost [lɒst]	verlieren

infinitive	simple past	past participle	German
make [meɪk]	made [meɪd]	made [meɪd]	machen, schaffen, herstellen, bauen, bilden
mean [mi:n]	meant [ment]	meant [ment]	bedeuten, meinen
meet [mi:t]	met [met]	met [met]	(sich) treffen
pay [peɪ]	paid [peɪd]	paid [peɪd]	(be)zahlen
put [pʊt]	put [pʊt]	put [pʊt]	legen, setzen, stellen, tun
quit [kwɪt]	quit [kwɪt]	quit [kwɪt]	aufhören, aufgeben
read [ri:d]	read [red]	read [red]	lesen
ride [raɪd]	rode [rəʊd]	ridden ['rɪdn]	reiten, fahren
ring [rɪŋ]	rang [ræŋ]	rung [rʌŋ]	läuten
rise [raɪz]	rose [rəʊz]	risen ['rɪzn]	steigen, wachsen
run [rʌn]	ran [ræn]	run [rʌn]	rennen, laufen
say [seɪ]	said [sed]	said [sed]	sagen
see [si:]	saw [sɔ:]	seen [si:n]	sehen; treffen
sell [sel]	sold [səʊld]	sold [səʊld]	verkaufen
send [send]	sent [sent]	sent [sent]	schicken, senden
shake [ʃeɪk]	shook [ʃʊk]	shaken ['ʃeɪkn]	zittern, beben, schütteln
shoot [ʃu:t]	shot [ʃɒt]	shot [ʃɒt]	schießen; (Film) drehen
show [ʃəʊ]	showed [ʃəʊd]	shown [ʃəʊn]	zeigen
sing [sɪŋ]	sang [sæŋ]	sung [sʌŋ]	singen
sit [sɪt]	sat [sæt]	sat [sæt]	sitzen
sleep [sli:p]	slept [slept]	slept [slept]	schlafen
slide [slaɪd]	slid [slɪd]	slid [slɪd]	rutschen
smell [smel]	smelled/smelt [smelt]	smelled/smelt [smelt]	riechen
speak [spi:k]	spoke [spəʊk]	spoken ['spəʊkn]	sprechen
spell [spel]	spelled/spelt [spelt]	spelled/spelt [spelt]	buchstabieren
spend [spend]	spent [spent]	spent [spent]	verbringen; ausgeben
split [splɪt]	split [splɪt]	split [splɪt]	trennen
stand [stænd]	stood [stʊd]	stood [stʊd]	stehen
steal [sti:l]	stole [stəʊl]	stolen ['steʊlən]	stehlen
swear [sweə]	swore [swɔ:]	sworn [swɔ:n]	fluchen; schwören
swim [swɪm]	swam [swæm]	swum [swʌm]	schwimmen
take [teɪk]	took [tʊk]	taken ['teɪkn]	nehmen; bringen; dauern
teach [ti:tʃ]	taught [tɔ:t]	taught [tɔ:t]	unterrichten, lehren
tell [tel]	told [təʊld]	told [təʊld]	sagen, erzählen
think [θɪnk]	thought [θɔ:t]	thought [θɔ:t]	denken, glauben
throw [θrəʊ]	threw [θru:]	thrown [θrəʊn]	werfen
understand [ˌʌndə'stænd]	understood [ˌʌndə'stʊd]	understood [ˌʌndə'stʊd]	verstehen
wake up ['weɪk‿ʌp]	woke up ['wəʊk‿ʌp]	woken up ['wəʊkn‿ʌp]	aufwachen
wear [weə]	wore [wɔ:]	worn [wɔ:n]	tragen
win [wɪn]	won [wʌn]	won [wʌn]	gewinnen
write [raɪt]	wrote [rəʊt]	written ['rɪtn]	schreiben

Lösungen Check-out

Unit 1 Seiten 26 – 27

1 New Yorkers and their jobs

1. Daisy is 22. She works for a computer company. She goes jogging every Saturday.
2. Tony is 55. He drives a cab in Brooklyn. He doesn't speak very good English.
3. Frank is 27. He cleans skyscraper windows. He sometimes has lunch 200 feet above the city.
4. Bruce is 15. He takes dogs for walks in Central Park. He doesn't get much money.

2 James in NYC

a)
8:00 Hotel Rome in Little Italy; 9:15 New York Harbor; 9:30 Statue of Liberty on Liberty Island; 10:45 Ellis Island; 12:00 Diego's Deli in Greenwich Village; 15:30 Empire State Building; 20:00 Chinatown
b)
At eight o'clock James had breakfast in his hotel in Little Italy. At quarter past nine he went to New York Harbor. At half past nine he went to the Statue of Liberty on Liberty Island. At quarter to eleven James visited the museum on Ellis Island. At twelve o'clock he went to Diego's Deli in Greenwich Village. At half past three he saw the Empire State building. At eight o'clock in the evening James went to Chinatown.

3 The history of Central Park

1. came
2. had lived
3. had been
4. started
5. wanted
6. could
7. had argued
8. decided
9. had drawn
10. talked
11. lived
12. had chosen
13. had left
14. destroyed
15. started
16. changed
17. worked
18. was
19. (had) started
20. took

4 9/11

1. been
2. in
3. worked
4. up
5. from
6. on
7. into
8. of
9. than
10. when
11. them
12. who
13. their
14. they
15. will

Unit 2 Seiten 44 – 45

1 Tiffany and her mom

a)
If you let me go to the disco, I'll wash your car.
If you drive me to school, I'll cook supper.
If you wash my sports clothes, I'll do the shopping.
If you lend me your digital camera, I'll clean the windows.
If you let me use your new laptop, I'll make the family website.
b)
If you don't wash the car soon, I won't let you go to the disco.
If you don't cook supper soon, I won't drive you to school.
If you don't do the shopping soon, I won't wash your sports clothes.
If you don't clean the windows soon, I won't lend you my digital camera.
If you don't make the family website soon, I won't let you use the new laptop (again).

2 A school project

2. Looking for
3. Using
4. Writing
5. Listening to
6. Answering
7. Talking
8. Working

3 Say what you think!

1. Joining the orchestra last semester was a good idea!
2. Going to the movies costs a lot of money.
3. Laughing when a student says the wrong answer is awful.
4. Drawing pictures of our teacher in Art class this morning was fun.
5. Going on a trip to the Space Center in Florida taught us a lot about Science.
6. Running every weekend is good for my dad.
7. Listening to my MP3 player on the bus helps me forget about school.
8. Smoking isn't cool.

4 The kids in 8th grade

1. Brittany loves cycling.
2. Scott likes swimming.
3. Joshua enjoys playing baseball.
4. Carol hates skateboarding.
5. Tiffany likes going to the movies.
6. Kate hates getting up early.
7. Steve doesn't like waiting for the bus.

5 Cheerleaders at the middle school

1. do
2. help
3. went
4. learned
5. Do you want
6. will be
7. will put
8. will receive

Unit 3 Seiten 62 – 63

1 A boy at Forest Springs

2. He was crazy about rowing on the Colorado River.
3. He got used to eating sausages every night.
4. He wasn't very good at singing around the campfire.
5. He wasn't crazy about getting up early every morning.
6. He was interested in finding out about animal tracks.
7. He got tired of listening to kids who weren't enjoying their time at summer camp.
8. Now he is looking forward to going back to Forest Springs next summer.

2 What would they do?

1. If I went to the Grand Canyon, I would wear a hat.
2. If I spent a week at Forest Springs, I would make a movie.
3. If I saw a spider, I would run a mile.
4. If I ate too many sausages, I would feel sick.
5. If I met a pop star, I would ask about his new CD.
6. If I won a lot of money, I would buy a fast car.

3 On vacation

1. "If I lost my cell phone on vacation, I would go crazy."
2. "I would go to a museum if it rained."
3. "If someone stole my bags, I would call the police."
4. "If I got lost on a hike, I would try to find my way back to the trail."
5. "I would send a text message to my friend if I got bored."
6. "I would call my parents if I missed my flight home."

4 Vacation problems

1. "If we'd checked the plane times, we wouldn't have missed our flight home."
2. "If I'd been more careful when I was free climbing, I wouldn't have broken my arm."
3. "If I'd taken a map on that hike, I would have got back to the cabin much earlier."
4. "If we'd taken our MP3 players, the long trip in the car wouldn't have been so boring."
5. "If I'd looked before I sat down, I wouldn't have got paint on my clothes."
6. "And if I'd listened to the weather report that morning, I wouldn't have got wet (I would have taken an umbrella)."

5 Abby's friend

1. question
2. lived
3. city
4. would
5. bored
6. far
7. miles
8. were
9. cabin
10. are
11. I'll
12. old

Unit 4 Seiten 80 – 81

1 A motel and its guests

1. The Roses always offer the President's Room to important guests.
2. They give a free map of the area to their guests when they arrive.
3. Mr. Rose often tells stories to his guests about people who have stayed at the motel.
4. They send Christmas cards to guests who have stayed more than once.
5. They don't show the town to guests.
6. Mrs. Rose gives the rooms on the quiet side of the building to older guests.

2 Signs

1. The apples cost 99 cents a pound.
2. You can drive at 55 miles an hour.
3. You can use the Internet here for $5 an hour.
4. The motel is open 24 hours a day.
5. The lemonade costs 25 cents a glass.

3 What is it called?

1. The satellite system for farmers is called GPS.
2. The technology some computer games use is called VR.
3. The strange things some people see at night are called UFOs.
4. The famous TV show about space travel is called *Star Trek*.
5. The two boys in 'Alien Invader' are called Roy and Zargon.
6. The people who travel into space are called astronauts.
7. The space station 217 miles above the Earth is called the ISS.
8. The Earth's satellite is called the moon.
9. The nearest star to the Earth is called the sun.

4 On the ISS

1. Sometimes satellites are repaired.
2. The equipment is checked every day.
3. Photos are taken of the Earth and the stars.
4. A report is written at the end of every day.
5. English is spoken on the ISS.
6. New parts of the space station are built.
7. Card games aren't played.
8. Tea is drunk from special cups.

5 Robots

1. is done
2. don't get
3. wash
4. is cooked
5. don't wash
6. is used
7. are done
8. is cleaned
9. are put away
10. repairs
11. does
12. think
13. are done
14. don't need
15. is

Unit 5 Seiten 96 – 97

1 An actor's things

1. His shoes were made in Italy.
2. His car was made in Germany.
3. His cell phone was made in India.
4. His guitar was made in Spain.
5. His bike was made in the US(A).
6. His sunglasses were made in France.

2 The first ...

1. The first books were printed by people in Europe 500 years ago.
2. The first photograph was taken by a man in France in the 1820s.
3. The first cars were built by a German in 1886.
4. The first plane was flown by two American brothers in 1903.
5. The first westerns were made by directors in the US in the 1920s.
6. The first rocket was sent to the moon by the US in 1969.
7. The first hip hop music was performed by DJs in the 1970s.

3 Oscar winners

1. He said that he was so proud. It was the best night of his life.
2. She explained that she had made lots of movies but that this was her first Oscar.
3. She said she wanted to thank her mom and dad for all they had done for her.
4. She told the audience she had really enjoyed making the movie and that she would never forget it.
5. He said that he was very happy. It was as if all his dreams had come true.
6. They said that they were glad to be in LA and that it was a wonderful surprise.

4 A date

1. He said (that) he was crazy about science fiction.
2. He asked me whether I had ever seen the movie *Tron*.
3. I said (that) I hadn't seen it.
4. He asked me what computer games I liked.
5. I said (that) I didn't really like games.
6. I said (that) it had been a nice evening.
7. He said (that) he would see me around.

5 A dangerous job

1. didn't
2. friends
3. dangerous
4. given
5. took
6. the
7. were
8. his
9. vacation
10. family
11. was
12. beach
13. playing
14. making
15. standing
16. hit
17. water
18. by
19. too
20. became

Lösungen Test practice

Test practice A Seiten 30 – 31

A Reading

1

a right

b wrong: Kids like Eddie have enough money problems of their own.

c wrong: Cristina is one of the organizers of Global Kids.

d wrong: Shelley is Eddie's classmate.

e right

f wrong: Lots of people were interested in the theater project.

2

a Global Kids started in 1991.

b Global Kids tries to get kids interested in the problems that people have in their own neighborhood and in other countries.

B Language

a to drop out of school
b to create something
c illegal immigrant
d poor
e neighborhood
f to make a difference

C Passing on information

a No, Hand-in-Hand don't make bread. They collect bread and other food which people would throw away. Then they give the food to poor people.
b You can help to collect, prepare and take the food to the poor people.
c They need people on / at the weekend.
d Yes, of course. A few hours is enough.
e No, they don't. The food is free.

D Listening

a one year
b water
c Central Park
d don't go to school regularly
e it was nothing really new
f get up on time

E Writing

1
I'd like to work on the theater project about illegal immigrants. We did a play at school last year and it was great. I'd love to perform a play on the streets and talk to people about the problem. A lot of immigrants have problems in Germany, too, and they often need help. I'd like to work on a project like that here, too.
2
In 1993 Rosa was born in a small town in Mexico. Between 1997 and 2000 her family tried to enter the US three times, and in 2000 they entered Texas. In 2003 Rosa moved to New York, where she went to school. In 2006 Rosa started to play the guitar, and in 2007 she started at high school in Brooklyn. In 2008 she joined Global Kids. She made a radio program about immigrants in New York. It was fun, and she learned a lot.

Test practice B Seiten 66 – 67

A Reading

1
a a new platform. b a member of a tribe.
c be bad for his tribe. d the tribe's water.
e important to the Hualapai.

2
• too many tourists • tourists not interested in culture of Hualapai • will take rocks as souvenirs, damage culture • will leave garbage and use water • land is very sacred to Hualapai • Skywalk does not show respect for ancestors

B Language

a tribe b ancient c garbage
d sacred e ancestors

C Passing on information

You: Is it true that we can't take any photos here?
You: Man kann hier keine Fotos machen, weil der Canyon für die Hualapai ein heiliger Ort ist.
You: Are there some postcards at least?
You: Im Besucherzentrum kann man welche kaufen. Das Zentrum hat außerdem Poster und Bücher über den Canyon zu bieten.

D Listening

1
a right b wrong c wrong d wrong e right
2
a, b, d, f

E Writing

1
I agree with this opinion. Older people often know what to do in difficult situations because they have been in situations like that before. Teenagers can learn from this if they talk to older people and listen to them. Many older people have made mistakes during their lives. If teenagers respect older people, maybe they won't make the same mistakes.
2
Dear Newtech,
I read the letter from Rory Quasala and I want to say that I don't agree with him. I think the future is more important than the past. Rory should think about the young people of his tribe. They need jobs and money. Lots of Native Americans are very poor and they need a chance in life. If the young people don't get that chance, they will leave the tribe and go and live in cities. They will forget about Native American traditions and the tribe will die. Yours,

Test practice C Seiten 100 – 101

A Reading

1
a right b wrong c right
d wrong e wrong f right

2

a … they wanted to get to know their country better.
b … went on a trip through the Canadian wilderness to Alaska.
c … hired her father and her brother …
d … had / got some nice surprises.

B Language

a someone who comes from another place to work in an area
b to work where you are not allowed to
c the way someone lives
d without stress or worries
e a fast and busy lifestyle
f a place where you can live and where you know you don't have to move

C Passing on information

a Nein. Es gibt sportliche Aktivitäten aber man kann auch malen, zeichnen und Musik machen.
b Nein. Es gibt einen Essensraum und Köche, die das Essen zubereiten.
c Das stimmt leider nicht. Man bekommt tagsüber zwei Stunden freie Zeit.
d „Counselors" schlafen in Kabinen, die sie mit zwei bis vier anderen Mitarbeitern teilen.

D Listening

right for the job: fantastic English, speaks French, can play the guitar and the piano, good at reading maps, loves climbing
not right for the job: can't stay out in the sun for long, must be careful with skin

E Writing

1
Dear …,
I arrived at summer camp in California last Friday. The kids here are nice, but some of the smaller ones are very loud. The food is OK, and we had some great sausages last nice. There's another student from France here. Her name is Julie. We're going climbing with the kids tomorrow. That will be fun!
Love,
Michelle
2
I don't agree with this opinion. Maybe it's true for a huge country like the US, but the parts of a smaller country like Germany are all very similar. You see the same cars, shops and buildings in every town. It's more important and interesting to see other countries, and meet the different people who live there. People who have visited other countries also look at their own country differently. They realize what is good about the country and what needs to change there.

Lösungen Grammar

G1 (Revision) Seite 123

A man from England decides to go and live in New York. "You'll love it in New York," people say. "The streets are full of gold!" So he takes the next ship to America. The journey is awful and he doesn't sleep very well. When he leaves the ship, he is very tired and hungry. He starts to look for a hotel. Then he looks down and sees a ten dollar bill in the road. He stops to pick it up, but thinks again. "No," he says to himself and smiles. "Why should I hurry? I am too tired now. I'll start tomorrow!"

G2 (Revision) Seite 124

1. I am getting hungry now. Let's buy something to eat!
2. Excuse me, do you speak English?
3. Excuse me, is anybody sitting here?
4. Hey, do you play baseball?
5. Not really, but my sister plays every weekend.

G3 (Revision) Seite 125

Friend: What did you do last summer?
Jack: We went on a trip downriver.
Friend: Did Chippy travel with you?
Jane: Yes, he did.
Friend: What did you see?
Jack: We saw lots of wild animals.

G4 (Revision) Seite 126

1. Chippy got up early yesterday.
2. After he had had breakfast, he went to play in the jungle.
3. When he had finished his game, he climbed into a tree.
4. He ate a banana. When he had eaten it, he slept for an hour.
5. Then it was time to go home.

G5 (Revision) Seite 127

They have collected some wood.
They have laid the tables.
They have put the candles on the tables.
They haven't finished / written the name cards.
They haven't found enough chairs.
They haven't started the fire.

G5 (Revision) Seite 128

1. Who invented the phone?
2. Ow! I've cut my finger.
3. What did you do yesterday?
4. In 1845 there was a famine in Ireland.

5. Look! There has been an accident.
6. When did they come home?

G6 (Revision) Seite 129

1. My dad will be 49 next week.
2. I think Paul is playing tennis with Linda this afternoon.
3. That's a heavy bag! I'll carry it for you.
4. I'm sure you will get a good grade in the test tomorrow.
5. We're going to spend our vacation in Florida this year.
6. The weather will change tomorrow.

G7 (Revision) Seite 130

1. If you don't take an umbrella with you, you will get wet.
2. If you ask Mrs. Smith, she will help you.
3. She will catch the plane if she hurries.
4. What will you do if you don't find your money?
5. Mum won't be happy if we don't go shopping for her.
6. If you don't work harder, you won't get a good grade.
7. We will have dinner together if Paul comes home early.

G8 (Revision) Seite 132

a)
1. You mustn't leave bottles (here).
2. You must leave the panther alone.
3. You mustn't swim in the lake at night.
4. You must ask Jack for help.

b)
1. You should go to the doctor.
2. You should buy a new CD for your friend.
3. You should take it to the police.
4. You should take it back to the shop.

G9 (Unit 2) Seite 133

1. Jane and Jack like playing the drums.
2. Chippy loves eating nuts.
3. Swimming in the river is sometimes dangerous.
4. Jack hates getting up early in the morning.
5. Living in the jungle is fun.

G10 (Unit 3) Seite 134

Dear Mr. Roberts,
I am writing because I am interested in working at Forest Springs Summer Camp this summer. I am used to working with younger children and I never get tired of playing games and singing with them. I am also quite good at sports and playing the guitar.
I am looking forward to hearing from you. Thank you.
Best wishes,
Caroline Baker

G11 (Unit 3) Seite 135

1. If I had more money, I would give you some of it.
2. I would live in Spain if I spoke Spanish.
3. My parents would help us if they were here.
4. If my computer was faster, I would be able to play more games on it.
5. If I needed a bike, my friend would lend me his.
6. I would watch TV more often if I wasn't so busy.

G12 (Unit 3) Seite 136

1. If I had had more time when the kids were young, I would have looked for a job.
2. I wouldn't have met your grandpa if I had stayed at home that night in 1952.
3. We wouldn't have married if our parents had said no.
4. I would have taken French classes if our school had had a French teacher.
5. If we had had more money, we would have moved to California in 1963.

G15 (Unit 4) Seite 139

2. I go to the movies once a month.
3. I use a computer twice an hour.
4. I eat fruit once a day.

G16 (Unit 4) Seite 140

1. The shopping isn't done.
2. The clothes aren't washed.
3. The sandwiches aren't made.
4. The floor isn't cleaned.

G17 (Unit 5) Seite 141

1. Three houses were damaged in stormy weather.
2. A UFO was photographed in California.
3. Jamie Foxx was seen in downtown Jonesboro.
4. Four teenagers were hurt in a car accident.

G18 (Unit 5) Seite 142

1. Paul said (that) he had acted in a short movie.
2. He added that he had only had a very small role.
3. He said (that) he hadn't had to say anything.
4. He added that he had worn a funny costume.

G19 (Unit 5) Seite 143

1. They wanted to know whether it had been a good movie.
2. They asked whether it had had a happy ending.
3. They asked what the name of the movie had been.
4. They wanted to know who the stars had been.

Bildquellen: Umschlagfotos: Corbis (March), Düsseldorf; S.4.1: Corbis (David Ball), Düsseldorf; S.4.2: Alamy Images RM (Steve Skjold), Abingdon, Oxon; S.4.3: Alamy Images RM (Chad Ehlers), Abingdon, Oxon; S.5.1: iStockphoto (RF/George Cairns), Calgary, Alberta; S.5.2: shutterstock (RF/Stephen coburn), New York, NY; S.10.1: Avenue Images GmbH (Michel Touraine/pixland), Hamburg; S.10.2: GOODSHOOT (Goodshoot), Annecy-Le-Vieux; S.10.3: shutterstock (RF/Christophe Testi), New York, NY; S.10.4: Corbis (Ed Kashi), Düsseldorf; S.10.5: laif (S. Falke), Köln; S.11.1: iStockphoto (RF/Pham), Calgary, Alberta; S.11.2: Getty Images (David McNew), München; S.11.3: laif (Finke), Köln; S.11.4: Comstock, Luxemburg; S.12.1: Alamy Images RM (D. Hurst), Abingdon, Oxon; S.12.2: iStockphoto (Lawrence Sawyer), Calgary, Alberta; S.12.3: Corbis (Craig Aurness), Düsseldorf; S.12.4: Corbis (Tim Thompson), Düsseldorf; S.12.5: MEV, Augsburg; S.13.1: Alamy Images RM (Content Mine Interna), Abingdon, Oxon; S.13.2: shutterstock (Christopher Penler), New York, NY; S.13.3, S.13.4: Alamy Images RM (Visions of America L), Abingdon, Oxon; S.13.5: Alamy Images RM (Ian Dagnall), Abingdon, Oxon; S.13.6: Alamy Images RM (Picture Contact), Abingdon, Oxon; S.14.1: Corbis (David Ball), Düsseldorf; S.15.1: Alamy Images RM (JTB Photo Communications, Inc.), Abingdon, Oxon; S.15.2: Avenue Images GmbH (image 100), Hamburg; S.15.3: iStockphoto (RF/Sami Suni), Calgary, Alberta; S.15.4: laif (Jonkmanns), Köln; S.17.1: iStockphoto (RF/Liv Friis-Larsen), Calgary, Alberta; S.17.2: iStockphoto (RF/aaron holbrough), Calgary, Alberta; S.17.3: MEV, Augsburg; S.17.4: iStockphoto (RF/Greg Nicholas), Calgary, Alberta; S.17.5: iStockphoto (RF/Cathleen Clappe), Calgary, Alberta; S.17.6: iStockphoto (RF), Calgary, Alberta; S.17.7: iStockphoto (RF/George Bailey), Calgary, Alberta; S.19.1: Corbis (Bettmann), Düsseldorf; S.20.1: JupiterImages (RF/photos.com), Tucson, AZ; S.20.2: iStockphoto (RF/stephanie phillips), Calgary, Alberta; S.20.3: shutterstock (RF/John Bailey), New York, NY; S.21.1: Getty Images (Mark Mainz), München; S.22.1: shutterstock (RF/Swartz), New York, NY; S.22.2: Picture-Alliance (Soeren Stache), Frankfurt; S.22.3: shutterstock (RF/Cribb), New York, NY; S.25.1: Klett-Archiv (Patrick Dembski), Stuttgart; S.25.2: Getty Images (Gorilla Creative), München; S.25.3: Getty Images (taxi/Goldmann), München; S.27.1: The Library of Congress, Washington , D.C.; S.27.2: MEV, Augsburg; S.28.1: Bananastock RF, Watlington/Oxon; S.31.1: iStockphoto (RF/Tilston), Calgary, Alberta; S.32.1: Avenue Images GmbH (Corbis RF), Hamburg; S.33.1: Avenue Images GmbH (Image Source RF), Hamburg; S.33.2: Alamy Images RM (Steve Skjold), Abingdon, Oxon; S.33.3: Alamy Images RM (Chad Ehlers), Abingdon, Oxon; S.39.1: Alamy Images RM (Ted Horowitz), Abingdon, Oxon; S.39.2: Corbis (ROB & SAS), Düsseldorf; S.39.3: Alamy Images RF (RF/David Davis Pho), Abingdon, Oxon; S.39.4: Alamy Images RM (Picture Partners), Abingdon, Oxon; S.41.1: JupiterImages (RF/Photos.com), Tucson, AZ; S.45.1: Getty Images (taxi/John Terence T), München; S.45.2: Getty Images RF (Photo Disc), München; S.45.3: Alamy Images RM (Telepix), Abingdon, Oxon; S.45.4: iStockphoto (RF/Daniel Brunner), Calgary, Alberta; S.45.5: Die Bildstelle (LEHTIKUVA OY), Hamburg; S.45.6: shutterstock (Wendy Kaveney Photography), New York, NY; S.46.1: Klaus Lienert, Appenweier; S.48.1: Corbis (David Kadlubowski), Düsseldorf; S.49.1: Corbis (Chris SattlbergerChr), Düsseldorf; S.49.2: Corbis (Jon Hicks), Düsseldorf; S.49.3: Alamy Images RM (Chad Ehlers), Abingdon, Oxon; S.50.1: Alamy Images RM (Visions of America, LLC), Abingdon, Oxon; S.51.1: Picture-Alliance (Keystone k94), Frankfurt; S.52.1: iStockphoto (RF/Danny Warren), Calgary, Alberta; S.53.1: Klett-Archiv (KD Busch Fotostudio), Stuttgart; S.53.2: iStockphoto (Galina Barskaya), Calgary, Alberta; S.54.1: iStockphoto (Kameleon007), Calgary, Alberta; S.54.2: PhotoAlto, Paris; S.54.3: Getty Images RF (Photodisc), München; S.54.4: laif (Piepenburg), Köln; S.55.1: laif (Heidorn), Köln; S.56.1: Alamy Images RF (RF/Purestock), Abingdon, Oxon; S.64.1: Cinetext, Frankfurt; S.66.1: Alamy Images RM (Lee Foster), Abingdon, Oxon; S.68.1: laif (Kurt Henseler), Köln; S.69.1: Corbis (George Logan/zefa), Düsseldorf; S.69.2: Alamy Images RM (Peter Widmann), Abingdon, Oxon; S.69.3: Fotofinder (PHONE Thiriet Claudi), Berlin; S.69.4: Corbis (Rick Friedman), Düsseldorf; S.70.1: iStockphoto (RF/George Cairns), Calgary, Alberta; S.71.1: Getty Images (Stocktrek), München; S.72.1: Corbis (Javier Pierini), Düsseldorf; S.74.1: Corbis (Birgid Allig/zefa), Düsseldorf; S.79.1: NASA, Washington, D.C.; S.80.1: iStockphoto (Bart Sadowski), Calgary, Alberta; S.80.2: Alamy Images RM (David R. Frazier Photolibrary, Inc.), Abingdon, Oxon; S.80.3: Alamy Images RF (Jack Sullivan), Abingdon, Oxon; S.80.4: Alamy Images RF (Philip Sayer), Abingdon, Oxon; S.80.5: Alamy Images RF (SuperStock), Abingdon, Oxon; S.81.1: Avenue Images GmbH (Alamy RF/Radius Imag), Hamburg; S.84.1, S. 94.1: Corbis (Mike Blake/Reuters), Düsseldorf; S.85.1: Picture-Alliance (Bandphoto), Frankfurt; S.85.2: Corbis (Bettmann), Düsseldorf; S.85.3, S. 94.2: Corbis (John Springer coll.), Düsseldorf; S.85.4: Picture-Alliance (Abaca), Frankfurt; S.86.1: Corbis (Bettmann), Düsseldorf; S.86.2: AKG, Berlin; S.87.1: Cinetext, Frankfurt; S.88.1: Getty Images (MIKE NELSON/AFP), München; S.88.2: Getty Images (JEFF HAYNES/AFP), München; S.89.1: Avenue Images GmbH (Image Source/RF), Hamburg; S.90.1: Corbis (Fabio Cardoso/zefa), Düsseldorf; S.90.2: shutterstock (Anna Chelnokova), New York, NY; S.90.3: Corbis (Holger Winkler/A.B./zefa), Düsseldorf; S.91.1: Picture-Alliance (Photoshot), Frankfurt; S.92.1: Getty Images (Stephen Shugerman), München; S.93.1: Alamy Images RM (AA World Travel Lib.), Abingdon, Oxon; S.95.1, S.95.2: Dream Maker Software (RF), Colorado; S.99.1: Corbis, Düsseldorf; S.99.2: Wikimedia Foundation Inc. (Public Domain), St. Petersburg FL; S.99.3: shutterstock (RF/Stephen coburn), New York, NY; S.100.1: Corbis (Jim Sugar), Düsseldorf; S.102.1: Corbis (James Leynse), Düsseldorf; S.106.1: Fotosearch RF (PhotoDisc), Waukesha, WI; S.106.2: MEV, Augsburg; S.106.3: Avenue Images GmbH (image 100), Hamburg; S.106.4: Panasonic Deutschland, Hamburg; S.107.1: iStockphoto (RF/Boulette), Calgary, Alberta; S.108.1: StockFood (Eising), München; S.108.2, S.108.3: Ingram Publishing, Tattenhall Chester; S.110.1: Getty Images (Botanica/Jack O`La), München; S.110.2: Picture-Alliance (ipol code), Frankfurt; S.110.3: AKG, Berlin; S.110.4: Alamy Images RM (Justin Leighton), Abingdon, Oxon; S.111.1: Fotosearch RF, Waukesha, WI; S.111.2: iStockphoto (RF/tness74), Calgary, Alberta; S.111.3: Corbis (Joseph Sohm; ChromoS), Düsseldorf; S.111.4: Getty Images RF (PhotoDisc), München; S.112.1: AKG, Berlin; S.112.2: Corbis (Bettmann), Düsseldorf; S.112.3: Wikimedia Foundation Inc. (PD), St. Petersburg FL; S.113.1: Corbis (Leonard de Selva), Düsseldorf; S.113.2: Corbis (Bettmann), Düsseldorf; S.113.3: Getty Images (AFP), München; S.114.1: Rockwell Museum of Western Art, Corning, New York; S.114.2: Süddeutscher Verlag, München; S.114.3: The Granger Collection, New York; S.114.4: Corbis (David Stoecklein), Düsseldorf; S.114.5: Süddeutscher Verlag, München; S.114.6: Corbis (Bettmann), Düsseldorf; S.115.1: Corbis (Alison Wright), Düsseldorf; S.146.1: Avenue Images GmbH (image 100), Hamburg; S.147.1, S.147.2: Getty Images RF (Photo Disc), München; S.147.3: MEV, Augsburg; S.149.1: Getty Images RF (PhotoDisc), München; S.152.1: MEV, Augsburg; S.154.1: Ingram Publishing, Tattenhall Chester; S.154.2, S.158.1: Corel Corporation, Unterschleissheim; S.158.2: Corbis (© Royalty-Free/CORBI), Düsseldorf; S.161.1: Mauritius (age), Mittenwald; S.162.1: MEV, Augsburg; S.164.1: Corbis (Digital image © 1996), Düsseldorf; S.169.1: creativ collection, Freiburg; S.172.1: Klett-Archiv (Silberzahn), Stuttgart

Textquellen: S.13: Sondheim, Stephen © Leonard Bernstein Music/Chappell-Co Inc., Universal Music Publ. GmbH, Berlin, Chappell & Co. GmbH & Co. KG, Hamburg; S.21: Bator, Stephen J. Jr/Diamond, Michael Louis/Horovitz, Adam Keefe/Madansky, John/Magnum, Jeff/O'Connor, Eugene Richard/Thomas, David Lynn/Yauch, Adam Nathaniel/Zero, Jimmy © Brooklyn Dust Music/Polygram International Publ. In/WB Music Corp. Neue Welt Musikverlag GmbH, Hamburg; S.22: Thomas, Roger © EMI Blackwood Music Inc., EMI Music Publishing Germany GmbH & Co. KG, Hamburg; S.41: Barker, Travis L./DeLonge, Thomas/Hoppus, Mark © Fun with Goats/EMI Music Inc/EMI Entertainment World Inc US. EMI Music Publishing Germany GmbH & Co. KG, Hamburg; S.57: © by Will Hobbs, Atheneum Publishers – Simon & Schuster, New York; S.61: Troup, Bobby © 1946 by Burke & Van Heusen Inc. Chappell & Co. GmbH & Co. KG, Hamburg; S.75: © by Merlyn's Pen, Inc. All Rights Reserved S.77: Burns, Michael Gerald/Glen, Steven Robert/Most, David © Ral Publishing Ltd./Save and Nickelodeon Ltd. Melodie der Welt J. Michel KG Musikverlag, Frankfurt/M.; S.91 From HAPPILY EVER AFTER: THE DREW BARRYMORE STORY by Elina Furman and Leah Furman, copyright © 2007 by Elina Furman and Leah Furman. Used by permission of Ballantine Books, a division of Random House, Inc.; S.93: Nobles, Vada J/Pugh, Rasheem Sharrief © Kilosheem Pub/VNM Publ., EMI Music Publishing Germany GmbH & Co. KG, Hamburg; S.100: © by Marlene Smith, Seventeen Magazine, 1977; S.106: Extract from Complete Physics by Stephen Pople (OUP, 1999), reprinted by permission of Oxford University Press.

NEW YORK
THE BRONX
W 155th St.
Harlem River Dr.
W 145th St.
HARLEM
W 125th St.
Henry Hudson Pkwy.
Broadway
7th Avenue
Lenox Avenue
MANHATTAN
Park Avenue
2nd Avenue
1st Avenue
Amsterdam Ave.
Central Park
E 106th St.
Hudson River
UPPER WEST SIDE
W 81st St.
E 96th St.
5th Avenue
UPPER EAST SIDE
E 84th St.
Lincoln Center
Broadway
Park Avenue
3rd Avenue
E 79th St.
2nd Avenue
1st Avenue
E 66th St.
Central Park St.
QUEENS
Lincoln Tunnel
10th Avenue
9th Avenue
W 42nd St.
Times Square
Avenue of the Americas
E 57th St.
Museum of Modern Art
Queensboro Bridge
12th Avenue
W 34th St.
8th Avenue
5th Avenue
Rockefeller Center
Chrysler Building
E 42nd St.
United Nations
MIDTOWN
E 34th St.
Queens Midtown Tunnel
Empire State Building
NEW JERSEY
9th Avenue
7th Avenue
Broadway
W 14th St.
E 23rd St.
West Side Highway
Bleeker St.
Greenwich Village
E 14th St.
Hudson St.
Holland Tunnel
Broadway
Avenue D
East River
LOWER WEST SIDE
Broome St.
Little Italy
E Houston St.
Canal St.
LOWER EAST SIDE
Chinatown
Bowery
Williamsburg Bridge
Site of World Trade Center
FDR Drive
Brooklyn Bridge
Manhattan Bridge
ELLIS ISLAND
Brooklyn Battery Tunnel
BERTY ISLAND
Statue of Liberty
BROOKLYN
MANHATTAN
THE BRONX
NEW JERSEY
QUEENS
STATEN ISLAND
BROOKLYN